The Clandestine Lives of Colonel David Smiley

Series Editors: Richard J. Aldrich, Rory Cormac, Michael S. Goodman and Hugh Wilford

This series explores the full spectrum of spying and secret warfare in a globalised world

Intelligence has changed. Secret service is no longer just about spying or passively watching a target. Espionage chiefs now command secret armies and legions of cyber warriors who can quietly shape international relations itself. Intelligence actively supports diplomacy, peacekeeping and warfare: the entire spectrum of security activities. As traditional inter-state wars become more costly, covert action, black propaganda and other forms of secret interventionism become more important. This ranges from proxy warfare to covert action; from targeted killing to disruption activity. Meanwhile, surveillance permeates communications to the point where many feel there is little privacy. Intelligence, and the accelerating technology that surrounds it, have never been more important for the citizen and the state.

Titles in the *Intelligence, Surveillance and Secret Warfare* series include:

Published:

The Arab World and Western Intelligence: Analysing the Middle East, 1956–1981
Dina Rezk

The Twilight of the British Empire: British Intelligence and Counter-Subversion in the Middle East, 1948–63
Chikara Hashimoto

Chile, the CIA and the Cold War: A Transatlantic Perspective
James Lockhart

The Clandestine Lives of Colonel David Smiley: Code Name 'Grin'
Clive Jones

Forthcoming:

Outsourcing US Intelligence: Private Contractors and Government Accountability
Damien Van Puyvelde

The Snowden Era on Screen: Signals Intelligence and Digital Surveillance
James Smith

The Problem of Secret Intelligence
Kjetil Anders Hatlebrekke

The CIA and the Pursuit of Security: History, Documents and Contexts
Hew Dylan

https://edinburghuniversitypress.com/series-intelligence-surveillance-and-secret-warfare.html

The Clandestine Lives of Colonel David Smiley

Code Name 'Grin'

Clive Jones

EDINBURGH
University Press

For Sally
(and the journey taken!)

Edinburgh University Press is one of the leading university presses in the UK. We publish academic books and journals in our selected subject areas across the humanities and social sciences, combining cutting-edge scholarship with high editorial and production values to produce academic works of lasting importance. For more information visit our website: edinburghuniversitypress.com

© Clive Jones, 2019, 2020

Edinburgh University Press Ltd
The Tun – Holyrood Road
12(2f) Jackson's Entry
Edinburgh EH8 8PJ

First published in hardback by Edinburgh University Press 2019

Typeset in 11/13pt Sabon by
Servis Filmsetting Ltd, Stockport, Cheshire

A CIP record for this book is available from the British Library

ISBN 978 1 4744 4115 5 (hardback)
ISBN 978 1 4744 4116 2 (paperback)
ISBN 978 1 4744 4117 9 (webready PDF)
ISBN 978 1 4744 4118 6 (epub)

The right of Clive Jones to be identified as the author of this work has been asserted in accordance with the Copyright, Designs and Patents Act 1988, and the Copyright and Related Rights Regulations 2003 (SI No. 2498).

All photographs reproduced by kind permission of David Smiley and Xan Smiley.

Contents

Preface	vi
Acknowledgements	xii
List of Illustrations	xiv
List of Abbreviations	xvi
1. From the Cradle to Palestine	1
2. From Palestine to Abyssinia	15
3. Desert Wars	39
4. From Regular to Irregular	58
5. A Matter Called 'Concensus'	78
6. Three Majors: Two for Politics, One for Fighting	111
7. Burnt but Alive	146
8. Between Ubon and a Hard Place	172
9. From Espionage to Sabotage	198
10. Subversion and the Ceremonial	221
11. As Tough as Teak	253
12. Our Man in Yemen	286
13. An Uncomplicated Patriot	323
Bibliography	339
Index	352

Preface

I felt bloody ill all day, either malaria or handling explosives and I was sick twice. I think it is a recurrence of malaria. I felt better in the evening. We set off at 11 [pm] to blow the bridge, and arrived at the bridge at midnight. We started to carry the explosives to under the bridge but got held up for half an hour while a Hun lorry proceeded to have a puncture on top of the bridge, while we waited under it. At last it left and all the explosives were carried under the bridge. I then sent all the Albs [Albanians] away except Veli and Ramiz who worked with Jenkins and I for about two hours while a continuous stream of traffic passed overhead. We set off time pencils as we had no safety fuze [sic] and went away from the bridge.[1]
David de C. Smiley, War Diary, 20 June 1944

Clandestine warfare and secret service during the Second World War and afterwards continues to exercise a fascination among academics, journalists and the general public alike. Indeed, it remains a paradox, when set against a conflict whose geographic scale and violent intensity denied strategic importance to all but a few actions carried out by both Allied and Axis special forces, that academic studies, biographies, autobiographies, unit histories and the study of particular incidents and events still grip the imagination. This is partly a reaction to the industrial scale of war wherein, from 1914 onwards, the global nature of conflict increasingly diminished the role of the individual. But the emergence of special forces, ironically, gave the narrative of war a more human face, an intimacy denied by the impersonal, almost mechanistic, reference to armies, corps, divisions, brigades and, indeed, battalions. This appeal continues to endure. From

Preface

T. E. Lawrence's beautifully written, if self-serving, narrative of the Arab revolt in the First World War to more earthy accounts of special forces in recent conflicts, how the individual or small group deals with adversity fires the popular imagination.

The life and career of David de Crespigny Smiley often proved the antithesis to the warfare of twentieth-century mass mobilisation. Until his death in 2009, aged 92, Smiley epitomised an officer whose values echoed an earlier age. Loyalty to friends, devotion to the institutions of his country and adherence to absolute honesty were themes of a life often lived on the physical edge. As Julian Amery, his wartime colleague in the Special Operations Executive (SOE) in Albania, who was greatly to influence his post-war career, noted of Smiley:

> He knew his own mind and spoke it on all occasions, not aggressively nor even bluntly, yet in a manner so direct that it left little room for argument and no doubt whatever as to his feelings and his views or his intentions. Seldom given to speculation, he lived firmly in the present, enjoying the good things of life and all that was agreeable or beautiful, though as an occasional patron rather than a connoisseur. He liked his friends and disliked his enemies, but was otherwise more interested in things than in men and found a rare satisfaction in organising a camp or testing the accuracy of a new weapon.[2]

This assessment is borne out in the diaries that Smiley wrote on his myriad journeys. While mainly focused on the operational side of his time 'behind the lines', from Abyssinia to Siam via Albania and the Middle East, these diaries vividly describe the landscape, the people and the flora and fauna he encountered. In Albania, Oman and Yemen, his writings, be they reports or diaries, also shed light on tribally based societies undergoing profound upheaval amid regional turmoil or, in the case of Albania, a world war. The difficulties of working in societies where sectarian identity, ethnic loyalty and religious persuasion often defied broader operational goals – what scholars of counter-insurgency would later refer to as the human terrain – are dominant themes.[3]

He remained, however, a professional soldier at heart, who took as much pride in being a regular soldier as he did in his clandestine operations. Indeed, the certainties of regular soldiering sometimes appealed more to him than the politicking and betrayals that he felt marked his time in the Balkans. Once, while holed up in Albania listening to the BBC in the aftermath of the D-Day landings, he caught mention of his old regiment, the Blues, and longed to be with them, free of the fear and intrigue in his Balkan backwater. Later, he was to command the Blues himself, riding beside the Queen at the head of her escort during the coronation of 1953, a role in which he took particular pride.

But it is as an exponent of clandestine warfare that Smiley is best known. For many years, his activities were subject to secrecy laws and it was not until the late 1970s and the opening up of official records that the more controversial aspects of the secret war conducted behind German, Italian and Japanese lines by SOE and other special units in the Second World War were unveiled. While the bravery of many of the men and women who served in SOE is beyond question, the wealth of new material has done little to end debates about the actual strategic contribution it made to the Allied victory. Tales of courage, sacrifice and ingenuity can be set against those of betrayal and incompetence across Europe, the Middle East and beyond. Bureaucratic rivalries in London and Cairo sometimes more than matched the enmity towards the Nazis. Smiley entered this world of intrigue in 1943 and, thereafter, controversy was never far behind.

Nowhere was this more evident than during his attachment to MI6 in the aftermath of the war. Smiley's involvement in Operation Valuable, a secret plan to infiltrate Albanian exiles back into their country to organise an insurrection against the communist regime of Enver Hoxha, was disclosed in 1984 with the publication of *The Great Betrayal* by Nicholas Bethell. In two of his own autobiographical works, *Albanian Assignment*, published soon afterwards, and *Irregular Regular*, Smiley fleshed out the details of this operation, blaming Kim Philby for the mission's failure. This explanation has since been questioned, with some historians arguing that poor field security was as much to blame for the disaster as any information supplied by the most notorious member of the Cambridge spy ring.[4]

Smiley remained coy, though, in detailing his involvement in the more controversial aspects of his secret service. In *Arabian Assignment*, published in 1975, he wrote of his time as Commander of the Sultan's Armed Forces in Oman between 1958 and 1961, and his later role supporting the Royalist cause in Yemen as a military adviser. But he omitted the tales of rivalries, intrigues and politicking that marked his service in Oman and which constrained what he could achieve. While his time in Yemen is also covered in detail, he gives only a tantalising glimpse of his involvement in a mercenary operation that had, by 1965, proved the nemesis of the Egyptian army and Nasser's regional ambitions.

Perhaps most controversial of all, Smiley remained tight-lipped until his old age over his own involvement in the sabotage of Jewish refugee ships seeking to break the British naval blockade right after the Second World War. An episode in late British colonial history that still stirs passions, it was only after the publication of the official history of MI6 by Keith Jeffrey in 2010 that Operation Embarrass became widely known. In 1947, Smiley was part of a team that planted limpet mines on these ships but, as he was keen to point out, they exploded before the ships could be loaded with their human cargo. The sensitivity surrounding this MI6 operation reflects the veil of subterfuge that denied the existence of the British secret service, as well as the need to prevent disclosure of operational capabilities that still might have been part of the MI6 repertoire.

In his last interview with the author, Smiley also recalled the controversy over the case of Roy Farran, a former member of the wartime Special Air Service (SAS) and a man he knew quite well, who was accused, and later acquitted in controversial fashion, of murdering a young Jewish activist in Jerusalem in 1947. A parcel bomb intended for Farran was later opened by his brother, killing him outright. For Smiley, the message was clear: some in Israel had long memories and scores to settle.[5] Only in his twilight years did he become relaxed enough to talk openly about this episode.

There may have been another sensitivity here. Smiley did collaborate with the Israelis under an assumed name in helping to organise 'Operation Mango', a series of thirteen clandestine parachute supply drops of arms and ammunition to the Royalist forces in Yemen, carried out between 1964 and 1966 by the Israeli air force. Because the Saudis were bankrolling the Royalist war effort, disclosure of Israel's involvement, when the allure of Egypt's President Nasser across the Middle East was in the ascendant, would have created a diplomatic storm. Smiley's view was that if Israeli help could be harnessed to defend British interests in Arabia, then the end justified the means. This illustrates a constant theme in his story: his profound belief that his involvement in secret service and clandestine activity was about the undercover advancement of British interests.

Of course, defining those interests is subjective. By aligning himself with Julian Amery and Neil (Billy) McLean, as much from sentiment as outright political conviction, Smiley was often at odds with the policies of the British Foreign Office in such places as Albania and, later on, Aden and South Arabia. Such tension, however, helps draw out a wider theme of this book: the reasons for the decline of British influence across the world and whether this was managed by design rather than by default. Smiley's clandestine career certainly reflected this. His later involvement in the mercenary operation in Yemen also portended a wider trend towards the privatisation of security that reached its apogee in Iraq and Afghanistan. Smiley fought to stem this decline and, until the mid-1960s, did not accept it as inevitable. He believed in the value of the British empire, a point he made with humour laced with sarcasm to Albanian partisans, including their leader, Enver Hoxha, alongside whom he fought during the war. He did become more diplomatic over time but speaking truth to power was always his hallmark, for he regarded integrity and honesty as the essence of his being.

Smiley certainly had his faults: he could be irascible and stubborn beyond reason. His bravery was matched by a loyalty to his friends, which could periodically blind him to the wider consequences of his actions. But if these were indeed flaws, they were very human ones that added to, rather than detracted from, the character of a man who remained modest and often self-deprecating about his achievements. He should have been more highly decorated, not least for planning and leading a counter-insurgency campaign in Oman that saved the al-Bu-Said dynasty

Preface

and, with it, wider British interests in the region. The fact that such honours were denied him was an injustice to a man whose commitment to his country and friends never wavered. This is his remarkable story.

Notes

1. David de C. Smiley, War Diary. Operation Concensus II, 1944. Entry for 20 June 1944.
2. Julian Amery, *Sons of the Eagle* (London: Macmillan, 1948), p. 50.
3. David Smiley Papers (hereafter DSP): Third Trip to the Yemen. Report on visit to the Yemen, 7 March 1964–3 April 1964. Appendix 'C'. Summary of what I told the Imam.
4. See for example, Roderick Bailey, *The Wildest Province: SOE in the Land of the Eagle* (London: Vintage/Jonathan Cape, 2009), p. 328; Tom Winnifrith, 'A Betrayal Betrayed: Kim Philby and Albania', in James Pettifer (ed.), *Albania and the Balkans: Essays in Honour of Sir Reginald Hibbert* (Cornwall: Elbow, 2013), pp. 96–118. A more recent BBC Radio 4 documentary substantiates this thesis: 'The Albania Operation', *Document*, BBC Radio 4, Broadcast on 4 April 2017. Available at <http://www.bbc.co.uk/programmes/b07j4ppw> (last accessed 10 December 2018).
5. Interview with David Smiley, London, 20 October 2008. On the Farran case, see David Cesarani, *Major Farran's Hat* (London: William Heinemann, 2009).

Acknowledgements

Writing any book, let alone a biography, is a journey, and as anyone who has travelled with children can attest, the end point can often seem a long way off. When the journey's end is reached, however, it is perhaps even sweeter for the difficulties encountered and overcome. Still, when I started this biography, David Smiley was still very much alive and it is to my great regret that he never lived to see its publication. I am sure there are interpretations of events and opinions in the book he would have disagreed with, perhaps profoundly so, but he would, I am sure, have respected the argument and analysis of events in which he often played such a pivotal role. During my visits to his flat in Earls Court, he and Moy treated me with kindness and a warmth that was unbounded, the hours spent interviewing him in his book-lined living room remaining fresh in my memory. I also enjoyed the indulgence of the wider Smiley family, and in particular Xan, whose forbearance of my efforts when progress was interrupted (and, on more than one occasion, derailed) was indulgence above and beyond the call of duty. He read the whole first draft, making invaluable corrections that improved the manuscript immeasurably. I remain deeply indebted to him.

This biography evolved through several stages of the journey and, along the way, I not only enjoyed the support, guidance and advice of longstanding colleagues and associates, but met individuals whose interest in the project often blossomed into firm and lasting friendships. It therefore gives me particular pleasure to acknowledge the help and support of Nahum and Nina Admoni, Roderick Bailey, Kirsten Daswani, General Sir Peter de la Billière, Anoush Ehteshami, Efraim and Hadassa Halevy, Lottie Johnson,

Acknowledgements

Rob Johnson, Robert McNamara, Bernard Mills, Beverly Milton-Edwards, Emma Murphy, Asher Orkaby, Ritchie Ovendale, Yehudit and Uzi Ronen, Mark Seaman, Yigal Sheffy, Simon C. Smith, Stephen Walton and James Worrall. I owe a particular debt of gratitude to Professor Richard Aldrich, Dr Noel Guckian and Jean Stevenson, all of whom read drafts carefully and whose guidance, corrections and advice proved invaluable. Alan Craig, Zach Levy, Rory Miller and Tore Petersen, all wonderful academics, provided much-needed encouragement throughout and I am proud and indeed fortunate to have them as close friends. Several others, formerly in government service, also cast a critical eye on the manuscript, and while they do not wish to be named, my debt to them is no less profound. They know who they are. Any errors that remain are, of course, my own.

Like David Smiley, my own father, Alan Jones, never got to cast his own critical eye over the manuscript, a source of lingering regret to me. But my mother, Anne, continued to offer gentle (if firm) encouragement to finish the book and happily read each chapter as it came off the printer. She never imagined she would know so much about Albania or Oman! I have been blessed too with having wonderful in-laws, Peter and Gill O'Leary, whose love and support for the family, not least when 'life' has been particularly challenging, has been unbounded. When I started this 'journey', I did so without children but, along the way, Sam and Alex arrived, two passengers who took me on a different voyage and one that, while longer, has proven to be immeasurably more enriching. And finally, for my wife, Sally. You truly are my world. This is for you.

List of Illustrations

Fig. 1.1	Taking a tumble.	7
Fig. 1.2	Lieutenant David Smiley, Royal Horse Guards.	11
Fig. 2.1	Behind the lines: Abyssinia, 1941.	30
Fig. 3.1	Smiley's 15 cwt truck and crew, Kermanshah.	52
Fig. 4.1	Breakfast in the Western Desert, October 1942.	65
Fig. 4.2	Smiley before his first parachute jump, Kabrit, Egypt, January 1943.	74
Fig. 5.1	Map of Albania.	79
Fig. 5.2	BLOs with partisans at Bixha. From left to right: Tony Neel, Enver Hoxha, Garry Duffy, Billy McLean, Sprio Moisi, Ramadan Çitaku, Andy Hands, Dali Ndren.	94
Fig. 5.3	Partisans signing for weapons and equipment. Note Smiley's gold 'pips'.	96
Fig. 5.4	With Billy McLean, Bixha, October 1943.	102
Fig. 5.5	Smiley and McLean with two female partisans.	105
Fig. 6.1	Julian Amery (left) and Said Beg Kryeziu.	122
Fig. 6.2	The bridge at Gjoles.	128
Fig. 6.3	Smiley with the Zogist guerrillas who helped destroy the Gjoles bridge.	129
Fig. 6.4	Smiley with his Turkoman '*Wehrmacht*' troops, 1944.	139
Fig. 7.1	Map of Siam/Thailand.	147
Fig. 7.2	Smiley with first-degree burns.	164
Fig. 7.3	On the Dakota back to India.	165
Fig. 8.1	With 'Pluto' and Gunner Collins, Ubon, 1945.	179
Fig. 8.2	Identifying Japanese war criminals with Captain Gneisau van Alting in attendance.	182

List of Illustrations

Fig. 8.3	From left to right: Rowland Winn, unknown Chinese colonel, Smiley and Peter Kemp.	193
Fig. 9.1	Moy Smiley in the uniform of a FANY.	200
Fig. 9.2	The 'cigarette smugglers' for Operation Embarrass. Clockwise: Jimmy Blackburn, Smiley, Don Bevers, Harold Perkins. The pictures were taken during 'Embarrass'.	213
Fig. 9.3	A secret MI6 reconnaissance photo of a ship suspected of being used by *Mossad Le'aliyah Beth* for taking Jewish refugees to Palestine, lying in Genoa harbour.	215
Fig. 10.1	The MI6 Training Team, Fort Benjimma, Malta, 1949. From left to right: Alistair Grant, 'Q' Howard, John Kelly, Smiley, Gunner Collins, Doc Zaehner.	229
Fig. 10.2	Four of the 'Pixies' in training, Malta, summer 1949.	231
Fig. 10.3	On ceremonial duty with 'the Blues', Windsor, 1953.	242
Fig. 10.4	Military attaché, Sweden, 1957.	246
Fig. 10.5	Moy on a 'bridge of interest', Jokkmokk, Sweden, 1957.	247
Fig. 11.1	Map of Oman.	254
Fig. 11.2	Smiley with Sultan Said bin Taimur, Salalah, 1958.	263
Fig. 11.3	An Omani 'fuddle' with the *Wali* of Buraimi.	269
Fig. 12.1	Map of Yemen.	287
Fig. 12.2	In the Khowlan mountains, Yemen, October 1963.	294
Fig. 12.3	With the Imam, Muhammed al-Badr (centre).	296
Fig. 12.4	Smiley's Land Rover during an Israeli resupply drop. Note the signal fire in the background.	303
Fig. 12.5	From left to right: 'Nanny', Smiley, Jim Johnson, Bernard Mills, unknown, James Knox (Smiley's bodyguard), Amara, Yemen, 1965.	306
Fig. 12.6	Self-portrait on Smiley's fiftieth birthday, 11 April 1966. Note the heavily bandaged left knee.	313
Fig. 13.1	Earls Court, London, summer 2008, aged 92.	335

List of Abbreviations

AK	*Armja Krajowa* (Polish underground army)
ARAMCO	Arabian–American Oil Company
BAOR	British Army of the Rhine
BLO	British Liaison Officer (SOE)
BMO	British Mercenary Organisation
BRIXMIS	British Commanders in Chief Mission to the Soviet Forces in Germany
CIA	Central Intelligence Agency (USA)
CSAF	Commander, Sultan's Armed Forces (Oman)
DIO	Desert Intelligence Officer
DSO	Distinguished Service Order
EDES	*Ellinikos Dimokratikos Ethnikos Stratos* (National Democratic Republican Greek League – Greece)
ELAS	*Ethnikos Laikos Apeleftherotikos Stratos* (National Population Liberation Army – Greece)
FANY	First Aid Nursing Yeomanry
FO	Foreign Office
FSA	Federation of South Arabia
GHQ	General Headquarters
HCR	Household Cavalry Regiment
KCMG	Knight Commander (of the Order) of St Michael and St George
KGB	*Komitet Gosudarstvennoy Bezopasnosti* (Russian Committee for State Security)
LNÇ	*Levizje Nacional Çlirimtare* (National Liberation Movement – Albania)
MC	Military Cross
MiD	Mention in Dispatches

List of Abbreviations

MI6	British Foreign Intelligence Service, officially known as the Secret Intelligence Service (SIS)
NATO	North Atlantic Treaty Organisation
NCO	Non-Commissioned Officer
NFR	Northern Frontier Regiment
NKVD	Narodnyy Komissariat Vnutrennikh Del (People's Commissariat of Internal Affairs – USSR)
OBE	Order of the British Empire
OPC	Office of Policy Coordination (USA)
ORA	Oman Rebel Army
OSO	Office of Special Operations
OSS	Office of Strategic Services (USA)
PD(O)	Petroleum Development Oman and Dhofar Limited
PoW	Prisoner of War
RAF	Royal Air Force
SAF	Sultan's Armed Forces (Oman)
SAS	Special Air Service
SEAC	South East Asia Command
SIS	Secret Intelligence Service
SOE	Special Operations Executive
STS	Special Training School
USAAF	United States Army Air Force
UVF	Ulster Volunteer Force
VE	Victory in Europe
YAR	Yemen Arab Republic

1 From the Cradle to Palestine

I

For a man whose career was shaped by conflict, it was perhaps appropriate that the fanfare of war – in this case, German Zeppelins dropping bombs on London – should usher the entry of David de Crespigny Smiley into a turbulent world. Born on 11 April 1916 at 55 Grosvenor Street, London, David Smiley was the youngest child of Major Sir John Smiley and of Valerie, daughter of Sir Claude Champion de Crespigny. In light of the reputation he was to earn for courage and daring both during and after the Second World War, it is hard not to draw parallels with the career of his maternal grandfather, in terms of his attitude to risk, hardship and the type of soldiering he came to experience and enjoy. Sir Claude, whose family, originally from Normandy, was ennobled in the late twelfth century before fleeing to England as Huguenots in 1685, embraced with an almost reckless abandon a range of dangerous sports, including steeple-chasing and ballooning. He was the first of the so-called aeronauts to cross the North Sea, from Essex to Flushing in the Netherlands in 1883. He combined conventional soldiering in India and Egypt with what might now be termed counter-insurgency against Fenian insurgents in Ireland in 1867.

This background resonated with Smiley's own experience as an 'irregular regular', a term he felt captured his own sense of pride as a professional soldier with the satisfaction he derived from his skill as a guerrilla. The uncanny echoes with Sir Claude do not stop there, for, like his grandson in later life, Sir Claude became what might be called a 'freelance soldier', attaching himself to a cavalry unit of the Prussian army besieging Paris in 1871. Later, he posed as a correspondent for *The East Anglian Daily Times* in the hope of witnessing the war against the *Mahdi*'s rebellion in Sudan in the 1880s. In 1882, his love of hunting also took Sir Claude, albeit briefly, to Albania to shoot woodcock and wild boar. Almost six decades later, his grandson was to enter this little-known Balkan state, although in vastly different circumstances, and where he was to find himself as much hunted as the hunter.[1]

Smiley's father, too, had been a regular soldier who fought in the Boer war before being recalled once more to colours at the beginning of the First World War. Sir John hailed from Ulster, where the family wealth had been built up in cotton and shipping. His father, Sir Hugh Smiley, who had been made a baronet in 1903, had been prominent in Ulster politics and owned a staunchly Unionist newspaper, *The Northern Whig*, which was vehemently opposed to Irish Home Rule. Sir Hugh's wife, Elizabeth Kerr, was a cotton heiress from Paisley in Scotland, whose grandfather, Alan Clark, owned reputedly the largest biggest cotton mill in the world. He was a forebear of Kenneth Clark, the art historian, and his son Alan, the MP and diarist. The Smiley family was close to the leader of the Ulster Protestants, Sir William Carson, and his Ulster Volunteer Force (UVF). In 1912, this close association saw the family allow arms for the UVF that had been bought in Germany to be secretly landed at a harbour they owned at Larne, north of Belfast. Sir John also signed the covenant at the Ulster Reform Club in Belfast on 28 September 1912, pledging to resist any devolution of power to the Catholic majority in Ireland. Such sentiment was shared by Sir John's Scottish mother, whose devotion to the 'Red Hand of Ulster' once saw her photographed presenting colours to the UVF alongside Carson.[2]

Rather than obey orders that would have seen units of the British army stationed in Ireland confront the UVF if Home Rule were passed, Sir John was involved in the Curragh mutiny in March 1914, an event named after the barracks outside Dublin. He was one of sixty cavalry officers who demanded a pledge from the Prime Minister, Herbert Asquith, that his Liberal government would not call upon the army to enforce the provisions of Home

Rule, should it become an act of parliament. But for the outbreak of war in August, civil war might well have broken out across Ireland.

But Britain's commitment to the defence of Belgium meant that tension in Ireland was held in check as British troops rushed across the channel to face the German army. The de Crespigny family had an early foretaste of the cost of a war that was soon to afflict families across the British empire. In one of the first engagements and one of the few between mounted cavalry during the whole of the war, Norman de Crespigny, Valerie's youngest brother, was killed. Three other brothers survived the war. One became a brigadier in the Grenadier Guards, winning a Distinguished Service Order (DSO), while another, Philip de Crespigny, served as a commander in the Royal Navy, being awarded a Croix de Guerre. Another brother, Vierville, also won a Croix de Guerre before dying of fever as a game ranger in Tanganyika, having been badly mauled by a leopard. The oldest of the brothers, Claude, won a DSO in the Boer war before shooting himself in 1910. This family history on his mother's side led Smiley to comment that 'All de Crespignys are brave, bad tempered and immoral!'

David Smiley was the youngest child by six years, his eldest brother Hugh having been born in 1906, his sister Patricia in 1908 and John in 1910. His arrival in the middle of the war led Smiley to remark in later life that he was 'my mother's war work in the 14–18 war, cannon fodder for the next one', a tongue-in-cheek remark that disguised his mother's love for her youngest child.[3] Smiley recalled a happy childhood and remained close to his siblings, but the relationship with his parents was remote. His father was not a man of strong convictions or ambition, seemingly more interested in country sports and sailing than earning his keep. Yet Smiley's grandmother kept Sir John on a tight leash; it was she, after all, who had money. The house in Grosvenor Street was rented, and it was not until 1927, on the eve of his mother's death, that Sir John was able to buy a family home, Great Oaks at Goring Heath, Oxfordshire. His own early death, aged fifty-three, in April 1930, when Smiley was thirteen, meant that he never developed any strong feelings for him. Despite her affection for her youngest son, Valerie left his day-to-day upbringing in the care of the butler and his wife, Mr and Mrs Cater, whom Smiley adored.[4]

This austere childhood may later have affected his own family relationships. His own children remember a loving father who was always 'on your side' but not always good at expressing emotion. Perhaps because of the lack of warmth from his parents, the strongest bonds Smiley forged in his early years were with his dogs. In his later diaries, animals, notably horses and dogs, are mentioned as much as his comrades in arms. Still, he generally got on well with his peers, who valued his honesty and loyalty as much as his plain speaking. He could be stubborn too: once decided on a course of action, he would not easily change his mind. Alan Hare, a close friend who served alongside Smiley in SOE in Albania, once remarked that he was not a particularly reflective individual. This may have led him to accept some assignments against his better judgement. Political skills, however, did not come naturally to him. Indeed, he often said he loathed politics and was quite quick to condemn politicians in general. But Smiley was no fool. He would not have survived without a canny sense of self-preservation, as events in Albania and Siam were to prove.

In September 1924, at the age of eight, Smiley was sent to board at Hawtrey's Preparatory School, Westgate-on-Sea, Kent, where his maternal uncles had all been educated. He was good at sport, excelling in football and cricket. His academic progress, however, was blighted by chickenpox, which, indirectly, was to dash his hopes of going to sea. From an early age, he had set his heart on a career in the Royal Navy. Entrance to the Royal Naval College at Dartmouth was by competitive examination, and in the winter of 1930, Smiley, along with 500 other hopefuls, sat the exam in Burlington House, London. However, his illness meant he was kept apart from the other students and forced to sit in the musicians' gallery, which looked down on the massed ranks of bowed heads, scribbling away at exam desks, transcribing English and French dictation. Sitting in their eyrie, Smiley and another pupil could not hear a word of the dictation but he was too shy to ask for the muffled sentences to be repeated. As a result, he failed the entire exam.[5] There was no right of appeal.

Instead, he was sent to Pangbourne Nautical College, an alternative if less prestigious route to the navy. But it had the advantage of being only 5 miles from Great Oaks, so he spent his weekends at home with his dogs and learned to ride and shoot. Again, he excelled in sport, gaining school colours in tennis, squash, fives and fencing, while the summer was dedicated to swimming, sailing and rowing on the Thames, activities thought to be more useful for those intent on a naval career than traditional summer pastimes such as cricket. The curriculum concentrated on navigation, shipbuilding and nautical engineering, as well as the more traditional subjects that informed a public school education.

Illness again intervened, however. This time, a serious heart ailment prevented him becoming a Royal Navy officer. It meant missing a whole term while he recuperated, putting him at a disadvantage when, at the age of seventeen, he sat his school certificate exam and the special entry exam for the navy. He passed both, finishing seventh out of twelve applicants in the special entry exam. But the navy board would accept only the five highest-scoring applicants, a bitter disappointment to him at the time. He had, as an insurance, also taken the exam for the Royal Military College, Sandhurst. Of the 500 applicants for admission in the summer of 1934, Smiley was placed eighteenth on the final list of successful candidates.[6]

By now, the family home at Great Oaks had passed into the hands of his elder brother, Hugh, while his mother moved to a house on the Wentworth estate close to Virginia Water, Surrey, in the summer of 1933. Now a baronet and an officer in the Grenadier Guards, Hugh had married Nancy, sister of the society photographer Cecil Beaton, earlier that year. Smiley acted as his best man at the wedding, his elder brother John having fallen ill before the ceremony at St Margaret's in Westminster.[7] A year later, having turned eighteen and with a substantial inheritance from his paternal grandmother that allowed him to pursue his passion for horses and racing, Smiley spent the summer of 1934 in Germany, as stable boy for Baron von Mitzlaff at Mecklenburg. Although he was there to learn German, he admitted that it was his horsemanship rather than his language skills that benefited most from his three months in a country in thrall to the siren appeal of National Socialism. Still, politics was far from his mind when, in September, he entered Sandhurst as an Officer Cadet.

II

Horses dominated Smiley's life at Sandhurst and almost ended it. The standard course for young officers lasted eighteen months and Smiley should have passed out in the spring of 1936. He had already decided he wished to join a cavalry regiment, although was unsure as to precisely which one. One of his de Crespigny uncles had won the DSO in the Boer war with the Life Guards, riding to the rescue of one of his troopers in the face of heavy enemy fire. Smiley too toyed with the idea of joining the Bays, in which Norman de Crespigny had become one of the earliest casualties of the Great War. He quickly realised, however, that having been earmarked for mechanisation, the Bays were, in all probability, a bad bet. He settled upon the Royal Horse Guards (the Blues), encouraged by a cousin on his mother's side of the family, Colonel Claude 'Jubie' Lancaster, who had been in the regiment. But after only six months of his course he collided with a tree in his first point-to-point race with the Garth Hunt near Sandhurst. He nearly died: a fractured pelvis, contused kidneys, a torn pericardial sac, three broken ribs, one of which penetrated his lung, and a fractured skull, resulting from being kicked in the head by another horse as he lay prone on the ground. Prompt evacuation to the Cambridge Military Hospital at Aldershot undoubtedly saved his life, but four months of convalescence meant that Smiley had to repeat his first term.

The experience did nothing to discourage Smiley from riding. Like most cadets intending to join the cavalry, he was expected to ride most afternoons, so he kept his own horse at stables in nearby Camberley. He also took up fencing and swordsmanship, for which he later won the Cadets Sabre Championship at the Royal Military Tournament at Olympia in the summer of 1936. A throwback to the martial skills of a bygone age, such activities did little to prepare cadets for the demands of modern mechanised warfare.

Fig. 1.1   Taking a tumble.

But if his training was antiquated, the friendships Smiley made at Sandhurst later influenced the course of his war. In particular, he became firm friends with Archibald Wavell, whose parents, General Sir Archibald Wavell and his wife, lived near his mother in Wentworth. Smiley later used this connection to lobby for a more active role in the war but his main aim now was to be accepted into the Blues. Despite his horsemanship, this was by no means assured. Along with the Life Guards, the Blues was and remains the most senior regiment in the British army, meaning that it could select rather than recruit its young officers. In 1936, its total strength stood at 15 officers, 419 men and 250 horses, rotating ceremonial duties with the Life Guards in London and Windsor. Other regiments used to joke that the Household Cavalry went on an 'overseas posting' if they went south of the Serpentine in Hyde Park or on exercises to Thetford or Tidworth on Salisbury Plain. Unlike other cavalry regiments, the Blues had never been used to police the outposts of empire in the inter-war years.[8]

Smiley was the only cadet from his year at Sandhurst to be commissioned into the Royal Horse Guards, passing out in August 1936, 'top', he noted proudly, 'in map reading and bottom in economics'.[9] Now a cornet, as subalterns in the Blues are known, Second Lieutenant David de Crespigny Smiley, army number P/6902, became one of the few officers to receive his commission from King Edward VIII, despite the hapless monarch never being crowned before his abdication. Life now revolved around Windsor, combining a mix of ceremonial duties with racing and debutante balls in London. He was twenty years of age, of wirily athletic build with clear blue eyes and blond hair. Rugged rather than conventionally handsome, he would none the less have appeared to have been a perfect suitor for many of the debutantes. But while he enjoyed a hectic social life, he was 'much more closer to my dogs than I was to any girl'.[10] This was true in the sense that his love of animals, not least horse racing, certainly dominated his immediate sporting horizons, but it also suggested a young man still trying to find his way in the company of women.

He much enjoyed his ceremonial duties and the relations with the troopers under his command. By contrast, he disliked the gulf between officers and men in the Brigade of Guards, which he viewed as pompous. He was well aware that such class differences existed in the Household Cavalry but felt they were less divisive because officers and troopers were mounted: both had to excel in horsemanship, which brought them closer together. This could be seen as sentimentality; after all, Smiley believed strongly in hierarchy as the guarantor of discipline and good order. But he was also a meritocrat, who disliked the way some officers, not least in his own regiment, had been accepted through connections rather than ability. This meritocratic ethos was to manifest itself most clearly during his years in Oman. Soldiers and guerrillas who served under and alongside Smiley throughout his career always gave him credit 'for leading from the front'.[11] He judged those he served with on their merits and never on the colour of their skin, class or faith. Any prejudices he had from childhood were soon erased by his military service. Of religion he noted, 'I was brought up with a rather strong anti-Catholic feeling but that went when

I joined the army. It didn't matter a damn what [religion] men were and I didn't care either.'[12] What mattered were ability and integrity.

His private income meant that he was able to indulge his fondness for skiing, horse racing and, as Amery observed, 'things'. Just after his twenty-first birthday and having attained a pilot's licence, Smiley bought a Miles–Whitney Straight aeroplane, which he used to fly across the channel to Le Touquet. And while his overseas service with the army may have been limited to 'just over the Serpentine', he took the opportunity every February and March to ski at Kitzbühel in the Austrian Alps. But it was riding as a jockey over the jumps that took up most of his time outside Windsor. By 1937, he owned four steeplechasers, as well as two hunters, riding winners at Kempton Park as well as Sandown. He now set his sights on riding his prize horse, Shanter, in the Grand National of 1939. To qualify under National Hunt rules, a jockey needed to have won five steeplechases, one of which had to be worth £200 (the equivalent today of £5,000) in prize money. This he did, helped in no small measure by his uncle, Philip de Crespigny, who, seeing him win at Sandown, presented Smiley with a cheque to pay his trainer's expenses.

But in October 1938, just as the steeplechase season was under way, Smiley's ambition was thwarted by typhoid. In an era before the mass use of penicillin, typhoid, whose bacteria attack the intestines, usually proved fatal. Given its incubation period, Smiley reckoned the culprit was a bad oyster he had eaten in Inverness. He was hospitalised at the London Clinic, his life being saved when he became a human guinea pig for a new drug, M&B693. He was undoubtedly in good hands: his doctor, Horace Evans, went on to become the Queen's physician, eventually taking a seat in the House of Lords. As the first person cured by this new wonder drug, Smiley become a minor celebrity, his remarkable survival written up in *The Lancet*. With his weight now down to 6 stone and looking like a skeleton, he recovered in the Bahamas and Miami, where he stayed with American friends, swimming and enjoying the company of beautiful women. But with war clouds now gathering on the horizon, Smiley was never to ride the Grand National at Aintree.[13]

III

On Sunday, 3 September 1939, the day Britain declared war on Germany, Smiley was in charge of the twenty-four-hour guard mounted at Windsor Castle. For over a year, most of his fellow officers had reckoned that war with Germany was inevitable and many had expected the outbreak of hostilities during the Munich crisis the previous year. The Blues had been partially mobilised then, some men digging slit trenches in Hyde Park while others filled sandbags in the Knightsbridge barracks. Even so, the brief period of peace did little to disabuse Smiley of his view that this was the calm before the storm. Having fully recovered from his illness and been declared fit for active service, Smiley, along with the Blues, was now given a rather belated introduction to the workings of the Bren light machine gun and the Boyes anti-tank rifle. Both appeared to be state-of-the-art weapons, but while the Bren gun was to enjoy great popularity among British and Commonwealth troops because of its reliability and accuracy, the anti-tank rifle was already obsolete before it even entered service.

Smiley was keen to join the fray, itching for an overseas posting that really would take him beyond the Serpentine.[14] Assessing his chances of surviving the coming conflagration, he decided to 'dispose of various possessions that I thought would be an encumbrance in wartime'. He sold his aeroplane and two of his horses, Diabutsu and Shanter, while he left his two remaining hunters at the de Crespigny family home at Champion Lodge near Maldon in Essex. He was never to see them again. Finally, in January 1940, just before setting off for Palestine, Smiley had his beloved dog Dizzy, a thirteen-year-old Dandie Dinmont terrier, destroyed. Having now dealt with his personal affairs, he felt he was ready for war.

While the bulk of the army, known as the British Expeditionary Force, was shipped over to France in the autumn of 1939, Smiley went north to Newark in November. The Blues and the Life Guards had amalgamated to become the 1st Household Cavalry Regiment (1HCR), and the move to Newark was to allow all units of what became the 1st Cavalry Division to form up before

From the Cradle to Palestine

Fig. 1.2 Lieutenant David Smiley, Royal Horse Guards.

being posted overseas. For the next ten weeks, Smiley trained hard with his troop of thirty-six men and forty horses, although by now most realised that their destination would be the Middle East rather than France. Albeit reluctantly, the senior officers in the division had come to realise that cavalry would have little part to play in the forthcoming land battles in Europe. This became clearer when their Bren guns were requisitioned for distribution among units heading to France. In February 1940, 1HCR began embarking men and horses on railway wagons to take the regiment from Newark to Dover, across the Channel to Dunkirk and on to Marseilles, then by ship across the Mediterranean to the port city of Haifa, in what was then the British Mandate of Palestine. Smiley was not to set foot in England for another four years.

It proved a horrid journey. Most of the men in his squadron sailed directly to Palestine, but Smiley, his squadron commander, Major Henry Abel-Smith, and the regimental medical officer were the only officers to accompany the horses all the way from Newark to Haifa. For the horses in particular, conditions were tough. The British railway wagons were too cramped for the eight horses each they carried on the relatively short journey from the Midlands to the south coast. While the French wagons proved much better, the bitterness of the mistral wind that blew down the Rhône valley towards the Mediterranean coast took its toll on the horses. While waiting to be loaded on a ship for Palestine, they remained tethered in the open grounds of the Château de la Reynarde, 10 miles from Marseilles. Their woollen blankets were scant protection against the elements and nine succumbed to pneumonia. Conditions for the accompanying troopers were hardly any better as they sheltered in tents erected in the castle grounds. Smiley recalled the officers' quarters in the château as squalid, dirty and unfit for human habitation. They had taken over the building from French Algerian troops, whose sanitary habits left a great deal to be desired. There were lice, fleas and no shuttered windows that could offer some respite from the chill of the mistral wind. As a result, Smiley and his fellow officers soon looked for alternative accommodation in Marseilles itself.

Any hopes that suitable billets could be acquired in the French port were soon dashed. A main artery for supplies and troops being rushed to reinforce British forces in the Middle East, Marseilles and its hotels were awash with British and French officers. While Smiley had been promoted to lieutenant, this was hardly sufficient to pull rank to obtain suitable lodgings. Instead, comfort that went beyond mere warmth and rest was found by renting rooms in a brothel, 'Miss Lucy's', whose hospitality Smiley enjoyed for the next three nights.[15] After nearly two weeks in Marseilles, he finally embarked for Palestine on a converted cargo ship, the *Rhona*. This vessel had the capacity to carry 500 horses in its hold and had been used to ship mules between Argentina and Europe. Again, pneumonia proved the main scourge, this time caused by the intense heat in the hold of the *Rhona*, which lacked ventilation. Smiley and his troopers spent most of this voyage giving oxygen to those horses who were suffering by sticking a tube attached to an oxygen cylinder into the nostrils of the afflicted beast. In this way, only three horses were ever lost, their remains thrown overboard to prevent the spread of disease. For Smiley, still to experience wartime human suffering, watching their upturned carcasses with legs pointing skyward disappear on the watery horizon as the *Rhona* sailed onward towards Palestine was a 'macabre sight'.[16]

After five days at sea, Haifa finally came in to view. Arrivals by sea would usually have seen the great massif of Mount Carmel before they spied the city itself, but the top of the mountain was wrapped in mist and rain as Smiley disembarked with the men and horses of 1HCR. Until now, he had led a privileged, indeed gilded existence, albeit not one without risks, but he had come through with a phlegmatic view of life. He was determined to live for the present and enjoy the opportunities fate brought his way. In the active theatre of operations in Palestine, he hoped his martial abilities would be tested, in a region whose defence was crucial not just to the British war effort, but to the survival of the nation itself.

Notes

1. Sir Claude Champion de Crespigny, *Forty Years of a Sportsman's Life* (London: Mills and Boon, 1910), p. 318. Sir Claude also had a reputation as a pugilist, although the use of his fists was not always confined to the ring. On several occasions, he found himself before magistrates, charged with affray brought about by an all too ready willingness to use his boxing skills to settle a dispute or slight, real or imagined, to his satisfaction.
2. Interview with David Smiley, London, 1 December 2005.
3. Imperial War Museum (hereafter IWM), Accession No: 10340/6 Interview with Colonel D. Smiley, Recorded 1989.
4. Interview with Xan Smiley, Taston, Oxfordshire, 30 June 2006.
5. Interview with David Smiley, London, 22 August 2005.
6. IWM, Accession No: 10340/6 Interview with Colonel D. Smiley, Recorded 1989.
7. Diana Souhami, *Greta and Cecil* (London: Phoenix Press, 2000), p. 107. Hugh Smiley had initially wanted to marry Nancy Mitford but his advances had been spurned.
8. Barney White-Spunner, *Horse Guards* (London: Macmillan, 2006), p. 490.

9. David Smiley, *Irregular Regular* (Norwich: Michael Russell, 1994), p. 4.
10. Interview with David Smiley, London, 22 August 2005.
11. Interview with Xan Smiley, Taston, Oxfordshire, 30 June 2006.
12. Interview with David Smiley, London, 1 December 2005.
13. Interview with David Smiley, London, 22 August 2005; see also Smiley, *Irregular Regular*, p. 6.
14. Smiley, *Irregular Regular*, p. 7.
15. Interview with David Smiley, London, 22 August 2005; see also Smiley, *Irregular Regular*, p. 11.
16. Smiley, *Irregular Regular*, p. 12.

2 From Palestine to Abyssinia

I

In 1940, an uneasy calm existed across Palestine. London was supposed to oversee the territory, a former slice of the Ottoman empire that had been awarded to the British under a League of Nations Mandate, as it moved gradually towards formal independence. In reality, the British Mandate authorities always struggled to reconcile the competing claims made by both Jews and Arabs to the same land and resources. Under the 1917 Balfour Declaration, Britain had promised a small but effective Zionist lobby under Dr Chaim Weizmann that it would allow for the establishment of a 'Jewish Home' in Palestine. The subjective nature of the semantics surrounding this promise heightened the already fraught relationship between the Jewish community in Palestine – the *Yishuv* – and the British Mandate authorities. Equally, the very idea that Britain would allow large numbers of Jews from the Diaspora to settle in a predominantly Muslim Arab territory provoked the increasingly violent ire of the Arabs.

Tensions only increased with the rise of Hitler and the growing number of Jews anxious to escape anti-Semitism in Europe. Many, although by no means all Jews looking for a new life in Palestine, were committed Zionists. But by the spring of 1936, the numbers migrating to Palestine were enough to spark serious unrest among the Arabs. When, the following year, a British government commission headed by Lord Peel recommended the partition of Palestine into separate Jewish and Arab polities, outright revolt broke out among large parts of the Arab community, led by the Grand Mufti of Jerusalem, Haj Amin al-Husseini. In an age when draconian security measures elicited little protest from the largely acquiescent media, the Mandate authorities ruthlessly crushed what was a nationalist revolt wrapped in the language of Islam. This included house demolitions, strict curfews, internment without trial, and expulsion, as well as capital punishment for those deemed guilty of terrorist offences. These ranged from murder to aiding and abetting the rebels, either through harbouring wanted individuals or through the storing of weapons. More passive security measures included the so-called Tegart Line, a continuous barbed-wire fence punctuated by fortified blockhouses and named after Sir Charles Tegart, a former Indian Police official, which prevented men and materiel from reaching northern Palestine from Syria and Lebanon. By the summer of 1939, Britain had crushed the revolt.[1]

But if the leadership of the *Yishuv* gained some advantage from the end of the Arab revolt, it certainly appeared to be sacrificed on the altar of broader British political expediency. Only too well aware that a European conflagration was fast approaching, Britain needed political stability across the Middle East if its oil assets were to be fully harnessed to the war effort. While the flames of the revolt had been extinguished, many in London felt that the embers still glowed and could easily be reignited across the Middle East by Nazi Germany and fascist Italy. As such, the publication of the White Paper in May 1939 was as much an attempt to assuage Muslim opinion across the Middle East and beyond as it was a genuine desire to promote its declared aim of establishing a single independent state that included both Jews and Arabs. At a time when European Jewry faced annihilation, however, the new immigration quota imposed by the paper of 75,000 over the next five years and with further numbers subject to Arab agreement, the White Paper effectively denied the main aim of Zionism: the establishment of a sovereign Jewish state in Palestine.[2]

By the time Smiley arrived in Haifa in the spring of 1940, the worst of the violence between the British and the Arabs had subsided but a substantial military garrison, numbering some 100,000 troops from Britain and the empire, was now expanded as Palestine became an important base from which British power could be projected across the Middle East. However, rather than being given a purely conventional military role, 1HCR was to relieve an infantry battalion on internal security duties, patrolling an area that had earned the sobriquet 'The Triangle of Death', between the Palestinian Arab towns of Tulkarm, Nablus and Jenin. The inhabitants of these towns mostly depended on olive farming for their livelihoods, and while the neatly tilled groves set amid the hilly terrain presented a bucolic idyll, tension was never far from the surface. Having arrived by train from Haifa, Smiley, along with the rest of his 1HCR squadron, disembarked at Tulkarm, where their camp, built in the grounds of an agricultural college, was located.

The camp was surrounded by barbed wire and protected by both static and roving sentries. Strict orders were issued regarding the movements of officers and men into the nearby towns and villages. No officer, for example, was allowed to enter Tulkarm unless accompanied by at least four armed soldiers, a legacy Smiley felt was entirely due to the hostility that had developed between previous military units and the locals rather than any animosity directed towards 1HCR. Indeed, he was struck by the hospitality he and his troopers enjoyed when entering the Palestinian towns and villages within the triangle. Over cups of mint tea, the officers of 1HCR passed the time of day with the village elders on subjects that had everything to do with the ebb and flow of everyday life but which studiously avoided politics. He was only too well aware that such hospitality, and indeed the impeccable manners displayed by the village *Mukhtars* (village elders), disguised a multitude of insurgent sins, but such visits rarely, if ever, produced intelligence of operational value.[3]

By contrast, Smiley at first held somewhat disparaging views of the Jewish population. The few he came across during weekend leave in Jerusalem, Haifa or Jaffa he found ill-mannered and somewhat arrogant. In later life, he conceded that making comparisons between Arabs and Jews on the basis of their social skills was 'odious' but equally, coming from a regiment and background where etiquette was all, such judgement inevitably swayed opinion among many of his fellow officers in favour of the Arabs. Being located amidst a predominantly Palestinian Arab area, however, gave Smiley little exposure to the wider Jewish *Yishuv* and the complexities it faced in forging a singular national identity from a largely immigrant population. Away from the coastal plain, where the majority of the Jewish population was concentrated, he found much to admire during a visit to Kibbutz Degania in the Galilee, close to the Syrian border. His troops had helped extinguish a fire that threatened to destroy the largely wooden buildings, and as a result, had been invited to share a meal with the Kibbutzniks. It was, he recorded, a most interesting experience to be among a community where 'communism was practised in its truest form', and while he was never to entertain sympathy for any form of socialism, he wrote later that 'I could not help but admire their energy, enthusiasm and high ideals.'[4]

The first few months in Palestine centred upon performing basic cavalry drills, punctuated by periods of activity supporting the work of the Palestine Police as they attempted to enforce the rule of law. Given their mounted role, 1HCR were ideally suited to covering the often rocky terrain in an area where access for vehicles was limited. It was on these patrols, with their emphasis on police primacy as a tangible demonstration of civilian as opposed to military rule in the wake of the Arab revolt, that Smiley first cut his intelligence teeth. Still, the means by which information was extracted from suspects shocked the young subaltern. He had been appointed as the assistant intelligence officer for 1HCR, a position he assumed without any formal training in intelligence work, but one that required him to act as a point of liaison with the Palestine Police. This often meant military support for arrest operations and involved throwing a cordon around any village suspected of harbouring fugitives. Suspects usually fled before the mixed military and police patrols could apprehend them, but occasionally, wanted individuals were caught.

During one such operation, Smiley was part of a mixed force hoping to arrest an individual accused of murder. The evidence against this man was based on information passed on by a not altogether trustworthy source, information which was used to disguise more personal vendettas. On this occasion, the suspect had fled the house in which he was believed to be hiding: not an unusual occurrence, as the patrol had had to make an approach march at night with all the pitfalls of poor navigation, accentuation of sound and that most reliable of early warning systems, the barking of dogs. Finding their prey gone, the leader of the patrol, a British non-Commissioned Officer (NCO) of the Palestine Police, none the less set about interrogating three men found in the building as to his whereabouts. Smiley now stood witness as one man was forced by two Palestinian Arab policemen on to his back and his feet held fast between a rifle and its sling while the soles of his feet were beaten with a leather strap. The next had a lighted cigarette applied to his testicles, while the third was subjected to a physical beating that left him with swollen eyes and several shattered teeth. Eventually, the information sought was provided but not before Smiley had registered his disgust with the sergeant in command over methods he felt would do justice to those practised by the *Gestapo*.

This was met with indifference by the British NCO. He replied that to have employed police methods as used in Britain would be seen as a sign of weakness and invited ridicule among a people nurtured under a system of law and order developed under centuries of Ottoman rule. He continued, as if offering some form of justification, that he never personally participated in the physical violence, allowing Arab police officers to interrogate Arabs and Jewish officers 'to beat up the Jews'. This was an abrupt introduction to the reality of counter-insurgency and one where the laws and norms of conventional war provided scant guidance as to the treatment of suspects and captives alike. Emphasis upon 'hearts and minds' in winning over the population, a central cornerstone of future counter-insurgency strategy in the post-war world, had yet to be realised. Indeed, later on, during his time in Oman, Smiley himself advocated harsh measures, including house demolitions, against villages suspected of harbouring insurgents. Even so, he was never to condone the harsh or inhumane treatment of the civilian population, irrespective of their affiliations or beliefs. Torture and unnecessary bloodshed certainly offended his own moral code as a professional soldier, as events in Albania later proved. It was a code that was to serve him well, providing a moral compass that helped him navigate the often bloody feuds in guerrilla wars where, all too often, the lack of clear political guidance dulled the senses of so many regarding the consequences of their actions.

In between supporting police operations, 1HCR continued to train for a more conventional role as mounted cavalry designed to exploit any supposed breakthrough in enemy lines. But for Smiley, such exercises increasingly had an air of unreality about them. It was a situation that made him frustrated, not because it heralded the end of mounted cavalry as an integral component of the British army, but because, due to its apparent aversion to armoured warfare, 1HCR was hardly ever likely to be sent to a real theatre of war. He was unaware, however, that moves were now afoot to convert 1HCR's role into an armoured one, a belated recognition by both the War Office and the more senior officers of his regiment that the days of mounted cavalry as a weapon of war were well and truly past.[5]

In time, 1HCR assumed an armoured reconnaissance role, being equipped with the mechanically reliable, if under-gunned, South African-built Marmon Herrington armoured car. But, itching to 'get into the war', Smiley now began to seek out other opportunities to join a conflict he felt was passing him by. His determination to transfer to a more active front of the war was also reinforced by what he considered to be a slight over an incident which he felt questioned his abilities as a cavalry officer. Having been seconded for a short spell as an instructor to the Middle East Cavalry School at Karkur in central Palestine, he found that, upon his return to Tulkarm, command of his old troop had been allocated to somebody else and he, in turn, had been given command of another. On the one hand, his pique was understandable; after all, he had commanded most of these men from the moment he joined the Blues. On the other, the rotation of officers between posts was regarded as normal; it helped develop a more rounded officer and enhanced future promotion prospects. Even so, intemperance born from both loyalty to his troop and frustration at a war passing him by saw Smiley heed calls for volunteers for new units being formed, most notably the Commandos and Paratroopers.

Having put his name forward, however, nothing happened. He found solace of sorts in his periods of leave, enjoying long weekends in Beirut, the destination of choice prior to the establishment of the Vichy regime in France, where he and his fellow officers indulged their love of fine French cuisine, nightclubs and the company of young Frenchwomen. Other enjoyable periods of leave were spent staying in the Windsor Hotel Annexe on Mount Carmel, run by a Palestinian family, the Boutagys, with whom Smiley became close. The patriarch of the family, Emil Boutagy, had worked for British intelligence behind Turkish lines in the First World War, and Smiley was to enjoy extended periods as a guest of the family, not least in the winter of 1942, when the hotel proved a more convivial billet than the wooden barrack hut he had been allocated when he started his training with SOE.

As welcome as such distractions were, they did little to hasten Smiley's entry into the war. In July 1940, and in a bid to develop his military skills beyond obsolescent cavalry tactics, he enrolled on a demolitions course near Gaza, where he learned the rudiments of explosives and mine laying. Acting as it did as a useful primer for skills he would come to hone during his time with SOE, his participation, much to his surprise, was now cut short. His attempts to play a more active part in the war now appeared to bear dividends as he and several other junior officers in the cavalry division were told to report to a new makeshift unit, the Somaliland Camel Corps, which was assembling in Ismalia in Egypt before onward despatch to what was then British Somaliland. Situated on the Horn of Africa, the territory had been invaded by Italian troops from neighbouring Italian Somaliland following the formal outbreak of hostilities with Italy on 10 June 1940. While hardly a unit at the cutting edge of technology, for Smiley and his fellow volunteers, it was a chance to enter an active theatre of war. He also suspected that his request for transfer away from 1HCR had the full support of his commanding officer, who had increasingly grown somewhat exasperated at this 'Bolshie' subaltern, a description of his attitude at the time with which he fully agreed.[6]

After a hot train journey from Palestine down to Ismalia, Smiley now joined eleven other officers at the beginning of August 1940 on a ship sailing down the Red Sea towards the port of Berbera. It was here that they were to assume responsibility for their new commands. The heat during the summer months in Palestine had made life uncomfortable, but despite the irritant of sandflies, which often resulted in a fever, the climate was bearable. The experience of his journey down the Red Sea, however, confronted Smiley with heat of an altogether different intensity. Without any form of air conditioning in their cabins, the temperature on one occasion reached 123 degrees Fahrenheit; only the simple expedient of lying on a bunk stripped naked offered any respite from the oven-like conditions. Two men succumbed to extreme heatstroke during the voyage, their bodies being buried at sea. But as the coastline of British Somaliland eventually came into view, any hope that Smiley and his fellow officers had of closing with the Italians were quickly dashed when their convoy was ordered to sail directly to the British-controlled port of Aden on the south-west tip of Arabia. Mussolini's troops had quickly overrun British Somaliland, despite stiff resistance from troops of the Black Watch.

Smiley's frustration only mounted, a sentiment shared by a fellow cavalry officer on the voyage, Neil McLean, of the Royal Scots Greys. McLean, who was known to all his friends as 'Billy', was from an old Scottish family whose clan roots could be traced back to the thirteenth century. Described by his friend and biographer, Xan Fielding, who himself served with SOE in Crete, as 'tall and slim, fair-haired and debonair', McLean had a natural charm that 'concealed a toughness of steel, great powers of physical endurance, and a needle sharp intelligence'.[7] It was this intelligence, coupled with a passion for political causes that belied his often languid approach to life, that captivated Smiley. Despite being two years older, he was often in awe of McLean, and while their relationship evolved into one of mutual respect and admiration forged on operations, it was McLean who held the whip hand in what became a lifelong friendship.

Both men were more determined than ever to avoid a return to internal security duties in Palestine as part of the Cavalry and Smiley now used his family connections to what he hoped would be good effect. Arriving back in Suez, he was ordered to report to his regiment in Tulkarm, an order he and several other officers decided to ignore. Instead, he carried on to Cairo, where, despite his relatively lowly commissioned rank, he sought a meeting with

General Sir Archibald Wavell, Commander-in-Chief of British Forces in the Middle East. Since the Wavells were family friends, Smiley was confident he would receive an audience. Such confidence was well placed. On meeting Wavell, Smiley was typically direct, telling the general that 'I don't think I'm going to do any good sitting on a horse in Palestine while all the battles are taking place in the Western desert.'[8]

Wavell proved sympathetic, sending Smiley to see his director of military intelligence, Brigadier John Shearer. Shearer, in turn, was impressed by Smiley's enthusiasm, which he was now all too eager to harness to a new unit he was seeking to establish: the Commandos. Smiley was not briefed in any great depth over what role the Commandos were expected to perform, other than being given a vague idea that they would operate independently, often behind enemy lines, and with a great emphasis placed on physical fitness, strong leadership and initiative. He was told to report back to 1HCR in Palestine and to await further instructions. At the end of October 1940, he finally received his orders to report to No. 52 Commando, which was in the process of being formed at Geneifa on the Suez Canal. Lest a final twist of fate prevent him from leaving Palestine, Smiley left 1HCR hastily and without any fond farewells to his fellow officers. He was twenty-four and now on the cusp of realising his ambition of seeing active service.

II

The very term 'commando' has come to signify a particular type of soldiering, requiring extremely high levels of fitness, intelligence, and the confidence and ability to operate independently in arduous conditions where initiative is all. Originally consisting of battalion-sized units of up to 600 men, the Commandos were seen by Winston Churchill as an effective tool that could hit back at German installations across the occupied coastline of Europe, the so-called 'butcher and bolt' strategy. While the Commandos were to achieve some notable strategic successes, most famously Operation Chariot, the great raid on the docks at St Nazaire in February 1942 that effectively denied Germany's battleships a home port on the west coast of France, their early reputation was anything but the epitome of the elite force they were to become. In the Middle East, three commandos were in fact raised, numbers 50, 51 and 52 (Middle East) Commando, the initial idea being that they would be used to attack enemy installations along the North African coast and across the wider Mediterranean. It was to No. 52 Commando that Smiley now reported on 2 November 1940, the very day this unit was formed.

For the first two weeks, he was trained alongside his fellow officers on the banks of the Great Bitter Lake in the rudiments of boat handling and unarmed combat, as well as demolitions and the use of mines, in which Smiley already had something of a head start. However, the training was rudimentary and there was no core curriculum determining the levels of proficiency expected in the commando skills required of officers, let alone men. After only two weeks, the new officers of 52 Commando were expected to take command of their first intake of recruits and induct them into the skills of commando warfare, in which they themselves were hardly more adept. Smiley nevertheless embraced this new regime, taking great delight in developing his fieldcraft skills, as well as being introduced to a new array of weaponry, most notable the .45 Thompson sub-machine gun, which later became emblematic of the Commandos.

Training his new charges was daunting. The later image of commandos as well-led, fit and resourceful was far removed from the assortment of volunteers that faced Smiley at the camp in Geneifa in mid-November 1940. 'When the men arrived, it was obvious that with few exceptions – notably the Brigade of Guards and the cavalry regiments – their commanding officers had seized the golden opportunity to get rid of their most undesirable characters.'[9] With some in possession of charge sheets up to eight pages long and others arriving with military policemen in tow, Smiley knew he had his work cut out to ensure that he produced a company of well-trained and motivated soldiers ready and willing to undertake 'butcher and bolt'-style operations. Time was of the essence, for under the command of Lieutenant Colonel Harry Fox-Davies of the Durham Light Infantry, 52 Commando was told it would soon be sent to an active theatre of operations.[10]

In the hope that the sheer physical demands of a commando unit would force some of the more undesirable elements to leave, Smiley led his recruits on a series of punishing route marches in full battle order across the Egyptian desert. But he also wanted to prove himself in front of his new command and to demonstrate that he was more than capable of the physical endurance expected of a commando officer. On one such march, he and his men covered 33 miles of desert in eleven hours, a considerable feat of endurance that saw a third of his company fall by the wayside. Smiley was not immune from feeling the effects of such physical effort. Internal security duties in Palestine had not been too arduous and he was not much fitter than the men he was now attempting to lead and inspire through example. While he completed this march, he did so with the heels of his feet completely rubbed raw. He none the less adapted quickly to the physical challenge of the Commandos, but he found the lack of parade-ground discipline the very antithesis of the military world to which he had become accustomed.[11] 'There was no saluting, no saying "Sir", no calling to attention on parades, and no marching in step,' he recalled. 'Some of the worst disciplined took advantage of this with disastrous results. When discipline had almost ceased to exist, normal army discipline was reintroduced with resulting improvements.'[12]

Smiley was undoubtedly well served by some experienced NCOs in his company, while the overall fighting quality of the Commando was enhanced by the arrival of seventy Spaniards who had deserted from French Foreign Legion units based in Syria. Having fought for the Republican government in the Spanish civil war, few had much sympathy for the French Vichy regime that was openly aligned with Berlin. Already immersed in the reality of battle, Smiley found their fieldcraft and fighting skills to be first-class, not least in their use of the 'Fanny', a commando knife that incorporated a brass knuckleduster in the handle and was adopted by some commando units as their official symbol.

The common belief among members of the Middle East Commandos was that they would be used to disrupt Italian lines of communication along the North African coast as the Italian army succumbed to a series of successful onslaughts by British and empire troops – the Western Desert Force – later expanded to become the Eighth Army. They soon threatened to evict the Italians from their colonial possession of Tripolitania in its entirety. On 16 December 1940, David Smiley, newly promoted to Captain and in command of 'C' Company, 52 Middle East Commando, embarked on the troopship *President Doumer* at Port Said for what most believed would be an onward voyage up the Suez Canal before deployment across the Mediterranean, either to raid Italian positions in the Dodecanese or to cut Italian lines of communication in Tripolitania. It was therefore something of a surprise that, on leaving Port Said, the *President Doumer* headed due south, arriving four days later at Port Sudan. Given his previous experience of steaming down the Red Sea, Smiley succumbed to a suffocating sense of déjà vu, given his all too brief service with the Somaliland Camel Corps. On this occasion, however, he was not to be disappointed.

III

The voyage down the Red Sea had been a tense affair and not just because of the fear of enemy attack. Accompanying 52 Middle East Commando on their journey had been the 2nd battalion, Highland Light Infantry, who took an instant dislike to a unit they knew little of and cared even less for. Pilfering of the Commando's personal supplies of beer and other Christmas comforts went unchecked by their officers, adding to tension between the units. It came as a relief, on reaching Port Sudan, that the two units went their separate ways. It was only now that Smiley and the rest of his Commando learned of their destination: Gallabat. A small village on the Sudanese–Abyssinian border, it was here that 52 Commando would join elements of the 10th Indian Infantry Brigade, part of the 5th Indian Division. Getting there, however, involved a rather circuitous route to the railhead of Gedaref, followed by an exhausting march of 100 miles to Gallabat. Disciplinary problems soon made themselves felt; on arrival at Gallabat, No. 52 Commando found they were not expected and were offered little in the way of protection from the cold of the desert night. To make matters worse, having been given their pay, many of the commandos, in the time-honoured tradition of soldiery down the ages, sought solace in the bottles and brothels of the village. Unable to control a situation that was increasingly getting out of hand, the Military Police called upon the officers of the Commando to help round up their men, a task Smiley recalled with particular displeasure.[13]

So it was with some relief that Smiley was able to lead his company to their assigned base for operations against the Italians: an encampment on the banks of the Atbara River, a tributary of the Blue Nile situated around 5 miles from the nearest known Italian positions across the border at Metemma in Abyssinia. The countryside certainly favoured troops trained in stealth and surprise, with the long elephant grass, abundant trees and thorn bush providing good cover on the ground, as well as camouflage from aerial observation. For someone fascinated by wildlife, this was the perfect location, and Smiley recounted the delight he took in spotting rhino, leopards, water buffalo and chimpanzee, as well as crocodiles, whose presence in the Atbara limited the otherwise welcome opportunities for bathing. Only the baboons really proved a nuisance, however, not so much because of any innate malfeasance on their part but because of their habit of peering around trees. At a distance, their faces could be mistaken for those of a human and added to the tension of those on patrol who were wary of enemy ambushes.

For the most part, the enemy facing No. 52 Commando were Italian-led colonial levies, many from Eritrea, who had achieved some success against the British when they had captured Gallabat on 6 November 1940. Troops from the Essex Regiment fled from the fort following an initial Italian aerial bombardment. Their rout was hushed up in official circles and the battalion was eventually withdrawn for retraining, with many of its officers replaced.[14] Now with Gallabat recaptured, No. 52 Commando was sent out on long-range patrols to probe the Italian defences, a role that Smiley felt was more suited to a regular infantry battalion than to commandos trained to 'butcher and bolt'. Pressing demands for British troops elsewhere, however, meant that few regular formations could be released for the Abyssinian campaign. Given its reputation as an 'odds and sods' unit, it is hardly surprising that No. 52 Commando was one of the few British units to be spared.

Despite being used in a more conventional infantry role, the skills that Smiley had managed to impart to his Raiders, as the commandos were called, were to prove useful in the bush and scrub between Gallabat and Metemma. This, and their undoubted superior fitness compared with their regular infantry counterparts, saw Smiley's company now committed to the fray. His first patrol was to reconnoitre a dry river bed along the frontier, enclosed on both sides of the bank by tall elephant grass. The intention was to probe the depth of any enemy defences and to note any gaps in their front lines that could, at a later date, be exploited. With two lead scouts up front, followed in turn by his lead section, then Smiley, his runners and three platoons immediately behind him, 'C' Company now embarked on its first patrol shortly before New Year, 1941. None of his men had seen action before and Smiley privately harboured some doubts as to whether all of them would be up to the task once the shooting started.

As he moved up the river bed or *khor*, his senses on edge for any ambush, Smiley became aware of a strange bird-like noise from the trees immediately in front of him. Suddenly, an Abyssinian jumped from the tree, followed immediately by a fusillade of rifle and machine-gun fire from both banks of the *khor*. This was Smiley's baptism of fire, in which he was at a distinct disadvantage. Confusion reigned as bullets passed overhead but miraculously seemed to miss his soldiers; most had been fortunate not to have been cut down in the first volley. Equally, few, if any, targets presented themselves and yet Smiley knew from his training that the only successful response to an ambush was to be aggressive and fight through it. Through his well-rehearsed hand-signals, he summoned up his Bren gunner, who immediately opened fire towards the elephant grass to his front. One Italian levy was hit running across his field of fire, while Smiley, with his two runners alongside, threw Mills bombs immediately to his front. He now signalled for his company to make a right-flanking movement, a manœuvre his Raiders executed with some aplomb, despite the fact that the elephant grass was now ablaze. Peering through the smoke, Smiley glimpsed the figure of an Abyssinian soldier, somewhat in panic, shooting wildly. But despite firing twice with his own revolver, he missed the hapless rifleman, who now fled into the bush.

One of Smiley's platoon commanders now reported that, having worked around their flank, the levies, reckoned to be fifty in number and led by an Italian officer, had been put to flight. Discretion being the better part of valour, Smiley decided not to pursue them but, instead, to conduct a quick search of the immediate area for any useful tactical intelligence before pulling back to base. He soon discovered the body of one dead Abyssinian to his front, felled by one of the grenades that had been thrown. He was lucky, for his death had been instantaneous. By contrast, his comrade, caught in the initial burst from the Bren gun, lay close to the river bank, clutching his stomach. In great pain and already having lost a great deal of blood, it was obvious he would die before he could be carried back to the aid station at Gallabat. Equally, he could not just be left because he would be burned alive by the ever-spreading fire in the elephant grass. Smiley faced an awful dilemma: not about saving a man's life but how to end it in the most humane way. One of his most able and trusted NCOs, Sergeant Harrison of the Scots Guards, suggested that the most humane thing would be to shoot him. Smiley reluctantly agreed and the wounded levy was despatched with a shot to the head. It was an incident that shook Smiley but, as agonising as the decision had been, he remained convinced that it had been the most humane thing to do.

He did, though, draw satisfaction from his own leadership and performance under fire. Not quite twenty-five, he had come through his first brush with the enemy, demonstrating powers of leadership, command and control that belied his initial fears of 'appear[ing] scared in front of my men'.[15] The demands made on him by fighting through the ambush denied him any time for reflective thinking or emotions that may have instilled indecision or panic. While his pistol shooting had scarcely improved since pre-war exercises on Salisbury Plain, he had made a favourable impression on his men, who now had confidence in his leadership. This did much to improve 'C' Company morale, despite the prevalent view that the senior commanders of the 10th Indian

Fig. 2.1   Behind the lines: Abyssinia, 1941.

Brigade remained indifferent to the concept underpinning the Commandos, seeing them as mere appendages to the conventional infantry.[16]

Plans were drawn up for 52 Commando to conduct long-distance raids on enemy lines of communication between Khor Kumar and Khor Abder Razzak, important Italian positions on the road between Metemma and Gondar. The idea was that, combined with a conventional assault on the main Italian logistics base at Gondar, the cumulative effect of this military pressure would clear the Italian positions from northern Abyssinia and open up a route for a thrust towards the capital, Addis Ababa. On the night of 19 January 1941 and carrying three days of supplies, two companies of 52 Middle East Commando left their base close to the banks of the Atbara river and, using old game tracks in a region devoid of accurate maps, set off towards the Italian lines. The approach march to 'C' Company's ambush point was some 15 miles and Smiley later recounted the mix of animal noises across the bush, amplified in the stillness of the night. Nerves were on edge but the troops were disciplined enough never to fire inadvertently on animals, whose nocturnal habits could so easily have been mistaken for the enemy. Smiley continued:

> Our ['C' Company] object was to get on to the only main road which led up from the Eytie positions around Metemma. We crept past several camps and even through the middle of an [Italian] mule company. Eyties were singing, the sentries idle, and we even heard women's voices – confirming the stories that the Eyties had women right up by the front lines. We blundered on to the road sooner than we expected and just as a supply convoy was coming down it. We had no time to get in to position, were challenged and on getting no suitable reply, were fired on. Then things became delightfully confused and everyone fired and everyone and my own company Headquarters was shot up from behind and my runner hit in the leg. We also successfully shot up the supply column and spare mules bashed around in all directions and we could hear the groans of the wounded. We even caught one mule.[17]

More by default than by design, 'C' Company had at least achieved its main objective of disrupting the lines of communication but it had come at a cost with the loss of one soldier, Raider Flood, who was fatally wounded. With the element of surprise gone, the company withdrew, gingerly retracing their steps through Italian encampments now only all too alert to their presence. One Raider bludgeoned an Italian sentry to death with the hilt of his 'Fanny', but through his skilful use of a compass alone, Smiley successfully brought the bulk of his company back to their start line. It was only then that Smiley discovered that Sergeant Harrison, a man upon whose wise counsel he had come to rely, was missing. He was never found, a loss Smiley felt deeply, not least because, as company commander, it had been his responsibility to ensure that all men were accounted for. It was a bitter lesson learned.

Despite the success of these raids, the size of such company attacks produced few tangible results, although the lack of accurate maps and proper intelligence were as much to blame. During the remainder of his time in operations with 52 Commando, Smiley and his company were committed only to small-unit reconnaissance operations, probing the Italian line, which occasionally resulted in brief if intensive fire fights. By the end of January, they were operating as regular infantry, replacing battalions along the line withdrawn for rest and recuperation. Occupying sangars and trenches along an often haphazard front that offered little protection from the occasional spasm of Italian artillery, it was an unpopular task among officers and men alike, who felt that their training and expertise were being wasted. Some recompense was had when, on 1 February, forward elements of 'C' Company reported smoke coming from the Italian positions.

Now, told to reconnoitre forwards, Smiley and his men discovered that the Italian unit before them, the 24th Colonial Brigade, had been ordered to retreat. Amid the paraphernalia of war that littered the abandoned Italian positions around Metemma, his runner found an Italian operational order that, carelessly, had not been destroyed. It revealed that the retreating troops were headed for the Chelga hills, a strategic position that commanded the approach to Gondar. This intelligence coup may have been invaluable to the Commander of the 5th Indian Division, Major General Heath, but it also marked the end of 52 Commando's participation in the Abyssinian campaign. With motorised transport at a premium but lacking their own, the Commando was not in a position to harry the Italian forces along their line of retreat. Instead, with morale already low owing to what many regarded as their misuse as line infantry, 52 Middle East Commando was ordered to march the 120 miles back to Gedaref and await further instructions.

After a week spent recuperating at Gedaref, the Commando now received orders to proceed towards Kassala, a border town just inside Sudan that had recently been recaptured from the Italians. The move was made by train, thankfully, although Smiley still had to lead his company on a 15–mile march at the other end to reach their new camp at the base of the Jebel Kassala. By now, malaria had begun to take an awful toll on the Commando, with some 70 per cent of the unit either sick or on sick leave. To all intents and purposes, 52 Commando was now combat-ineffective, an indictment of the commanders who had not provided the troops with anti-malarial drugs. Given the ad hoc nature of the unit's formation and the original expectation that it would be deployed from the sea for 'butcher and bolt' operations, its logistical needs were regarded almost as incidental and were expected to be met from whatever larger formation they were attached to. They had had no proper quartermaster staff upon which to rely, remaining very much a Cinderella unit, dependent on the munificence of others or what they could beg, borrow or steal.[18]

The decision was now taken to withdraw 52 Commando back to Egypt to rest and regroup. From Kassala, the remaining commandos, along with some Italian prisoners, were taken by truck to the port of Wadi Halfa on the Nile. Courtesy of a requisitioned Thomas Cook paddle steamer, they slowly made their way northwards towards Egypt. After the heat and danger, and no little frustration with their fighting in Abyssinia, this enforced wartime cruise came as a welcome relief. Again, the splendour of the African wildlife was there for all to enjoy and Smiley delighted in spotting the crocodiles sunning themselves by the Nile. Time was also spent exploring ancient Egyptian sites at Abu Simbel, where the huge figures and intricate stonework much impressed the troops. Not prone to deep philosophical reflection, Smiley was nevertheless impressed by the size of the carvings and the grandeur of this testament to an ancient civilisation, whose scale seemed only to emphasise the mortality of those gathered in awe.[19]

Eventually, their steamer docked at Aswan, before the whole Commando boarded a train for Tel el-Kebir, where, on arrival, they were given two weeks' leave. Smiley chose to go to Cyprus, a choice he perhaps came to rue, for on returning to the main commando base at Geneifa, he succumbed to a bout of scarlet fever and was promptly hospitalised. He had, of course, hoped that 52 Commando, once rested and replenished with fresh recruits, would be allocated to a theatre of operations more suited to its particular skills. Indeed, rejoining the Commando in Alexandria after his recovery, he expected that this would happen. In and around the harbour, amphibious assault exercises continued, and with the arrival of Layforce, a brigade-sized commando unit named after its commander, Brigadier Bob Laycock, whom Smiley had known as an adjutant in the Blues, the portents looked promising that 52 Commando would be part of a broader campaign across the eastern Mediterranean. It was not to be. Instead, much to his chagrin, Smiley and the men of 52 Commando found themselves guarding the docks at Alexandria.

IV

In March 1941, the British position in the Middle East was relatively stable. The Western Desert Force under Lieutenant General Ritchie O'Connor had chased a much larger Italian force from the borders of Egypt all the way back to Tripolitania, where only the arrival of two German light armoured divisions, soon to be called the Afrika Korps, prevented the total rout of Italian forces in North Africa. But having almost achieved a decisive military victory in the Western Desert, and in the face of German threats to the Balkans, and Greece in particular, British, Australian and New Zealand troops were pulled from the front line to support the Royal Hellenic Army against the expected invasion. It was a strategic blunder. Under the command of General Erwin Rommel, the Afrika Korps, supported by Italian troops, quickly counterattacked a British force now depleted of men and facing a foe whose superiority in term of equipment, mastery of armoured warfare and ability to fight a war of manœuvre in a largely flat, featureless desert was pronounced. Such superiority now produced similar results in Greece. On 6 April 1941, Axis forces launched their invasion from neighbouring Yugoslavia and Bulgaria. Despite stiff resistance in places from Greek and Commonwealth troops, the British government decided to evacuate the expeditionary force from the Peloponnese by sea on 21 April.

It was the remnants of this force that Smiley now watched disembarking in Alexandria in late April and early May. He was hugely impressed by the achievements of the Royal Navy, which, despite heavy losses, had managed to rescue over 50,000 Allied servicemen from Greece, but such praise was in stark contrast to his thoughts and feelings about some of the troops as they left the ships. Much like the breakdown in discipline among British and Commonwealth troops on Crete so memorably fictionalised by Evelyn Waugh in his *Sword of Honour* trilogy, the behaviour of some of the troops on the dockside bordered on anarchy. Some, most notably the Kiwis, retained a bearing and discipline that impressed all who saw them leave the ships, in marked contrast to the Australians. Having been badly mauled and with many of their officers and NCOs killed, wounded and captured, some had lost their good order and discipline. Many taunted Smiley's men with shouts of 'Yellow bastards, why weren't you in Greece?' While he later lauded their martial skills on the offensive, he opined, 'They (the Australians) were absolutely awful in any defeat – look at Singapore when they shot their officers.'[20] Applying the standards of a professional soldier to troops who had suffered appalling casualties in Greece might seem unfair. After all, in echoes of the heroics long associated with the Spartans at Thermopylae, New Zealand and Australian troops fought savage rear-guard actions, notably at Tempe Gorge and Brallos Pass, which proved instrumental in enabling the bulk of the Allied forces to reach Egypt.

But appreciation of the wider operational environment in Greece and Crete passed most of 52 Commando by. They literally fought street battles to contain a mass of Antipodean soldiery intent on banishing their recent experiences of combat through drink and women on the dockside and in the side streets of Alexandria. For over a week, Smiley and his men had running fist fights as they attempted to restore a semblance of law and order. Given their own rather indifferent record towards military discipline, many of the commandos were undoubtedly treading a fine line between law enforcement and outright thuggery. In such an environment, the fact that so many Australians had lost their personal weapons was seen by the Military Police and the commandos as a blessing in disguise. They had few doubts that, given the chance, they would have used them.

But Smiley's ire against the Australians was not limited to the survivors of the Greek debacle. Many of the anti-aircraft units responsible for the aerial defence of Alexandria docks were manned by Australians, who proved adept at petty theft from warehouses along the quaysides. Even when presented with evidence of their larceny, Australian officers were reluctant to discipline their own men. So 52 Commando meted out their own particular form of military justice in a flurry of boots, fists and the odd truncheon, a practice Smiley condoned. During the course of the war, experience on special operations in the Balkans and Siam saw Smiley take a more relaxed view of formal military discipline, but this was among men who were his peers or where clandestine missions instilled a sense of self-discipline. Even so, he firmly believed that such discipline always remained contingent on respect for the leadership qualities of officers and NCOs. In the spring of 1941, such virtues were, in his view, decidedly lacking in some British and Dominion units.

Alexandria did, however, afford opportunities for Smiley to socialise with other officers, often with friends from Sandhurst serving in the Western Desert. Conscious that their lives might be cut short, Smiley and his friends frequented various clubs, bars and, indeed, Mary's House, a brothel whose attraction lay as much in the availability of alcohol after the proscribed time of 10 p.m. as in its more obvious comforts. Mary's eventually received a direct hit in one air raid, and while the proprietor escaped unhurt, several officers were killed. To save the blushes and embarrassment of the next of kin, but notable too for a rather black-humoured double-entendre, they were listed as 'killed in action'.

As agreeable as he found his social life in Alexandria, hearing tales of fighting in the desert reminded Smiley that, yet again, the war was passing him by. It was now that he learned that, divested of their horses, 1HCR had been earmarked to invade Iraq to oust the Prime Minister and former army officer, Rashid Ali, whose pro-Axis sympathies threatened to disrupt British oil supplies provided by the pipeline that stretched from Mesopotamia to the oil refineries at Haifa. Along with two other officers, Smiley asked permission from the commanding officer of 52 Commando, Lieutenant Colonel George Young, to rejoin his regiment, a request that Young granted. It proved fateful. Two weeks after he left the Commando to track down the whereabouts of 1HCR, 52 Commando, alongside the rest of Layforce, was committed to the disastrous defence of Crete. Disembarked too late to affect the outcome of the German airborne landings that, despite their heavy losses, had still seen Hitler's forces emerge triumphant, Layforce was sacrificed in a rear-guard action to secure the coastal rim of yet another Allied seaborne evacuation in the eastern Mediterranean. But for Young's indulgence, Smiley's war might well have ended on the shores of Crete.

Reflecting on his time with No. 52 Middle East Commando, Smiley later wrote, 'I am certain the experience left me a wiser officer.' If so, it was also an experience he found frustrating and one that indicated the incompetence of the British wartime establishment. Enthusiasm alone was meagre recompense for inadequate training, poor logistical support and the wasted deployment of troops in a role to which they were ill suited. This hurt the morale and cohesion of a unit whose raison d'être had been to pioneer a new type of warfare. Recognising the role and limitations of irregular warfare was a key observation made by Smiley of his time in the Commandos. In his subsequent campaigns behind enemy lines, he was at pains to ensure that the manpower at his disposal played to their particular strengths, while avoiding actions for which they were ill prepared, poorly equipped and, most importantly, lacking in effective leadership. Yet, despite the frustrations of serving in the Commandos, it had at least given Smiley the confidence to lead a disparate group of men into battle and, by his own example, to instil them with the confidence and courage to perform well. Now, his appetite whetted by the prospect of seeing action with his own regiment, it was with relief mixed with excitement that he bade farewell to his erstwhile comrades at the end of April 1941. He had been a commando officer for six months.

Notes

1. For a detailed account of the methods used by the British to defeat the Arab revolt in Palestine, see Simon Anglim, 'Orde Wingate, the Iron Wall and Counter Terrorism in Palestine 1937–39', *The Strategic and Combat Studies Institute*, Occasional Paper No. 49 (2005), pp. 1–54.
2. See Ashley Jackson, *The British Empire and the Second World War* (London: Continuum, 2006), pp. 137–43.
3. IWM, Accession No: 10340/6 Interview with Colonel D. Smiley, Recorded 1989. See also Smiley, *Irregular Regular*, pp.13–14.

4. Smiley, *Irregular Regular*, p. 22.
5. White-Spunner, *Horse Guards*, pp. 506–8.
6. Interview with David Smiley, 22 August 2005.
7. Xan Fielding, *One Man in His Time: The Life of Lieutenant-Colonel NLD ('Billy') McLean, DSO* (London: Macmillan, 1990), p. xii.
8. IWM, Accession No: 10340/6 Interview with Colonel D. Smiley, Recorded 1989.
9. Smiley, *Irregular Regular*, p. 23.
10. Charles Messenger, *The Commandos 1940–1946* (London: Grafton, 1985), p. 71.
11. Charles Messenger, *The Middle East Commandos* (London: William Kimber, 1988), pp. 25–6.
12. Interview with Colonel David Smiley, London, 22 August 2005.
13. Smiley, *Irregular Regular*, p. 26; Interview with Colonel David Smiley, London, 22 August 2005.
14. Michael Asher, *Thesiger* (London: Penguin, 1995), pp. 190–1.
15. Smiley, *Irregular Regular*, p. 29.
16. Messenger, *Middle East Commandos*, p. 55.
17. Smiley quoted by Messenger, *The Commandos 1940–1946*, p. 77.
18. IWM, Accession No: 10340/6 Interview with Colonel D. Smiley, Recorded 1989. See also Smiley, *Irregular Regular*, pp. 35, 39.
19. Smiley, *Irregular Regular*, p. 34.
20. Interview with Colonel David Smiley, London, 22 August 2005.

3 Desert Wars

I

The fighting across North Africa has long overshadowed that other desert campaign fought by British, Indian and Dominion troops in the spring and summer of 1941: the invasion and occupation of Iraq, Syria and Iran to prevent the rise and consolidation of pro-Axis regimes. In April 1941, the emergence in Baghdad of the 'Golden Square', a cabal of military officers led by a charismatic nationalist lawyer, Rashid Ali el-Ghalani, removed the pro-British government under Nuri es Sa'id, and announced that British troops would no longer enjoy free transit across Iraq. By the end of the month, the main British base in Iraq, Royal Air Force (RAF) Habbaniyah, had been encircled by the Iraqi army, while at the same time, the Golden Square increasingly looked to Berlin to provide military support against what they knew would be a British reaction. A limited number of German bombers deployed to Syria to support the Junta, a move backed by the French Vichy authorities under General Henri-Fernand Dentz in Damascus, who now extended material aid to Rashid Ali. For while the defence of the Suez Canal zone rightly attracted the lion's share of men and equipment, the loss of Iraq and Iran and the disruption of oil supplies would have quickly brought Britain to her knees. In his book, *The First Victory*, Robert Lyman notes that the success of a rather ad hoc force in preventing the consolidation of pro-Axis regimes in Baghdad and Tehran, as well as the defeat of the Vichy government in Syria and Lebanon, which had threatened Palestine, was crucial in allowing Britain to secure its oil supplies across the Middle East. Had such oil supplies been disrupted, the United Kingdom, he argues, might well have lost the war in 1941.[1]

His awareness that 1HCR had been earmarked for the relief of Habbaniyah was not, however, matched by Smiley's knowledge of their actual whereabouts. The regiment had, in fact, already left for Iraq and had reached the first of five pumping stations, named H1, H2 and so on (the H signified Haifa), along the length of a pipeline over 500 miles long that carried oil from Kirkuk in the north of Iraq to Palestine. An identical system was used to designate the pumping stations of the T pipeline, which again ran from Kirkuk all the way to the northern Lebanese port of Tripoli. Now, after a lengthy journey by train down to the Jordan Valley, and another tedious trip by convoy on a bus that had been requisitioned from its Jewish owners to carry supplies forward for 1HCR, Smiley eventually reached H4. His relief at finding two former officers from his regiment was more than matched by the relative comfort of his new surroundings, a welcome respite from the oppressive heat of the barren desert. From the outside, these pumping stations resembled a 'Beau Geste' fort, but alongside their heavy machinery, they contained a level of comfort – air conditioning, electricity and a ready supply of cool water from adjacent wells – designed to make life bearable for those European engineers posted to oversee these desolate outposts.

It was here that Smiley first met Colonel John Glubb, better known as Glubb Pasha, commander of the Trans-Jordanian Arab Legion. Though small in stature, Glubb had a quiet dignity that deeply impressed Smiley. He wore a chequered red and white *keffiyeh* on his head, held in place by an *aqal* or silk rope, which, when set against his blue eyes and sandy complexion, personified his loyalty to two kings and two kingdoms. With their knowledge of the desert and its tribes, his legionnaires proved invaluable as guides to the main body of British troops now known as the Habbaniyah Task Force or Habforce. This was very much an ad hoc military formation, with 1HCR part of a smaller column of 2,000 men commanded by Brigadier John Kingstone, known as 'Kingcol', which acted both as a strike force and as a forward reconnaissance unit mounted on 15 cwt open-topped trucks. Unknown to Smiley, by the time he had reached H4, the lead elements of Kingcol had already raised the siege of Habbaniyah and were now looking to advance on Baghdad and remove the pro-Axis regime of Rashid Ali. Once the news reached Smiley that the RAF base had been relieved, he looked for a more effective way of reaching the front line without having to endure the hardship of his previous journey to reach H4, so he accepted a lift on a Vickers Valentia troop carrier that had landed on a small, parched airstrip close to the pumping station and was now preparing to depart for the air station at Habbaniyah.

It was a lift he soon came regret. With a top speed of 80 knots, the Valentia, a twin- engine bi-plane, was hardly a state-of-the-art aircraft and was certainly no match in speed and agility for the German fighters and bombers based in Syria and Mosul. To compensate, the pilot decided to fly at no more than 200 feet in the hope of avoiding the *Luftwaffe*, although this increased the risk of being hit by ground fire. The Valentia finally took off carrying three cavalry officers, whose fears were assuaged only by the liberal consumption of whisky. In the event, the *Luftwaffe* failed to materialise, although a failure to raise Habbaniyah on the radio, an engine fire and the pilot's eventual admission that he was lost hardly helped to settle frayed nerves. Eventually, Lake Habbaniyah, which bordered the RAF base to the south, was spotted and, using this for navigation, the Valentia at last made a safe landing.

The following day, 19 May 1941, Smiley caught up with 1HCR, camped on the southern shore of the lake. Over the next week, he got to know his new command, a troop of thirty Life Guards, as well as the workings of the 15 cwt trucks. While glad to be back with the regiment, he was only too aware that his command, again, lacked adequate equipment, not least in terms of firepower. Instead of being equipped with Bren guns for fire support, the troop had to make do with the obsolete French-made Hotchkiss machine gun, which, in the harsh climate, was prone to jamming. A battery of 25-pounder guns manned by sixty Field Regiment Royal Artillery accompanied 'Kingcol' but their availability depended on immediate need. The only other fire support came in the form of venerable Fordson armoured cars, manned by No. 2 Armoured Car Squadron RAF and sporting a .303

inch Vickers heavy machine gun. This unit was led by Squadron Leader Michael Casano, who, Smiley recalled, relished the role of skirmishing ahead of his own thin-skinned vehicles, even though the armour on Casano's own Fordson scarcely offered any more protection. These equipment shortfalls failed to dampen the morale of his men as they awaited battle, although, as Smiley realised, few, if any, had seen actual combat. This was soon to change.

On 26 May 1941, Kingcol received orders to advance on Baghdad. Split into two columns, one was to cross the Euphrates close to Fallujah before advancing on Baghdad from the west, while the other was to ford the great river further north, crossing the desert, then cutting the Baghdad–Mosul railway line before advancing on Baghdad. It was Smiley's troop who were to lead this column, with members of the Arab Legion as 'guides, scouts, skirmishers, guerrillas and agents' for the column.[2] They soon earned the sobriquet 'Glubb's Girls' from British troops on account of their wild, unkempt hair and flowing robes, but no one doubted their bravery or their use in gaining tactical intelligence from local tribes. In a desert devoid of recognisable landmarks and where maps were poor, their role as guides was highly prized.

Now, having crossed the Euphrates by ferry under the cover of darkness, Smiley relied on their knowledge to bring him within striking distance of a small railway station at Taji, where it was reckoned that elements of the Iraqi army were stationed. Led by Casano's armoured car, Smiley and his troop got to within half a mile of the station before coming under fire. With the armoured car providing cover, he ordered his men to dismount into a nearby ditch and the trucks to move out of small-arms range. Splitting his troop into two and using a railway embankment as cover, he got to within 200 yards of the station before firing from the station suddenly stopped. With Casano's car still providing covering fire, Smiley and his men charged the station – an audacious act in the circumstances – only to find that its defenders had escaped in four trucks that had remained out of sight of the attacking force.

The view that Iraqi troops had little stomach for the fight was, however, dispelled the next day. Smiley was tasked with capturing the brickworks at Al-Kadhimain station, only 6 miles to the north of Baghdad. There was little hard intelligence on the strength of the Iraqi positions, as the men of Kingcol, commanded by Lieutenant Colonel Andrew Ferguson, prepared to attack. Having dismounted from their vehicles, Smiley and his men found themselves at the forefront of an assault across open ground and with little cover. Once within range, the Iraqi defenders opened up with an all too accurate barrage, which followed Smiley and his men mercilessly as they tried to press home their attack on the brickworks.

But any hope of repeating his charge of the previous day was dashed by the intensity and accuracy of the small-arms and machine-gun fire he now faced; only the fortuitous presence of a ditch, in which he ordered his men to take shelter, saved his troop from serious casualties. His own ability to return fire was limited to a 2 inch mortar, which, after the first bomb had been fired, was discarded, as the firing pin in the tube broke and nobody had an immediate replacement to hand. With no artillery on call to lay suppressing fire, Smiley and his men had to endure intense heat with very little water throughout the rest of the day, trusting to luck that Iraqi shells would miss them. It was with undoubted relief that the order to withdraw was finally given. But his grim association with Al-Kadhimain was not yet finished.

That evening, Ferguson ordered him to take a small patrol back towards the brickworks to try to ascertain the real strength of the Iraqi forces and, if possible, capture a prisoner for interrogation. With the enemy fully alert after the day's fighting, it was a patrol fraught with danger but, given his experience in Abyssinia, one that Smiley was more qualified than most to lead. Navigating by compass and moonlight, he now led six volunteers back over the same open ground in silence until, magnified by the stillness of the night, they heard voices conversing in Arabic. From his time in the Commandos, Smiley was well versed in the importance of noise discipline, but the faintest of coughs from one of his men proved enough to provoke a cacophony of firing from the Iraqi positions. Thankfully for the patrol, most of the Iraqi shooting was too high, and while the taking of a prisoner was now nigh impossible, the gun flashes from the brickworks at least gave some indication as to the location and strength of the

Iraqi positions. It later transpired that Ferguson's column of 700 men had, in fact, been attacking a defending force of Iraqi troops of brigade strength, around 1,800 troops. Given the intensity of the fire faced that day, the lack of casualties was near miraculous. In a campaign otherwise known for a series of British military victories, Al-Kadhimain was, none the less, a tactical defeat.

Even so, the cumulative pressure of such operations was enough to convince the government of Rashid Ali that the British forces closing in on Baghdad were far larger than was the case. On 29 May, he fled from the Iraqi capital, along with forty other members of his Junta, hoping to find sanctuary in Iran. At the same time, the German Ambassador to Baghdad, Dr Fritz Grobba, widely regarded as the *éminence grise* of the nationalist government and who had helped orchestrate the removal of Nuri es Sa'id, looked to escape to neutral Turkey. Smiley and his squadron of 1HCR were detached from Kingcol and sent to join a new flying column, called Gocol, after its commanding officer, Lieutenant Colonel Eric Gooch, but not before he was to experience the elation of a desert charge with Glubb and the Arab Legion. With the Iraqi forces in a near state of collapse, Smiley and his troop were now ordered to capture the railway station at Mashaida, just to the north of Taji. This time, they were supported by a single 25-pounder field gun, which softened up the target before the main assault. After it had found its range and men were seen fleeing from the station, Smiley formed his trucks into a line abreast and charged across the desert, the Arab Legionnaires firing their rifles in a *feu-de-joie*. It was, he recalled, an exhilarating experience, the nearest he got to a full cavalry charge in his military career. It also provided a valuable lesson in the vagaries of tribal politics, for Glubb lost little time in recruiting some of their erstwhile opponents into the Arab Legion through the simple expedient of bribery. He explained to Smiley that they 'bore no bitterness against us, and providing we paid and fed them [they] were just as happy to fight on our side'.[3] It was an education in the eddies of tribal politics but, although his later experience of service in Albania, Oman and Yemen would involve similar transactions, it was one with which Smiley was never entirely comfortable.

Ordered now to race to the Turkish–Iraqi border to block

Gobba's escape, Smiley's troop covered 200 miles that were notable for the changing landscape as the desert escarpment of Iraq gave way to the lush valleys of Kurdistan, and a people, he soon discovered, only too anxious to be rid of their Arab overlords in Baghdad. He was particularly taken by the beauty of the Rowanduz Gorge, whose steep red cliffs made an impressive contrast with the clear blue waters of a river running below. In the event, locals informed the British troops that Gobba had, in fact, made for the Syrian border town of Kameshle, no doubt in the belief that he would be protected by the Vichy regime still ensconced in Damascus. Gooch had strict orders not to violate the boundary but, whether by design or a map-reading error, his column now pressed on towards Kameshle, cutting telephone lines as they went to prevent news of their approach reaching the German fugitive. In the event, Gocol was forced to a halt on the outskirts of the town by the threat of being shelled by French guns. Unknown to both parties, however, the British had, in fact, launched an invasion that very night into Lebanon and southern Syria from Palestine.[4]

II

The invasion of Syria by British, Australian and Free French Forces, aided and abetted in some instances by members of the Jewish underground, the *Haganah*, acting as guides, was a natural progression from the success of deposing the pro-Axis regime in Baghdad. The use by the Germans of airfields in Vichy-controlled Syria, which could have threatened British communications across the region, was self-evident. But with 45,000 troops at their disposal, including local and colonial troops, as well as units of the French Foreign Legion, the Vichy French forces under Dentz were a more formidable foe than the largely ill-trained and poorly led Iraqi army. Indeed, having advanced to the outskirts of Damascus, a brigade comprised of two Indian and one British battalion was forced to surrender on 19 June 1941. Two days later, however, the Syrian capital fell to units of the Australian 6th Division, supported by some of General de Gaulle's Free French Forces.

Now reintegrated as part of Habforce, Smiley and his trucks formed part of a wider thrust designed to clear Vichy troops from the ancient city of Palmyra before heading north and cutting the main road between Homs and Syria's second city, Aleppo, close to the Turkish border. Although this was a primarily a diversion, Habforce also sought to secure the T pipeline that ran from Kirkuk to Tripoli and, if necessary, to destroy it, should the war swing in favour of the Vichy forces.[5] On 22 June, Habforce crossed the border, making good progress towards their first objective, the pumping station at T1. Here, however, Smiley and the rest of Habforce were confronted by what he politely called a 'shambles'. The station had been thoroughly looted by guerrilla bands led by Fawzi al-Din al-Qawuqjji, a Syrian whose experience as an officer in the Ottoman army during the First World War had already been used against the British in Palestine during the Arab revolt of 1936. While the parochial nature of Arab society thwarted his efforts to develop a more coherent insurgency against the Mandate authorities, al-Qawuqjji gained the grudging respect of his enemies for his skill in irregular warfare, which he now harnessed in support of the Vichy regime.[6]

Like many guerrilla bands before and since, al-Qawuqjji's forces rarely took prisoners. With their preferred tactic of picking off stragglers as, inevitably, military columns became extended across the desert, tales soon circulated of the bloody fate that awaited those who became separated from their units. Smiley referred to such treatment as 'not attractive': in fact, it was appalling. Some of those captured were murdered by having petrol poured over them and set alight; others were stripped naked and abandoned to their fate under a blistering desert sun. But the conventional threat was more pressing. As vehicles crossed the rocky desert en route to Palmyra, they threw up dust which quickly attracted the attention of the French Vichy air force. As Habforce worked its way along the pipeline from pumping station T1 to T3, this become more and more of a hazard, the column coming within range of Vichy air power, which appeared to have complete control of the skies. More galling for Habforce was the knowledge that these aircraft were American-built Glenn Martin bombers, using British-manufactured 200 and 500 lb bombs and supplied before the capitulation of France. The effect, when dropped on the flat, rocky landscape, was to increase their lethality as stones and shrapnel scythed through the air in unison. The lack of clear cover – even slit trenches were difficult to dig in such an environment – meant that casualties were inevitable.

Against this, Habforce could employ only small-arms fire, which, while mostly ineffective, did occasionally bring moments of triumph. One French fighter plane, probably a De Woitine D.520, was shot down by one of Smiley's troopers using an unreliable Hotchkiss machine gun while standing in full view of the enemy, an action for which he received a Military Medal. Later on, accompanied by members of the troop, Smiley went to the crash site to try to retrieve the pilot's body but found only a pair of feet 'with neither shoes or socks that had been neatly severed at the ankle'. These were none the less buried and a cross was erected over the spot. It was a pyrrhic triumph, however, since debris from the falling aircraft hit and killed one of his men, Trooper Fowler, a robust professional soldier whom Smiley greatly admired.

Having endured the danger and discomfort of a journey across the Syrian desert, Smiley and his troops found themselves within striking distance of the French garrison at Palmyra. Little was known of the enemy defence of the town, and since no intelligence was available from aerial photography, signals intelligence and, perhaps surprisingly, even from the Arab Legion that had accompanied Habforce, reconnaissance patrols were the only option. With his previous experience in the Commandos, Smiley was again chosen to lead the first of these patrols.

By now, though, he was feeling quite ill but chose not to disclose what he knew were the signs of malaria to his commanding officer. Instead, he selected ten men and in two trucks they set out for the outskirts of the town, dismounting about a mile from the famous Roman ruins. Under the cover of darkness, the patrol moved through the ancient architecture before entering a side street that marked the beginning of the garrison town proper. They took note of the physical location of defences, the number and registrations of vehicles – in fact, anything to indicate troop numbers and strength. Two men were sent to reconnoitre a small ruined Turkish fort overlooking the town, but when they failed to reappear at the appointed rendezvous before sunrise, Smiley began to fear the worst.

Now he was caught in a dilemma: to hang around much longer in the lee of the French defences clearly risked capture or death. But responsibility for his men trumped all, and after his experience in Abyssinia, he was determined not to leave anyone behind. Daybreak brought no reunion and Smiley reluctantly decided to head back to his own lines. However, exiting from the ruins, they were spotted by French sentries and it was only after an hour of crawling, cowering and running that they managed to make good their escape without further loss. Despite the personal congratulations of Major General George Clark, the commander of Habforce, on the intelligence he had gathered, Smiley was, by his own admission, crestfallen to have lost two men. So it was much to his relief and surprise that the pair reappeared 48 hours later without weapons or boots. They claimed to have been robbed by local Arabs but, given their rather nefarious characters, Smiley suspected they had fallen asleep on reaching the fort, before being relieved of their kit.[7]

In his memoirs, Smiley makes no mention of the risks he took in this night-time excursion. But the intelligence he provided was of such value that he was recommended for the Military Cross. In the event, he was mentioned in despatches for leadership and gallantry around Palmyra. By now, though, he was seriously ill. A fellow officer, Gerry Fuller, suspecting heat stroke, suggested he shelter inside a cave, where, while reading an old copy of the *Tatler* magazine, he saw a society photograph of his only sister, Patricia, getting married. As he noted, 'So erratic was the mail in the Middle East that I had not even heard she was engaged.'[8] During the night his condition worsened, and in the morning he was ordered to report to the dressing station with suspected malaria. He was now covered in blankets and placed in a slit trench until transport could be arranged to take him back to Palestine.

Here he witnessed for the first time a demonstration of Allied air power as six Glenn Martins of the Vichy French, confident in their dominance of the skies, were shot down by six Tomahawk fighters flown by the Royal Australian Air Force. For Smiley and the men of Habforce it was a massive boost to morale, not least when parachutes appeared as the crew bailed out from the stricken aircraft. But his immediate joy at this spectacle was soon put in perspective. One of the captured French aircrew had been badly burned and Smiley witnessed his arrival at the aid station as a medical officer carefully removed the burnt skin. This memory came to be imprinted on his mind because, while he was to bear witness to terrible events throughout the war, he too was to suffer horribly from burns that he was lucky to survive. The French pilot was less fortunate. He passed away the following morning, a Roman Catholic chaplain having given him the last rites, a sight that moved Smiley, though he was not particularly religious. As he noted, 'close proximity to the enemy, as often happens in war, aroused feelings of sympathy rather than hate'.

Now, with an escort of Arab Legionnaires to fend off the unwanted attentions of al-Qawuqjji's guerrillas, Smiley was lifted into the back of 3 ton truck with fifteen other sick and wounded men for the long, slow journey to a casualty clearing station in an old monastery in Nazareth. It was a 'journey from hell'. He had been diagnosed with malignant malaria, was already delirious and now had to travel through the heat and dust over roads that were little more than rutted tracks. Three times, his small convoy attracted the attention of the remnants of the Vichy French air force, who showed little respect for the Geneva conventions, as they attacked trucks clearly marked with the Red Cross. Yet he felt so sick that, even amid bomb attacks and strafing, Smiley had neither the strength nor the inclination to remove himself from his transport. After a journey of three days, he was eventually transferred to an ambulance in Mafraq in Jordan, before reaching Nazareth. There his spirits were lifted by the 'angels', Australian nurses whose kindness was unbounded. The same affection hardly extended to their male counterparts, who promptly relieved Smiley of his compass, binoculars and prized Mauser pistol, which he never saw again. He was finally transferred to a hospital at Sarafand, close to Tel Aviv, to complete his convalescence. He and the other wounded had travelled over 600 miles since leaving Palmyra.

III

Bouts of malaria afflicted Smiley for the rest of the war, but in two weeks of convalescence close to the Mediterranean he quickly recovered. The forces under Dentz had by now agreed to surrender under the Acre Convention, the terms of which, much to the chagrin of General de Gaulle, were particularly generous to the Vichy French. With its signing on 14 July 1941, hostilities across Syria formally ended, although tension between the British and the Free French continued as de Gaulle came to regard the British association with nationalist causes in Beirut and Damascus as naked political opportunism designed to remove French influence across the Levant. Later events confirmed his suspicion.[9] Such political intrigue, however, was a world away from Smiley's immediate concerns. Having made what he thought was a full recovery, he took time to visit a fellow officer from 1HCR, Captain Somerset de Chair, who had been evacuated to a hospital in Jerusalem after being wounded outside Palmyra. He then boarded a train to Cairo for an extended period of leave.[10] On finally rejoining 1HCR, now garrisoned outside Aleppo, in August 1941, he was greeted by the news that his regiment had now been earmarked to take part in an invasion of Persia.[11]

Although Persia was ostensibly neutral, its ruler, Shah Reza Pahlavi, had kept close ties with Nazi Germany. Indeed, it was estimated by the British that up to 3,000 Germans were working on various industrial projects across the country. While pro-Axis regimes had been removed in Damascus and Baghdad, the British feared that future reversals in North Africa could spark new nationalist rebellions. Persia's annual oil output of 8.4 million tons was crucial to the British war effort, so a pliant regime in Tehran free from Axis influence was vital. Other considerations favoured direct British intervention. With the Nazi invasion of the Soviet Union on 22 June 1941, Persia remained one of the few routes by which American Lend-Lease supplies could be transported in relative safety to the Soviet forces now suffering crippling losses on their eastern front. On 21 August 1941, Churchill demanded that the Shah, despite his declared policy of neutrality, expel all Germans from Persia, a demand that both powers knew he would resist, as it would clearly violate his neutrality as well as undermining any vestige of Persian sovereignty. Four days later, Soviet and British forces entered Persia from the north and south-west, respectively, forcing the Shah to abdicate in favour of his son, Mohammed Reza Pahlavi. The country was now run, in effect, as a joint Anglo-Soviet condominium until the end of the war.

Smiley actually saw relatively little action in the invasion, his recollections of this time being more notable for the socialising that took place in Tehran than anything else. Even so, he painted a vivid portrait of a country where the splendour of the monarchy stood in stark contrast to the filth and poverty of a largely disenfranchised populace. His parent unit was now part of the renamed 10th Armoured Division, although it contained precious few armoured vehicles; once again, 1HCR went to war with their venerable 15 cwt trucks. The monotony of the journey from Syria to the Iraqi border with Persia was, however, broken by the discovery of a railway rest-house just outside Kirkuk, whose comforts extended not just to electricity, a bathroom and fan-cooled rooms but also to a supply of Heidsieck 1928 champagne. It was not quite the desert watering hole that Smiley had come to expect in the Middle East and he was quick to take the opportunity to volunteer for the temporary position of Railway Transport Officer.[12]

When orders finally came through to cross the border and take the town of Kermanshah via the Pai-Tak pass before advancing towards Tehran, it was, Smiley recalled, more a procession than an invasion. Under laws passed by a corrupt potentate hoping to ape the reforms of Kemal Ataturk in neighbouring Turkey, the Shah had forbidden the wearing of local dress in favour of Western clothes, so Smiley was struck by the incongruous sight of emaciated locals in ill-fitting pinstripe suits worn down by a tough agrarian existence. As the peasants could hardly afford meat, British troops happily bartered tins of bully beef for fresh eggs, fruit and vegetables. The condition of the people starkly contrasted with country's natural beauty. Mountains, some over 10,000 feet high, punctuated the skyline, their slopes covered in

Fig. 3.1   Smiley's 15 cwt truck and crew, Kermanshah.

trees and colourful shrubs that made a welcome contrast with the desert. This appreciation of the bucolic extended to the small towns and villages on their advance where, in sharp contrast to Syria and Iraq, bougainvillea abounded, making a crimson splash against whitewashed walls.

Resistance from the Persian forces remained slight. What danger existed came from the odd pot-shot from the Persian Gendarmerie, which was more loyal to the reigning Shah than was his army. Seeing the ravines and passes of the Zagros mountain range through which the 10th Armoured Division journeyed, the military incompetence of the Shah and his forces was just as well. On 28 August 1941, 1HCR reached Kermanshah, where, upon taking over an abandoned army barracks, officers and men alike engaged in a looting spree. This brought a sharp reprimand from a brigadier whose admonition Smiley hardly took seriously, given his own involvement in securing the spoils of war. Finally, 1HCR was told to advance towards the capital, reaching Tehran on 17 September.

The time Smiley and his fellow officers spent in the Persian capital hardly conformed to wartime conditions. Despite evidence of German influence – 1HCR were billeted in a former German armaments factory – the owners, along with their compatriots, had long fled. Instead, Smiley encountered officers of the Soviet Red Army and was impressed by what he saw. The turnout and bearing of these troops, with their 'green tunics, gold epaulettes and black butcher boots', contrasted with the rather careworn appearance of his own regiment, whose uniforms, after nearly four months of continuous operations across thousands of miles of desert, were hardly fit to wear, let alone grace a parade ground. Smiley recalled Soviet and British officers getting 'tight' in the mess on copious amounts of vodka, an evening of fraternisation that culminated in boisterous renditions of the 'Internationale', 'God Save the King' and the 'Eton Boating Song'.[13]

Smiley was frank about his time in Tehran: 'We probably behaved fairly badly and over-indulged, but we had an enjoyable time.' He and his fellow officers (and, no doubt, men) took full advantage of Tehran's nightlife, which compared favourably with Cairo's, enjoying the company of desirable young women from the more affluent sector of Persian society. But on one occasion, things went too far. With the expulsion of the German delegation from Tehran, Berlin's interests and its embassy premises were now looked after by the Swedish legation. A party from 1HCR, having one night consumed too much vodka, broke into the German embassy, vandalised furniture and pictures of the *Führer*, and returned to their billet with a bust of Hitler and a Nazi flag as trophies. The bust found itself being used as a target of sorts in a urinal in the NCOs' temporary mess.

As amusing as this was, the incident was a serious breach of diplomatic protocol and the repercussions for those involved could have been severe. Instead, the squadron commander, Major Gerry Fuller, managed to protect the perpetrators. The return of the bust, suitably cleaned, was the only admission of guilt. It also indicated, though Smiley never admitted as much, that discipline among the troops was in danger of breaking down, so news that the regiment would be returning to Palestine, if not entirely welcome, was perhaps necessary to restore a modicum of military authority. On 27 September, 1HCR left Tehran, travelling over 1,000 miles in trucks whose chassis, by now, had seen far better days. Two weeks later, they arrived in Jerusalem, with each truck having covered an average of 6,300 miles since leaving Palestine the previous May. Given that few troops in 1HCR had had any mechanical training before handing over their horses, it was a remarkable achievement in the harshest of conditions. Casualties overall in 1HCR had been remarkably light too: 22 killed and 42 wounded. In light of the importance of Persian oil to the war effort, it was a small price to pay for securing such a strategic asset.[14]

IV

Smiley, though, never made it back to Palestine. In Baghdad, he succumbed again to malaria and was evacuated to the hospital at RAF Habbaniyah. When finally declared fit to travel, he could not be certain – and nobody could tell him in Baghdad – whether 1HCR was still in Jerusalem. With memories of the awful trip in the back of the truck from Palmyra to Palestine still fresh in his mind, he hitched a lift in a Blenheim bomber to Cairo, squashed into the seat usually occupied by the rear gunner. On arrival, no one in authority could tell him the whereabouts of his regiment; General Headquarters (GHQ) suggested unhelpfully that it was in Persia, while others suggested it was, in fact, at Habbaniyah. Exasperated with a headquarters staff unable to locate his unit, he eventually asked the barman at Shepheard's Hotel, who, with great certainty, informed him that 1HCR was now billeted in Jerusalem.[15]

In early November 1941, Smiley finally rejoined his regiment at Allenby barracks on the outskirts of the city. Rumours now abounded that 1HCR was at last to be retrained as an armoured car regiment, but until this was settled, Smiley took special delight in the seasonal change from the heat of the desert to the bitter cold of the Judean hills as deep snowfalls greeted the onset of the festive season. A busy round of cocktail parties and mess dinners still punctuated the more mundane aspects of regimental duties but, in a foretaste of things to come, Smiley was selected to attend what he called a 'cloak and dagger' course run by an organisation called G(R) in the grounds of Emwas Monastery near Latrun, halfway between Tel Aviv and Jerusalem. Although G(R) was, in fact, a subunit of SOE, its origins lay in an organisation called MI(R) (Military Intelligence – Research), which had been formed under the auspices of the War Office in 1938. Under its founder, Lieutenant Colonel J. F. C. Holland, MI(R) was charged with researching and developing guerrilla warfare and tactics, including sabotage and subversion as part of the broader repertoire of the British army.[16] In July 1940, MI(R) merged with Section D of the Secret Intelligence Service (SIS) to form SOE, under the control of the Ministry of Economic Warfare headed by Hugh Dalton.

While a synergy of sorts marked the establishment of SOE in London, its regional offshoots became victims of bureaucratic turf wars. In Cairo, GHQ (Middle East) insisted that SOE operations should remain subordinate to wider British military operations across the Mediterranean theatre, a policy that often starved SOE of the resources to perform their primary function: raising, training and supporting indigenous resistance against Axis occupation across Europe. As such, G(R) still very much saw itself as beholden to GHQ(ME). It was not until late 1941 that it became formally absorbed into SOE. But the training of guerrilla bands in Europe remained a distant prospect when set against the more immediate threat to Palestine from Rommel's forces in North Africa. While a stalemate now marked the fighting between the British Eighth Army and the Afrika Korps in the winter of 1941, preparations were in hand for a scorched earth policy in Palestine, should Axis forces ever cross the Suez Canal.[17] Smiley gained a rare satisfaction from this course, in effect a continuation of the instruction that he had briefly undergone in Gaza in July 1940 before the lure of the Commandos had cut short his participation. On his return to 1HCR, he imparted his knowledge to twelve selected men, who thoroughly enjoyed 'letting off bangs and setting up booby traps'.

Having enjoyed life in and around Jerusalem in the winter of 1941–2, Smiley was told in February that 1HCR would move to Jericho to convert to a proper armoured car regiment. It was a prospect all relished. At last, the culture of 'mend and make do' with inadequate transport and obsolete equipment would be a thing of the past. Indeed, while some of the fighting in Iraq and Syria had been fierce, the quality of the opposition mercifully had not exposed the undoubted shortcomings of British and Dominion forces in training, kit and leadership. The Germans, however, were much tougher opposition and Smiley and his fellow officers knew it. Even so, he was confident in his abilities and, now approaching twenty-six, was recognised as one of the more accomplished troop leaders in 1HCR. War in the Western Desert now beckoned.

Notes

1. Robert Lyman, *First Victory: Britain's Forgotten Struggle in the Middle East, 1941* (London: Constable, 2006), pp. 2–3.
2. Smiley, *Irregular Regular*, p. 44.
3. Smiley, *Irregular Regular*, p. 48.
4. IWM, Accession No: 10340/6 Interview with Colonel D. Smiley, Recorded 1989.
5. Lyman, *First Victory*, pp. 214–15.
6. Martin Thomas, *Empires of Intelligence: Security Services and Internal Disorder after 1914* (Berkeley: University of California Press, 2008), pp. 249–50.
7. Smiley, *Irregular Regular*, pp. 54–5.
8. Smiley, *Irregular Regular*, p. 55. His Mention in Dispatches (MiD) was posted in the *London Gazette* on 13 December 1941. By coincidence, it appeared alongside an MiD awarded to his future wife, Moyra Francis Scott, for her work as a 'cipherene' in Signals Intelligence, based in Nairobi.
9. See, for example, Meir Zamir, 'The "Missing Dimension": Britain's Secret War against France in Syria and Lebanon, 1942–45 Part II', *Middle Eastern Studies*, 46/6 (2010), pp. 792–3.
10. Somerset de Chair, *The Golden Carpet* (New York: Harcourt Brace, 1945), p. 235. De Chair had been the intelligence officer for Kingcol. Smiley visited him twice in hospital in Jerusalem, one suspects more out of regimental duty than personal friendship, as he confided to the author that he found him rather an aloof figure.

11. IWM, Accession No: 10340/7/3 Interview with Colonel D. Smiley, Recorded 1989.
12. Smiley, *Irregular Regular*, pp. 56–7.
13. IWM, Accession No: 10340/7/3 Interview with Colonel D. Smiley, Recorded 1989.
14. White-Spunner, *Horse Guards*, p. 517.
15. Interview with David Smiley, 22 August 2005. How this barman knew the locations of individual units was, Smiley recalled, the source of some bemusement to his fellow officers. Some speculated that he might be in the pay of the German *Abwehr* but, given the loose nature of bar-room chat among British officers, this information was hardly difficult to come by.
16. See Simon Anglim, 'MI(R), G(R) and British Covert Operations, 1939–42', *Intelligence and National Security*, 20/4 (2005b), pp. 634–7.
17. Smiley, *Irregular Regular*, pp. 60–1.

4 From Regular to Irregular

I

Reflecting on his time in the Western Desert, Smiley was to recall,

> There was something very satisfying to me about being in contact with the enemy, whether visually or violently, and an armoured car regiment often drew the fire of the enemy or attracted unwelcome attention of his fighters. I believe that in desert warfare an armoured car unit had the most exciting and interesting role of all.[1]

It was a time he looked back upon with pride, not least the small part played by the Blues in the Battle of El Alamein, long regarded, perhaps unfairly, as the engagement that decided the war in North Africa. But his initial expectations of seeing action mounted in armoured cars were confounded when, in February 1942 and still based outside Jericho, Smiley and 120 other officers and men from the Blues were selected for 'special duties' in the Western Desert.

By this time, the front line extended from Gazala, just beyond the coastal town of Tobruk, down to Bir Hakeim in the south, a post held largely by Free French Forces. It was the last Allied defensive position before the Qattara Depression, a huge expanse of quicksand over which few vehicles, let alone medium or heavy armour, could pass. The forces defending Tobruk, mainly Australian and British but supported by contingents of Czech and Polish troops, had achieved an iconic status among the Eighth Army since they had held this vital port between April and November 1941, despite being entirely surrounded by Axis forces before being relieved. Now, as Smiley and his composite squadron made their way in trucks past Tobruk, they encountered the debris of war all around them, testament to the intensity of the battles that had been fought around the carcass of this shattered town. Many of the tanks, both Allied and Axis, still contained the mutilated bodies of their crew, which inevitably attracted flies that added to the risk of dysentery among troops. Many of these eviscerated corpses were now cremated to prevent the spread of this debilitating illness by the simple expedient of pouring fuel over what, in effect, now became armoured tombs.

Most men serving in armoured regiments felt their chances of survival were far better than those of the infantry, since they had some protection, however illusory. But such protection, illusory or not, was now denied to Smiley and his troop. Having arrived at Tobruk in early March 1942 and having been renamed 101 Royal Tank Regiment (101RTR), they discovered their fate: deployment as a decoy squadron equipped with eighteen dummy tanks, designed to fool any German aerial reconnaissance as to the strength and likely intentions of the Eighth Army. Though Smiley never expressed outward dismay at being allocated this task, it was somewhat disheartening to know that the rest of the Blues were being introduced to the Marmon–Herrington armoured car. Equally, his new command of armoured dummies, made to look like Crusader tanks yet comprised of wood and canvas, and mounted on the back of a Ford 3 ton chassis – were as attractive to air attack as real armoured vehicles. To disguise the wheeled-tyre imprints that these vehicles left in the desert sand from aerial reconnaissance, one or two genuine Crusader tanks were attached to the unit to make the tracks, while the thicker clouds of dust thrown up by a tank squadron when on the move were replicated by the simple expedient of dragging chains behind the trucks.[2]

The ruse proved frighteningly effective, for 101RTR endured more than its fair share of air attacks from the German *Luftwaffe*. With the use of incendiary rounds from their canons wreaking havoc among the plywood and canvas shells, the ensuing fires reduced the dummy tanks to skeletal frames in no time, with the regiment losing several men. It was frustrating for Smiley and his men not being able to hit back, although he and his fellow officers drew some pleasure from their new surroundings. Unlike the campaigns in Iraq and Syria, he found the Western Desert a more comfortable place in which to live and fight. The climate was more to his liking, the heat of the day often contrasting with the cool breeze of the evening that blew inland from the Mediterranean. Indeed, winter in the desert of North Africa was decidedly bitter and those who could do so soon got hold of thick Hebron sheepskin coats to ward off the cold at night.

Amid the attempts to fool the Afrika Korps, relief of sorts was to be had in a brief attachment to the Royal Dragoon Guards. Because they would eventually be equipped with armoured cars, all officers and senior NCOs attached to 101RTR had to familiarise themselves with the reconnaissance expected of an armoured-car regiment. Their role was to act as a screen for the forward units in the desert, providing real-time intelligence as to enemy dispositions and strength, as well as trying to identify weak points in the enemy defences. As Smiley explained:

> A troop would operate in no man's land between our own and the enemy forward positions – both of which were usually protected by stretches of wired and marked minefields. All enemy activity observed by the troop was immediately reported back by wireless to the squadron leader, whose HQ of two armoured cars was a mile or so in the rear. He in turn would report anything of importance to the colonel, whose regimental HQ was even further to the rear.[3]

Their key weapon was speed and little else, for the Marmon–Herrington had terribly thin armour and Smiley knew that its main armament, the Boyes anti-tank rifle, was obsolete. Many crews managed to scrounge abandoned German or Italian 20 mm cannon from the battlefield, although when Smiley approached the salvage depot in Tobruk that acted as the depository for captured Axis weapons, he was, much to his annoyance, refused by the officer in charge. Later in the desert campaign, Smiley was to command a troop of Daimler armoured cars, which, with their thicker armour and 2-pounder gun, proved a more formidable weapon. But beyond the hard coastal escarpment of North Africa, the Daimler struggled to cope with the softer desert terrain as, one after the other, their transmission systems gave out. By October 1942, on the eve of the Battle of El Alamein, the Blues were again equipped with the Marmon–Herrington.[4]

Much was to happen to Smiley before this crucial engagement. A brief period of leave in Cairo at the end of April 1942 was followed by 101RTR being re-equipped with a new range of dummy tanks, this time replicas of the newly arrived American Grant. Their role was the same but this time their arrival back at the front line was to coincide with a major offensive by the Afrika Korps. On 26 May, Rommel launched his forces against the British lines and, in a series of daring manœuvres, outflanked the Free French position at Bir Hakeim before forcing the Eighth Army to withdraw from Gazala. On 21 June 1942, Tobruk finally fell to the Axis forces. Only the air cover provided by the Western Desert Air Force prevented the retreat by the Eighth Army from turning into a rout, allowing the British, after yet another setback at Mersa Matruh, to establish a new defensive line named after the small railway station of El Alamein.

Amid the confusion of armoured warfare in the desert, Smiley and the rest of 101RTR were fortunate not to have been captured by the advancing Axis force, for they had their fair share of narrow escapes, most notably from air attack. He recalled vividly the stench of death across the battlefield as corpses, burnt and bloated by the sun, lay unburied. On one occasion, having snatched a few hours of precious sleep on the desert floor, he awoke to find he had been dozing only yards away from a half-buried German soldier.[5] Even so, it was clear to Smiley that trailing his dummy tanks around the battlefield appeared to have had little impact on the momentum of the battle, which was moving in favour of the Afrika Korps. But at least now, he could hand in his dummy tanks and train properly for the role that he had long hankered for: armoured reconnaissance.

II

In preparation for their new armoured reconnaissance role, 1HCR were given orders to embark for Cyprus. In the brief lull before his departure, Smiley happened to meet up again in Cairo with Billy McLean, the young, rather unconventional officer in the Royal Scots Greys with whom he had formed a strong bond while headed towards Somaliland in 1940. Unlike Smiley, McLean had avoided rejoining his parent unit once the Italians had been removed from East Africa. The excitement of irregular warfare, with its scant regard for more formal military rules and regulations, had proved much more appealing to a man described in one report as a 'born leader of "irregulars"' who 'should not be left to cool his heels in the Middle East, if there are similar jobs to be done'.[6] Instead, by March 1942, McLean had found employment with the Yugoslav section of SOE in Cairo. Much to his chagrin, however, his only operational experience remained limited to acting as a conducting officer for a group of Yugoslavs dropped back into their homeland one month later.

This lack of action weighed heavily on his shoulders, prompting him to seek a transfer to MI9, the secret organisation responsible for the 'escape and evasion' of Allied servicemen on the run behind enemy lines. McLean soon found himself posted to Istanbul and the port of Smyrna, where he helped oversee the exfiltration in Turkish-built *caiques* of British and Australian troops from Greece and Crete, who had managed to evade capture by the Germans for over a year. By the autumn of 1942 and with this task largely complete, McLean requested that he be posted back to the Yugoslav section of SOE, where he now lobbied for an operational role.[7]

He quickly suggested to Smiley that he might like to join what many referred to as 'the firm', since it was looking for operatives to work behind enemy lines in the Balkans. McLean most likely exaggerated the appeal of such work; in the late spring and early summer of 1942, SOE operations into the Balkans were few and far between, as resources, particularly aircraft, were increasingly committed to the defence of Egypt. Those missions that were authorised tended to focus on Greece and, anyway, with the prospect of imminent action, serving with 1HCR remained the more attractive proposition for Smiley.[8] Even so, it was a meeting that planted the seed of interest in his mind, a seed that was to germinate far sooner than he ever expected.

Over the next two months, amid the relative calm of Cyprus, he and his fellow officers and men got to know the Marmon–Herrington, admiring its speed and agility over rough ground but deriding its main armament, which lacked sufficient punch. Smiley was glad, though, to be back under the command of Gerry Fuller, an officer he had come to admire for his leadership and tactical skills. As veterans of the fighting in Iraq, Syria and Egypt, their knowledge of desert warfare was much prized by those in 1HCR yet to experience combat. But training for the armoured reconnaissance role only partly occupied their time on Cyprus. Any repetition of the debacle of Crete in May 1941, when British and Dominion forces had been unable to withstand a determined German airborne assault, was to be avoided at all costs. Days were now spent identifying strategic choke-points and digging trenches from where counter-attacks could be launched. Again, given his experience of irregular warfare in Abyssinia, it was a role for which Smiley was particularly suited, although many in his squadron felt it was a distraction from the real war. Still, if distraction were indeed needed, it took the form of visiting nightclubs on the island, where Smiley and his fellow officers vied for the attention of cabaret girls, many of whom had fled from Central Europe. A decision by the military authorities to intern these entertainers as enemy aliens was met with undisguised outrage.[9]

But the German airborne threat to Cyprus never materialised. Although the British may not have realised it at the time, the grievous casualties inflicted upon the German paratroopers and glider-borne troops in Crete made Hitler uncharacteristically cautious regarding future airborne operations. Instead, at the end of August 1942, 1HCR sailed from Famagusta in Cyprus to Port Said. Issued with their new armoured cars at Tel el-Kebir, they were now at last a fully-fledged armoured reconnaissance regiment. By the end of September, 1HCR was deployed on the southernmost flank of the Eighth Army, relieving the 11th Hussars, whose own experience of armoured reconnaissance was deemed more useful in identifying and exploiting gaps in the German and Italian front lines.

These preparations were now overseen by General Bernard

Montgomery, who, despite his later reputation, was at first regarded with suspicion by officers in 1HCR. Some suspected this went back to 1938. On arrival in Palestine, elements of the Royal Dragoon Guards, whose ties with the Blues were close, had been ordered by Montgomery, then a little-known divisional commander, to forgo their horses and patrol on foot a stretch of railway line between Tel Aviv and Jerusalem. Moreover, because of his own family ties, Smiley held a particular affection for Montgomery's predecessor as Eighth Army commander, General Sir Archibald Wavell. He had helped him join the Commandos and many felt that Wavell's subsequent removal following the Greek debacle and Rommel's initial gains in Libya had been unfair since he had scant resources at his disposal and these were spread across three active fronts in North Africa, Iraq and Syria, as well as Greece.

An element of snobbery also affected views of Montgomery and his relative humble origins in a county line regiment, the Royal Warwickshires. Some disliked his habit of talking to officers and men together, rather than briefing them separately. Unlike some of his contemporaries, Smiley did not mind this approach, although he did feel Montgomery to be a 'bullshitter'. But his pursuit of self-publicity, with his remarks about 'knocking Rommel for six', was aimed as much at stiffening the resolve of the whole of the Eighth Army as it was a reflection of his own arrogance. Still, Montgomery's habit of wearing an Australian slouch hat festooned with the regimental badges of units under his command did not endear himself to the officers of the Blues. They soon noted the absence of their own insignia on his Antipodean headdress.[10]

This contrasted with the overwhelming admiration for Rommel, whom Smiley and the officers of 1HCR 'thought the world of'. In fairness to Montgomery, his self-belief, which at times bordered on arrogance, was needed to puncture this aura of invincibility, and most officers in 1HCR realised this. Certainly, the massive build-up of men and new matériel, not least the arrival the new American-built Sherman tank, underpinned Montgomery's strategy of attaining a clear superiority in equipment and troop numbers before he would be prepared to go on the offensive.

From Regular to Irregular

Fig. 4.1   Breakfast in the Western Desert, October 1942.

After a brief period of training that included instructing his squadron in the use of the sun compass, an invaluable aid to navigation in the often featureless wastes of the Western Desert, Smiley and the rest of 1HCR were sent south to a line just to the north of the Qattara Depression as the designated armoured-car regiment for the 7th Armoured Division, known as the Desert Rats. Here, 1HCR manned a series of extended observation posts, with three troops of armoured cars serving each post and a further two held in immediate reserve. For the most part, direct contact with the enemy was restricted by the intricate pattern of minefields laid by each side around their respective positions, although both sent out probing patrols in an effort to identify points of strength and weakness along their opponents' lines. One such encounter saw the second-in-command of Smiley's squadron wounded in a sharp encounter with a reconnaissance unit of the Afrika Korps, whose use of M-3 Stuart reconnaissance tanks captured from the Eighth Army on a previous engagement caught 1HCR by surprise.

Smiley consequently took over as squadron second-in-command, but now received orders to return to the base area behind the front lines where, for the next ten days, 1HCR was fully rehearsed in the part it was to play in the forthcoming Battle of El Alamein. The training, Smiley recalled, was intense. Not only did 1HCR have to rehearse its own role in the forthcoming operation, but also it had to perform the role of enemy forces. Of particular concern to Montgomery were the German minefields, which, if not properly cleared, would act as channels in which his armour could be picked off by the dreaded German 88 mm guns. Dummy minefields based on aerial photographs were laid in preparation for the night assaults as sappers and supporting infantry practised clearing pathways marked by white tape. Smiley knew that, even without the distraction of a massive artillery barrage that presaged the actual assault on 23 October 1942, poor navigational skills at night invariably led to confusion as disorientated units 'strayed from one place to another'.[11] The use of white tape to identify routes for the armour was therefore critical to the success of the planned British offensive.

Nevertheless, a growing sense of optimism prevailed. It was born from both the clear material advantage that had been accumulated prior to the battle, and the knowledge that Rommel had incurred severe losses at the Battle of Alam Halfa in September, when he had attempted to outflank the Eighth Army. Pushed back by a combination of tanks and artillery on the Alam Halfa ridge and harried by continuous bombing by the Western Desert Air Force, the Afrika Korps had suffered a severe setback. Retrained, re-equipped and under a commander who exuded confidence, the British now prepared to take the offensive. Intent on capitalising on his superiority in men, artillery and armour, Montgomery had a relatively simple plan: a feint attack against German and Italian positions close to the Qattara Depression aimed to draw Rommel's forces away from the coastal plain. Here Montgomery was to breach Rommel's defences and push through the gaps and into the desert beyond. The whole onslaught would be preceded by a massive artillery barrage. It was a plan born from Montgomery's reluctance to incur unnecessary casualties, a legacy of his own experience in the First World War.

III

Filled with trepidation, Smiley none the less eagerly awaited the coming battle, for while he had by now accumulated considerable combat experience, this was to be his first real test of modern mechanised warfare and, indeed, his first real opportunity to close with the Germans on anything like an equal footing. On 21 October 1942, 1HCR received word that the battle would commence in forty-eight hours; they would be part of the feint in the south to help draw Rommel's forces away from the main assault further to the north. In reality, however, 1HCR remained mainly static for the first six days of the battle, allowing them the luxury of enjoying the spectacle of a massive artillery barrage accompanied by what Smiley remembered as a 'galaxy of searchlights', whose beams were designed to blind and disorientate fixed enemy positions as infantry and sappers negotiated the minefields.

On 30 October, Smiley was ordered to probe the enemy defences to his front and next to the Qattara Depression. This was not easy as the soft going, much of which concealed quicksand, was widely regarded as impassable for wheeled and tracked vehicles. Only British special forces, most notably the Long Range Desert Group, learned to navigate this desert swamp with any degree of certainty, so Smiley's orders to press forward with his squadron carried clear risks. In the event, the squadron advanced over 35 miles across the depression and reported the presence of German tanks and vehicles to the north in fixed positions on firmer ground. The unit's Marmon–Herringtons coped well with the conditions but Smiley's own Daimler less so. Unable to deal with the intense pressure of driving through a sea of gluten-like mud, the transmission broke and set light to the ammunition panniers for its 2-pounder gun. Although the fire was extinguished, such was the damage that Smiley had to abandon the Daimler.[12]

The next day, 1HCR was told to re-attach itself to the 7th Armoured Division, which had been tasked with breaking through the German positions on the Himeimat feature, a desert outcrop that protected its southern flank. The division was then ordered to reinforce the main attack along the coastal plain in the north but

1HCR remained to support an infantry battalion, whose dogged persistence in attack, despite the casualties suffered, finally broke the German defences.[13] Now 1HCR set off to harry the retreating enemy, an experience recounted by some of those involved through the liberal use of hunting metaphors.[14] Smiley used similar language in his own account, recalling that the 'best kill of the day' was a group of thirty German paratroopers. He later learned that their tenacity in defence resulted from the belief that, as elite troops, the British would shoot them out of hand.[15]

Thrilling as the pursuit of the retreating Germans and Italians may have been, Smiley was not immune to the desolation and loss across the battlefield. Having pushed through the minefields around Himeimat, he recalled seeing ' dead everywhere. I can remember seeing a man in his trench with his mess tin in front of him. He was dead. The barrage had opened up so suddenly it had caught them well and truly unprepared.'[16] But it was the volume and condition of the Italian troops that left the greatest impression upon him. As 1HCR pushed further west, these troops, often in their hundreds and deserted by their officers, looked to surrender to any Allied unit or, indeed, soldier. At first, Smiley and his crews merely pointed eastwards, shouting to these confused and dispirited soldiers that they would be picked up by troops following on behind, for their main task was to reconnoitre the expanse before them and push on westwards.

Most, poorly equipped and many starving or acutely dehydrated, were a pitiful sight to Smiley. On one occasion, sixteen Italians clambered on to his armoured car for transportation back to the British lines, grateful that their war was now over. Smiley found them a world apart from the tough Italian colonial troops he had encountered in Abyssinia. These were poor wretches, grateful to the British more as liberators than captors.[17] In total, 1HCR took over 10,000 prisoners, including most of the Italian Folgore Division. Even so, the order given for the regiment to halt their pursuit left many, including Smiley, with a bitter taste. To be sure, the 'thrill of the chase' blinded many to the wider logistical challenges facing Montgomery, though he has since been accused of being over-cautious in his pursuit of Rommel's forces. But for 1HCR, the news was worse. It was to be pulled out of the line altogether. With great regret, it drove all the way back from the battlefield to a holding base at Tel el-Kebir, with command of the regiment passing from Colonel Andrew Fergusson to Eric Gooch, Smiley's former squadron commander in Iraq.[18]

The officers and men of 1HCR grasped the opportunity to take some well-earned leave in Cairo, but amid the socialising Smiley had other ideas. He now sought out his old friend, Billy McLean. Amid the comforts of the Egyptian capital, McLean readily agreed to help Smiley join SOE as part of his planned mission to Yugoslavia. It was an offer Smiley hoped would materialise, since he had just been told that, rather than returning to North Africa, 1HCR had been earmarked to patrol the Turkish–Syrian frontier, hardly an active theatre of war. While this was justified as a necessary precaution against a German attack through neutral Turkey, many in the Household Cavalry believed it to be further evidence of Montgomery's bias against the regiment. Whatever the reasons, it was enough to decide Smiley on a path towards special operations that was to define the rest of his war and, indeed, his military career.

IV

In 1942, the headquarters of SOE in Cairo was better known by its cover name, MO4. Still, this bland nomenclature never fooled even the most humble Cairene taxi driver, who always referred to the MO4 office in Rustem Buildings in the city centre as the 'secret building'.[19] While beholden politically to the Foreign Office in London, its operations in the Mediterranean and the Balkans were under GHQ Cairo and its Special Operations Committee, which exercised some control of SOE's activities in support of the wider war effort. Unbeknownst to Smiley, the secret world of SOE was a hive of jealousies and personal rivalries, described memorably by Bickham Sweet-Escott in his account of working with 'the firm' as an 'atmosphere of jealousy, suspicion and intrigue which embittered the relations between the various secret and semi-secret departments in Cairo'.[20] Sweet-Escott, a banker who knew the Balkans well before the war, was referring in particular to the rather vexed relationship between SOE and the SIS, better known as MI6 but which operated in the Middle East under the cover name of the Inter-Services Liaison Department.

Such tension was partly due to their different philosophies. With its remit from the Prime Minister, Winston Churchill, to 'set Europe ablaze' through acts of sabotage, subversion and resistance, the actions of SOE often appeared the very antithesis of the stealthy collection of intelligence associated with MI6. These differences have often been overplayed: in several theatres, most notably Norway, both organisations did enjoy close relations. In the Middle East, however, such rivalry was often because of the pressure on scarce resources, notably aircraft, as both organisations tried to prioritise their respective missions.

Ideological differences inside SOE, especially over policy towards Yugoslavia and Albania, also soured relations among and between operatives. But in December 1942, Smiley knew nothing of these internal disputes. He was more concerned with persuading the staff at Rustem Buildings that he was a suitable candidate for special operations in the Balkans, before getting permission from his commanding officer in 1HCR to join SOE. In the event, he easily persuaded his interviewing panel that he had the skills and motivation to organise and conduct guerrilla warfare. His experience of battle, his service in the Commandos, his training in mines and explosives, and his brief stint as an intelligence officer in Palestine were ideal for the type of officer SOE wished to recruit for the Balkans. Unlike that of their counterparts dropped initially into France, the Low Countries and Scandinavia, the main task of SOE in the Balkans was to raise, equip and train guerrillas to attack and harass enemy lines of communication. Referred to as British Liaison Officers (BLOs), they mostly operated openly in various forms of British battle dress. Many BLOs came to spend as much time trying to reconcile competing ideological and political agendas between various partisan and guerrilla groups as they did fighting the Germans and Italians.

Smiley was duly accepted as a candidate but told to report back to his regiment, now stationed in the Syrian town of Raqqa on the banks of the upper Euphrates, and await orders. Eventually, he was summoned to see his commanding officer, Lieutenant

Colonel Gooch, who had received a request from MO4 for Smiley to be released from 1HCR. He knew Gooch thought highly of him but he was unsure how well he would take the loss of one of his most able troop commanders, for Smiley was now on the cusp of taking over his own squadron. In the event, Gooch gave his benediction, accepting Smiley's plea that 1HCR was unlikely to see action for some considerable time against a threat that seemed to diminish by the week. His explanation that Gooch was possibly 'glad to be rid of a Bolshie' was too modest. Gooch appreciated an officer anxious to remain in 'the war' and admired his spirit of adventure.[21] With his personal affairs quickly settled, Smiley reported for duty with SOE in Cairo on New Year's Day 1943. He was not to rejoin his regiment until after the war.

As soon as he arrived in Cairo, Smiley was sent back to a place he knew all too well: Haifa. In the grounds of an old monastery atop the panoramic splendour of Mount Carmel, SOE had set up Special Training School (STS) 102, where its students were subjected to an intense curriculum involving all aspects of irregular warfare. Over the next three months, alongside candidates drawn from Yugoslavia, Greece and France as well as Britain, Smiley faced a regime of intense physical training interspersed with lessons in the use of German and Italian weapons, equipment and vehicles, recognition of their unit formations, insignia and badges, explosives, demolitions and the use of time pencils (delayed detonators that initiate an explosion). He was also trained in wireless communications (including transmission in Morse code), the encryption and decryption of messages, advanced field security, resistance to interrogation, the use of secret inks, the tapping of telephone lines and how to pick locks, blow a safe and even drive and sabotage a locomotive.

Already versed in the use of explosives, Smiley proved a quick learner and soon became expert in assessing the amount needed – be it amatol, dynamite or gelignite, or a mix of all three – to collapse a structure such as a pylon, bridge or electrical generator. He and his fellow students were also introduced to an array of special weapons designed by SOE's army of scientists. The most useful, Smiley recalled, was the 'tyre buster', a ring of explosive barely 2 inches wide, fitted with a small pressure-switch that could be scattered easily on roads, either at the point of an ambush or to prevent follow-up operations by motorised troops. Any ground pressure heavier than 150 lb would activate the switch, and the tyre buster proved remarkably effective.[22]

Smiley was also taught to set limpet mines, which, with powerful magnets, could be attached below the waterline to the hulls of enemy ships. To satisfy his instructors, one winter's night amid pouring rain, he and a fellow student had to paddle out to put dummy mines of the wreck of the *Patria*, a ship that had been abandoned once its human cargo of illegal Jewish immigrants had been brought ashore in Haifa. Smiley never had cause to use this particular skill during the war but it was one he was called upon to employ soon after as part of a highly sensitive covert operation designed to stem the flow of refugees to Palestine.[23]

Lessons to help students evade capture were also taught by a range of staff whose previous employment in civilian life had been rather exotic. Major Jasper Maskelyne, a magician, taught Smiley how to secrete various items of escape kit – button compasses, silk maps, and pencil clips that doubled as magnetic needles, as well as money sewn into his clothing. When asked to search Major Maskelyne for such items after his lecture, his students were amazed to find that they had missed over twenty items, despite an apparently thorough search of his person.[24]

The curriculum much appealed to Smiley, for he took a real delight in the minutiae of military weapons and equipment, a result of his overriding interests in the 'material aspects of life'. This, however, highlights one key flaw in the training of BLOs. With its emphasis upon the paramilitary skills to train guerrillas behind enemy lines, little attention was paid to honing the diplomatic skills needed to deal with disparate groups whose agendas often undermined the coherence needed to meet wider operational or strategic aims. Most BLOs were soldiers by inclination and training, but they were poorly prepared to understand the vagaries of local rivalries, with their often bitter mix of sectarian and religious differences, tribal loyalties and ideological rivalries. Most BLOs had to learn these skills on the job but Smiley was never entirely comfortable with this aspect of his work and, certainly in Albania, deferred to the greater political nous of

McLean and, later on, Julian Amery. On more than one occasion in Albania, it was McLean's tact in smoothing partisan feathers ruffled by Smiley's blunt comments that prevented their mission being badly, even violently, undermined.

Knowing that a life with few comforts in the field lay ahead, Smiley had no wish to endure the Spartan conditions that made up the billets for most trainees atop Mount Carmel. Instead, during his training at STS 102, he stayed again in the Windsor Annexe Hotel, whose Palestinian owners, the Boutagys, had remained good friends. Increasing tension between Jews and the Mandate authorities, though, was never far from the surface and one incident in particular, with serious ramifications for Anglo-Jewish relations in Palestine, occurred soon after he left STS 102. On the night of 6 March 1943, a British army truck drew up outside the training school armoury, having passed through camp security. On board were locally recruited Jewish soldiers tasked with providing base security. They disembarked under the instruction of a Jewish intelligence officer responsible for field security around the base, and promptly emptied the contents of the armoury before disappearing into the night, never to be seen again.[25] Smiley admired the 'cunning' of the subterfuge and recalled that the camp commandant received a 'terrible bollocking' before being removed from his post. The raid had been carried out by the *Palmach*, the elite strike force of the *Haganah*, who justified the raid on the grounds that, following the end of any immediate German threat to Palestine, they were reclaiming their own arms, which had been illegally confiscated by the British.[26] But they took more than just their own arms. The haul included Italian and German weapons used by students to familiarise themselves with such arms in the expectation that they would have to use them too.

Six weeks after entering the school, Smiley was one of twenty candidates who passed the course and were allowed to proceed to the next phase: parachute training. Of those who failed, some were deemed technically maladroit in the use of explosives and others failed to achieve the required standard in wireless telegraphy, while a few were found to be temperamentally unsuited to working behind enemy lines. Now, Smiley headed south once

Fig. 4.2 Smiley before his first parachute jump, Kabrit, Egypt, January 1943.

more to Egypt and the training camp at Kabrit on the Suez Canal, for parachute training alongside some who had been recruited into the SAS. Parachute training during the war was still rudimentary. Students had to leap off the back of a small truck travelling along the stony desert at 40 mph, a method that, it was felt, best replicated an actual parachute landing. Injuries, some of them serious, were common, particularly among those who failed to keep their feet together in order to maximise stability to their knees and ankles upon impact.

Those who were deemed to have mastered this skill then had to make six jumps over the course of a week from a Lockheed Hudson aircraft. Given that most operational jumps into the Balkans were initially made from converted Halifax bombers, the Hudson was a poor choice because its slowest speed of 120 mph was rather fast for a comfortable exit through a doorway never designed for parachuting. But the RAF was still reluctant to dedicate Halifax bombers to special duties so the Hudson offered the only available platform from which would-be parachutists could gain their wings.[27]

Not knowing what to expect, Smiley was excited by the prospect of his first jump. It was British practice to jump with only one parachute, which was attached by a static line to a strong wire running the length of the fuselage. Since operational jumps were supposedly to be made from between 800 and 1,000 feet, reserve parachutes were deemed unnecessary since the student would hardly have time to open a second canopy before hitting the ground, should the main parachute fail. Such failures were usually the result of 'Roman Candles', when a poor exit from the aircraft let the rigging lines of the parachute fold over the top of the canopy and prevent its proper deployment. While such occurrences were rare, one trainee did suffer a Roman Candle during Smiley's training, a visceral reminder of the risks taken by those using a technology still very much in its infancy.

Smiley completed his six jumps without mishap, four during daylight from the Hudson and two at night from a Dakota, which he found to be a much more stable aircraft from which to exit. He found his second jump the most frightening because ignorance had very much been bliss during his initial jump. Like most airborne troops, he approached his future jumps with trepidation born of experience. But he always felt delight and exhilaration once the canopy had opened safely. By mid-March 1943, having completed all his required jumps and having been duly awarded his parachute wings, he was deemed a fully trained member of MO4 and, after a brief period of leave, ready to be despatched to the Balkans.

This leave was spent with his elder brother, John, an officer in the Middlesex Yeomanry, hitchhiking from Cairo to Eritrea on the back of a string of RAF trucks. It was a time to catch up on family news, for he had not been back in England for over three years and he knew there could be no guarantees that he would ever see his family again. But the omens were on his side. He had arranged to fly back from Asmara in Eritrea to Cairo in a Dakota. Having taxied to the end of the runway waiting for the all-clear to take off, Smiley was looking forward to his final few days of leave in Cairo before his operational assignment. Instead, the plane was ordered back to the makeshift terminal where a brigadier, pulling rank, ordered Smiley off the plane, claiming that his need to get back to Egypt was more pressing. While extremely annoying, it was an order that saved Smiley's life, for while he was to catch a later flight and arrive late but otherwise fit and healthy, his original flight crashed in the desert on its approach to Cairo. There were no survivors.[28]

Notes

1. Smiley, *Irregular Regular*, p. 66; IWM, Accession No: 10340/7/4 Interview with Colonel D. Smiley, Recorded 1989.
2. Smiley, *Irregular Regular*, pp. 62–3.
3. Smiley, *Irregular Regular*, p. 66.
4. IWM, Accession No: 10340/7/3 Interview with Colonel D. Smiley, Recorded 1989.
5. Smiley, *Irregular Regular*, p. 67.
6. Fielding, *One Man in His Time*, p. 25.
7. Fielding, *One Man in His Time*, p. 31. A detailed account of MI9 operations in the Mediterranean theatre can be found in TNA WO208/325, Top Secret: Summary of MI9 Activities in the Eastern Mediterranean 1941–1945: Section E, Middle East. Brief History of IS9(ME) Balkan Operations.
8. David Smiley, *Albanian Assignment* (London: Chatto & Windus, 1984), p. 2.
9. Smiley, *Irregular Regular*, p. 69.
10. IWM, Accession No: 10340/7/4 Interview with Colonel D. Smiley, Recorded 1989; White-Spunner, *Horse Guards*, p. 527.
11. IWM, Accession No: 10340/7/4 Interview with Colonel D. Smiley, Recorded 1989.
12. Smiley, *Irregular Regular*, p. 72.
13. White-Spunner, *Horse Guards*, p. 526.
14. White-Spunner, *Horse Guards*, p. 526.
15. Smiley, *Irregular Regular*, p. 73.
16. IWM, Accession No: 10340/7/4 Interview with Colonel D. Smiley, Recorded 1989.
17. IWM, Accession No: 10340/7/4 Interview with Colonel D. Smiley, Recorded 1989.
18. White-Spunner, *Horse Guards*, p. 527.

19. Artemis Cooper, *Cairo in the War 1939–1945* (London: Hamish Hamilton, 1989), p. 262.
20. Bickham Sweet-Escott, *Baker Street Irregular* (London: Methuen, 1965), p. 73.
21. Smiley, *Albanian Assignment*, p. 3; Interview with Colonel David Smiley, London, 1 February 2005.
22. Interview with Colonel David Smiley, London, 1 February 2005; Bailey, *The Wildest Province*, p. 52; Frederic Boyce and Douglas Everett, *SOE: The Scientific Secrets* (Stroud: Sutton Press, 2003), p. 54.
23. Interview with Colonel David Smiley, London, 1 February 2005; Smiley, *Albanian Assignment*, p. 4.
24. Bailey, *The Wildest Province*, p. 52; Smiley, *Albanian Assignment*, p. 15.
25. Interview with Colonel David Smiley, London, 1 February 2005.
26. See Yehuda Bauer, *From Diplomacy to Resistance: A History of Jewish Palestine 1939–1945* (Philadelphia: Jewish Publication Society of America, 1970), pp. 266–7.
27. Smiley, *Albanian Assignment*, p. 5.
28. Smiley, *Albanian Assignment*, pp. 5–6.

5 A Matter Called 'Concensus'

I

Smiley had assumed that his eventual destination would be somewhere in Yugoslavia. Keen to ensure that German and Italian troops remained in the Balkans while the Allies prepared to invade first Sicily and then mainland Italy, GHQ Cairo had begun to examine closely the extent to which SOE could help resistance groups across the Balkans to tie down Axis forces. Since September 1942, SOE missions had been probing the possibilities of building up an effective resistance network in Yugoslavia, assuming that Royalist forces that had survived the German invasion of Yugoslavia in the spring of 1941 could form guerrilla bands. Led by Colonel Draža Mihailović, these guerrillas, known as *četniks*, were predominantly Serbian nationalists whose animus towards the Nazis came to be more than matched by their hatred of the communist partisans, led by a Croatian, Josip Broz, better known as Tito. The government in London at first reckoned that Mihailović's politics were more suited to British interests in the Balkans. But by the beginning of 1943, reports reaching GHQ Cairo, mainly through intelligence supplied through 'Ultra', the top secret Enigma decrypts of German military traffic, suggested that forces under Tito, of whom London and Cairo knew little, were increasingly effective.[1]

SOE missions dropped into Yugoslavia, led by William Deakin and Brigadier Fitzroy Maclean, served to confirm this intelligence: Tito's partisans not only were the more active against the Germans but also evidence had emerged of collaboration between Mihailović and Axis forces.[2] The British decision to abandon

A Matter Called 'Concensus'

Fig. 5.1 Map of Albania.

the *četnik* leader still remains controversial. Some have argued that any collaboration between Mihailović and the Germans was purely tactical. Indeed, the *četniks* did help SOE demolish the railway bridge during an SOE mission at Višegrad in October 1943, which disrupted the supply of chrome from Albania and Yugoslavia. Moreover, some key SOE officers in Cairo, including James Klugmann, a committed communist, and Basil Davidson, later a noted a left-wing journalist, have been blamed for the shift in British policy towards the partisans by distorting or indeed withholding information that portrayed Mihailović and his *četniks* in a more favourable light.[3]

This volatile mix of competing ideologies, religious sectarianism and ethnic politics had a similar resonance in neighbouring Albania. This small Balkan state on the Adriatic coast, surrounded by the provinces of Yugoslavia to the north and east, and by Greece to the south, was a country of which the British knew little and cared less. A tribal monarchy of just over a million inhabitants, Albania was dominated by mountains that ran along the spine of the country, interspersed by deep valleys and rivers that snaked down to the coastal plain before meeting the sea. Ethnically divided between two main groups, the Ghegs in the north, and the Tosks in the south, most Albanians were Muslim, divided equally between Sunnis and Bektashis. Further to the north towards the border with Yugoslavia lived the majority of Albania's Catholic population, numbering some 120,000, while close to the frontier with Greece, around 80,000 Albanians considered themselves Greek Orthodox.[4]

A former province of the old Ottoman empire, Albania had gained its independence in 1913, although in the aftermath of the First World War its borders were ratified by a treaty that failed to include the Yugoslav province of Kosovo, whose million people were ethnic Albanians. The inter-war period was one of continuous political unrest in Albania as competing tribal clans vied for influence and power amid the avaricious designs of fascist Italy and Yugoslavia. A Gheg chieftain, Ahmed Bey Zogu, proclaimed himself president in 1925 and king in 1928. But as King Zog, he faced immediate opposition. Many Albanians, particularly the Tosks, resented the imposition of a fiefdom dominated by

Ghegs, while the Italian government, which had initially given Zog economic and military aid, became alarmed as the 1930s progressed by his increasing independence, especially after he set up his own gendarmerie overseen by a handful of British officers. Mussolini forced Zog eventually to dispense with these 'advisors', but wider fascist ambitions in the Balkans, which the Italian dictator viewed as part of his natural domain, saw Italian forces invade the country on 7 April 1939.[5]

Albanian resistance quickly collapsed. Only a rear-guard action around the port of Durazzo by Major Abas Kupi, a member of the gendarmerie, helped King Zog and his family to flee, eventually finding exile in Britain. Attempts by London to raise resistance against the Italians once Rome declared war on Britain in June 1940 eventually foundered on the rocks of Albania's ethnic and political realities. Amery, son of the British colonial secretary, Leo Amery, whose enthusiasm for intrigue and adventure saw him quickly recruited into Section D of MI6, the forerunner of SOE, sought to stir up a rebellion. While working under diplomatic cover at the British embassy in Belgrade and trading on his experience of travel in the Balkans before the war, he established a network of contacts and couriers. Working with the Kryeziu brothers from Kosovo, as well as with Kupi, Amery hoped to raise the Gheg tribes against the Italians in the north of Albania.[6] But the German invasion of Yugoslavia in the spring of 1941 dashed such hopes as Amery's networks quickly crumbled. Indeed, most Albanians remained aloof from attempts to resist either the Italians or the Germans because Axis forces were clearly triumphant.[7]

But by 1943, with the tide of war in the Mediterranean turning in favour of the Allies, GHQ Cairo now looked to harness aid to resistance across the Balkans to the wider British war effort. While the focus was on supporting movements in Greece and Yugoslavia, reports reaching Cairo suggested that resistance was also beginning to stir in Albania. SOE in Cairo turned to a remarkable woman, Margaret Hasluck, known as 'Fanny'. Resembling an English governess with her 'pink complexion and bright blue eyes', and her greying hair held tightly in a bun, she was a noted anthropologist who had studied Albanian folklore and customs all her life. After the death of her husband, Frederick, an ethnographer who had researched the Bektashi, she dedicated herself to editing his papers. From 1923 onwards, she had lived in Elbasan, just south of the capital, Tirana, until expelled in 1939 by the invading Italians, who suspected her of espionage.[8]

But despite her academic credentials and unique knowledge, Hasluck knew little of what had been happening inside Albania since joining SOE in 1940. Attempts to recruit exiles in Turkey or Palestine foundered. The British had precious little to offer Albanians, reluctant to side with the Allies at a time when Axis fortunes were in the ascendant, apart from bribes. Furthermore, the Germans had been politically adroit in hiving off Kosovo from Yugoslavia and awarding it to Albania, assuaging a territorial grievance long regarded by Albanians as a national humiliation. Hasluck's attempts to persuade London to recognise the changed status of Kosovo were brushed aside. The Foreign Office regarded Yugoslavia and Greece as far more influential players in Balkan affairs.[9]

All the same, it was felt that organised resistance in Albania could help hasten Italy's collapse. In early 1943, the British chiefs of staff ordered SOE to conduct 'An intensified campaign of sabotage and guerrilla activities in the Balkans' to help disrupt the deployment of German forces to the eastern front and 'to disrupt Axis supplies from the region of oil, chrome and copper'.[10] SOE's interest in Yugoslavia and Greece only increased McLean's curiosity about Albania, which he came to regard as a 'unique challenge'. He now submitted a sketchy plan to Brigadier C. M. 'Rolo' Keble, Chief of Staff of SOE in Cairo, an effective staff officer despite his temper and bullying manner, who had acquired something of a reputation for bureaucratic 'empire building'.[11]

Keble's decision to sanction an exploratory mission to Albania was based as much on an assumption of pan-Balkan resistance to the Germans and Italians as it was on any hard evidence of resistance. The Albanian section in Rustem Buildings was tiny. Aside from Hasluck, it consisted only of Major Robert Cripps, a former officer in Zog's gendarmerie before the war. It was to this small section that McLean and Smiley now reported. Hasluck did her best to brief them on the politics, history and social structures of

A Matter Called 'Concensus'

Albania, and suggested four men – Abas Kupi, Baba Faja, Myslim Peza and Muharrem Bajraktar – around whom she believed resistance could be organised, but their exact whereabouts remained unknown. Smiley remembered Hasluck with great affection as 'a wonderful old woman' but her attempts to impart even a basic understanding of a language that Smiley found wholly alien to most European tongues proved impossible. In time, most BLOs acquired a smattering of Albanian, enough to issue basic instructions and make rudimentary enquiries. Sometimes translators were employed. For the most part, though, Smiley used French, in which he was well versed and which was understood by those few Albanians who knew a Europe beyond the Balkans.[12]

From the outset, Smiley regarded the mission as military rather than political. Though conservative in his leanings, he was largely uninterested in politics. McLean, by contrast, saw diplomacy and, later, politics as the essence of the mission, and crucial if the aim of stirring up an insurrection across Albania was to be harnessed to Allied interests. Circumstances required that Smiley engage in negotiations between and within various factions in Albania, but it was not a role for which, initially at least, he was particularly suited. This was to expose tensions, not least when Smiley felt that talking with various guerrilla leaders produced little of tangible benefit other than to delay or impede operations. Actions, he felt, spoke louder than words. In time, his views were tempered by a deeper understanding of the challenges facing SOE missions across Albania. He never challenged the views or orders of McLean and the close friendship between the two men never wavered. He did, however, come to harbour doubts over the merits of trying to court particular Albanians, including Kupi. But he never let such feelings cause friction with McLean and, later, Julian Amery as disagreements over the wider trajectory of SOE policy in Albania and the wider Balkans emerged.

Smiley and McLean now had to assemble the rest of their team. Lieutenant Gavan (Garry) Duffy, originally from Leeds, was an explosives expert in the Royal Engineers and, like Smiley, a graduate of 102 STS. He was accompanied by Corporal William (Willie) Williamson from Leith, the mission's main radio operator. The operation had been named the 'Concensus' mission (thus spelled), with the team members allocated code names based upon a play or pun on their actual surnames. McLean's was PASTE after the well-known brand of toothpaste, Duffy was PLUM after the pudding and Smiley's was GRIN. Some SOE code names in Albania fell into abeyance but in Smiley's case his stuck and was used in other theatres where he later served, up to and including the Yemen civil war in the 1960s.

II

On the night of 17 April 1943 at 20:30 hours, the Concensus team boarded a Halifax bomber at Derna airfield in Cyrenaica for the three-hour flight to their drop zone in Albania. It was the first time Smiley was to set foot in mainland Europe for over three years.

At 23:00 hours, the RAF dispatcher signalled for his charges to put on their parachutes. Smiley had spent most of the flight reading a recently acquired copy of *Horse and Hound* and the *Tatler*, as it was too noisy to converse above the noise of the engines. Perhaps it let Smiley gather his thoughts for the task ahead, as well as reflect on its inauspicious start, for their Albanian interpreter, Faik Elmaz, a former officer in King Zog's Royal Guard, refused to board the plane, claiming that he required written orders from King Zog himself. McLean took the snap decision to leave him behind. The hapless Albanian spent the rest of the war exiled in Sudan as a security risk.[13]

Despite this setback, comfort was drawn from the fact that the pilot of the Halifax bomber was Squadron Leader Jimmy Blackburn of 148 Special Duties Squadron, whose reputation for accurately dropping men and supplies on to designated drop zones was unsurpassed. His skill was now tested, as the Halifax headed for the Epirus mountains in northern Greece, close to the Albanian border, where another SOE team, known as the Starling Mission, waited for them 12 miles north-east of a small town called Jannina. McLean had at first wanted to parachute 'blind' into Albania, but given the lack of reliable information, he had wisely heeded the advice of Hasluck and decided to cross the frontier on foot, but only after he had been briefed by Starling.[14]

Glancing around the dimly lit interior of the Halifax, Smiley described his comrades as looking like trussed chickens, puffed out by one-piece jump suits and parachute harnesses, under which they wore standard battle dress. Stitched into this were various escape items, such as button compasses and silk escape maps, as well as gold sovereigns sewn into the trouser turn-ups of a pair of corduroys that Smiley had had specially tailored in Cairo. Even his captain's 'pips' on his shoulders were made of solid gold. Should the need arise, they could be used for barter.

With the drop zone fast approaching, the dispatcher removed the cover from the floor of the Halifax. Each member of the team, having ensured their static lines were securely fastened, shuffled to the hole, their legs dangling out, awaiting the green light to jump. This is Smiley's diary entry:

> Eventually, we saw our fires on the ground – nine in all in the shape of a 'V'. We did a circle over the ground and then we got 'Action Stations', and a few seconds later 'go'. At 23:30 we jumped. Bill first, myself second, Williamson third and Duffy fourth. . . . We dropped between 2000 and 3000 feet and I nearly collided with Bill on the way down. It was a wonderful sensation after the parachute had opened – first the engine of the Halifax growing fainter and fainter in the distance and then silence – the snow-capped mountains on either side – then on getting near to the ground the noise of the bells on the sheep and goats – then the shouts of men on the ground and then the bump.[15]

The bump was harder than he admitted. While he had landed within five yards of one of the signal fires, it was in a dry riverbed strewn with rocks. As a result of his uneven landing, Smiley tore a muscle in his leg. Any self-pity was swept away by being picked up, hugged and kissed on both cheeks by a bearded Greek guerrilla, or *Andarte*, one of fifty who, under the guidance of SOE officers, had secured the drop zone. A signal was flashed to the circling Halifax that all men and most of the containers had landed safely. Unfortunately, Williamson's set had been smashed, forcing Concensus to depend on Starling's radio until a replacement could be sent from Cairo.

McLean at once conferred with Starling's leader, Brigadier Eddie Myers, whose headquarters were an hour and a half away in an old Greek Orthodox monastery near the village of Romanon. Smiley and the rest of the party collected their supplies, which were loaded on to mules. Then, led by a BLO, John Cook, the team and their accompanying *Andartes* made for a farm, where it was agreed they would rest before proceeding the next day to Romanon. Smiley confided to his diary that sleep that night came easily, due more to the mental strain of being dropped into enemy territory than to the pure physical effort of recovering the heavy canisters containing weapons, ammunition, food and clothing to equip the mission.[16]

By keeping a diary, Smiley broke all the operational rules regarding security. Even so, in his no-nonsense prose, his various entries give glimpses into his innermost thoughts and feelings as the mission progressed. Despite the excitement and glamour of special operations, he was well aware of the huge risks. While BLOs worried about parachute malfunctions and the possibility of a compromised drop zone, they also knew that evacuation would be difficult, if nigh impossible, should they be wounded or fall seriously ill. Betrayal was an ever-present danger: loyalty was a commodity that could be bought and sold with consummate ease. If they were captured, the wearing of British uniform offered scant protection under the Geneva conventions. The Germans and Italians regarded the bands of guerrillas or partisans as little more than terrorists. More likely, they would be tortured and, once any useful information was extracted, summarily executed. Such were the psychological strains on the BLOs.

The day after his arrival, Smiley and his colleagues proceeded towards Romanon. Despite his injured leg and a splitting headache caused partly by the change in altitude, he took great delight in the journey. 'After three years in the Middle East', he wrote, 'it is wonderful to be in such a beautiful country. The mountains are green and wooded, with snow on the tops, and the valleys have very blue rivers flowing in them; the air is quite different from the Middle East.' After a couple of hours, they arrived at the monastery, where Smiley found McLean deep in conversation with Myers and Guy Micklethwaite, another member of Starling whom McLean knew from his time in Abyssinia. Over the next three days, the Concensus mission tried to get a sense of local conditions and decide on a plan of action. Myers could provide little in the way of intelligence on Albania, although this was not for want of trying. He had sent Cook to reconnoitre the border area with Albania, but apart from warning of the open hostility between Greeks and Albanians, who regarded the Epirus mountains as theirs, he gleaned little of practical use.

Neither McLean nor Smiley was impressed with the squalid conditions in which Starling lived. McLean held little regard for Myers, noting in his diary that he had 'quite a good brain but [was] limited. He seemed weak yet obstinate and certainly ambitious. He was selfish with the selfishness of many regular army officers.'[17] This was harsh. Myers had won a DSO for his destruction of the Gorgopotamos Viaduct, whose single-tracked railway had been vital for carrying Axis war supplies to Greek ports for sending on to North Africa. It demonstrated what SOE could do at a time when doubts in Cairo and London were being raised about its operational, let alone strategic, worth. It also achieved the unique feat of bringing together competing factions to cooperate in a single guerrilla operation. As in neighbouring Yugoslavia, there was bitter rivalry in Greece between the largely pro-communist guerrillas of *Ethniko Apeleftherotiko Metopo* (ELAS) and the staunchly Royalist forces of *Ellinikos Dimokratikos Ethnikos Stratos* (EDES).[18] The difficulties in persuading ideological foes to put aside such differences for the sake of the wider war effort would soon become apparent to the Concensus mission. But now, buoyed by the attraction of the unknown and keen to move on from what they saw as the lacklustre atmosphere of Myers's camp, Smiley and McLean prepared to set off towards Albania.

Williamson was to remain at Romanon until a replacement radio set could be dropped. In the mean time, Smiley and McLean would press ahead and try to contact the Albanian resistance. With their kit loaded on to mules and accompanied at first by guides from EDES, the two men, accompanied by Duffy and Cook, left the monastery on 21 April and headed towards territory where ideological loyalties were decidedly mixed. On the outskirts of a village called Moshpina, this became all too apparent, as their escort bade them farewell, reluctant to venture further into an area where ELAS held sway. Much to their relief, the communist guerrillas who met them proved friendly enough, although in their haste to make quick progress, both men now threw caution to the wind.

Reaching the Jannina–Egoumanitsa road close to the border with Albania, which was a major supply artery for the Italians, their guides became increasingly nervous and reluctant to press ahead. With no sign of the enemy and believing that their escort had become 'windy', Smiley and McLean began to cross the road when they were suddenly challenged. Throwing themselves on the ground, they drew their pistols but neither of them knew or understood Greek. In their exposed position only darkness afforded them any protection. The tension was broken by their hitherto timid escort realising that it was, in fact, another ELAS patrol that had been sent out to meet them. While they made light of the incident, it was a salutary reminder that doing 'advance guard' was not 'worth getting killed [for] just because we were impatient to get on'.[19]

Over the next three days, they inched closer to the Albanian border, enjoying the hospitality of the locals along the way. On 25 April, they reached Drymades, a village only a few hundred yards from the border. That evening, the Concensus mission was introduced to two Albanian partisans, who were quickly sent back across the border to contact their leaders and spread word that a British military mission wanted to meet them. After three days and in the absence of any news from the two partisans, McLean decided to head into Albania. On 28 April, they crossed the border at an unmanned customs post, Smiley jovially brushing past McLean so that he could claim to be the first British officer to enter Albania during this phase of the war. They again received a warm welcome in the villages of Sopcic and Poliçan, a pleasant surprise, given that they had been warned previously of the taciturn nature of Albanians. Smiley noted, however, that most of the villages they passed through near the border were ethnically Greek. Finally, on 1 May 1943 in the small village of Nivan, they finally met with Bedri Spahiu, the leader of the local Albanian communist *çeta*, or partisans, whose members greeted the British delegation with clenched-fist salutes.

Spahiu, though, viewed McLean and Smiley with deep suspicion. Communicating in French, which many of the communist leadership spoke, he claimed that *une réaction fasciste* close by made it impossible for the Britons to continue on their way and advised them to return to Greece. Reluctantly, the Britons agreed, but not before McLean had persuaded Spahiu to pass on a letter to the leadership of the *Levizje Nacional Çlirimtare* (LNÇ), or National Liberation Movement, outlining the purpose of the mission. While an umbrella organisation representing all elements of the Albanian resistance, it was from the outset dominated by the communists, headed by a former school teacher, Enver Hoxha. Spahiu did, albeit with some reluctance, agree to pass on McLean's letter and, with this, the mission returned to Drymades.

But, frustrated at the slow pace of progress, McLean decided on a division of labour. He and Williamson, who had by now received a replacement radio, would stay in Drymades; Duffy would head towards the southern town of Gjinokaster, roughly 15 miles away; and Smiley would head much farther north, towards the large town of Korcë, some 40 miles to the north-east. Splitting the mission up was risky. It could, for example, make the LNÇ command suspect the motives behind the Concensus mission before a formal meeting had been arranged. Smiley and Duffy were, in effect, going in blind, with little appreciation of the political and military landscape. Even so, anxious to contact the partisans and any others in the Albanian resistance, McLean felt the potential rewards outweighed the risk.

After a short stay at the border village of Visani, Smiley proceeded to Konitza, just inside the Greek border, arriving on 9 May. It had been a miserable journey: incessant rain had made crossing rivers hazardous, although once again he was welcomed by the Greek inhabitants, most of whom, he quickly realised, resented the control that ELAS exercised over the town. He was struck too by the number of Greeks who spoke with an American drawl: some had lived in North America before returning home. 'The American-speaking villagers are not usually a good type,'

Smiley noted, 'having been civilised enough to know what dishonesty means.' He was soon confronted with chicanery of an altogether different magnitude. Having interviewed a local Greek man accused of informing for the Italians, he found out later that day that the individual concerned had been summarily shot. While he made light of this incident in his diary, it made him nervous about his own security. Early the next morning, he slipped out of the town and, with two members of ELAS, headed once more into Albania.

On the morning of 12 May, after a six-hour march, Smiley finally made contact with a *çeta* leader, Sulo Kozelli, in the small village of Molyploskastion. Accompanied by twenty members of his guerrilla band, all wearing caps with red stars and armed with captured Italian weapons, Kozelli proved more amiable than Spahiu. He gladly showed Smiley a map of Italian military dispositions in and around the town of Leskovik, which he informed Smiley they soon intended to attack. His curiosity aroused, Smiley asked for permission to join the partisans in their assault. Agreeing to his request, Kozelli prepared to move off with his *çeta* while Smiley hurriedly wrote a message to McLean, informing him of his plans. Such messages were invariably delivered by local runners with no guarantee that they would reach their intended recipient. Even if delivered, they would often have been opened and read 'by mistake'.

This necessarily rudimentary form of delivering information and orders among the Concensus team and, later, between other missions in Albania often determined the scope and pace of what could be achieved. It handicapped SOE's efforts across Albania and, as political rivalries increasingly sharpened, even sowed divisions among British members of these missions that were to fester long after the war. Indeed, acting as a communications hub, SOE headquarters in Cairo, and later in the Italian city of Bari, exercised an unusual degree of operational command and control over the missions in Albania since all radio messages had to passed through them.

These difficulties lay in the future. For now, Smiley was keen to make a reconnaissance of Leskovik. After another long approach march and suffering from a heavy cold, he climbed a series of hills overlooking the town before quickly sketching various Italian military positions. On 14 May, the partisans launched an attack, which they claimed killed 200 Italians over the next three days with the loss of only 2 dead partisans and 12 wounded. The Italian losses were inflated but the assault did allow Smiley to witness the partisans in action and assess their worth. In his diary on 16 May he noted,

> I had the pleasure of watching the *çetas* ambushing an Italian convoy. This was the one returning to Korça from Leskovik. It was most amusing, and as a result the *çetas* got 13 Italian prisoners with their rifles, four machine guns, 20 boxes of ammunition and a truck. They shot the prisoners.[20]

The Italians were quick to exact revenge. Two nearby villages, Germenj and Vodice, which Smiley had passed through with the partisans, were burned to the ground. 'I seem to leave a trail of fire behind me,' he noted in his diary. Still, his spirits remained buoyant. He took great delight, now dressed in the apparel of a partisan with the requisite cap with its red star on his head, in giving 'the communist salute to whomever I meet. I consider this very infra dig for an officer of His Majesty's Royal Horse Guards!'[21] But this upbeat mood was not to last long. After arriving at the village of Vithkuq on 18 May, he was arrested and held for the next three days in solitary confinement. This was a rude awakening for Smiley. He now understood that the partisans he had accompanied during the attack on Leskovik thought that he might be a Greek spy. Confiding in his diary that he was 'very bored and depressed', it was only with the arrival of the officer commanding all partisan units in the Korçë district, Nexhip Vinçani, that his true identity as a BLO was confirmed.

A lawyer before the war, Vinçani held considerable sway across the district and, with 500 men under his command, had commanded the attack on Leskovik. He now agreed to take Smiley farther north in the expectation that they would meet up with members of the central council of the LNÇ. This proved frustrating, for while Smiley did eventually meet a member of the council, Skender Dine, in the historic town of Voskopoj, both

Dine and Vinçani remained sceptical of British intentions and of their ability to help, as Smiley expressed all too clearly: 'If only I had a wireless set with me and could get a supply drop, I could convince these obstinate people I really can help them. They seem a bit doubtful at the moment.'[22] The value of the supply drops was now not just in their military purpose but as a tool of diplomacy to shore up the credibility of the Concensus mission in the eyes of the partisans.

After over a month apart, Smiley met up again with McLean and Williamson in the mountain village of Leshnjë on 10 June. Like Smiley, McLean had experienced great frustration, not least with Bedri Spahiu, who also remained deeply suspicious of the British. McLean readily agreed on the urgent need for a supply drop to boost the influence and prestige of the mission. It was now arranged with SOE Cairo for their first supplies to be dropped on to a plateau some 5,000 feet above sea level on Mount Leshnjë, far from prying eyes. Bad weather postponed the initial sorties but eventually, in the early hours of 23 June, Smiley heard the distant engines of a Halifax approaching. Cairo had failed, though, to give precise notice that the drop was 'on'. Stumbling barefoot from the shepherd's hut that acted as his headquarters, it was only with great difficulty that Smiley was able to organise the lighting of signal fires to guide the aircraft in over the drop zone. Help in collecting, carrying and storing the parachuted supplies had been arranged with a local commissar, Ramiz Aranitas, to whom Smiley had given 200 gold sovereigns to pay for mules and mule men. At the sound of the Halifax approaching, Smiley had sent one of his guards to alert Aranitas to the coming drop; Aranitas, however, had been shot and robbed of his sovereigns by another camp guard, who had witnessed Smiley giving him the payment. Smiley considered himself fortunate, for in a small recess under the floorboards of the hut over which he had unrolled his sleeping bag, Smiley had stashed 4,000 gold sovereigns in two bags, of which, to his great relief, the assassin had remained unaware.

III

Over the next six months, the volume of supplies dropped to the Concensus mission was relatively small: 128 rifles, half a million rounds of small-arms ammunition, 177 light and medium machine guns, 65 Boyes anti-tank rifles, 349 Sten sub-machine guns.[23] Their true value, however, was the diplomatic traction and credibility they gave to the mission. Alongside over 30,000 gold sovereigns to help pay for supplies, accommodation, food, mules and indeed bribes, they demonstrated to the various parts of the Albanian resistance that British and Allied assistance was tangible and geared solely towards defeating the Axis powers. McLean had by now managed to meet the central committee of the LNÇ, leading to an agreement that the mission could begin to train what would become the First Partisan Brigade, comprising the hitherto disparate *çetas* in and around the area of Korcë. Overseeing the training of these men and the logistics to support them was to form the bulk of Smiley's work in the coming months. This entailed moving the mission's headquarters to an abandoned mosque in the mountain village of Shtyllë, a day's march from Leshnjë. Set deep in a range of mountains dominated by its highest peak, Mount Ostravica, Shtyllë proved a far more suitable base from which to expand the mission. Situated at a confluence of two great plains, one of which made an ideal drop zone accessible only by mule, the village could be reached directly only along one passable road that led down the mountain to the town of Vithkuq.

As the summer went by, Smiley began to take a more critical view of the partisans, an approach that eschewed the diplomatic niceties that marked McLean's dealings among and between the disparate groups that comprised the Albanian resistance. This was to be expected. After all, he was here to prosecute a war against the Germans and Italians first and foremost. But acting as a quarter-master responsible for the distribution of arms and supplies to the various *çetas*, Smiley was often dismayed at the avarice of commanders whose gratitude for the material aid given was often grudging at best. He insisted that all weapons handed

Fig. 5.2   BLOs with partisans at Bixha. From left to right: Tony Neel, Enver Hoxha, Garry Duffy, Billy McLean, Sprio Moisi, Ramadan Çitaku, Andy Hands, Dali Ndren.

over to guerrilla groups should be signed for by the leaders, both to maintain proper accounts and increasingly as leverage over the scope, scale and tempo of partisan operations. Equally, he was not impressed by the partisans' leadership and military skills. Two days after moving to Shtyllë, he accompanied Vinçani on a supposed night attack on an Italian camp near a place called Kuqar, only for both men to be caught in the crossfire between the partisans. But for the inaccurate shooting of both sides, the results could have been a lot more lethal than the reported two partisans dead.[24]

Returning from this haphazard mission, Smiley encountered for the first time a *çeta* belonging to the *Balli Kombetar*, or Balkom, led by Safet Butka. While opposed to the restitution of the Albanian monarchy, the nationalist Balkom was even more fiercely anti-communist than the Royalists. Even in the summer of 1943, it regarded the LNÇ with ill-disguised hostility. Still, this meeting was notable for another reason. Smiley had seen smoke rising from villages in the distance and assumed that they had been victims of Italian retribution. The truth was more macabre. The village of Barmash had been surrounded and destroyed by German troops, with women and children burned alive in their houses or shot when they tried to escape. As Smiley noted laconically, 'This was the first news of the Germans in Albania,' and a foe of an altogether different calibre.

By the end of July, the British mission at Shtyllë had been expanded with the arrival of two RAF officers, Flight Lieutenant Andy Hands and Squadron Leader Tony Neel, two new signallers and two former army commandos, Sergeants Jones and Jenkins, lifelong friends from Liverpool. McLean sent many of the new arrivals farther north, hoping to proliferate missions across Albania and to help any group, irrespective of ideological hue, willing and able to attack Axis lines of communication. By now, Shtyllë had received several visits from the *Shtab*, the general staff of the LNÇ, and Smiley began to form a view of its two most formidable leaders, Enver Hoxha and Mehmet Shehu. A man he recalled as 'very capable', Shehu had received an extensive military education in Albania and Italy, and had fought in Spain with the International Brigade before escaping to France. While Smiley respected Shehu's grasp of military affairs, he had little time for his politics or his plain antipathy towards the British. Relations between the two men quickly soured when the Albanian accused Smiley of giving most of the arms dropped by the RAF to Balkom *çetas* rather than to the partisans. Smiley's meticulous records of where and to whom he gave supplies, complete with their signatures, gave the lie to such accusations, and he took great delight in reading out, slowly and deliberately, each record sheet in front of the *Shtab*. By his own account, Shehu never forgave him for this humiliation.[25]

As for Hoxha, Smiley was kinder in his pen portrait of the Albanian leader than he was in later taped interviews. He recalled his intelligence and, over a glass of local raki, his sense of humour. Later, however, he remembered a 'rather fat slob of a man' with a 'flabby handshake' and a violent temper. He certainly enjoyed goading the future dictator. While poring over a map of the world, Hoxha opined that, after the war, he would like to see it

Fig. 5.3 Partisans signing for weapons and equipment. Note Smiley's gold 'pips'.

all painted red. Smiley retorted: 'I [too] would like to see, after the war, the whole world painted red on the map – and not the kind of red you think either.'[26] While this passed without incident, Smiley later acknowledged that often his own frustrations threatened to get the better of him, when, after several months in the field, he tired of being confronted with what he saw as deliberate delay, obfuscation and the cowardice of the communist leadership. It was only McLean's timely interventions in such heated discussions that prevented such rancour taking a more violent turn. After one such incident, he noted in his diary, 'Bill as usual restrained me and probably saved my life, as he has done on many similar occasions.'[27]

The greed, too, of many Albanians and their lack of gratitude for services rendered rankled with many BLOs. Even so, Smiley's attitudes towards the Albanians was at first somewhat condescending. One camp retainer who wandered into his quarters

A Matter Called 'Concensus'

early one morning was, according to McLean's account, met with the following invective from Smiley: 'Get out you bastard – I will not have Albanians in here before breakfast!'[28] Harsh words undoubtedly, but such comments have to be placed within the wider context of service in an environment where the physical and psychological demands on all BLOs were immense. The distances covered, often on foot across rugged terrain, amid communities where loyalty was a commodity to be sold to the highest bidder or given to the strongest party, all took their toll. Smiley's diary entry for 4 August gives a vivid insight into the stress that affected other BLOs in Albania:

> In the middle of the night I heard odd noises and woke up and saw two people fighting in the middle of our room. I quickly pulled my .45 from my pillow and cocked it, but could not see well enough to fire at anyone so luckily did not. It turned out that Williamson was going out to relieve himself and accidently stepped on Bill (McLean). Bill was having a nightmare at the time as though we were being murdered in our sleep by [an] Iti (Italian) deserter, so he leapt and seized the wretched Williamson by the throat and half-strangled him. Williamson was yelling, Bill was making queer animal like noises and I was longing to shoot somebody. I suppose it is really all the result of a high mental strain. I myself quite often have nightmares.[29]

Throughout the summer of 1943, training of the First Partisan Brigade continued apace. The curriculum concentrated on weapons training rather than tactics, as it was reckoned that the guerrillas already knew the terrain and were capable of launching small-scale ambushes to cut Axis lines of communication. While Duffy, Jones and Jenkins trained selected *çetas* in demolition, Smiley gave instruction on heavier weapons, including 3 inch mortars and the 20 and 47 mm cannon. While the bulk of this training was for the pro-communist *çetas*, McLean was keen to harness the energies of other guerrilla groups. To this end, he agreed with Safet Butka that, should his men help ambush an Axis convoy, SOE would look favourably on future requests from Balkom for military support. This met with fierce opposition from Fred Nosi, an English-speaking liaison officer appointed by the

Shtab to coordinate with McLean but whose real aim, the BLOs suspected, was to spy on Concensus.

Waving these objections aside, McLean now tasked Smiley with leading an ambush to test the Balkom guerrillas. Smiley was particularly keen to do this, since a previous attempt to ambush a convoy on the Korcë–Leskovik road had proved a fiasco. His partisan bodyguards proved to be 'decidedly windy', while his attempts at mining the road were defeated by the tough surface. The new target selected was again on the same road but was on a stretch on a bend cut out of the mountainside. The near-vertical sides of the cliff denied cover to anyone seeking shelter, while the other side of the road dropped down a sheer ravine. The steep sides of the mountain opposite afforded an excellent view of the ambush site and it was here that Smiley planned his attack. The preparations were not without incident. Nosi had informed a partisan *çeta* of the planned operation and they now claimed to be organising a similar action at the same place and time. It was only after Smiley threatened to withhold future British supplies, which he had no authority to do, that the partisans stood aside.

In the very early hours of 13 August 1943, and accompanied by a party of ten men from Balkom and three Yugoslav deserters from the Italian army, Smiley laid sixteen mines in two clusters of eight, 250 yards apart, each being obscured by a sharp bend in the road. At 06:30 a German convoy, led by a half-track carrier towing an 88 mm gun, approached. Mistaking the gun for a tank, some of the Balkom *çetas* turned tail and ran, much to Smiley's great disgust. What happened next, however, is recorded in his diary:

> The troop carrier blew up on the mines I had laid and I took a photograph as it went up. All the Germans were killed, 12 by mines and 20mm fire, six were shot running away. I had much pleasure in personally getting direct hits on the troop carrier with the 20mm. The braver guerrillas went on to the road and got identifications from the dead Huns and murdered any wounded ones. They had a wonderful time looting the troop carrier and I tried to get them to push the 88mm gun over the ravine, but somehow when the mines went off they damaged the wheels of the gun and they could not move it. They

threw all they could in the ravine. [H]alf an hour later, a convoy from Leskovik was heard coming and so we got into position again. The first lorry was blown to pieces on mines and five Germans killed but by this time all the *çetas* had run away, which was heart-breaking as the Germans all ran back down the road and the three of us were left to destroy the lorries they left behind. . . . It was most enjoyable seeing the fruits of one's labour and the mines go up. We got good identifications – they are all from the 1st Alpine Division – and quite a lot of loot as well. It would have been a perfect ambush if the Albs had not run away. If only I had a dozen British instead.[30]

IV

The ambush on the Korcë–Leskovik road marked the apogee of his first mission to Albania. His own determination to press home the attack was in marked contrast not only to that of his Balkom retainers but also to that of some of the *çetas* of the First Partisan Brigade. Ten days after that successful ambush and accompanied by McLean and Peter Kemp, a recently arrived BLO, he watched with growing dismay as the brigade, under the command of Mehmet Shehu, fail to press home an attack on an isolated German outpost of just twenty men. As he noted, 'We were disgusted to think that 800 Albanians could not take on 18 Germans.'[31]

Such martial reticence was not, however, due to fear of a superior enemy. Smiley and McLean were later presented with a letter intercepted by Balkom guerrillas in which Hoxha had urged partisan leaders not to waste arms and ammunition on Axis forces. Rather, it should be conserved for the future struggle against the Zogists and the *Balli Kombetar*.[32] It was now clear that the Italian grip on Albania was slipping fast. At the end of August, a last desperate effort by the Italians to capture the members of the mission had only just failed, although they ransacked the base at Shtyllë. While, later on, Smiley managed to retrieve a cache of explosives that he had carefully camouflaged, he was again scathing of the partisans: 'Considering how ideally Vithkuq and Shtyllë are sited for defence, the [First] partisan brigade has put up a very poor show, apart from making no effort to help us when they are supposed to be protecting us.'[33]

The mission relocated to the monastery of Santa Maria on the side of a mountain to the west of Lake Ohrid, close to where the borders of Greece, Yugoslavia and Albania met. The nearest village, Llengë, was fairly secure for a new headquarters but it lacked a good drop zone suitable for receiving new BLOs, who had continued to arrive throughout the summer. Aside from Kemp, Bill Tillman, a noted mountaineer, Gerry Field, George Seymour and a handful of paramilitary experts and wireless operators had all been dropped at Shtyllë before being despatched by McLean to train various groups – Zogist, Balkom and communist alike – across Albania.

But Italy's capitulation on 8 September 1943 set a new tone for Concensus. Seizing the initiative, Smiley the following day tried to negotiate the surrender of the Italian garrison in the strategic town of Pogradec on the south-west shore of Lake Orchid. While he had hoped that the Italian commander might be inveigled into joining the partisans, this proved a forlorn hope. Instead, it was agreed that the Italians would evacuate the town for Korcë and throw their heavier weaponry into the depths of the lake, thus denying their future use to the Germans and partisans alike. Smiley warned the Italians that they would probably be attacked by the partisans along the way and last saw them piling into lorries for the hazardous journey south. Amid the losses inflicted subsequently on the convoy, many of these Italians, veterans of the Alpini Division, did indeed go over to the partisans. Given their alternative fate, this was unsurprising.

The uneasy alliance between the communist-dominated LNÇ, the Balkom and the Zogists now unravelled alarmingly fast. The first breakdown occurred between the Balkom and the LNÇ, but by November 1943, Abas Kupi, the leader of the Zogists and one of the few non-communist members of the LNÇ council, split from the movement and founded *Legaliteti*, which, while espousing an anti-fascist platform, sought an accommodation with the nationalist but avowedly anti-monarchist Balkom.[34] SOE in Cairo remained committed to helping any group willing to fight the Germans, but in reality, attacks on enemy lines of communica-

A Matter Called 'Concensus'

tion came to depend more on the actions of the BLOs than on the guerrilla bands themselves. As if to prove the point, on 12 September, Smiley mined the road from Pogradec to the chrome mines at Kafe-Thanes. Using 'Beehive charges' plus 25 lb tins of ammonal, he blew eight large craters in the road, sending part of it tumbling in to the waters of Lake Ohrid below.

Three weeks later, he demolished a large bridge over the River Shkumbin, which linked the main road from Elbasan to Pogradec. This was his riskiest operation to date, since the approaches to the bridge were garrisoned by German troops on either side. Aided by two partisans, he placed charges against the two main piers, using time pencils as the main detonators set with ten-minute-delay fuses. Having set the first fuse, he had just initiated the second and was about to recross the bridge when he was blown off his feet. The first charge had gone off after only two minutes. This left him stranded on the wrong side of the bridge, facing the prospect of being blown up by the second time pencil going off prematurely. He had no alternative but to sprint over the second pier, scramble down the bank and then swim across the river. The current was strong and at one point appeared to drag him back towards the bridge. It took all his might as a naturally strong swimmer to reach the comparative safety of the bank and pull himself exhausted on to dry land, just as the second charge exploded.

By now, German patrols had unleashed accurate machine-gun and rifle fire that swept the hillsides. They kept up their pursuit for another twenty-four hours, until Smiley and his escort reached the comparative safety of a partisan base at Labinot after a particularly arduous march, chased by German patrols over mountainous terrain. It had been an exhausting operation but its outcome was little appreciated by Enver Hoxha, who claimed that no permission had been given by the *Shtab* for the bridge to be destroyed. In his published memoir, Smiley recalled that Hoxha 'stomped away' from this encounter. His own short diary entry for Friday, 7 October reflected a more personal bitterness because the operation, carried out at huge personal risk, had been little appreciated: 'They [the *Shtab*] are becoming very much above themselves, now that we have given them lots of arms and money. A pity there is little else to show for it.'[35]

Fig. 5.4   With Billy McLean, Bixha, October 1943.

Moreover, the capricious nature of the partisans increasingly rubbed up against the sensibilities of a regular officer who, while used to the bloody excesses of irregular warfare, still maintained a sense of decency towards the enemy. He and McLean were taken aback by the senseless execution of four German soldiers who had survived a partisan ambush near Pogradec in mid-September. As McLean noted in his diary, the commander of the partisan *çeta* had them shot not because of any vendetta but because 'he was ashamed to steal their clothes and yet leave them alive to walk about half clad, as a continued reminder of his theft'.[36] Just before he demolished the bridge over the River Shkumbin, Smiley was presented with another three German prisoners – two medical orderlies and a military policeman – who had survived a Balkom ambush. He knew all too well that the partisans would have them summarily executed once any intelligence had been extracted. Smiley first dressed their wounds then took them down to the main Kafe-Thanes road. With a small Balkom *çeta*, he watched a large German convoy approach and told the prisoners, who claimed to be Austrian, to flag the vehicles down. They promised not to reveal Smiley's position, situated less than a hundred yards from the road. They kept their promise to the letter, a just reward for this act of chivalry.[37]

His growing disillusion at working with Albanian guerrillas (and with the partisan leadership in particular) was understandable. The risks and physical endurance required to fight the Axis forces, with little support from the various factions more interested in personal vendettas, soon disabused many BLOs of any romantic notion they may have had of irregular warfare in this little-known country. Reginald Hibbert, a BLO dropped into northern Albania in December 1943, whose account of SOE in Albania is among the most thoughtful, noted of Hoxha that the

> role that he wanted to assign to them [the BLOs] was exclusively that of purveyors, under LNÇ direction, of arms and equipment to Partisan forces. Insofar as they [BLOs] represented an imperialist power, by definition one hostile to communism, he tolerated rather than facilitated their presence.[38]

But it was a presence that SOE in Cairo wanted to expand, with the various missions controlled by a new headquarters commanded by a more senior officer. With a brigadier, Fitzroy Maclean, now firmly established with Tito's headquarters in Yugoslavia, Albania was considered worthy of the same accolade.

This expanded SOE presence in Albania reflected a belief in Cairo that intensifying operations across Albania would help divert German forces from the eastern front and Italy by giving the impression that the Allies were contemplating an invasion of the Balkans. A new base to accommodate this expanded mission, code-named 'Spillway', was now established on a plateau at Bixha, located high in the Chermenika massif, surrounded on two sides by towering mountains and protected by a dense forest of beech trees. The plateau ran down to the west towards Tirana, the closest that the Concensus headquarters had been so far to the Albanian capital. It lacked suitable accommodation but, with partisan and Italian labour to hand, a series of wooden shacks was hastily built to accommodate the expanded mission.

Spillway was led by Brigadier Edmund F. Davies, better known by his sobriquet, 'Trotsky', on account of his reputation as a young subaltern for being truculent towards authority. A regular infantry officer by training, Davies was dropped into Albania on 15 October 1943, with five officers – Arthur Nicholls, Marcus Lyon, Jim Chesshire, Frank Trayhorn and Alan Hare – and two NCOs. Two more teams were dropped alongside Spillway, including Major Alan Palmer, whose views on the various guerrilla groups were later to influence British policy in favour of Hoxha and his partisans. Smiley's immediate impression of Spillway was its size. It was too large and logistically cumbersome for the type of irregular warfare being fought across Albania: 'I have never seen so much kit as they have brought – camp furniture and even two containers of stationery. There is a clerk among the NCOs.'[39]

If the new headquarters was more suited to a running of a regular army unit, it seemed that some of the new arrivals expected something similar in the appearance and bearing of the BLOs. Smiley and McLean overheard Nicholls, second in command of the Spillway mission and a Lieutenant colonel in the Coldstream Guards, 'giving Alan Hare a rocket' for being as unkempt and untidy as 'those fellows Smiley and McLean'. Given McLean's earlier observation of Eddie Myers and the scruffy conditions at his lair in Greece, this illustrates how the demands of guerrilla warfare over time inevitably altered sartorial standards. The choice of dress adopted by most BLOs in Albania was very much left to the individual, dictated by comfort and durability. Smiley invariably wore a British battle-dress blouse, usually with his prized corduroy trousers, which concealed his paraphernalia of escape and evasion. While he sometimes wore the forage cap of the Blues, he often sported a white Albanian fez, while McLean made do with a woollen cap comforter emblazoned with the cap badge of his parent regiment, the Royal Scots Greys.[40]

It was therefore with something akin to relief that, a week after his arrival, Davies told Smiley and McLean to exfiltrate Albania via Italy and report back to SOE in Cairo. Smiley noted in his diary,

A Matter Called 'Concensus'

Fig. 5.5 Smiley and McLean with two female partisans.

We are very pleased at this news as neither of us fancied hanging about this new headquarters much. It seems most unsafe too, as it is so large and immobile. I also feel that the Brigadier is believing rather too much of what Khadri Hoxha (a member of the partisan *Shtab*) and others are telling him.[41]

They spent the next few days preparing to leave Bixha. While McLean briefed Davies thoroughly on what he saw as the political and military vices and virtues of the guerrilla groupings, Smiley handed over his inventories of arms and supplies to Alan Hare, who, like Smiley, was a regular officer in the HCR. He also passed his mule, Fanny, of whom he had grown quite fond, into his care, hoping that, as a good cavalry officer, Hare would look after her. As things turned out, Fanny did not survive the winter. Neither did many of the Spillway mission.

The journey to the coast by car, mule and foot took a little under two weeks. It was not without incident. The men left Bixha on 23 October with Williamson, the route chosen meaning that they had to cover 200 miles, heading south through Labinot, Berat and Përmat, before swinging west towards the town of Kuç and on to a small coastal cove close to the town of Dukati. In Labinot, Smiley again nearly came to blows with several communist members of the LNÇ and admitted that, but for McLean's ability to smooth ruffled feathers, his war might well have ended then and there. As it was, he survived a close call when traversing a narrow path around Mount Nemerçke. The horse he was riding slipped and fell over a precipice, meeting its demise after a drop of over 100 feet. Only because he had been riding with his feet out of the stirrups did Smiley manage to slide off the unfortunate beast in time.

As they got near to the coast, they passed through several burning villages, whose supposed allegiance to Balkom had wrought this partisan vengeance. McLean and Smiley had long suspected partisan malfeasance but now they believed they had the material evidence to prove it. Passing through the Balkom village of Quereshnik, they were given a captured document, a directive from the *Shtab* to the local communist branch in the town of Berat, ordering all military efforts to be directed against the *Balli Kombetar* and not the Germans.[42] They believed the veracity of the document and quickly made a copy, aware that its contents might well affect future SOE policy towards both the partisans and the LNÇ.

Eventually, on 7 November, the party reached the headquarters of another British mission, code-named Sapling, headed by Major Jerry Field. Smiley was soon struck by the number of vagrant Italian soldiers wandering aimlessly around the camp area, hoping against hope that they might be evacuated back across the Adriatic to Italy. Many were nearly starving and, with a bitter winter in the offing, few had decent shelter. Only Field's headquarters, located in a cave overlooking the sea, provided some shelter and succour to a handful of Italian retainers. He refused to employ Albanians, whose avarice he regarded as a national characteristic. 'He won't', Smiley wrote, 'have an Albanian near him, and shoots at them all on sight.'[43]

In truth, Field needed to be replaced, his mission's sole value now being to ensure that 'Seaview', as his troglodyte dwelling was known, remained accessible to seaborne missions to and from Italy.[44] Seaview itself was cramped and dirty. While it offered some protection from the incessant rain that swept across the cliff face, its cold, fleas and lice made it impossible to sleep at night. Food supplies were perilously low and only the relief of a bottle of raki brought the illusion of warmth. This was the first time Smiley began to experience real pangs of hunger, which led to a surreal, if macabre, culinary experience. Wandering across the cliffs close to Seaview, he came across a half-burnt-out house. Among its ruins, a handful of Italian soldiers were enjoying a spicy stew and beckoned Smiley to join them, which he did, believing the meat to have been cut from a dead mule. Only after he had taken his fill did his hosts disclose that the meat was human flesh. 'It's Giuseppe,' they told him.[45]

Eventually, on the night of 17 November, Smiley and McLean were picked up by a Royal Navy motor torpedo boat. Paddling out amid a heavy swell in a dinghy that was fast sinking, they only just made it, flinging their briefcases with their invaluable documents on to the deck moments before the dinghy sank. Once on board, they alerted the commander, Lieutenant David Scott, to Field's predicament. It was with great skill that Scott managed to manœuvre his craft within feet of the rocky shoreline to throw supplies of food ashore to Field and his grateful Italians. Three hours later, after crossing the Adriatic, they entered the Italian harbour of Brindisi.

With Albania behind them, Smiley and McLean looked forward to a period of well-earned leave after being debriefed. Both could reflect on a job well done. Within six months, they had assessed the scope of Albanian resistance hitherto unknown to Allied war planners and raised a partisan brigade virtually from scratch. Equally, by their individual actions, both men had showed extraordinary bravery and physical stamina amid fickle loyalties and under severe psychological strain. Both were convinced that, amid such internecine rivalries, Britain would have to choose sooner rather than later which side to back. For Smiley, the choice would prove as much aesthetic as political. After all, he held the martial prowess of most Albanians in fairly low regard, irrespective of their political colouring. His choice, influenced by his allegiance to McLean and Julian Amery, was to shape his next encounter with Albania, against the shifting tides of SOE policy in what previously had been dismissed as a Balkan backwater.

Notes

1. For the most detailed account of SOE in Yugoslavia, see Heather Williams, *Parachutes, Patriots and Partisans: The Special Operations Executive and Yugoslavia 1941–1945* (London: Hurst, 2003).
2. See F. W. D. Deakin, *The Embattled Mountain* (London: Oxford University Press, 1971); Fitzroy Maclean, *Eastern Approaches* (London: Penguin, 1991).
3. Basil Davidson, *Special Operations Europe: Scenes from the Anti-Nazi War* (London: Victor Gollancz, 1980).
4. Smiley, *Albanian Assignment*, p. 9.
5. See Bernd J. Fischer, *Albania at War* (London: Hurst, 1999), pp. 6–32.
6. Richard Bassett, *Last Imperialist: A Portrait of Julian Amery* (York: Stone Trough, 2015), pp. 68–81.
7. Bailey, *The Wildest Province*, pp. 28–34.
8. Bailey, *The Wildest Province*, pp. 38–9.
9. Bailey, *The Wildest Province*, p. 41.
10. Bailey, *The Wildest Province*, p. 45.
11. One former SOE officer, Xan Fielding, wrote of Keble that he was a 'A globe shaped choleric little militarist' who 'did his best to conceal his natural and professional shortcomings by a show of bloodthirsty activity and total disregard for the agents in the field whom he treated like so many expendable commodities'. Quoted in Nigel West, *Secret War: The Story of SOE, Britain's Wartime Sabotage Organisation* (London: Coronet, 1992), pp. 221–2. See also Cooper, *Cairo in the War 1939–1945*, pp. 262–3; Sweet-Escott, *Baker Street Irregular*, p. 170.
12. Interview with David Smiley, London, 18 February 2005.
13. Major N. McLean, Diary Notes, Entry for Saturday, 17 April 1943, McLean Papers Imperial War Museum (hereafter MP-IWM); Major David Smiley, Diary entry for 17 April 1943, The National Archives (hereafter TNA) HS 5/143. This version of the Smiley diary kept by

the TNA contains redactions. However, an uncensored copy of the same diary is held by the Imperial War Museum.
14. Bailey, *The Wildest Province*, pp. 56–7.
15. Major David Smiley, Diary entry for 17 April 1943, TNA HS 5/143.
16. Major David Smiley, Diary entry for 17 April 1943, TNA HS 5/143.
17. Major N. McLean, Diary Notes, 'British Mission at Romano', MP-IWM.
18. Eddie Myers wrote his own account of his mission to Greece. See E. C. W. Myers, *Greek Entanglement* (London: Rupert Hart-Davis, 1955).
19. Major David Smiley, Diary entry for 22 April 1943, TNA HS 5/143.
20. Major David Smiley, Diary entry for 16 May 1943, TNA HS 5/143.
21. Major David Smiley, Diary entry for 17 May 1943, TNA HS 5/143.
22. Major David Smiley, Diary entry for 24 May 1943, TNA HS 5/143.
23. See the final SOE mission report on Albania, 'Albania', TNA HS 6/79. RAF records for the months June, July and August 1943 stated that 44,242 lb or 19.5 tons of supplies were dropped to the Concensus mission. See Reginald Hibbert, *Albania's National Liberation Struggle* (London: Pinter, 1991), p. 53.
24. Smiley, *Albanian Assignment*, pp. 51–2.
25. Smiley, *Albanian Assignment*, pp. 55–6; IWM, Accession No: 10340/6 Interview with Colonel D. Smiley, Recorded 1989.
26. Diary Concensus I mission, MP-IWM.
27. Major David Smiley, Diary entry for 23 October 1943, TNA HS 5/143.
28. Diary Concensus I mission, MP-IWM.
29. Major David Smiley, Diary entry for 4 August 1943, TNA HS 5/143.
30. Major David Smiley, Diary entry for 13 August 1943, TNA HS 5/143.
31. Major David Smiley, Diary entry for 23 August 1943, TNA HS 5/143; Smiley, *Albanian Assignment*, p. 67. Peter Kemp, a BLO who had just been dropped into Albania and to whom Smiley became a close friend, recalled that he made clearly 'audible comments' in the direction of Shehu over what he regarded as a clear act of cowardice. See Peter Kemp, *The Thorns of Memory* (London: Sinclair-Stevenson, 1990), p. 192.
32. Smiley, *Irregular Regular*, p. 90.
33. Major David Smiley, Diary entry for 29 August 1943, TNA HS 5/143.
34. See Bernd J. Fischer, 'Abaz Kupi and British intelligence in Albania',

in John Morison (ed.), *Eastern Europe and the West* (London: Macmillan/St Martin's Press, 1992), p. 131.
35. Major David Smiley, Diary entry for 7 October 1943, TNA HS 5/143.
36. Diary Concensus I mission. Diary entry for 14 September 1943, MP-IWM.
37. Major David Smiley, Diary entry for 5 October 1943, TNA HS 5/143.
38. Hibbert, *Albania's National Liberation Struggle*, p. 54.
39. Major David Smiley, Diary entry for 16 October 1943, TNA HS 5/143. According to Davies's own account, McLean and Smiley recommended that every officer and NCO serve no more than six months at any one time in the field before being allowed 'to rest and refit'. See Brigadier Trotsky Davies, *Illyrian Venture* (London: Bodley Head, 1952), p. 66.
40. Smiley, *Albanian Assignment*, pp. 85–6.
41. Major David Smiley, Diary entry for 21 October 1943, TNA HS 5/143.
42. Major David Smiley, Diary entry for 28 October 1943, TNA HS 5/143.
43. Major David Smiley, Diary entry for 10 November 1943, TNA HS 5/143.
44. Field was eventually evacuated after blowing himself up with gelignite while fishing. His replacement was Major Anthony Quayle, better known as the actor and founding member of the Royal Shakespeare Company, later Sir Anthony Quayle.
45. Smiley, *Irregular Regular*, p. 97.

6 Three Majors: Two for Politics, One for Fighting

I

By the winter of 1943, SOE had moved the command of its Balkan operations to Bari, although the Albanian section, under Major Philip Leake, was still in Cairo, where Smiley and McLean were to return after their debriefing in Italy. First, however, both had the indignity of being deloused, but in the haste to prevent the spread of any infectious disease, what now passed for their uniforms were incinerated while the pair lay soaking in carbolic baths. Smiley was furious: not only was he rather attached to his pair of tailor-made corduroy trousers, but they still contained a button compass, gold sovereigns stitched into the turn-ups and other escape equipment. His battle-dress blouse too was thrown on to the pyre, including his captain's pips made of solid twenty-four-carat gold, as well as a prized silk escape map secreted in the waistband.[1]

The next three days were spent in a whirlwind of debriefings. Both men handed over a raft of documents, notably the pay books of dead German soldiers, which disclosed their units and troop strength. This material was supplemented by newspapers and reports that would help military intelligence and SOE build up a more detailed picture of the German order of battle. They identified new targets inland for strikes by the RAF, including infrastructure around the oil fields at Kuçove. In his last few days at Seaview, Smiley had also carefully mapped all the nearby coastal defences, including minefields and shore batteries. Best of all, they brought out with them a set of German maps of Albania, given to them by Italian deserters, which proved more accurate than anything the British had at the time.[2]

On 23 November 1943, both men arrived back in the Egyptian capital, where they were debriefed in more detail. This marked for Smiley the start of what he later remembered as his happiest few months of the entire war. At first they stayed at Shepheard's Hotel but such were the pressures on their time from a now-expanded Albanian section that meetings inevitably overran and their schedule soon became unmanageable. As a result, they were allocated a conducting officer, a tall, handsome captain in the Coldstream Guards, William 'Billy' Stanley Moss. His languid charm appealed to both men and before long he had invited them both to visit Tara, a large villa in the upmarket district of Zamalek at the northern end of Gezira island. Moss shared the villa with two other occupants: Patrick Leigh-Fermor, later to gain renown as a writer, had already spent considerable time behind enemy lines with SOE in Crete, helping to organise resistance, while Sophie Tarnowska, a Polish aristocrat and noted beauty, had helped set up the Polish Red Cross in Cairo.

The atmosphere at Tara in the winter of 1943–4 was irreverent and bacchanalian. As they were spending so much time at the villa, ostensibly writing up detailed reports on Albania, McLean and Smiley abandoned Shepheard's for their new, intoxicating surroundings. It also made financial sense: every time they visited Tara – a name chosen by Leigh-Fermor in reverence for his Irish ancestry – Smiley was tapped by Abdul, the household *suffraghi* (butler), for contributions to household expenses.[3] They were soon joined by other young SOE 'blades', including Rowland Winn, Xan Fielding and Arnold Breene. Their elite status, both military and social, was parodied in the aliases they engraved on a nameplate at the entrance to the villa: Princess Dneiper-Petrovsk (Tarnowska), Sir Eustace Rapier (McLean), the Marquis of Whipstock (Smiley), the Hon. Rupert Sabretache (Winn), Lord Hughe Devildrive (Fielding), Lord Pintpot (Breene), Lord Rakehell (Leigh-Fermor) and Mr Jack Jargon (Moss). For a while, Tara was *the* place to be seen, the revelry often matching the excesses of a 1970s rock band on tour: sofas were thrown out of windows and a piano was 'liberated' from an Egyptian officers' mess while games of indoor golf saw smashed windows. During one party, a group of drunken Polish officers decided to

Three Majors: Two for Politics, One for Fighting

test their marksmanship by shooting out light bulbs. Artemis Cooper, in her chronicle of wartime Cairo, described Tara thus:

> They were all under 30, back from enemy-occupied territory and rejoicing in the fact of being alive. A fortune in back pay sat in their bank accounts, ready to be spent on slaking appetites sharpened by months of hardship, and the glamour of secret operations meant that they were greeted as heroes.[4]

Presiding over proceedings was Tarnowska, whose separation from her husband, an officer in the Polish Carpathian Brigade, added to the allure she held for several young blades, Smiley included. While he had had several girlfriends, none had been serious. Being unattached helped make his decision to join SOE that much easier.[5] Now, during the winter months, along with Fielding and Moss, he bid for her affections, though this appeared not to harm individual friendships.[6] Tarnowska kept a cavalry sabre beside her bed to deter the more forward of her admirers while happily toying with their emotions. Smiley had certainly begun to develop strong feelings for a woman whose looks, independence and *joie de vivre* enchanted so many. Moss wrote an affectionate portrait of Smiley at Tara:

> David – English squire? with a difference – the difference has to be brought out of him, and then he becomes impish and adventurous and full of prank playing – always well-mannered and almost always in the best of humour – reliable and I'm sure a very true friend and quite sincere. I shall never forget the two of them (McLean and Smiley), trying to compile their report on their Albanian adventure, papers, loot, sovereigns, cavalry swords and a sulky faced typist – my wretched study suffered in those days. The two of them scratching their heads ... and then they would snap at each other and David would say 'You bloody communist!', and Bill would retort 'You bloody Fascist' ... Paddy's (Leigh Fermor) primary observation that they were quite definitely more mightier with the sword than the pen seemed fairly correct. The writing of that report had gone on for a whole month.[7]

The detail required of the reports only partly explains the slow progress for, as Smiley happily conceded, they were having the time of their lives. Moss recalled Smiley sitting in a steaming bath pronouncing 'This is a good war – I hope it last much longer.' This, of course, was more a reflection of life at Tara than any fond memories of Albania. Amid brief trips back to STS 102 in Haifa to lecture new recruits on the practicalities of guerrilla warfare, he continued to enjoy life in Cairo. He wrote:

> I stayed in Tara all over Christmas when we had a series of wonderful parties, the best of which was on New Year's Eve when we went to a ball given by Princess Chevikar who was one of King Fuad's (of Egypt) wives. It was like a court ball, it was so grand. Wonderful food, unlimited champagne and Scotch whisky, lovely women smothered in jewels, wonderful looking Sudanese men servants in livery and lovely looking Circassian maids and all presided over by an English butler. At midnight the lights went out and I kissed Sophie.[8]

This idyll was not to last, as Tara's inhabitants embarked on new operations. In February 1944, Moss and Leigh-Fermor departed for Crete on an operation to abduct the garrison commander, General Heinrich Kriepe.[9] Smiley had played a small if unorthodox part in planning this operation. The condensation on the tiles in one of Tara's large bathrooms allowed him to provide for the semi-naked Moss and Leigh-Fermor an outline of the ideal spot for an ambush and the tactics required to ensure its success.[10] However, before they set off for Crete on what SOE's official historian, M. R. D. Foot, later referred to as 'a late, almost absurd coup', Smiley and McLean had left for London to report directly to SOE headquarters in Baker Street and to the Foreign Office. After further debriefings, they expected to be given another period of extended leave.[11]

In January, Smiley landed at RAF Lyneham in Wiltshire. It was his first time back in England for nearly four years. His journey to London, however, disabused him of any lingering nostalgia. Despite buying a first-class ticket, he lamented that he had to stand all the way to the capital. On arrival, he was taken aback by the reaction of the taxi driver when he asked to be taken to Berkeley

Three Majors: Two for Politics, One for Fighting

Square: 'The place where all them aristocrats live? They ought to be shot in my opinion.' He longed 'to return to Cairo straightaway'.[12] Still, he was happy to stay at the Ritz for the next month on account of his personal family allowance; McLean preferred Claridge's. During the next month, both men were interviewed by a series of officials, notably Lord Selbourne, the Minister in Charge of SOE, as well as the Foreign Secretary, Anthony Eden. They also officially briefed the exiled King Zog, who left a deep impression on Smiley as highly intelligent and capable but who was never considered by the Foreign Office as being representative of the Albanian people or as the acknowledged head of a government-in-exile.

A division of labour marked these briefings: McLean delivered detailed appreciations of Albanian politics while Smiley dealt with the military–technical aspects of their mission, drawing heavily on his report compiled at Tara. He highlighted correct procedures for the dropping of supplies; percentages of supplies lost to defective parachutes; the importance of personal mail and food supplies for keeping up the morale of BLOs in the field; and the need for adequate explosives and mines, and for regular supplies of petrol, message pads, cipher paper and up-to-date maps, which, although requested continuously by the mission, were never sent. He also noted the need for heavier weapons – 81 mm mortars, heavy machine guns and more rifles – to be supplied, but he was clear that 'grenades, Tommy guns, light machine guns and light mortars' should not be sent 'owing to the Albanian dislike for close range fighting'.

Smiley was typically blunt in his criticism of SOE's supply chain: unneeded equipment was sent; when it was required, it was often inadequate. Mortars were delivered with the wrong base-plates and incorrect sights; a consignment of boots for the partisans were all size 6, 'which did not even fit the female partisans'. Ammunition sent was often in poor condition or did not fit the calibre of weapons to hand. Finally, he addressed the issue of personal kit:

> Take nothing with you that you value and treat everything that you take as certain to be lost. Always keep a haversack filled with your

most valuable equipment and essential necessities, so that, in the case of an emergency, you can grab it and fly.[13]

It was prescient advice that his compatriots back in Albania were now very much having to put into practice.

II

In the early spring of 1944, it was not at all clear that Smiley would return to the Balkans, let alone Albania. With his next posting yet to be decided, his practical experience of guerrilla warfare was now imparted to the 'Jedburghs', three-man special forces teams of a Briton, a Frenchman and an American, who were to be dropped behind German lines in northern France in the run-up to D-Day to carry out acts of sabotage with the various resistance groups.[14] Smiley's experience of this kind of more organised partisan warfare was much valued by his audience. His reward was a .30 semi-automatic carbine, which, alongside his trusted Colt .45, he was to find the best small arms for guerrilla warfare. Until then, he had equipped himself with a German 9 mm Schmeisser machine pistol or with the ubiquitous Thompson sub-machine gun. He cared little for the British-made Sten sub-machine gun, 'not a good advertisement for British manufacturing', whose design on safety grounds alone, as he was soon to experience, left much to be desired.[15]

Visits to other SOE establishments were also arranged, but by the end of the month and despite experiencing some of London's bomb-battered nightlife, he was looking forward to what he thought might be a month's leave, staying at his mother's house at Virginia Water in Surrey. But, after just a week, he was suddenly recalled to Baker Street to be greeted with tragic news: the Spillway mission had been betrayed to the Germans by traitors in Balkom. Brigadier Davies had been wounded and captured, while the rest of the mission was on the run. News of the whereabouts of Hare and Nicholls was scant but it was obvious that all would be in great distress, high up in the mountains, and facing a bitter Albanian winter with insufficient clothing, food or shelter.

Nicholls eventually succumbed to frostbitten feet that became so gangrenous they had to be amputated. His stoicism and fortitude in the most appalling conditions were recognised in the award of a posthumous George Cross. Hare avoided capture but barely survived the ravages of winter. Clearly malnourished, with frostbitten toes that had to be amputated, his survival was a triumph over adversity. While all ran the risks of betrayal, the concerns that Smiley and McLean had committed to paper regarding the size of the mission had been tragically realised. The need to have a haversack that 'in the case of an emergency you can grab . . . and fly' had never been more keenly felt.

In the face of the wider German offensive across Albania, those BLOs not on the run were lying low in the hope of re-establishing a presence in their allotted areas, come the spring. It was largely in light of their experience that the head of the Albanian section of SOE, Philip Leake, now asked for Smiley and McLean to return and, in Smiley's words, 'take over all the missions in Albania again'. This would be only part of the endeavour, as McLean was now keen to ensure that the reports he had drafted in Cairo (with the help of Julian Amery) should now determine government policy towards Albania. He made two key observations. First, the communist-dominated LNÇ was, without doubt, the most effective fighting force in the south and centre of Albania but it was already engaged in fighting the nationalists and Zogists, mainly in the more tribal north. Second, the nationalists, defined broadly as anyone not directly under the control of the LNÇ, were increasingly reluctant to fight the Germans. With the tide of war clearly turning, they remained keen to preserve their military strength for a civil war now in its infancy. The Balkom betrayal of the Spillway mission had been an early manifestation of this.[16]

McLean's recommendation mixed pragmatism with his own political leanings: SOE, he advised, should continue to support the LNÇ militarily but should maintain contact with the Zogists and Balkom in the belief that, with the right inducements, they could be reconciled with the communists. This would dampen the flames of an internecine conflict that could only benefit the Germans.[17] Before his capture, Brigadier Davies had profoundly disagreed with this assessment and had signalled accordingly.

While his time in the field had been limited before his capture, he had come to the conclusion by December 1943 that only the LNÇ was offering any real resistance to the Germans. On this basis alone, Britain had to give its overwhelming backing to the partisans.

The Special Operations Committee in Bari, which oversaw British missions in the Balkans, baulked at such wholesale support. Siding with Hoxha and the LNÇ meant committing to one side, possibly the wrong side, and with the wider aim of ensuring that, at the very least, the efforts of the BLOs were aimed at maximising attacks on German lines of communication across Albania, it was decided to maintain contact with all factions. Moreover, to declare British support for the partisans might endanger the lives of British officers stationed in areas controlled by rival political factions. Equally, however, the Zogists had to demonstrate that they were willing to take up arms alongside the British before military aid would be released. So the task of what was code-named Concensus II was to persuade the Zogists and other nationalists to fight the Germans and to try to effect some form of reconciliation between the Zogist leader, Abas Kupi, and the LNÇ. It was also meant to reorganise those missions in the north that had been so badly scattered by the German offensive.[18]

These directives were backed by the Foreign Secretary, Sir Anthony Eden, who had given permission for Concensus II to approach him personally if he could promote their mission. In reality, McLean knew the difficulties in trying to reconcile any of the political factions, Smiley regarding the mission from the outset as more political than military. He was therefore relieved to be told that Julian Amery would now join them, largely on the strength of his knowledge of the Balkans and of Albania in particular. It helped, too, that Amery was a close friend of McLean's, and while he was an ardent admirer of King Zog, it was felt that his diplomatic skills could help buttress McLean's efforts in brokering an agreement between the warring factions that might bring London around to offering military support to the Zogist cause. Amery reckoned that Kupi offered the best bulwark against the LNÇ and, by extension, the spread of Soviet imperialism across the Balkans.[19] But, as Roderick Bailey, author

Three Majors: Two for Politics, One for Fighting

of a definitive history of the SOE in Albania, notes, the wider dilemmas faced by nationalists and Zogists alike on the ground did not necessarily tally with the objectives of the Concensus II mission:

> To counter the growing communist threat, a good number of Nationalists, including many of the BK (Balkom) were now slipping into open collaboration with the German who were only too pleased to encourage civil war. But as BK forces fought side by side with the Germans against the partisans, other Nationalists, including Kupi, would choose to remain aloof, maintaining contact with both SOE and collaborators but staying neutral until concrete evidence showed the better option.[20]

This proved a serious bone of contention, not least because McLean, Smiley and Amery came to believe that official policy towards Kupi and the Zogists had been influenced by communist sympathisers and fellow travellers at SOE's headquarters in both Cairo and Bari. But timing too decided the fate of the Concensus II mission. The German drive south to secure its main lines of communication between Albania and Greece in the winter of 1943 had severely disrupted the LNÇ, but the nature of guerrilla warfare and the training they had received from McLean, Smiley and other SOE missions had allowed the partisans to weather the storm. When McLean had first written his reports in Cairo, a small window of opportunity as the partisans melted away before the German offensive might have offered the prospect of a truce between the Zogists and the LNÇ. But by the time Concensus II was ready to be dropped back into Albania in the spring of 1944, that window had well and truly closed.

The delay in sending the mission back to Albania can be explained partly by the fragmentary information flowing back to SOE in the aftermath of the German offensive. But having flown back to Cairo at the end of February 1944, both Smiley and McLean had no immediate desire to leave Tara any time soon. Smiley again tried to capture Sophie's affection and both men even tried to prolong their stay by wiping off their smallpox vaccine, knowing full well that a week had to pass by before it could be administered safely again.[21] But for Amery's insistence that the mission now fly to Bari before being dropped back into Albania, Smiley and McLean would have undoubtedly stayed even longer. By design or by default, these delays meant that any hope of a reconciliation between the warring parties was already gone, overtaken by events that, by April 1944, saw the LNÇ in the ascendant. Reports too from BLOs with the partisans, notably Lieutenant Colonel Alan Palmer, the most senior British officer present, highlighted the military worth of the partisans, which stood in marked contrast to the paucity of effort by the Zogists and the Balkom. In short, given its rather contradictory orders and the subsequent delay in its despatch, Concensus II was probably past its sell-by date before it was despatched.[22]

During the flight from Egypt to Italy at the beginning of April, Smiley was despondent for other reasons. 'I have never been so miserable as I was on that trip leaving Tara, Sophie and Cairo,' he later wrote, despite his recent promotion to major and the award of the Military Cross for his actions at Barmash the previous August. Affairs of the heart, however, were pushed to one side on arrival in Bari. A series of intense briefings focused on the growing strength of the partisans compared with the Nationalists' and Royalists' resistance. All three remained frustrated that the Foreign Office continued to prohibit the mission from carrying any written communication from King Zog to Kupi, urging him and his men openly to join the fray against the Germans. This, Smiley noted, tied their hands in any future negotiations with the Zogists. As if to remind them of the difficulties that awaited them, they visited a fellow SOE officer, Anthony Quayle, whose attempts at reconciling the factions in and around the evacuation point of Seaview had largely failed. Having been evacuated, he now lay in a hospital bed in the Italian port, recovering from acute dysentery, jaundice and malaria. Quayle, Smiley recalled, had 'nothing good to say about the Partisans'.[23]

On 19 April, almost a year to the day after he had first parachuted into the Epirus mountains of northern Greece, Smiley and his accomplices set off for the short flight across the Adriatic to Albania, this time in a Dakota of the United States Army Air Force (USAAF). Their parachute drop close to Bixha confirmed

Three Majors: Two for Politics, One for Fighting

Smiley's low opinion of the flying skills of the USAAF. While the fires below clearly indicated the drop zone, all three men ended up landing just over a mile away in what Smiley referred to as a 'bloody awful drop' into a beech forest. His parachute caught on overhanging branches, causing him to swing violently back into a tree, badly bruising his back. Had the forest floor not been carpeted in thick snow, his injuries would have been a lot worse. Much to Amery's and McLean's anger, they discovered too that their parachutes were made of cotton rather than silk, a type usually reserved for dropping supplies rather than bodies. The failure rate of such parachutes was notorious.

After a brief rest, the party pushed on towards the main base at Xhiber, some four days' march away, where the remnants of some of the BLO missions had gathered. Progress along the mountain tracks was slow, for even though signs of spring abounded, deep piles of grey snow blanketed everywhere, thanks to volcanic ash from Mount Vesuvius drifting across the Adriatic. It was on this march that Smiley met Abas Kupi for the first time in the small village of Derije. He warmed immediately to the Zogist leader but observed that 'he does not seem particularly clever'.[24] This view was to change as he came to know a man whose standing across the more tribal region of the Mati remained high. In his forties and of stocky build with greying hair, Kupi came across as a calm and reflective individual. His refusal to throw his lot in with the Balkom underscored, in Smiley's eyes, his pro-British credentials. Certainly, Kupi's observation that the Concensus II mission consisted of *Tre majora, dy për politikë nji për luftë* (Three majors: two for politics and one for fighting) chimed with Smiley's summary of the mission's division of labour.[25]

The fact that King Zog was exiled in Britain appeared to underscore Zogists' support for the Concensus II mission.[26] But later entries in Smiley's own diary reveal another, more sober assessment. As the mission progressed in the summer of 1944, Smiley came to doubt the Zogist leader's real commitment to expending men and matériel at the instigation of the British in wholehearted guerrilla action against the Germans at a time when the LNÇ were clearly in the ascendant. While he was to claim that Kupi had been let down badly by the British authorities in both London and

Fig. 6.1   Julian Amery (left) and Said Beg Kryeziu.

Bari, this view was influenced by Amery and McLean, to whom he instinctively deferred in matters of diplomacy and politics. As events were to prove, his own gut instincts proved the better guide to Kupi's motives.

Still, the immediate problem facing the Concensus II mission on arrival at Xhiber was to determine the fate of those BLOs who had survived both the German offensive and the privations of a bitter winter. Morale among many was low, and McLean quickly saw that many needed to be evacuated. Aside from physical injuries, many suffered from dysentery and jaundice while the mental strain had caused one signaller to break down completely. Smiley had every sympathy: 'We must get them sent out for a rest,' he noted, 'as their nerves are bad and they are run down physically and mentally, six months is quite long enough for a normal person on this job.'[27]

McLean despatched over a dozen back to Italy, although the increasing difficulties of exfiltration amid a growing civil war

Three Majors: Two for Politics, One for Fighting

meant that most did not set foot in Italy until August. Those judged fit to remain included Alan Hare, John Hibberdine, Ian Merrett and the indomitable pairing of Sergeants Jones and Jenkins, whose intelligence and toughness Smiley particularly valued. These individuals were to be the mainstays of his existence over the next two months. While McLean and Amery headed north on a tour of the Mati in the hope of reconciling, however temporarily, Kupi with the LNÇ, Smiley was tasked with securing the headquarters at Xhiber and overseeing, once again, the reception of men and matériel from Italy. This included a new signaller, Sergeant William (Gunner) Collins, whose association with Smiley was to prove particularly longstanding.

While important work, it did little to satiate Smiley's desire for action. Nor was there much training of guerrilla forces: SOE in Bari refused to supply weapons and ammunition to Kupi until he had proved his fidelity to the British cause. This meant that the BLOs were, in the main, interested observers rather than active participants in the events unfolding around them. With time on his hands, Smiley began to brood, with thoughts of Tarnowska to the fore. On 8 May, he bared his emotional state to Hare, a man whom Smiley deeply respected and whose decision to stay with the Concensus II mission was remarkable in light of his own injuries. A man of charm, grace and tact, Hare had been entrusted with Smiley's reliable steed 'Fanny' on leaving Albania the previous year. That winter, Smiley had even sent a signal to Hare, an officer in the Life Guards, enquiring as to Fanny's welfare. Hare's reply was admirably direct – 'Have eaten Fanny' – leading Smiley to note later in jest that Hare 'could not have been a true cavalryman'. Now he listened as Smiley, clearly despondent, 'spilt out my heart about all the complications in Cairo'. His mood could not have been helped by the theft of a personal canister that contained fresh clothing, secret documents, a camera and a precious photograph of Tarnowska that had been dropped in advance of the mission. The uncertainty in his love life, coupled with the petty theft of the camp retainers, only seemed to magnify the vagueness of Kupi's plans. Until these were known, offensive action by the Concensus II mission was stymied.

Smiley therefore had to content himself with reorganising the base camp, sorting out stores from a series of parachute drops from the USAAF, whose accuracy still left much to be desired, and occasionally soothing relations between BLOs when these had turned sour after so long in the field. He stayed fit with long walks in the mountains surrounding Xhiber, the highest of which offered a panorama down to the capital, Tirana. Observing him at such close quarters during this period of waiting led Amery to capture the more martial side of Smiley's character in his book *Sons of the Eagle*: 'Smiley lived for action alone and was happiest on a dangerous reconnaissance, or on those expeditions which gratified his passion for blowing things up.'[28] This particular passion was soon to be fulfilled. While the target was a bridge vital to German lines of communication in northern Albania, the true impact of its destruction would, it was hoped, be felt in SOE headquarters in Bari and London.

III

McLean and Amery had spent considerable time in cajoling Kupi to fight the Germans. In an effort to persuade him that his best interests lay in demonstrating his commitment to the Allied cause, a meeting was held at Xhiber on 13 June 1944. Talks made slow progress, with the Albanian insisting on a demonstration of British good will up front in the form of arms 'which we [the BLOs] won't do until he does fight'. McLean had signalled Eden, hoping that the Foreign Secretary's apparent commitment to Albania would override the Foreign Office's objections and allow for a message from King Zog to be passed to Kupi ordering him to fight. The Foreign Office remained, none the less, firm in their opposition to any such communication. All Eden would offer was the empty blandishment in a signal to 'keep the pot boiling'. Knowing they had few cards to play, it was only after several hours of careful persuasion on the part of Amery and McLean – and to the obvious delight of Smiley – that Kupi finally relented. 'In the evening he [Kupi] agreed to allow me to carry out demolitions,' wrote Smiley with clear relief in his diary.[29]

The target chosen was Albania's third-largest bridge at a place

Three Majors: Two for Politics, One for Fighting

called Gjoles, just north of Tirana, at a spot where the road from the capital forked north to the town of Durazzo in one direction and towards Scutari in the other. The BLOs believed that the campaign in Albania was primarily about disrupting the enemy lines of communication, and the attack at Gjoles had real strategic worth. Accompanying Smiley to the target would be a *çeta* of sixty Zogists, an interpreter, Veli Hasan, and Sergeant George Jenkins, whose bravery and sardonic sense of humour Smiley greatly appreciated. Amery described Smiley's rather unorthodox preparations:

> When the Zogist leader had gone from the camp, Smiley had set about sorting out his demolition devices or 'toys' as he called them in preparation for the attack on the bridge. He was well versed in the qualities of the different explosives and knew exactly which required to be treated with respect and which might be handled with rougher intimacy. The rest of us, however, were imperfectly initiated in these mysteries; and Smiley took a malicious pleasure in filling us with alarm and despondency by dropping sacks of dynamite with seeming carelessness or tossing them to his bodyguards to be loaded onto the mules. The sweet, plasticine-like smell of explosives pervaded the camp; and to our horror, and this time to Smiley's, one of the mules began rolling to free itself from the unwelcome burden. There were no accidents, however and towards evening Smiley set out with Sergeant Jenkins ... followed by a few bodyguards and a string of pack animals.[30]

The approach march to the bridge took two days, followed by a further day of reconnaissance when, having changed into civilian clothes, Smiley walked brazenly down the Tirana–Scutari road with German vehicles passing by all the time and made his way down to the piers supporting the bridge. Once there, he discovered that not only had German sappers prepared demolition chambers for the bridge to be blown, but had helpfully inscribed the amount of explosives needed to bring down the bridge next to each cavity; he soon realised that the amount he had brought was insufficient to do the job.

He sent word back to Xhiber for more 'toys' and, for the

next forty-eight hours, carefully noted the insignia, types and volume of German transport moving along the Tirana–Scutari road before retiring to a nearby farm on land belonging to Kupi. By the time the extra explosives arrived, however, Smiley had begun to feel increasingly ill. At first he thought it was the effects of dealing with plastic explosives; the odour often induced severe headaches in those handling it over a sustained period. He soon realised, however, that it was the recrudescence of malaria. By the time the extra explosives arrived on the afternoon of 20 June he was over the worst of his shakes and, with Jenkins, begun to divide the explosives into the necessary packets for the chambers. Finally, under the cover of darkness, he set out with Jenkins and his Zogist bodyguards for the bridge. In summer, the river was little more than a stream and, with the two main piers on dry land and with good cover to hide the mules only a hundred yards away, the portents were good.

Smiley knew that speed and silence were of the essence; sadly, both were absent as, in ever more voluble whispers, he urged both haste and caution on his Zogist retainers as they manhandled the explosives to the piers. At one point, with several of the saboteurs, including Smiley, directly under the bridge, a German staff car stopped for half an hour to repair a puncture. The tension was palpable, not least because, even though the staff car eventually moved off, a constant flow of German transport vehicles continued to cross the bridge in their efforts to avoid daylight attacks by the RAF. Finally, Smiley sent the bulk of the *çeta* away, with just himself and Jenkins remaining to do the 'technical work' and two bodyguards, Veli and Dani Ramiz, keeping watch. Into the six demolition chambers, three on each pier, Jenkins and Smiley placed a 100 lb mix of gelignite, plastic explosive and ammonal, plus a further four Beehive charges in the gap of the curved aperture between the piers and the bridge. All were linked via a junction box initiated by two time pencils with ten-minute fuses. The whole effort took two hours to complete. In the early hours of 21 June, Smiley now squeezed the time pencils to initiate the charge, then dashed back to the top of the bridge to scatter tyre busters on the road. Given the notorious unreliability of the time pencils, this was at considerable personal risk, but within five minutes two German vehicles had been brought to a halt by these devices.

Having withdrawn to what they thought a safe distance, the saboteurs now watched with increasing intensity at their watches as the minutes ticked by. Nothing. Frustration being the better part of valour, Smiley now set off back towards the bridge, his movements slow and deliberate lest he draw the attention of the Germans pondering the fate of their damaged vehicles. But once he had covered just half the distance, a tremendous roar and a flash ripped through the night sky, lumps of concrete falling like bloated hailstones in and around the saboteurs, which miraculously hit no one. Of the Germans on the bridge there was no sign.

Their adrenalin still pumping, this elated band with their *çeta* in tow now headed back to base, although Smiley narrowly avoided serious injury when Veli, in his haste to clear an area now quickly filling with Germans, dropped his Sten gun, which promptly fired rounds in all directions.[31] This mishap aside, Smiley was now convinced that his actions would persuade SOE Bari of Kupi's fidelity to the Allied cause. Still, his diary entry for 21 June reveals the immense pressure under which he had laboured over the Gjoles operation:

> Very glad to be back and have some food and see Billy, Julian and Alan [Hare]. Had the shivers twice today and am sure I have malaria. Sat up late drinking cherry brandy and do not feel very tired in spite of an 18 hour march, no sleep for 36 hours and much mental and physical strain.[32]

For this action, McLean recommended Smiley for the immediate award of the DSO.

McLean believed the destruction of the Gjoles bridge proved beyond doubt Kupi's pro-British bona fides. On 23 June, he sent a signal to SOE headquarters informing them of the Gjoles operation and requesting enough arms and ammunition to equip 2,000 men to be despatched to Kupi. The hope was that other nationalists in the north of Albania might now rally around, once word spread. This would create the momentum to harry German communications as the *Wehrmacht* began to redeploy its forces

Fig. 6.2 The bridge at Gjoles.

to stem the Allied advances in France after D-Day and the Soviet push into Eastern Europe. To support their argument further, McLean and Amery emphasised the distinctive social character of northern Albania. Across the Mati and beyond, the largely Gheg tribes looked to their tribal chiefs for protection. Failure to provide security 'leads either to the rejection of the leader by society or to the radical modification of the social order on which the leader's power is based'. When combined with a topography that McLean felt was inimical to the type of slow-burning guerrilla campaign that had marked partisan operations in the south, he concluded that only a general uprising supported by the nationalist population could succeed. This, in his view, justified the volume of arms and ammunition he requested.[33]

This cut little ice in Bari. True, Concensus II had identified several nationalist leaders, notably the Kryeziu brothers, Gani Bey, Said and Hassan, operating across the border into the province of Kosovo; Fiqri Dine in the Dibra region; and Luma Meharrem, who, while anti-Zogist, was prepared to overlook such differences since he shared the antipathy of all towards the LNÇ. Gani Bey Kryeziu, in particular, had a reputation as a particularly resolute guerrilla commander. SOE office in Bari, however, was swayed by reports from other BLOs, notably Palmer, over the growing strength of the partisans, who, having survived the German onslaught over the winter of 1943/4, were now on the offensive. This resilience in the face of adversity was, in no small part, due

Three Majors: Two for Politics, One for Fighting

Fig. 6.3 Smiley with the Zogist guerrillas who helped destroy the Gjoles bridge.

to the training that Concensus I had imparted to the partisans the previous summer, a legacy that now had a bitter irony, since the partisans became increasingly belligerent in their demands of Kupi and the Zogists.[34] In particular, Hoxha failed to understand why BLOs continued to be attached to a movement that, so far, had offered little tangible opposition to the Germans. The Gjoles operation therefore was meant to assuage all these concerns, a visible demonstration of the Zogists' good will and willingness to take the fight to the Germans. Still, it was notable that Kupi was reluctant to have his name associated with the operation.[35]

This was linked to Kupi's ties to the puppet government in Tirana, led briefly by his close associate Fiqri Dine. Clearly, Kupi was trying to keep all options open. His overwhelming concern was to 'raise effective resistance forces with which to oppose the communists', while at the same time hoping to 'convince the allies of the neutrality of Albania in the hope of gaining some material and diplomatic support'.[36] The reasoning behind Kupi's position is understandable, and the wider communist threat posed to British influence throughout the Balkans, should Hoxha emerge triumphant, explains the support he continued to receive from McLean and Amery.

By contrast, Bari remained adamant that military considerations, rather than any future political exigencies, should drive strategy in Albania and the wider Balkans. As such, Kupi's impact on the guerrilla war against the Germans paled in comparison with the partisan effort. In their later accounts, Smiley, Amery and others blamed the presence of pro-communist sympathisers at SOE headquarters in Bari for the overwhelming political and material support given to Hoxha and the partisans.[37] Long after the war, it remained an episode mired in bitter controversy and recrimination. Amery was convinced that Albania had been sacrificed on the altar of limited strategic gains at best, and communist subversion at worst. Smiley agreed, and in later years felt that the partisan successes against the Germans had been exaggerated, while British policy was flawed in its failure to appreciate the true intent of the LNÇ.[38] There certainly were communist supporters in SOE Bari. Captain John Eyre of the Albanian section and Major James Klugmann, who oversaw wider SOE operations across the Balkans, were pronounced in their ideological sympathies.[39] Klugmann, a brilliant Cambridge graduate who had been a close pre-war friend of the infamous Soviet spies, Donald Maclean, Guy Burgess and John Cairncross, was always frank about his politics. Smiley met Klugmann several times in Bari. He recalled:

> [a] hardened Communist but in fact he was a very nice chap. He used to keep our relatives happy as there was little contact [when on operations]. He would send messages to my mother and tell her I was well but unable to make contact and that sort of thing. He was a good chap except he was 100% communist. As I say, we knew his beliefs; he never pretended to be anything else.[40]

Klugmann later had dealings, albeit fleeting, with Soviet intelligence in London but accusations that he and Eyre, a dissolute intellectual, could have manipulated information to influence a

Three Majors: Two for Politics, One for Fighting

pro-partisan policy in Bari have since been challenged. Some evidence does exist suggesting that cables to London via Bari taking a pro-Zogist line were suppressed or delayed. Undoubtedly, opinions in Bari were also swayed by BLOs in theatre, a large proportion of whom were attached to the partisans and who, in the winter of 1943, witnessed first-hand the treachery of the Balkom. Their reports alone may have influenced opinion in Bari. Roderick Bailey has argued that the reports of Alan Palmer, hardly a fellow traveller in the communist cause, carried considerable weight in deciding where SOE's resources were likely to attract the greatest return. Arguing that he too had urged Kupi unsuccessfully to act against the Germans in the spring of 1944, Palmer signalled his complete disagreement with McLean's proposals to instigate an uprising in the north of Albania: 'Surely by now Kupi's unwillingness to fight the Germans is clear. There is no time for Kupi to take action against the Germans before he is attacked by the partisans.'[41]

Whatever the sympathies of SOE staff in Bari, policy towards Albania was now determined by the newly formed Balkan Air Force under the command of Air Vice-Marshal William Elliot. McLean described him as an 'intelligent and civilised man but something of courtier. . . . He had the then fashionable pinkish attitude and as a result was pro-partisan and pro-communist.'[42] This seems far-fetched. More likely, Elliot simply chose the most effective means of prosecuting the war in the Balkans and he certainly had the authority. He oversaw a committee that included representatives of the SOE and Foreign Office. Importantly, the actions of the Balkan Air Force were determined by immediate military strategy and not by gainsaying the future political and diplomatic calculations towards Albania and the wider Balkans.[43] In any case, the BLOs in the field were largely removed from this level of decision-making. Still, perception was all, and the actions of Bari certainly came to fuel a view among Amery, McLean and Smiley that the Zogist cause was sacrificed unnecessarily. From the ground, evidence for this view was keenly felt. Ten days after the operation at Gjoles, Hoxha ordered his 1st Partisan Brigade to attack Zogist forces.

This smacked of a deliberate attempt to thwart British support for the Zogists, as it undermined the efforts of Amery and McLean to persuade Kupi once again to cooperate with the LNÇ. It remains unclear when or how Hoxha heard of the proposed arms supplies to Kupi or if Bari was involved. Smiley recalled 6 July as being the worst day so far for the Concensus II mission. The partisans had taken the town of Shëngjergi, just to west of Bixha, and were now rumoured to be heading north towards Xhiber and Bastar. Smiley had received a message from Bari on 2 July stating clearly that, should the partisans attack, they would be denied further arms and supplies, which by now averaged around 100 tons a month: 'This means', Smiley wrote, 'we have some office support after all which we doubted.'

But such hopes were soon dashed. With the partisans advancing and seemingly immune to threats and censure from Bari, McLean now sent Hare to try to negotiate with Hoxha. By now, the bulk of the Concensus II mission had moved further north to Macukall, close to the frontier with Kosovo, where, on 9 July, they heard that the partisans had captured their advanced headquarters, which had recently been moved from Xhiber to Bastar, and with it, Alan Hare. This very bad news was compounded by reports that the Germans were advancing on the town of Burrel. In effect, the Concensus mission was now surrounded on at least three sides by foes intent on seeking its demise. Far from harnessing the various guerrilla groups towards one defined end, by the summer of 1944 British policy towards Albania seemed only to exacerbate their differences. Indeed, it placed BLOs on opposite sides of an internecine conflict that brooked no compromise.

IV

Amid this confusion, members of the Concensus II mission spent the next ten days, sometimes together, at other times apart, trying to head north back across the Mati valley towards the relative safety of a base at Macukall. Smiley spent two days in the small village of Karice, still surrounded on all sides but enjoying the food and drink of a Zogist supporter, whose family took delight in watching him perform his ablutions each morning. By 17 July,

Three Majors: Two for Politics, One for Fighting

however, he was beginning to get increasingly bored, and only an evening spent watching 'masses of tortoises copulating' brought any sense of light relief in his attempts to reach Macukall. In the early hours of the next morning, he was awoken by his hosts and told to gather his belongings, as fifty partisans were reported to be moving towards the village. He now headed for Kafe-Thanes, where he had been told that McLean was now located, but along the way he bumped into a Zogist *çeta* that had been conducting anti-partisan operations alongside the Germans in the Mati valley.

McLean was, in fact, in nearby Meneres but, on arrival there, Smiley discovered that his compatriot had actually sent word for him to remain at Karice, an order he never received. Both now suspected that Kupi, anxious to disguise the extent of Zogist cooperation with the Germans in the area, had prevented the message from being delivered and had concocted the story of a partisan presence to get Smiley out of the way. It says much for their indulgence of Kupi that this incident was not allowed to sour relations or their continued support for the Zogists.[44] But it does question Smiley's later assertion in *Albanian Assignment*, written four decades later, that 'We well knew that at no time did Kupi collaborate with the Germans.'[45]

On 20 July, the mission reached Bastar and from there intended to regroup and assess the situation, while signals were sent to Bari urging it to order BLOs attached to the partisans to exercise a restraining influence on Hoxha. SOE headquarters had, in fact, tried to arrange a cease-fire, and had dropped Captain Victor Smith to McLean in the hope that, untainted by previous association with the mission, he could mediate between partisans and Zogists, and persuade both to send delegates to a conference in Italy to reach a *modus vivendi*. Kupi accepted the proposal at once; Hoxha, with the tide of war in his favour, rejected it out of hand. By now, Smiley was convinced that the mission was effectively over. While he expressed sympathy for Kupi, in his diary, on 20 July 1944, he was also more forthright: 'Had talks again in the afternoon with Kupi but personally I think Billy and Julian are wasting their time and the sooner we return to Italy the better. I am sure these people [Zogists] have no intention of fighting the Huns any more than the partisans.'[46]

It is unclear whether Smiley confided these doubts to Amery and McLean, and his published memoirs make no mention of his concerns. Loyal to both Amery and McLean, he tended to defer to what he regarded as their greater political expertise. At the same time, he hoped to extract at least something of military worth from the mission. This was not easy. On his arrival, Smith told the 'three musketeers' that Bari had come to an arrangement with the LNÇ whereby any BLOs captured serving with nationalist forces would be immediately 'evacuated under escort. The swine in the [Bari] office had deliberately not told us.'[47] Now, amid both Albania's internal bloodletting and SOE's own internecine feuds, it was decided that Smiley should embark on a reconnaissance of the northern coast, both to gather intelligence on German positions and, discreetly, to identify a suitable place for the mission to be exfiltrated.

Smiley's progress towards the coast was aided by Zogist sympathisers, notably Ihsan Toptani. A man of great social standing, Toptani was from a family of wealthy Muslim landowners and was one of the few Albanians to have enjoyed a higher education outside his country as a student at Vienna University before the war. He also had good contacts in the Albanian Gendarmerie, a paramilitary organisation that, while enjoying the indulgence of the Italians and now the Germans, had remained pro-Zogist. It was sympathetic to the BLOs too, as former British army officers, recruited in the 1920s, had overseen its training under King Zog.[48]

Part of Smiley's journey to the northern coast was in a car provided by Toptani, a rare luxury. He was accompanied by two bodyguards he had come to trust: Ramiz and Bardhok. This carried its own risks, however, for as dusk fell on the night of 23 July, a German soldier signalled the car to stop. Smiley, in full uniform in the back seat, 'heartily wished I could make myself smaller' but luckily the German was merely slowing traffic down because of an earlier accident and waved them on without a glance inside. Perhaps this made the driver too frightened to carry on for, soon after, he stopped the car, indicated that the coast was only two hours' march away, and promptly left the trio by the roadside. What happened next Smiley recalled as one of his more bizarre experiences in Albania:

Three Majors: Two for Politics, One for Fighting

[M]y guides and I were joined by a Hun soldier who jumped off his bicycle and started walking along with us. It was dark but I had on a full battledress with Major's crowns, my parachute badge, medals etc, and he never realised who I was. I spoke Albanian to him and got some useful information. In the end he gave me a cigarette and we parted. Little did he know! We did not murder him as this is a recce of the coast, and I do not want to attract attention.[49]

Having changed into civilian clothes, his trademark fez still firmly on his head, Smiley now reconnoitred the Milot–Luz road, around 20 miles to the north-west of Tirana and a major supply artery for the German occupiers, marking 'Hun positions' on his map as he passed. This was a risky endeavour in its own right for, should he be caught in civilian dress, the Germans would have been within their rights to execute him as a spy. He also faced the risk of daylight sorties by the RAF, who 'shot up absolutely anything they saw on the roads, including wretched peasants in ox carts'.

One month later, however, running such a risk almost caused his downfall. Still hoping to persuade Bari of Kupi's worth to the allies, Amery and McLean had inveigled him into attacking the coastal port of Durazzo, a town vital to German control of the coastal plain. Before such an attack, it was decided that Smiley would 'recce the place'. On 29 August, he again put on his civilian garb. With Captain Rifaat Tershana of the Albanian Gendarmerie, he left the house of Toptani in Luz for Durazzo in a truck, along with several other gendarmes. The presence of the gendarmes enabled them to negotiate two roadblocks before being dropped off, along with Halit Kola, his interpreter, 5 miles from Durazzo. Without the protective cloak of their official uniformed escort, they were now more vulnerable. After passing several German soldiers on the approach road without incident, they were suddenly stopped and asked to produce identity papers:

I was in plain clothes but even so always fail to look like an Alb (sic) as they do not have fair hair or blue eyes. I had a pistol in my hip pocket but remembered I had not got one up the spout like a fool. Anyway, when I could produce no card I talked in Albanian for some minutes which of course the Huns could not understand. Halit had already passed as he had a card and was about 20 yards away. He shouted at me to come so I turned my back on the Huns and walked away. Halit says the Hun corporal then drew his pistol, pointed it at me, then shrugged his shoulders and put it back in the holster again. Little did I know![50]

Smiley was quite shaken by this incident and saw it as a warning that in his efforts to wage war for the Zogist cause, which seemed increasingly forlorn, he had to be more calculated about the risks he should take. As it was, he felt German strength in Durazzo and the surrounding area was too great for the guerrillas to hold the town for more than a couple of days. Moreover, as the Germans grew more uneasy about the loyalties of the Gendarmerie, they began to round up dozens of their number. Given the casualties involved in an attack that would be unlikely to enhance the credentials of the Zogist cause in Bari, he argued that it be abandoned, recommending instead the sabotage of the Tirana–Scutari road.[51]

Such actions had, however, become increasingly few and far between. Smiley knew that the nature of the Concensus II mission had always been avowedly political. Even so, amid the internecine conflict and the need to shift camps and headquarters, often at short notice, throughout the summer and early autumn of 1944, he saw little evidence of any tangible military reward: 'I have now completely wasted four months here and although Billy and Julian have all the politics they want, life for me is bloody; nobody talks of fighting Huns these days.'[52] Much of this he blamed on Bari, which, having suspended arms supplies to the LNÇ following their attacks on Kupi, now resumed them, much to the disgust of the Concensus II mission. This served only to embolden the partisans still further. Towards the end of August, Hoxha sent an ultimatum to Bari that McLean, Amery and Smiley should surrender themselves within five days or face capture and trial before a military tribunal. This was too much, even for Bari. But while Hoxha was forced to rescind the order or face a complete suspension of supplies from SOE, it did little to assuage the concerns of the mission over Hoxha's intentions or the pro-partisan line in Bari.

Still, by the late summer of 1944, Smiley's certainty over the malign intent of the partisans could not disguise his often conflicted view of Kupi and the Zogists. On the one hand, he felt that Kupi had been let down by SOE headquarters, especially after the Gjoles operation, which he felt should have unlocked supplies to Kupi: 'I feel very sorry for him', he wrote on 13 August 1944, 'as he is a real patriot and genuinely pro-British and it makes me sick seeing him thrown over for a lot of very anti-British communists.'[53] Equally, he knew that Kupi's commitment to fighting the Germans remained weak. The Zogists still preferred to marshal their resources against the partisans as it became increasingly clear that the Germans were preparing to evacuate their forces entirely from Albania. Thus, Smiley's recommendation that Zogist *çetas* should sabotage the Tirana–Scutari road, along which the retreating German forces would have to pass, was met yet again with evasion: 'I feel Kupi is stalling again.'[54]

The British had by now decided to give exclusive support to the LNÇ. The historian David Stafford noted that this 'represented both a recognition of the LNÇ's power, and that by supporting it, Britain could hope to retain some form of post-war influence' that would prevent Albania from falling into the Soviet orbit.[55] The Zogists did eventually undertake a series of ambushes against the Germans, one of which, on 16 September, destroyed a convoy of nine lorries, but this was too little, too late. The Balkan Air Force now dictated the allocation of resources accordingly and few now valued the Zogist effort. With Kupi a busted flush, it says much for Smiley's professionalism that he continued to seek every opportunity to engage the Germans as evidence of their withdrawal from Albania became ever more apparent. This included the increasing desertions of scores of Turkestanis and Tajiks, who, having been captured on the eastern front while serving in the Red Army, had been conscripted into the *Wehrmacht* to help lessen manpower shortages.

At the beginning of September 1944, some of these troops in northern Albania contacted Kupi. They brazenly claimed to have murdered their German officers and wanted to come over and fight alongside Concensus II and the Zogists, most of whom were fellow Muslims. While the fate of the German officers caused some unease among Smiley, McLean and Amery as to their true loyalties, it was decided to test their martial instincts sooner rather than later. Such an attack, if combined with the Zogists, might go some way to refuting the partisan claims that Kupi was collaborating with the Germans and buy some political capital in Bari. The target chosen was an artillery unit of thirty Germans and an equal number of Italians who had remained loyal to Axis. Situated in a hollow between two hills, the camp was poorly sited for defence. A plan was now drawn up for McLean, accompanied by the Zogists, to attack from one side and Amery, with thirty Turkestanis and Tajiks, to assault from the other. Smiley, in turn, would give covering fire. In the event, the attack only just avoided disaster. After opening fire, the Zogist *çeta* 'proved too yellow to charge', leaving McLean and three others dangerously exposed. By contrast, Amery's 'troops' threw themselves enthusiastically into the fray, with Smiley giving fire support from a captured German Spandau machine gun. Amery had a fragment of his chin shot away but, for the loss of one Zogist and a Turkestani, 10 Germans were killed and 13 Italians captured; the rest fled.[56]

As gratifying as this attack had been – Smiley took some pride in having commanded former *Wehrmacht* soldiers in battle – such actions did little to obstruct German plans for withdrawal, plans that had been procured by one of Kupi's men and passed on to Smiley from a disaffected German NCO at the headquarters of the German 21 Mountain Corps in Tirana. In return for his safe conduct, he now passed over the complete *Wehrmacht* order of battle and the order for the withdrawal of German forces across Albania, as well as maps detailing German installations right across the Balkans. This was intelligence gold dust and was quickly encoded before being signalled to Bari. Kupi's part in this intelligence coup, alongside the Zogist role in attacking the German artillery unit, was heavily flagged.[57]

But British policy towards Albania was already fixed. Despite an upturn in the tempo of air attacks against German targets resulting from this intelligence coup, the Zogist cause had run its course. The momentum was with the partisans, who enjoyed the lion's share of supplies dropped by the Balkan Air Force and the backing of BLOs, notably Palmer, whose advice remained greatly

Three Majors: Two for Politics, One for Fighting

Fig. 6.4 Smiley with his Turkoman '*Wehrmacht*' troops, 1944.

prized in Bari. Despite this, Smiley and the Concensus II mission continued to attack German targets where they could. On one occasion, he used Hawkins grenades to destroy a truck, killing three Germans north of Tirana. He followed this up soon after by demolishing two more bridges. The first and larger of these was on 11 September, not far from his previous triumph at Gjoles, aided and abetted by thirty Turkestanis and the ever-resourceful Jenkins. Spectacular as these feats undoubtedly were, they could not mask the end of a mission that had failed to reconcile Kupi with the LNÇ. Nor did it succeed in harnessing a guerrilla movement whose hatred and fear of Hoxha trumped any clear commitment to the Allied cause until too late. Smiley's diary entry for 21 September captured the sense of dejection felt by all:

> AK (Abas Kupi) in confidence told us he was finished, which had been obvious for some time. I was very sorry for the poor old boy who has been continuously let down by the British (ie us) who in turn have been let down by the office. . . . I am certainly not going to stay with the firm (SOE) when I return as I resent receiving orders from such fools.[58]

The wheels for that return were soon set in motion. Throughout September, the mission received several messages from Bari ordering them to cross over to partisan lines and give themselves up before being evacuated. Mindful of Hoxha's previous orders to have them arrested, this the mission was not prepared to do. Instead, Smiley once more reconnoitred the coast, examining beaches around the northern port of Shengjin for a suitable embarkation point. This was a prohibited military zone, but judging the risk to be worth it, Smiley crawled through the surrounding barbed wire and mapped the entire German defences before making good his escape.

During all this time, the physical and mental demands on him had been immense. Because of the civil war, headquarters frequently had to be moved, creating an itinerant existence that made the mission dependent on the good will of villagers and townspeople. But fear of the partisans made this an increasingly precious commodity. More than once, Smiley felt it safer to hide in fields, often cold and wet, rather than risk betrayal. While much of his travel was done on mule, long distances still had to be negotiated on foot, especially in the mountains around Lesh and at the mission's final base at Velijë, close to the coast. His diary entry for 4 October 1944 recalled an eight-hour march, some of it in the dark and much of it over precipitous terrain. The inadequacy and scarcity of the local food would have tested the most resolute operatives. Bitten relentlessly by mosquitoes and fleas, and occasionally succumbing to worms, dysentery and malaria, Smiley none the less proved remarkably resilient.

He had hoped that Toptani might have been able to use his influence to obtain a boat large enough to evacuate the whole of the Concensus mission. In the event, this proved unnecessary, as Bari signalled on 13 October that a Royal Navy launch would evacuate the group. This was carried out eleven days later on two consecutive nights from a small beach just north of Cape Rodonet. Smiley went first, along with Jones, Jenkins and another long- serving SOE officer, Captain Ian Merrett, who, like many other BLOs, had suffered the most appalling hardship. McLean and Amery were evacuated from the same spot twenty-four hours later. While Smiley was glad finally to leave, his relief was tinged

Three Majors: Two for Politics, One for Fighting

with deep sadness and foreboding. Bari had made it clear that no Zogists, including Kupi, were to be evacuated, an order that had prompted an increasingly acrimonious exchange of signals between McLean and SOE headquarters. For the sake of appeasing the LNÇ, it seemed that Kupi, Toptani and the Kryeziu brothers, as well as the mission's loyal interpreters, Shaqir, Halit and Veli, would be left to the mercy of the partisans. McLean even tried to signal Eden via Bari for this order to be countermanded, only for Smiley later to be told that the signal was literally 'binned' in SOE headquarters, allegedly by Eyre. Such incidents fuelled the ire of a mission who, in the ensuing days and months, became convinced that a pro-communist conspiracy had thwarted them from the outset.

In the event, Toptani's efforts to find a boat finally bore fruit. He, along with Kupi and his close followers, were eventually picked up in the Adriatic on 1 November 1944 by a British minesweeper. Soon after, Smiley, McLean and Amery then experienced first-hand what they regarded as the pro-partisan bias at SOE headquarters in Bari. Smiley warned McLean and Amery of the extreme hostile attitude they could expect from the Albanian section, some of whom were 'even using the word Fascist when referring to us'. It was a friendly secretary who told Smiley that Eyre had delayed or destroyed signals that McLean had tried to send to Eden.[59] On 28 November 1944, Hoxha and the partisans entered Tirana, ushering in almost five decades of the most totalitarian and isolationist rule anywhere in the Balkans.

The three musketeers expressed their disgust in their post-operational report on the Concensus II mission. Smiley's immediate future was uncertain, so he returned to Cairo, while McLean and Amery headed for London. While in Albania he had entertained thoughts of returning to his regiment, whose progress through Belgium and the Netherlands he had occasionally followed in BBC bulletins. He eventually rejoined the Blues after the war but this was not to be his final association with 'the firm' nor, as it turned out, was it to be his last association with special operations and Albania.

Notes

1. Smiley, *Irregular Regular*, p. 99.
2. Major David Smiley, Diary entry for 18 November 1943, TNA HS 5/143.
3. Captain William Stanley Moss, Diary entry for 8 January 1944, IWM OS/74/1. Tara was the legendary home of the High Kings of Ireland. The most vivid account of life in Tara is to be found in Cooper, *Cairo in the War 1939–1945*, pp. 285–90.
4. Cooper, *Cairo in the War*, p. 286.
5. Peter Liddle, *Captured Memories 1930–1945: Across the Threshold of War – The Thirties and the War, Volume II* (Barnsley: Pen & Sword, 2011), p. 222.
6. Colonel David de C. Smiley, Operational Diary Concensus II Albania, p. 3, Papers of N. L. D. McLean, IWM.
7. Captain William Stanley Moss, Diary entry for 8 January 1944, IWM OS/74/1.
8. Colonel David de C. Smiley, Operational Diary Concensus II Albania, p. 83, Papers of N. L. D. McLean, IWM.
9. While a spectacular operation in terms of the audacity and courage required, the abduction of Kriepe was of little strategic significance. It has been argued that the retribution visited upon the Cretan population by General Friedrich-Wilhelm Müller in the aftermath of the abduction was out of all proportion to Kriepe's actual worth. See Wes Davis, *The Ariadne Objective* (London: Corgi/Transworld, 2014).
10. Cooper, *Cairo in the War*, p. 301.
11. M. R. D. Foot, *SOE: The Special Operations Executive 1940–46* (London: Pimlico, 1999), p. 336.
12. Colonel David de C. Smiley, Operational Diary Concensus II Albania, p. 3, Papers of N. L. D. McLean, IWM.
13. 'Notes on Supply and Equipment in the Field', March 1944, Major Smiley', Papers of N. L. D. McLean, IWM.
14. On the Jedburghs, see Jay Jakub, *Spies and Saboteurs: Anglo-American Collaboration and Rivalry in Human Intelligence Collection and Special Operations, 1940–45* (Basingstoke: Macmillan, 1999).
15. 'Special Technical Appendix by Major Smiley', February 1945, p. 63, in Colonel David de C. Smiley, Operational Diary Concensus II Albania, Papers of N. L. D. McLean, IWM.

16. Rod Bailey, 'SOE in Albania: The "conspiracy theory" reassessed', in Mark Seaman (ed.), *Special Operations Executive: A New Instrument of War* (London: Routledge, 2006), p. 180.
17. Major N. McLean, 'Memorandum on Albania', December 1943, Papers of N. L. D. McLean, IWM.
18. Bailey, *The Wildest Province*, p. 163.
19. IWM Sound Archive Accession No: 8980 Interview with Julian Amery; Bassett, *Last Imperialist*, pp. 101–2.
20. Bailey, 'SOE in Albania', in Seaman (ed.), *Special Operations Executive*, p. 181.
21. Colonel David de C. Smiley, Operational Diary Concensus II Albania, p. 3, Papers of N. L. D. McLean, IWM.
22. Palmer was perhaps the most effective and certainly the most influential of the BLOs sent to Albania. His reports on the effectiveness of the partisans, compared with their nationalist rivals, wielded considerable influence in SOE headquarters in Bari. He impressed all those he came into contact with, including senior officers, as a natural leader and fine soldier, and was awarded the DSO. See Bailey, *The Wildest Province*, pp. 303–4.
23. Smiley, *Irregular Regular*, p. 101. Watching Quayle's performance as a captured intelligence officer lying in a hospital bed in the film *Guns of Navarone*, Smiley remarked on how similar he looked to his ailing self in Bari over a decade earlier.
24. Colonel David de C. Smiley, Operational Diary Concensus II Albania, 23 April 1944, Papers of N. L. D. McLean, IWM.
25. Smiley, *Albanian Assignment*, p. 111.
26. NA HS5/126, Albania: Report Top Secret by Lt Col. McLean DSO, Major D. de C. Smiley MC and Captain Julian Amery in 'Concensus Mission II 28 November 1944'.
27. Colonel David de C. Smiley, Operational Diary Concensus II Albania, 26 April 1944. Papers of N. L. D. McLean, IWM.
28. Amery, *Sons of the Eagle*, p. 50.
29. Colonel David de C. Smiley, Operational Diary Concensus II Albania, 13 June 1944, Papers of N. L. D. McLean, IWM.
30. Amery, *Sons of the Eagle*, p. 179.
31. Smiley, *Irregular Regular*, p. 105.
32. Colonel David de C. Smiley, Operational Diary Concensus II Albania, 21 June 1944, Papers of N. L. D. McLean, IWM.
33. Concensus II to SOE Bari w/t message, 18 June 1944, Papers of N. L. D. McLean, IWM.
34. Interview with Colonel David Smiley, London, 18 February 2005.

35. NA HS5/126, Secret: Comments on Report by Lt Col. McLean DSO, Major Smiley MC and Capt Amery dated November 28 1944 (February 1945), p. 5; Bailey, 'SOE in Albania', in Seaman (ed.), *Special Operations Executive*, p. 183.
36. Bernd J. Fischer, 'Abaz Kupi and British intelligence in Albania, 1943–44', in Morison (ed.), *Eastern Europe and the West*, p. 134.
37. Smiley, *Albanian Assignment*, pp. 151–4; Kemp, *The Thorns of Memory*, pp. 231–2.
38. Interview with Colonel David Smiley, London, 18 February 2005.
39. See Geoff Andrews, *The Shadow Man: At the Heart of the Cambridge Spy Circle* (London: I. B. Tauris, 2015). The biography of Klugmann provides the most detailed account of the scope and limits of his espionage activities. While he was involved in Albanian affairs during his time with SOE, his main focus was Yugoslavia.
40. Interview with Colonel David Smiley, London, 18 February 2005.
41. Quoted in Bailey, *The Wildest Province*, p. 262.
42. N. L. D. McLean, Draft Notes for Diary 1944/45 (Reconstructed 1984), Papers of N. L. D. McLean, IWM.
43. Roderick Bailey, 'Smoke without Fire? Albania, SOE and the "Communist Conspiracy Theory"', in Stephanie Schwandner-Sievers and Bernd J. Fischer (eds), *Albanian Identities: Myth and History* (London: Hurst, 2002), p. 150.
44. Colonel David de C. Smiley, Operational Diary Concensus II Albania, 18 July 1944, Papers of N. L. D. McLean, IWM.
45. Smiley, *Albanian Assignment*, p. 133.
46. Colonel David de C. Smiley, Operational Diary Concensus II Albania, 20 July 1944, Papers of N. L. D. McLean, IWM.
47. Colonel David de C. Smiley, Operational Diary Concensus II Albania, 27 August 1944, Papers of N. L. D. McLean, IWM.
48. See D. R. Oakley-Hill, *An Englishman in Albania: Memoires of a British Officer 1929–1955* (London: Centre for Albanian Studies, 2002).
49. Colonel David de C. Smiley, Operational Diary Concensus II Albania, 23 July 1944. Papers of N. L. D. McLean, IWM.
50. Colonel David de C. Smiley, Operational Diary Concensus II Albania, 29 August 1944. Papers of N. L. D. McLean, IWM. See also Smiley, *Albanian Assignment*, p. 137.
51. Amery, *Sons of the Eagle*, p. 272.
52. Colonel David de C. Smiley, Operational Diary Concensus II Albania, 16 August 1944. Papers of N. L. D. McLean, IWM.

53. Colonel David de C. Smiley, Operational Diary Concensus II Albania, 13 August 1944. Papers of N. L. D. McLean, IWM.
54. Colonel David de C. Smiley, Operational Diary Concensus II Albania, 1 September 1944. Papers of N. L. D. McLean, IWM.
55. David Stafford, *Britain and European Resistance 1940–1945: A Survey of the Special Operations Executive with Documents* (Toronto: University of Toronto Press, 1983), p. 172.
56. Colonel David de C. Smiley, Operational Diary Concensus II Albania, 6 September 1944. Papers of N. L. D. McLean, IWM.
57. NA HS5/126, Albania: Report Top Secret by Lt Col. McLean DSO, Major D. de C. Smiley MC and Captain Julian Amery in 'Concensus Mission II 28 November 1944'; Smiley, *Albanian Assignment*, p. 139.
58. Colonel David de C. Smiley, Operational Diary Concensus II Albania, 21 September 1944. Papers of N. L. D. McLean, IWM.
59. Colonel David de C. Smiley, Operational Diary Concensus II Albania, 31 October 1944. Papers of N. L. D. McLean, IWM; Letter from David Smiley, *London Review of Books*, 18/24 (12 December 1996).

7 Burnt but Alive

I

Having spent November 1944 in Bari writing up post-operational reports, Smiley flew back to Cairo. The exuberance of life at Tara the previous winter was long gone and the mood felt like the morning after a good party. Many old friends had moved on, and while he 'had the usual good time', Smiley's words lacked conviction. He learned too that Sophie Tarnowska had decided to marry Billy Moss: 'Xan (Fielding) has taken it very hard and I must say I am not too pleased myself.'[1] In Albania, he had seriously given thought to rejoining the Blues, who were pushing through Belgium and the Netherlands as part of the advance guard of Montgomery's 21st Army Group. It seemed a more fruitful way of fighting the Germans than guerrilla warfare with its political vagaries. Smiley's belief that the Concensus II mission had been let down by the political prejudice of some SOE people in Bari still weighed heavily on his mind.[2] In Albania he had confided to his diary: 'I am certainly not going to stay in the firm when I return as I resent receiving orders from such fools.'[3]

But happenstance again determined otherwise. While concluding his affairs in Cairo, he met by chance an old family friend, Prince Subha Svasti, brother-in-law to the exiled monarch of Siam (now Thailand), King Prajadhipok, who, forced to abdicate after a failed putsch in 1935, had settled with his family circle close to Virginia Water, where Smiley's mother lived. King Prajadhipok was a keen Anglophile and had held a commission in the Royal Horse Artillery before the First World War. It is not surprising that his family and wider entourage fitted seamlessly into the

Burnt but Alive

Fig. 7.1 Map of Siam/Thailand.

upper-class social circles of this corner of Surrey. Subha Svasti – or 'Chin', as he was more widely known – became a great friend of Smiley and they shared an interest in aviation; they had flown together in Smiley's private plane before the war.[4] A graduate of the Royal Military Academy at Woolwich, Chin had been recruited into the Far East Section of SOE (Force 136) and was now a lieutenant colonel. Like Smiley, he was in transit, in his case to India, where he was responsible for infiltrating agents into his home country to organise resistance against the Japanese.

While Siam was formally an ally of Tokyo, Chin assured Smiley of the widespread dislike across the country, both of the Japanese and of Field Marshal Pibul Songgram, Prime Minister and Commander-in-Chief of the Siamese armed forces, whose avowed anti-colonialism masked his own territorial claim against Malaya. When Chin suggested that his old friend join him in Force 136, Smiley needed little persuading. Having packed up his belongings in Cairo and shipped them back to England, he reported back to SOE headquarters in Baker Street just before Christmas 1944. Chin had already signalled ahead requesting Smiley's transfer, and Baker Street was happy to oblige. Not only was he a highly experienced BLO but the award of a bar to his Military Cross (MC) for blowing up the Gjoles bridge the previous June (despite McLean's recommendation that he be awarded a DSO) singled Smiley out as a singularly brave and audacious officer, whose technical experience in organising resistance behind enemy lines was now deemed invaluable.

One of the few independent states in the region before 1941, Siam had signed treaties of non-aggression with Britain and France in 1940, despite having claims to territories administered by France in French Indo-China. Though he claimed neutrality, Pibul quickly sided with Japan when, in December 1941, Japanese troops landed in Thailand, a name preferred by Pibul over Siam because it was shorn of its subservient overtones to the European powers that had marked its foreign relations. Thai forces had offered only token resistance to the Japanese invaders, allowing them to secure their lines of communication quickly as they pressed south into British Malaya and the colonies of the Dutch East Indies, and north-west into Burma. On 25 January

1942, Thailand declared war on both Britain and the United States. London returned the compliment but Washington, believing that the Thai government was acting under duress, desisted. The difference – the one seeing Thailand as an outright enemy, the other as an enemy-occupied country – soon marked serious discord over policy between the British and Americans. Pibul's support for the Japanese was rewarded with suzerainty over four northerly states of Malaya. This was grist to the mill of those in London who wished to punish Bangkok, a position summed up by Foreign Office officials who argued that, because of their supposed quisling behaviour, the Thais 'must work their passage home'.[5]

Thai support for the Japanese was nowhere near as solid as these Foreign Office assessments suggested. Pibul had appointed a political rival, Nai Pridi Bhanomyong, as Regent, partly to keep him quiet but mainly to clip his political wings. By 1943, however, Pridi had secretly founded the Free Siam Movement, whose membership had infiltrated the organs of the Thai state – the military, police, regional governors and civil service – upon which Japanese control and Pibul depended. Initially, Force 136 treated the Free Siam Movement with some scepticism. Because Pridi had been made regent under the auspices of the Japanese, many questioned his true loyalties. Only after a hesitant start, including two failed missions, was the Regent's sincerity established beyond doubt. By 1943, increasing numbers of young Thai men, many from elite families that had sent them to British public schools and universities before the war, were being spirited out to India, where Force 136 had its headquarters under Colin Mackenzie in Calcutta. Given their social standing, SOE staff referred to these recruits as 'the Old School Thais'.[6]

Still, British policy towards the Free Siam Movement and the future of post-war Thailand remained opaque. Echoing the debates and intrigue that had blighted British policy towards Albania, inter-departmental divisions across Whitehall muddied policy towards Thailand. The Colonial Office, the India Office and the Foreign Office offered competing views on how best to secure British interests. This, in turn, hamstrung efforts on the part of South East Asia Command (SEAC), established in October

1943 by President Franklin Roosevelt and Winston Churchill at the Quebec conference. Under the command of Admiral Lord Louis Mountbatten, SEAC tried to be creative in its approaches towards Pridi, not least in what London could offer as terms for a post-war settlement. In light of the animus towards Thailand and the suspicion in some quarters in Washington that Britain had territorial designs beyond the Malay–Thai border on the Kra Isthmus (which official British denials did little to allay), the ability of Force 136 to marry political weight with the supply of military hardware to help the Free Siam Movement was handicapped from the outset.

By contrast, Washington had a clearer view of its interests in Thailand and, in Pridi, saw the opportunity to meet them. Unencumbered by any active declaration of war against Thailand, the United States could afford to take the moral high ground and oppose the re-establishment of European colonial influence across the region. One wag declared that SEAC stood for 'Saving England's Asian Colonies'. In reality, the Office of Strategic Services (OSS), the counterpart to SOE and forerunner of the Central Intelligence Agency (CIA), was keen to usurp British influence in Thailand and considered Pridi the instrument for doing so.[7] As the historian Richard J. Aldrich observed, by 1945, 'OSS now regarded themselves as being in a straight race for Pridi's affections.'[8] Under the umbrella of SEAC, the activities and policies of the OSS and Force 136 should have been coordinated. In reality, both services ran separate operations into Siam with little joint planning. Only late in the day did Mackenzie and his OSS counterpart in SEAC, John Coughlin, came to realise that Pridi and the Free Siam Movement were 'neither pro-British nor pro-American but instead pro-Thai'.[9]

SOE none the less stole a march on its OSS counterpart when, in April 1945, it managed to infiltrate Brigadier Victor Jacques (code name Hector) into Thailand for talks with Pridi. Jacques, a veteran of the First World War, had practised law in Bangkok before the Japanese invasion and, at 6 feet 4 inches tall, was regarded literally as a towering intellect. Jacques was accompanied by Chin and another SOE officer, Tom Hobbs, and the meeting was meant to persuade the Free Siam Movement to support

Operation Priest, the Allied capture of the island of Phuket off the Thai coast, from where air attacks could be mounted against Japanese targets before an Allied invasion of Malaya. Operation Priest was eventually cancelled, much to the chagrin of many among the Siam section of Force 136, but it did allow resources to be concentrated on developing guerrilla groups across Thailand.[10] Force 136 had been attempting to do just this from the beginning of 1945 but information on conditions on the ground was patchy. The Siam section war diary for 22 January noted that contact had been made with the Free Siam Movement and it was proving a valuable source of intelligence. But its guerrilla units remained an unknown quantity; nor was it clear in which areas such guerrillas were operating or under whose orders.[11]

Smiley knew little of this when he accepted his assignment. Indeed, he was unaware that Chin, with his royal pedigree, was regarded with some suspicion by the Americans, who saw his closeness with the British as part of a plot to reimpose dynastic rule across Thailand.[12] In London, McLean and Alan Hare had urged Smiley to accompany them as part of an SOE mission to China, but a compromise of sorts was reached. Upon arrival in India, they would all take stock of the wider eddies of the war against Japan and decide where they would like to be posted. Thus, in March 1945, after an extended period of leave, Hare, McLean and Smiley boarded a flight to India via Cairo. They stayed at Tara for just over a week, catching up on gossip and meeting old friends, among them Peter Kemp, whom Smiley had last seen in Bari before he was dropped back into Albania the previous spring. After his own hazardous experiences in this Balkan wilderness, including a foray into Kosovo, Kemp had been parachuted into south-west Poland in December 1944 to assess the *Armja Krajowa* (AK), the Polish Home Army, as it struggled to re-establish itself in the aftermath of the failed Warsaw uprising. Organised by Lieutenant Colonel Harold Perkins of the Polish Section of SOE, the mission achieved precious little. The mass advance of the Red Army across Poland soon swept up the mission and Kemp was interned by the Soviet NKVD before pressure from London secured his release. An avowed anti-communist to his very core, Kemp returned from captivity to

Cairo via Moscow, Baku and Tehran. Smiley had long admired Kemp from their Albanian days and now urged him to travel out to India.[13]

Kemp had to return to London for a full debriefing, but in the mean time, Smiley and his companions continued on their way to Delhi. His close family link with the Wavells again paid dividends. Lord Wavell, by now Viceroy of India, was travelling back to Delhi from London when he chanced upon Smiley at a dinner party in the Egyptian capital. Hearing of Smiley's intentions, he arranged for him to be quartered at the Viceroy's Lodge in the Indian capital. Designed by Lutyens, the lodge was a symbol of the grandeur of the Raj and stood in marked contrast to the heat and discomfort of the administrative headquarters of Force 136. Hare and McLean, meanwhile, found similar salvation in a comfortable hotel in Old Delhi. Still, their arrival had been unexpected and was resolved only by posting the trio to Ceylon, where Force 136 had its operational base and jungle training schools. Smiley's brief sojourn in Delhi, however, confirmed Siam as his preferred area of operation. While the appeal of accompanying Hare and McLean to new vistas in China was undoubtedly strong, Colonel Peter Fleming, head of D Division of Force 136, which dealt with deception operations, persuaded Smiley that his war should now take him from his colleagues. Fleming (brother of Ian), whose knowledge of the Far East theatre Smiley greatly respected, believed that growing political rivalries in China would stymie SOE operations as Washington flexed its diplomatic and military muscles. Siam now beckoned.[14]

II

At the end of March 1945, Smiley swapped the luxury of Viceroy's house for the rigours of ME 25 on the island of Ceylon, the training camp for BLOs and agents destined for Japanese-occupied territory in South East Asia. Located in a rubber plantation two hours north of the capital, Colombo, its Spartan conditions, with coconut matting for beds, were meant to introduce students to the harsh conditions they could expect in the jungle. The students on the intense three-week course were a kaleidoscope of nationalities and tribes: Kerens, Malays, Siamese, Koreans, Kachins, Annamites (from Vietnam), Chinese and even a few Japanese. Among these were scattered the Europeans, mainly British, French and Dutch. Smiley reckoned that at least twenty-nine nationalities and ethnic groups made up the student body, but it also included many veterans of SOE operations in the Balkans, several of them former associates and friends from Tara. These included Rowland Winn, Xan Fielding and Billy Moss, as well as Hare and McLean, while later recruits included John Hibberdine and Peter Kemp.

All experienced operators in their own right, they were still subjected to the rigours of a jungle warfare training regime, with Gurkhas often acting the part of the enemy. The ability to shoot instinctively rather than take steady aim was impressed upon students, as targets in dense foliage often appeared only fleetingly. The students learned how to deal with tropical diseases and snake bites, and to identify edible fruits, as well as to hunt in a jungle environment. While happy to eat wild boar, deer and jungle fowl, Smiley drew the line at a monkey that had been 'shot for the pot' by a French SOE candidate. He remained highly proficient in demolitions and signals but took the opportunity to hone these skills further. As the course progressed, more time was spent in the jungle, culminating in a five-day exercise designed to instil into the students the fact that their environment was neutral. Making it work to their advantage would be key to their survival.

Towards the end of course in April 1945, Smiley was told he would be dropped into Siam under the next full moon, likely to be near the end of May. In the mean time, he was to choose a team to go with him before travelling to the Siam Country Section in Calcutta for a more detailed briefing. Smiley selected two former police inspectors who had worked in the Bangkok CID and whom he had observed close up during his own jungle training: Sudhi Sudisakdi (code name 'Chat') and Santa Sintavi (code name 'Pun') would be his bodyguards and interpreters. They possessed four skills he prized highly in operations behind enemy lines: they were fit and tough, spoke passable English and, above all, were cheerful, a 'most important requirement under guerrilla conditions'.[15] The final member of the team was Sergeant William 'Gunner' Collins, a skilled wireless operator recruited to SOE from the Royal Horse Artillery, who had been dropped into northern Albania in 1944. Smiley much admired his intelligence, bravery and fortitude on operations. Hearing that he had returned to the UK, Smiley immediately signalled London requesting his services. It was a prescient choice, for Gunner was soon to save his life.

In Colombo, he bid farewell to Hare, who had been given a staff position with Force 136 in Kandy, and to McLean, who had been posted to the Chinese province of Sinkiang. Together with Chat and Pun, he now flew to Calcutta. After his experiences of SOE office politics in Bari, Smiley was anxious to meet the Siam Country Section head and staff. He was not disappointed. The GI (General Staff Officer I), Major Ben Hervey-Bathurst of the Grenadier Guards, he knew from their time together at the same prep school; the head of section, Lieutenant Colonel Peter Pointon, was an old East Asia hand who had worked for the Bombay–Burma Trading Company before the war; the section intelligence officer, Lieutenant Commander 'Hoppy' Hopkinson of the Royal Naval Volunteer Reserve had previously been an employee of the Swedish Match Company in Bangkok. All instilled a confidence in Smiley that greatly reassured him. They never let him down.

Post-colonial politics was, however, making itself felt. Siam was now to be called Thailand, and Smiley noticed that Force 136 agents of the Siam section wore shoulder flashes with the words 'Free Thais'. The office now gave Smiley a thorough immersion in the complexities of Thai politics, which was much needed if diplomatic incidents were to be avoided. He learned what Force 136 considered to be the scope and scale of the Free Siam Movement and was given a detailed briefing on Pridi, who, somewhat incongruously, had been given the code name Ruth. By now, Calcutta had a far more detailed picture of the Free Siam Movement, thanks to the inconspicuous work of Jacques who, along with his signaller, was now operating from a safe house in the Thai capital as part of the Panicle mission under the very noses of the Japanese.

As regent, Pridi continued to hold high-level meetings with his Japanese interlocutors; information from these meetings was invariably passed directly to Jacques and swiftly forwarded via coded signal to SEAC in Kandy. Though of varying quality, this intelligence gave Mountbatten's staff a valuable insight into Japanese war plans. Panicle's biggest coup was to gain complete access to their order of battle across South East Asia, which Smiley later believed saved countless Allied lives but for which Jacques (and, indeed, Pridi) never received the credit they deserved.[16] Meanwhile, Jacques, under strict orders from London, saw his relationship with Pridi as primarily military. It was therefore much to the irritation of his Thai benefactor that Jacques refused to be drawn on Britain's post-war commitments to Thailand.[17]

By the spring of 1945, SEAC had decided that Force 136 should harness the potential of the Free Siam Movement, particularly across northern Thailand, to harry Japanese lines of communication as British and Indian forces pushed down through Burma and to be held ready in the event of a seaborne landing on the Malay Peninsula. Mountbatten, however, urged that such action should be closely coordinated with SEAC. If bands of guerrillas attacked the Japanese before the main offensive, this would only alert Tokyo to Allied intentions while exacting a terrible price on the Free Siam Movement and the civilian population as the Japanese army sought revenge.[18] This was exactly the same reservation expressed by the British authorities in Bari when the Concensus II mission advocated military support for the Zogists. Pridi, however, was keen to test the mettle of the resistance, a position that Mackenzie felt was partly driven by the need of the Thais to be seen 'to be working their passage home' and gaining political leverage that might help ensure the country's future independence.[19]

The insertion of Force 136 teams into northern Thailand was therefore as much about staying the hand of Free Siam Movement and ensuring their full integration in SEAC strategy as it was about liaison and training. Thailand was divided up into vast areas of Force 136 operations, the most northerly given the code names 'Candle' and 'Coupling'. Already, the Free Siam Movement had made much progress in organising guerrilla training camps in both these areas to an extent that was probably not fully appreciated by either Force 136 or, indeed, SEAC. Smiley was now designated to lead his mission, code-named 'Felt', across Candle, an immense area, covering about one-third of Thailand's land mass, which encompassed

> That part of north-east Thailand bounded on the west by the railway running north from Korat to Udon and the road on to Nong Khai, on the north east by the Mekong River (where it forms the frontier between Thailand and French Indo-China) and on the south by the railway from Korat to Ubon.[20]

To the west of Candle was Coupling, an area of similar size assigned to Lieutenant Colonel Sidney ('Soapy') Hudson, a decorated veteran of SOE operations in France.[21] Across the Mekong river, Free French Force 136 officers were active, much to the chagrin of the OSS, whose own officers were believed by SOE to be operating to the south of both Coupling and Candle. The fact that this could not be confirmed at the time of Smiley's briefing illustrates the lack of cooperation at the planning level between the OSS and SOE.

The Felt mission now received its orders, most of which were familiar to Smiley from his time in Albania: to organise and train guerrillas, to receive air drops, to gather intelligence on Japanese dispositions, and to locate prisoner of war (PoW) camps while helping escapees, be they downed Allied aircrew or civilian refugees. They included, however, the following order: '[T]o remain clandestine and on no account to take any action against the Japanese'.[22] Pointon continually impressed on Smiley that the Felt mission should exercise the utmost restraint towards the Free Siam Movement in its area of operations until ordered otherwise. Having just turned twenty-nine, with a wealth of experience in special operations, Smiley now had his first command over an SOE mission. It was a challenge he relished, while anxious to avoid the political intrigues that, from his perspective, had so blighted Concensus II.

As more intelligence in his area of operations was gathered, he acquired additional skills. Some 90 miles north-east of Calcutta lay Jessore, the base for long-range air sorties into South East Asia. Here Smiley joined the 'pick-up' course, to identify and organise landing strips behind enemy lines, a skill taught to only a select few BLOs dropped into Albania, Collins among them. It was here that Smiley recalled the rather muted celebrations of Victory in Europe (VE) Day, 8 May 1945:

> The day itself created little impression in India, where the majority of the inhabitants were concerned about the war on their own doorstep. Nor were the British troops madly enthusiastic, when their efforts in Burma had received such scant attention in the British press.

Midway through his pick-up course, Smiley accepted an invitation to accompany the crew of a B24 Liberator dropping supplies to Thailand, including the Candle area of operations. In a converted bomber modified to carry extra fuel tanks for the twelve-hour round trip, this flight almost proved Smiley's last. An hour after take-off, a fire broke out in the fuselage after an incendiary device, designed to prevent its secret radar falling into Japanese hands if the aircraft was forced to land, exploded prematurely. It took Smiley and the rear gunner fifteen minutes and all the fire extinguishers on board to douse the flames that had, in the mean time, destroyed their parachutes. Despite this, the pilot pressed on. An hour later, the ill-fated bomber developed a fuel leak, forcing the pilot to fly on three engines, the minimum to keep the plane air-borne. It was a relief to Smiley and the rest of the crew when the pilot finally decided to return to Jessore.[23]

But Smiley was so determined to familiarise himself with his area of operations that on 20 May he subjected himself again to the experience of a supply drop over Thailand, happily this time without incident. The pilot even flew him over his designated landing area at Sakon Nakon, allowing him to photograph the drop zone and identify any immediate hazards to be avoided on his descent; clearly, he had not forgotten the two painful drops into Albania. At thirteen and a half hours it was an exhausting flight but it brought home to Smiley the huge risks the RAF Liberator crews took in resupplying resistance groups across Burma, Thailand, Malaya and farther afield. The weather was often erratic; the violence of sudden thunderstorms and thick cumulus cloud had been known to flip aircraft or cause a sudden loss of instrument readings, often with catastrophic results. When this was combined with the ever-present threat of being bounced by Japanese fighter aircraft, these crews took extraordinary risks in supplying missions and agents who, Smiley later opined, 'might or might not be doing a good job'.[24]

III

On 29 May 1945, the Felt mission of 'Grin, Gunner, Chat and Pun' boarded its Liberator for the seven-hour flight to their drop zone. The journey was memorable only for the intense cold felt by the Candle members as the Liberator levelled out at 15,000 feet to fly over mountain ranges and circumvent threatening clouds. Finally, the silvery outline of the Mekong river and the lake close to Sakon Nakon could be seen from the port side of the Liberator as the light of dawn crept over the eastern horizon. The plan was to drop the team close to the village of Ban Non Han, and soon Smiley spotted the signal fires on a drop zone that was swarming with men. Exit from the Liberator was via a slide under the turret of the rear gunner, a method much preferred by Smiley to jumping from the side door or, as in the case of a Halifax, dropping through a hole in the fuselage, as the slipstream proved less turbulent.

With the red light on, the team was ready on the slide: Smiley first, then Chat, to be followed by Pun, with Gunner last. The green light flashed and Smiley pushed himself down and out, quickly feeling the heavy tug of the static line deploying his canopy. Looking over his shoulder, he glimpsed the fast-disappearing silhouette of the despatcher against the dim interior light of the aircraft giving the thumbs up to confirm a smooth exit. Disconcerting, however, was the absence of the three other parachutes in close order behind. But having been dropped from a height of only 500 feet, the more immediate concern was to land safely as the ground rushed up to meet him.

It proved to be wet and muddy but otherwise the softest of landings, as Smiley came down in a paddy field, leaving the two bottles of whisky in the pockets of his jump-suit firmly intact.

Burnt but Alive

Two Thais rushed towards him and immediately introduced themselves by their code names as Pluto and Kong. But before further pleasantries could be exchanged, the Liberator flew in for another pass, this time disgorging three bodies dangling from their canopies, followed by another two runs that dropped the mission's weapons and supplies. Smiley later learned that Chat had frozen on the slide, forcing the pilot to make a second run, while the gentle persuasion of the despatcher and the not-so-gentle persuasion of Pun and Gunner decided the issue.

The presence of a known Japanese garrison close to Sakon Nakon was doubtless a concern, but Smiley's subsequent journey on the back of a bullock-drawn cart, accompanied by a hundred armed guerrillas returning to their camp 2 miles away, demonstrated the limits of Japanese control over the surrounding countryside. Smiley soon discovered from Pluto and Kong that, in the Candle area, some 5,000 members of the Free Siam Movement had received paramilitary training, a number far higher than the estimates of SEAC. Moreover, it seemed that the movement had managed to inveigle itself into the civil administration. District governors passed on political information, post-office workers tapped communications and railway workers reported on Japanese troop movements, while teachers and doctors were numerous in its ranks. Such was the influence of the Free Siam Movement that large numbers of police and soldiers of the regular Thai army had to be ordered to remain in place, lest their sudden desertion to swell the ranks of the resistance alert the Japanese.[25]

Pluto, whose real name was Nai Tieng Sirikhandra, was an elected member of the Thai house of assembly or parliament for the province and town of Sakon Nakon. A close associate of Pridi, he regarded Pibul as little more than a Japanese puppet; he was in overall charge of all guerrillas across Candle. Smiley took to him immediately. Kong, whose real name was Kris Tosayanonda, was also impressive. Fluent in English, having studied medicine at Edinburgh University before the war, he had been dropped to Pluto by Force 136 as a wireless operator and, like many Thais recruited into SOE, held a British army commission. Over the next two weeks, these men quickly immersed Smiley in his area of operations, taking him to see a variety of training camps where he could appraise the training and equipment needs of his new charges. Pluto also informed Smiley of a lone OSS officer operating in an area around the small town of Ban Han on the way to Ubon, Major John Holladay. A former Christian missionary who knew Thailand well and spoke its language fluently, Holladay was a natural choice for what he told Smiley on their first meeting was purely an intelligence-gathering mission. He appeared to Smiley 'kind, hospitable and co-operative', and allayed his concerns that, in an area of operations under his immediate command, toes would be trodden on.[26]

In fact, Holladay's presence in the Candle area had hastened the despatch of Felt; SEAC believed that Pluto's ties with the OSS were purely instrumental and meant to secure more supplies. In turn, Force 136 also suspected that the OSS looked to use such aid to gain greater influence over Thai politics. That Smiley was unaware of Holladay's presence when he left India underscores the simmering rivalry at staff level between the two Allied secret organisations, but it also suggested something of an intelligence lapse on the part of Force 136.[27] After this initial encounter, which Smiley remembered fondly, Holladay signalled back to his own headquarters in Kandy, recounting Smiley's '[i]nitial pessimism about his situation', reporting that he 'spoke of a desire to return to India but he [Smiley] apparently changed his attitude after touring Tiang's [Pluto's] camp'.[28] As Smiley had yet to assess guerrilla capabilities anywhere in Candle, this is surprising, because in his own memoirs he never expressed any doubts about the mission. If such doubts were aired before Holladay, they were quickly dispelled. On 11 June, just ten days after the landing, the Force 136 war diary recorded that 'Smiley reports that everybody is helpful and enthusiastic. There are 10 training camps in area UDORN-SAKOL, SAKOL-NAKAWM-NAKON, PHANOM-POIET [sic] each capable of training 100 men per week in rifle, carbine and grenades.'[29]

In the following days, Smiley took stock of the operational needs of his large jungle parish. His ability to move from camp to camp virtually unhindered by any meaningful Japanese military presence emphasised the almost complete control now exercised by Pluto and the Free Siam Movement. But the lack of security at

Burnt but Alive

many of the camps worried Smiley, not least because falling into the hands of the feared *Kenpeitai* – Japanese military intelligence – was 'something I didn't care to contemplate'. Pluto tried to allay these fears, pointing to the paucity of Japanese troops in his area and the fact that his own network of agents was so closely entwined with the Japanese garrison that they would receive plenty of warning of troop movements in their area. At some of these camps, local villagers had been enlisted to help build airfields that, once the Allied landings had taken place, would serve as forward air bases for transport aircraft and medium-range bombers. One such airfield was already under construction close to a small hamlet at Maha Sarakham. Unfamiliar with the Thai language, Smiley code-named the airfield 'Heston' after the grass airstrip from where he had flown his private aircraft before the war. Bases at Ban Tao Ngoi and Ban Non Han nearby were called 'Kempton' and 'Ascot', names that reflected Smiley's pre-war equestrian interests and were decidedly easier to remember.

Far from experiencing the jungle privations that Felt had been conditioned to expect, Smiley and Collins lived and ate rather well as they travelled on their ponies across the Candle area, inspecting camps and making plans. The flora and fauna enchanted him: large deciduous trees played host to wild orchids while huge butterflies of the most vivid blue provided a stark contrast along paths under a jungle canopy illuminated only by irregular shafts of sunlight. Eventually, Smiley decided to set up his headquarters at Ascot: it already housed 1,000 guerrillas, had clean running water from a nearby stream and was sited close to a suitable drop zone. Pluto quickly had living quarters built on a nearby hill that afforded Smiley and Collins some privacy and security; they also came equipped with the luxury of real beds, a far cry from the expected bamboo mats. From Ascot, Smiley could reach most of the dozen training camps in the Candle area within three days. The only impediment to training the guerrillas was the lack of arms and BLOs. Smiley was sure that, once these were received, the resistance would give a good account of themselves when SEAC gave the order to attack.

This bucolic idyll was not to last. Back in Calcutta, SEAC had heard, most likely from Pridi via Jacques, that the Japanese had become aware of the Felt mission and had despatched the *Kenpeitai* to Sakon Nakon to track Smiley down.[30] Most of the Japanese patrols were accompanied by Thai officials working for Pridi, who either led them up the jungle equivalent of blind alleys or, where the Japanese knew the location of specific camps, forewarned the inhabitants to evacuate the area immediately. In most of these cases, Pridi ordered the camps to be destroyed.

On 23 June, Smiley received the news that one of his agents had contacted a large PoW camp at Ubon. Hoping to exploit this opportunity, he travelled to Heston, where he intended to stay the night, before proceeding to the outskirts of Ubon the next day. But once he arrived at Heston, news was received that a large Japanese force was approaching the camp and was less than a mile away. Speed was of the essence. Collins quickly packed up the precious transmitter while Smiley gathered his code books and copies of signals from SEAC and hurriedly threw them into a specially designed briefcase. It almost proved fatal:

> I had with me a brief case which was made by the special effects people in SOE. It had six pounds of thermite in the bottom and could be used as a booby trap. You could leave it. Whoever opened it blew themselves up. Or, if you wanted to destroy secret documents and things you could put the documents in the brief case, press a button and after five seconds it would explode. I was packing my code books and various signals I'd been receiving into this brief case. It exploded in my hands. Must have short circuited somewhere. Six pounds of thermite blew up. I was extremely badly burnt. ... My hands and knees were burnt. My face was burnt, my eyes were closed. I couldn't open them. I shut my eyes when the thing went off. I couldn't open them again.[31]

Whether he accidently triggered the mechanism in his haste or the briefcase short-circuited is unclear, but the entry in the Force 136 war diary for 5–7 July 1945 recalled that Smiley's condition was 'not serious'. This totally belied the extent of his injuries. He had first-degree burns on his face, chest and neck, and second- and third-degree burns on his inner arms, hands and knees; four fingers of his left had burned to the bone. With only enough

Burnt but Alive

morphia to dull the excruciating pain for a day, his situation was desperate, as Collins led Smiley by the hand to evade the Japanese. The irony was that the report of the impending Japanese presence proved false. Returning to Heston, Smiley was placed on the floor of a bamboo hut, Kong gently rubbing coconut oil into his burnt flesh to alleviate the pain. Collins radioed Calcutta, who replied that a Dakota transport aircraft would be sent to Heston as soon as possible but could give no precise date. With only basic medicines available and with no hope of being admitted to a hospital in towns still under Japanese control, Smiley's chances of survival looked slim. Medical advice radioed back from Calcutta advised Collins to keep the burns covered but to bathe them frequently in salt water. Soon, however, maggots found their way into the wounds and began to eat the dead flesh on Smiley's body. Clearly, they did not have their fill, for they began to feast on his live flesh. This added to Smiley's acute pain but the medical advice from Calcutta was to leave them be: the maggots not only were helping to keep the wounds clean but were preventing gangrene from taking hold, which, in the jungle conditions, would have been fatal.

Still, the pain pushed Smiley to his limit. After three days, the burnt skin on his neck, arms and legs had begun to blister and burst. While able to see through slits in his eyelids, he could draw sustenance only from sucking gently on a straw. He even tried to dull the pain by smoking an opium pipe, which made him drowsy. But when news came that the Dakota would not be sent after all, his spirits, by his own account, dropped. He now assessed his situation: marooned behind enemy lines, he was devoid of proper medicine, a hindrance to his mission and therefore, by his own reckoning, a handicap to all and sundry. His burnt fingers searched for his holster and his Colt .45, a desperate remedy but one that had the hallmarks of the rational thinking of a professional soldier. Collins, who had been with Smiley throughout his ordeal, along with Chat and Pun, saw what Smiley intended to do and gently but firmly removed the side arm from his reach. 'By their nursing care', he later wrote, 'Gunner [Collins], Kong, Chat and Pun undoubtedly saved my life, for without their attention, I would have died of shock.'[32]

Fig. 7.2   Smiley with first-degree burns.

Events now took a new course. Hearing of Smiley's plight, Pridi arranged for an aircraft of the Thai air force to land at Heston and evacuate him to an airstrip further west, from where it would be easier to take him to India. On 30 June, a Japanese Nagoya fighter–bomber landed at Heston, piloted by two Thai air force officers. In what must have been a surreal experience, Smiley was bundled into the navigator's seat for a journey of 200 miles that took him to a clandestine landing strip at Non Han. Despite the pain of his wounds and cramped as he was into such a tiny space, he was none the less grateful for the risks taken on his behalf, and even more so because, as a British officer flying in a Japanese aircraft, his pilot had avoided the attentions of any marauding RAF fighters. After three days at Non Han, where his wounds were attended to by a doctor, Smiley was flown to another airstrip even further west. After fitful bouts of sleep because of the continued pain, he drank a whole bottle of strong rice spirits or 'Thai Whisky . . . I passed clean out – it was wonderful'.[33]

Burnt but Alive

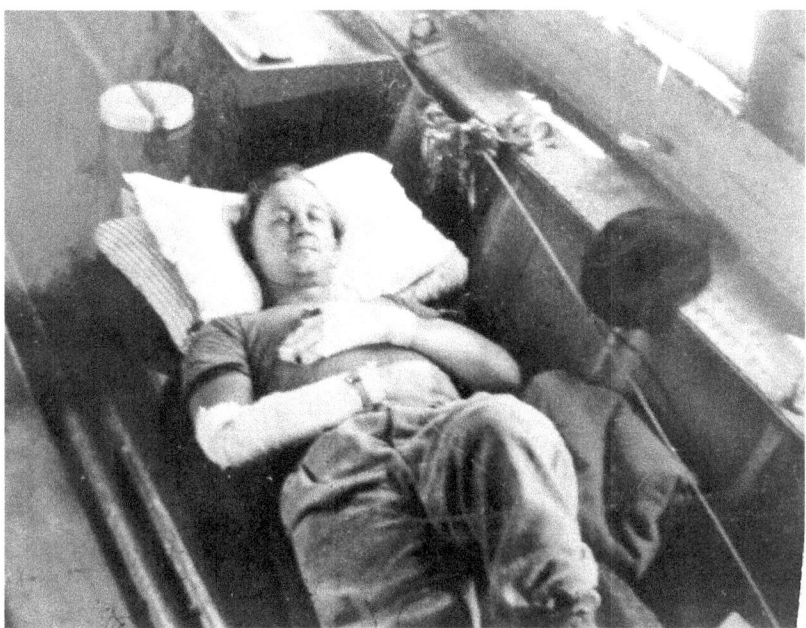

Fig. 7.3 On the Dakota back to India.

For the next five days, Smiley was looked after as well as the Free Siam Movement could manage. Eventually, a Dakota landed and, along with twenty Thais sent for training in Ceylon, Smiley was gently placed on a stretcher and loaded into the fuselage. After a stopover of two days in Rangoon, only recently recaptured from the Japanese, where his wounds were again dressed, the Dakota reached Alipore, close to Calcutta. To the amazement of awaiting friends and colleagues from Force 136, who had been told to expect the worst, Smiley walked from the aircraft, his pain eased by heavy doses of morphine.

IV

Recuperation from burns is often a long, painful process. On arrival in India, it was not at all clear if Smiley's war was now over. He spent two weeks immersed in a series of saline baths in a military hospital in Calcutta, after which he had to undergo the laborious and painful process of having his wounds treated and dressed. His recuperation was again helped by family connections since the wife of the Governor of Bengal, Sir Richard Casey, an Australian, was a friend of Smiley's mother. Hearing of his plight, they set aside the Curzon suite in Government House, a far more comfortable and discreet setting than a military ward. Because Force 136 was still a top secret unit, the privacy here allowed Smiley to discuss the progress of Felt, as well as to brief SEAC on what he knew of the Japanese order of battle in the Candle area. Incredibly, by the end of his two weeks in Calcutta, he needed bandages only on his hands and arms, although the severity of the burns still cast doubt on a future operational role.

He was determined, however, to rejoin Felt but needed to be declared fit by a medical board. His appetite had been whetted by his experience of working with the Free Siam Movement, which, despite his short time in theatre, made a deep impression upon him, and he was further encouraged by messages of support from Collins, Pluto, Chat and Pun. He also again took advantage of his Wavell connection. Hearing of his injuries, Lord Wavell's wife, Eugenie, invited him to convalesce as their guest at the viceregal lodge in Simla, among the grandeur of the Himalayan foothills. It was a welcome relief from the summer heat of Calcutta. Amid such beautiful surroundings and enchanted by the 'birds in full song . . . the war seemed far away', Smiley later recalled.[34]

This brief period of recuperation in Simla was memorable for another reason: it brought Smiley into contact with the key protagonists in the unfolding drama of Indian independence. Between games of tennis to help build up his fitness and an entertaining social scene, he mixed with Mahatma Gandhi, Jawaharlal Nehru and Muhammad Jinnah, who had come to Simla to press their political views on Lord Wavell. He found Gandhi most amusing, while Nehru was deemed charming, possessing the manners and grace of the English upper classes. Jinnah, by contrast, 'went out of his way to be rude to Wavell and everybody else and we took a great dislike to him. I think his behaviour must have harmed the Muslim cause.'[35]

The lodge had a private cinema, where Wavell invited his guests to watch the latest newsreels from Europe. With Jinnah, Nehru and Gandhi all there, the audience watched in silence as British troops liberated Bergen–Belsen and stood amid the emaciated bodies of the living and the dead. Immediately the lights went up, Smiley recalled Jinnah approaching Wavell and exclaiming, '"That was fantastically good propaganda. How did you manage to get those people looking like corpses?" They didn't believe it was true. It was quite extraordinary. It was an awful film.'[36]

By August, Smiley felt he had recovered enough to face a medical board, despite having to wear thin cotton gloves and dressings around his forearms. He had already been making plans with Kemp, now in India, to return to Candle and his desire to do so was sharpened by the news that the Japanese were becoming more active in this area. Reinforcements had been sent to Sakon Nakon to intensify the tempo of anti-guerrilla operations, and signals received by Force 136 reported that Collins and Pluto were seeking sanctuary deeper in the jungle: 'When I heard that the Japanese were getting more active and there were distinct possibilities that we might be allowed to take more aggressive action against them, I made my grateful farewells to Simla and returned to Calcutta.'[37]

The problem of the medical board remained, however, and, to his consternation, he failed. In part, he blamed his mother. Lady Wavell had sent her a signal informing her of Smiley's circumstances. In return, unbeknown to her son, Lady Smiley had sent several telegrams to Lady Wavell, asking her to ensure that the medical board declared him medically unfit to return to active duty. This can clearly be seen as the concern of a mother, painfully aware that her youngest son had tempted fate on too many occasions throughout the war. But in a fit of pique at this 'pulling of strings', Smiley signalled in a rather unusual way his determination to be master of his own destiny. In Calcutta, the medical staff attending to his burnt hands and arms had cut around the back of his wrists and 'pulled the dead skin off like a glove', giving Smiley his 'own grown gloves' as a macabre souvenir. He put them in an envelope and sent them back to Virginia Water. 'This', he recalled, 'didn't go down very well', but 'eventually I passed the medical board although I was still wearing [cotton] gloves and

I had a few bandages on my arm – I still had to wear trousers of course because of my knees.'[38]

Having overcome this maternal interference, Smiley reported back for duty with Force 136. He was just in time, for another officer had been assigned to replace him and take over Felt. This appointment was cancelled. Instead, Peter Kemp and Rowland Winn, a fellow cavalry officer whose own service with SOE in Albania had been blighted by his breaking a leg on his first operational jump, were assigned to Smiley's command. All were very close friends, which Smiley valued greatly, for he was aware from his time in Albania that poor personal relations between BLOs had ruined some of the missions. He also hoped that the rules of engagement would now be changed to let Felt be more aggressive. But events elsewhere now decided other priorities for Candle.

On 6 August 1945, the United States dropped its first atomic bomb on Hiroshima and, three days later, a second on Nagasaki. In Force 136, confusion reigned. Few in SEAC had any prior inkling of these events and it was unclear if the Japanese Imperial Army across South East Asia would fight on regardless. Amid this uncertainty, most pressing was the need to ensure the safety of Allied PoWs and to protect them from retribution by an army approaching its death throes. Seeing the acts of barbarity of Japanese troops elsewhere, this fear was well founded. Moreover, from reports smuggled out of the camps by members of the Free Siam movement, it was clear that many of these prisoners were in an appalling physical state and needed urgent help.

Kemp, Winn, his signaller, Sergeant 'Spider' Lawson, and their mission interpreter quickly left for Jessore, from where they expected to be dropped into the Candle area. Smiley was scheduled to parachute in soon after, although, with his hands still swathed in cotton gloves, he was probably in no fit state to handle a canopy with its requirement to pull down firmly on rigging lines both to steer and to ease the speed of descent. He was saved from this by the appearance of Hector Jacques, who, like Smiley, had been in India when news of the atomic bombs had broken. SEAC was keen that he should return to Bangkok as soon as possible and had laid on a special Dakota to take him. Offered the opportunity to accompany the Brigadier as far as Rangoon, Smiley needed no second invitation.

On 14 August 1945, with just a Thai wireless operator and the crew for company, Smiley and Jacques headed towards the Burmese capital. A delay caused by engine trouble gave Smiley twenty-four hours to explore Rangoon but he finally arrived on 16 August at the clandestine airstrip in Thailand from which he had been evacuated only seven weeks before. Met by Hudson, who had remained in the Coupling area, the pair flew to Non Han, while Jacques continued via a clandestine flight to Bangkok. On arrival, Smiley had approached the Governor of Khon Naen, a known associate of Pluto, to arrange a reunion as soon as possible. This occurred sooner than he expected: while travelling by car to Pluto's last known location, Smiley met him by chance along the road. It was a joyous reunion. Pluto told Smiley that Winn and Kemp had dropped safely the previous day. Collins, Chat, Pun and Lawson, too, were safe and enjoying the hospitality of the Free Siam Movement in the small village of Phannikhom. The next day, Smiley and Pluto were joined by Kemp and Winn, marking the occasion with a boisterous party to celebrate a happy reunion and Kemp's thirtieth birthday. All went to bed that night the 'worse for wear'. The following weeks, however, would bring challenges of a very different kind, challenges that would not only test Smiley's leadership and diplomacy, but require acts of personal bravery in situations that were as emotionally taxing as they were politically charged.

Notes

1. Colonel David de C. Smiley, Operational Diary Concensus II Albania, November–December 1944. Papers of N. L. D. McLean, IWM.
2. Colonel David de C. Smiley, Operational Diary Concensus II Albania, 11 October 1944. Papers of N. L. D. McLean, IWM.
3. Colonel David de C. Smiley, Operational Diary Concensus II Albania, 21 September 1944. Papers of N. L. D. McLean, IWM.
4. IWM, Accession No: 10340/6 Transcript of Interview with Colonel D. Smiley, Recorded 1989, p. 46.

5. Smiley, *Irregular Regular*, p. 116.
6. Richard J. Aldrich, *Intelligence and the War Against Japan: Britain, America and the Politics of Secret Service* (Cambridge: Cambridge University Press, 2000), p. 195.
7. Max Hastings, *The Secret War: Spies, Codes and Guerrillas 1939–1945* (London: William Collins, 2015), pp. 514–15.
8. Aldrich, *Intelligence and the War against Japan*, p. 199.
9. Aldrich, *Intelligence and the War against Japan*, p. 200; E. Bruce Reynolds, *Thailand's Secret War: OSS, SOE and the Free Thai Underground during World War II* (Cambridge: Cambridge University Press, 2005), p. 299.
10. West, *Secret War*, p. 269.
11. TNA HS1/68, Top Secret: Force 136 Siam Country Section: Forward Plans and Estimates 22 January 1945.
12. Smiley, *Irregular Regular*, p. 117.
13. Kemp, *The Thorns of Memory*, pp. 255–65.
14. Liddle, *Captured Memories 1930–1945*, p. 227.
15. Smiley, *Irregular Regular*, p. 122.
16. TNA HS1/68, Top Secret War Diary – Report on Force 136 Activities; Charles Cruickshank, *SOE: Special Operations Executive in the Far East* (Oxford: Oxford University Press, 1983), pp. 113–14; Liddle, *Captured Memories 1930–1945*, p. 228.
17. Aldrich, *Intelligence and the War against Japan*, p. 322.
18. TNA HS1/68, Top Secret War Diary – Report on Force 136 Activities: Tasks for Staff Country Section; Sweet-Escott, *Baker Street Irregular*, pp. 250–1.
19. Cruickshank, *SOE: Special Operations Executive in the Far East*, pp. 116–17.
20. Smiley, *Irregular Regular*, p. 126.
21. Hudson later wrote an interesting account of his time in South East Asia with Force 136. See Sydney Hudson, *Undercover Operator: An SOE Agent's Experiences in France and the Far East* (Barnsley: Pen & Sword, 2003), pp. 116–55.
22. Smiley, *Irregular Regular*, p. 126.
23. IWM, Accession No: 10340/6 Transcript of Interview with Colonel D. Smiley, Recorded 1989, p. 48; Smiley, *Irregular Regular*, p. 128.
24. For a vivid account of special operations flights across South East Asia towards the end of the Second World War, see Terence O'Brien, *The Moonlight War: The Story of Clandestine Operations in South-East Asia, 1944–5* (London: William Collins, 1987).

25. Cruickshank, *SOE: Special Operations Executive in the Far East*, pp. 118–19.
26. Smiley, *Irregular Regular*, pp. 136–7.
27. Reynolds, *Thailand's Secret War*, pp. 321–2.
28. Reynolds, *Thailand's Secret War*, p. 322.
29. TNA HS1/68, Siam: Operations War Diary 27/11/43–12/10/45. Entry for 11 June 1945.
30. TNA HS1/68, Siam: Operations War Diary 27/11/43–12/10/45. SITREP 17/23 June Field Sigs N.288 from Kandy 24.6.45.
31. IWM, Accession No: 10340/6 Transcript of interview with Colonel D. Smiley, Recorded 1989, p. 50.
32. Smiley, *Irregular Regular*, p. 146.
33. Interview with Colonel David Smiley, London, 22 February 2006.
34. Smiley, *Irregular Regular*, p. 150.
35. Interview with Colonel David Smiley, London, 22 February 2006; Liddle, *Captured Memories 1939–1945*, p. 229.
36. Interview with Colonel David Smiley, London, 22 February 2006.
37. TNA HS1/68, Siam: Operations War Diary 27/11/43–12/10/45 SITREP to 11 Aug. Smiley, *Irregular Regular*, p. 150.
38. Interview with Colonel David Smiley, London, 22 February 2006.

8 Between Ubon and a Hard Place

I

The belief that dropping the atomic bombs on Hiroshima and Nagasaki heralded the end of the war against Japan was not shared by Force 136 and its missions spread across South East Asia. Communications between Tokyo and the Imperial Japanese Army in the field were haphazard at best and loyalty to Emperor Hirohito absolute. The prospect that its field commanders would continue to fight on was very real, while nobody could be certain that, in a fit of revenge, Japanese troops would not massacre British, Dutch, American, Indian and Australian PoWs scattered in numerous camps across Thailand, Malaya and Singapore. Securing the camps was a priority, then, that had to be managed carefully, lest precipitous action by Force 136 or the Free Siam Movement provoke the Japanese before the terms of a formal surrender had been agreed.

In the background was the vexed question of competition in South East Asia between the old colonial powers of Britain, France and the Netherlands on the one side, and the United States on the other. It was no longer clear, operational and strategic exigencies aside, that political cooperation between London and Washington would continue. The British were at something of a diplomatic disadvantage: the end of the war had undercut the Free Siam Movement and its stated desire to fight the Japanese, although it was uncertain that an uprising would have been militarily effective. Still, having stayed the hand of the Free Siam Movement, SEAC had prevented the Thais from a visible display of 'working their passage home'. Washington, by contrast, felt that the resistance had cooperated with the Allies as well as could be expected and continued to be suspicious regarding British demands for reparations from Bangkok and revisions to the Thai–Malay border.[1] Unsullied by making any such punitive demands, the OSS enjoyed better relations with the new political order in Thailand. As the historian of SOE's war in Asia, Charles Cruickshank, has observed of the British position,

> The Free Siam Movement was instructed by Mountbatten not to go into action before he gave the word – and therefore had no chance to prove it meant business. If words were not enough and deeds forbidden how could the unfortunate Siamese get absolution?[2]

These intrigues and rivalries would impede Smiley's mission. But more immediately, he had to decide where best to send Kemp and Winn. This was not so simple because the uneasy armistice now signed between the Allies and the Japanese did not guarantee any formal acceptance of the terms of surrender. Moreover, Smiley found that his orders from SEAC appeared ambiguous beyond the need to remain covert and restrain the Free Siam Movement from hostile acts. He had two immediate priorities: to safeguard the only known prison camp in the Candle area at Ubon and to disarm Japanese troops. Ubon contained the largest known Japanese garrison in Candle and so Smiley made this his main concern. He made Kemp (code name Sackcloth) responsible for the north-east of Candle, an area bounded by the Mekong river, with his base at Nakhon Phanom. He allotted Winn (code name Georgette) the north-west, with his headquarters at Nong Khai, again on the bank of the Mekong, with Indo-China just a short boat trip across the river for both missions. Smiley wanted them to contact the Free French officers from Force 136, who he knew had been dropped close to the Laotian capital, Vientiane, and Thakhek, opposite the Candle area. Like the British, the French were anxious to re-establish control over their old colonies. Smiley had also heard rumours that French civilians who had survived the war at the hands of the Japanese still remained across the river and he was anxious to locate their whereabouts.[3]

But Smiley was still under strict orders to remain covert until he received the code word 'Gold Fish'. Only then would he be at liberty to disclose his presence to the Japanese, organise their surrender and take over the camp at Ubon. This was now his primary concern, and news from 'Sackcloth' suggested that some urgency was needed. Kemp reported rumours that the Japanese in his area had executed some PoWs; further death sentences were prevented only by Kemp, who threatened, through the use of intermediaries, future retribution against those Japanese found responsible.[4] Most of the prisoners at Ubon camp had worked on laying the strategic railway across Thailand, including over the River Kwai, in conditions that became a byword for human cruelty. Information regarding conditions in the Ubon camp was scant, but Smiley knew it was crucial to find out the number and state of health of the prisoners if proper relief was to be organised. Pluto again proved his worth. Trusted by the Japanese, he was able to move freely in and around Ubon and arranged for Smiley, along with Collins and his radio, to be smuggled into a room above the officers' mess in the Thai garrison. He assured Smiley that, should the Japanese try to murder the prisoners, he would immediately surround the camp with his own guerrillas.

Smiley was grateful too to be reinforced by another Force 136 officer, Major Chris Blathwayt, seconded from Hudson's mission. Using the services of a girl of mixed Thai–Chinese parentage who supplied rice to the Ubon camp guard on a daily basis, Smiley smuggled in a series of notes addressed to the 'senior British medical officer', asking for details of the camp inhabitants and their medical needs. It was an incredibly brave act, for had this girl been discovered, Japanese retribution would have been swift and bloody, even though Smiley later learned that the Japanese officer in charge of the Ubon garrison was keen 'to surrender to the British officer whom he had been chasing for the past six months'.

Smiley discovered that the camp strength stood at 3,035: 1,458 British, 1,472 Dutch, 101 Australians and 4 Americans. Clothing, blankets and washing kit was needed for 3,000 men, plus urgent medicine that included 50,000 Atabrine tablets and 100 ampoules of ephedrine. Some 500 tins of condensed milk were also required.

The overall health of the camp was described as good (this was, of course, relative), with 20 stretcher cases and 300 sitting cases needing prompt attention. The list had been complied by Major E. A. Smyth of the Royal Army Medical Corps, who had signed the letter. Since most of these men had been forced to work in the most appalling conditions and subjected to acts of callous brutality, the survival rate was remarkable.

Still ordered to remain undercover, Smiley was none the less eager to meet the senior British officers in overall command. He now sought the help of Colonel Prom Pot of the Thai army, a good friend of Pluto, to arrange a series of secret meetings. Under the pretext of security, Pot now claimed to want to interview the British officers in Ubon camp. Usually, all British officers had to be escorted by Japanese guards outside the camp confines; while waiting for an audience with Colonel Pot, each Briton asked in turn to visit the lavatory, not an unusual request given the sanitary conditions. Being in their own officers' mess allowed the Thais to pull rank and 'escort' the British officers to their ablutions, which in turn let Smiley interview each separately amid the sanctity of the men's lavatory. By this subterfuge Smiley managed rushed meetings with Smyth, his colleague, Captain L. D. Stone, and the camp's remarkable Regimental Sergeant-Major, Sandy McTavish of the Argyll and Sutherland Highlanders. An unsung hero of the Ubon camp, McTavish had maintained the discipline and morale of the prisoners and had suffered for it: he was beaten on several occasions by the camp guards, including on his birthday, when the prisoners sang him 'Happy Birthday'.[5]

From these three, Smiley learned that most of the officers had been taken to other camps, although some thirty medical officers and orderlies had remained to tend the sick and starving. They added to the list of urgently needed supplies, which Collins relayed to Calcutta. But Smiley, much to his own personal frustration, had to remain hidden until he received the requisite code word from SEAC. On leaving, he promised he would return as soon as he could. In the mean time, he would do all he could to hasten the arrival of the promised supplies. Finally, on 26 August, 'Gold Fish' was received. He was now 'free to swim' in more propitious waters.

This was not before time. Unbeknown to Smiley, McTavish had been summoned to the office of the camp commandant, Major Chida, who, in an act of surrender, offered the Scot his sword, proclaiming that the war was now over, although nobody else in the camp had been told. In an act of measured calm, McTavish told Chida to organise the handover of all Japanese weapons and have them locked away and secured. Only then, and after the men had returned from their daily work, was the camp informed of the Japanese surrender. The relief and joy among the prisoners was unbounded but, other than the front gate being torn down, order and discipline were maintained and no serious retaliation against their erstwhile captors was recorded. Only later, when he had returned to England, did Smiley hear rumours that some of the Australians had murdered two of the guards who had been particularly cruel, but wholesale acts of revenge were largely conspicuous by their absence.[6]

The officers who had been separated from their men soon returned to Ubon, led by the brave and dignified figure of Lieutenant Colonel Philip Toosey, a gunner whose quiet leadership but firm resolve had ensured the survival of so many of the men from an array of units who had come under his command following the fall of Singapore in 1942. Later, he was stereotyped as the inspiration for 'Colonel Nicholson', the flawed character played by Alec Guinness in the 1957 film, *Bridge on the River Kwai*. But for Smiley, he was a 'quite magnificent man', whose leadership and care of the men in the most terrible circumstances had been remarkable. Next day, 27 August, Smiley met this impressive soldier for the first time and, at his invitation, agreed to take the salute at a specially organised camp parade. It was an event that those present would never forget.

II

Accompanied by Soapy Hudson and his OSS counterpart in the Coupling area, who had come up to Ubon, Smiley entered the camp as Toosey called the parade to attention. Looking around him, Smiley was confronted by men in various states of dress, ranging from the few in newly pressed uniforms, to the scores in ragged shorts and the pitiful many clad only in what Smiley called a ball-bag, an improvised loin cloth held together with string to cover the genitals. Some wore home-made straw hats, others were bare-headed but all, in Smiley's eyes, embodied a proud dignity despite their years of cruel captivity. The Japanese flag was lowered and a Union Jack, concealed throughout his captivity by an enterprising British prisoner, was raised in its place soon after, along with an improvised Dutch flag. Smiley had great difficulty holding back tears as the assembled throng sang the national anthem, followed by its Dutch counterpart. Some said tears did indeed roll down his cheeks. Whatever his bearing, it was for Smiley the most emotional moment of his war. Given his previous experiences of conflict from the scrub of Africa to the mountains of Albania, this was some admission.[7]

After the parade, Smiley and his entourage were surrounded by prisoners wanting to shake their hands and hear news from home. To his horror and disgust, Smiley discovered that, in violation of the Geneva conventions, Chida had withheld hundreds of family letters sent to the prisoners via the Red Cross:

> The Commandant asked whether the prisoners would like their letters. I said what do you mean like their letters? He said well I'll show you. He took me to a room and it was piled high with letters. None of these had been given to the prisoners and I asked why the hell not? He (Chida) said I haven't got an interpreter to read them. These were letters that had accumulated over three years and those poor devils had heard nothing. So that's why they asked me [all these questions]. Of course I had them dished out immediately but at least half the people were dead already, some dying not knowing what happened to their families. It really was disgraceful. He showed no signs of being in any way embarrassed or regretful by his actions. He was eventually tried as a war criminal.[8]

That evening, Smiley mounted the stage of the makeshift camp theatre and for two hours did his best to answer a barrage of questions from the assembled PoWs regarding the conditions at home and, most importantly, when they might be repatriated. This he promised to facilitate as quickly as he could but, in the mean time, he had to attend to more immediate humanitarian concerns. A tour around Ubon camp revealed the primitive conditions in which the prisoners lived: long bamboo huts 50 yards long with atap roofs made of palm leaves and matting sides accommodated 150 men, each sleeping shoulder to shoulder. There were no beds; men slept on mats infested with bugs. The prisoners, however, had been particularly inventive in fashioning their own water supply, including the construction of bamboo pumps that tapped aquifers below the camp. The hospital Smiley found full, with dysentery cases and malaria the most common ailments, but an outbreak of smallpox was also now reported.[9]

Help was soon at hand. Thanks to the signal sent by Collins back to SEAC asking for relief supplies and medicines, two Liberators flew low over the neighbouring Thai barracks, dropping blankets, clothes, toiletries and longed-for cigarettes on the day of the parade. The next day, another pair of Liberators dropped more medical supplies, accompanied by two medical officers and two orderlies. These were from a newly formed team, the Relief of Allied Prisoners of War and Internees (RAPWI). Given the dysentery in the camp, one account reckoned that Smiley's prompt action saved at least 100 lives.[10] Despite the two dozen medical officers and orderlies among the prisoners, their years in captivity had denied them knowledge of advances in field medicines, including penicillin. From the moment the RAPWI teamed arrived, no prisoner died in Ubon camp.[11]

By now, Smiley had moved his headquarters to an airfield built by the Japanese close to Ubon camp. While repatriation was being organised, discipline, although relaxed, still needed to be upheld. Toosey's leadership and his moral authority ensured the camp remained ordered, the PoWs accepting the need to perform light duties. Under a rota, the inmates themselves collected and distributed supplies dropped on to the airfield and organised their own camp entertainment. It was only in the matter of sex that Smiley now became involved. After three years of enforced celibacy, many of the prisoners feared that their incarceration and poor health might have made them impotent. Smiley recalled:

Between Ubon and a Hard Place

Fig. 8.1   With 'Pluto' and Gunner Collins, Ubon, 1945.

The gates were thrown open and they [the prisoners] could go into [Ubon] town; the officers in particular wanted to have a tart as they had been in prison for three-and-a-half years and didn't know if they could make it or not so I arranged with the chief of police for a brothel – there were plenty more for the other ranks but the police chief got a very good lot [of prostitutes] – I had to meet the head madam of the brothel to arrange payment but there was not enough money around. Eventually payment was done through strips of parachute which were made into 28 strips. Each time a girl went with a man she got three strips of parachute silk for services rendered. This silk was very much in demand – one of the parachute silks was bright yellow and this was very much in demand from the Buddhist priests. They were delighted and grabbed them all.[12]

Venereal disease was, however, a threat. Toosey, while he could not prevent his men from satiating their sexual desires, was worried about the dire consequences for the longed-for family reunions, so he asked Smiley to signal SEAC: 'Please send 10,000 French letters at once.' The contraceptives were dropped in bulk the following day.[13]

In the coming weeks, the PoWs were sent in batches by train to Bangkok and from there boarded ships for home. Only for the Dutch prisoners was there uncertainty. Most were from the Dutch East Indies, so were faced with the prospect of returning to a country in the early throes of a bloody insurgency that later resulted in the founding of Indonesia. Smiley was ordered by SEAC to rearm these prisoners with Japanese weapons and then send them on their way, testament again to the British desire to restore the old colonial orders that were now swimming against the tide of nationalism across South East Asia. Three weeks after entry into Ubon, all Allied prisoners, bar a handful who had volunteered to remain under Smiley's command, had gone. As they left the camp, their former Japanese captors lined up by the gate and bowed as each truck passed by. Smiley noted the spontaneity of the gesture, which not only recognised their military defeat but acknowledged too the PoWs' moral triumph over appalling adversity.

While the well-being and repatriation of the prisoners was Smiley's priority, ensuring justice for the crimes committed against them by their captors and taking the formal surrender of the remaining Japanese troops of the 22nd Imperial Japanese Division were equally pressing. Smiley had held the rank of major on returning to Thailand, but given the scope of his command, with its diplomatic as well as military responsibilities, he had been promoted in the field to acting lieutenant colonel. Rank carried weight in terms of protocol and politics, if the surrender of 10,000 Japanese soldiers in the Candle area was to run smoothly. Accompanied by Philip Toosey and an eccentric Old Etonian and former employee of the Bombay–Burma Trading Company, Major John Hedley, the surrender of the division was accomplished with few difficulties, helped by the iron discipline that Japanese officers still exercised over their men. Only on one occasion, when the commander of the Ubon garrison, Colonel Hosumi, proved somewhat truculent, were more forceful measures taken. On 18 September, accompanied by Toosey, Smiley entered Hosumi's office, to be met by the said officer sporting a bandaged head following a drunken brawl with one of his own men over the services of a prostitute. Smiley had given Toosey two revolvers: if the Colonel proved recalcitrant, he was to slam them both down on the desk in front of Hosumi in a show of force. Smiley would follow suit.

Hosumi did, indeed, prove obstinate but the agreed demonstration of intent quickly produced the desired results. In an act of obsequious contrition, Hosumi produced a bottle of whisky and the surrender and disarming of his men proceeded without further incident. Most of the weapons were handed over to the Thai army; a few were retained by Japanese soldiers to protect themselves and vital petrol supplies while their own repatriation was settled by higher authorities. Smiley invited Toosey to take a Japanese officer's sword as a souvenir from a pile that had been surrendered, helping himself to some fifty, most of which he distributed among Thai and British officers as mementoes. These were not, however, the finest ceremonial swords the Japanese possessed. Smiley suspected that these had been hidden or dumped in the Mekong river rather than let their owners face the ignominy and shame of handing them over to their foes.[14]

After the surrender and disarming of 22nd Division, Smiley began to identify those among the Japanese who should be arrested and tried for war crimes. Prisoners attested to, or at least said they had witnessed, beatings with bamboo canes, floggings, and the forcing of men to stand to attention in the searing sun for hours on end, often holding heavy objects above their heads until they fainted through exhaustion and dehydration. Others told of prisoners being tied spread-eagled to trees and poles or confined in cramped positions for hours on end in corrugated pens, which, under the sun, simply cooked the prisoner inside. Such punishments were often inflicted for the most trivial of perceived crimes. One British soldier had been murdered by being drowned in a deep trench latrine for trying to escape. The worst offenders were the Korean guards. Smiley had already had Chida and Lieutenant Hoseda, responsible for the latrine murder, arrested and taken to Bangkok to await trial, along with a number of Koreans.[15]

Among the prisoners that had suffered most, those from the

Fig. 8.2 Identifying Japanese war criminals with Captain Gneisau van Alting in attendance.

Dutch East Indies had endured particularly sadistic treatment while being forced to build the airfield at Ubon. Smiley was keen to see the ill-treatment of all Allied prisoners punished, irrespective of nationality. He quickly identified the Japanese unit responsible for overseeing the construction of the airfield and, with a Dutch officer, Captain Gneisau van Alting, and the Japanese officer commanding the unit, Major Sensui, in attendance, walked down the lines of men, identifying those to be arrested. When this had been completed, Smiley turned to Sensui and quietly but firmly told him,

> 'Major Sensui, you are the last. Hand over your sword.' His face fell and he protested that he had been ordered to beat the prisoners. In spite of his pleas he was marched off, much to the delight of the Dutch, for he had been quite the worst offender.[16]

Most of those arrested and tried served lengthy prison sentences. Lieutenant Hoseda was court-martialled, found guilty and summarily executed. Smiley took satisfaction from the part he played in seeing these acts of justice carried out. Not only was it for the murder, however callous, of the soldier concerned; it also embodied a wider retribution, however symbolic, for the brutality that had been meted out by the many, to the weak, for so long.[17]

One final act regarding the surrender of Japanese forces was particularly loathsome for Smiley. Despite the mechanised nature of the Second World War, armies in the field still relied heavily on horse-drawn transport and the Imperial Japanese Army was no different. Having already walked some 1,500 miles from the Chinese border to Ubon, their horses were in a pitiful condition, ill treated and starved. With the help of Major Tom Phillips of the Royal Norfolk Regiment, captured in 1942 with the fall of Singapore but who had been a racehorse trainer before the war, Smiley immediately condemned 700 of the 1,200 horses he inspected. Over a dozen a day were dying with saddle sores so deep and infected with pus that they could easily accommodate a man's fist: 'I had never in my life seen such ill-treated horses,' wrote Smiley.

Huge pits were dug where the condemned animals were led before being shot in the head. But a deputation of Thais objected to this slaughter since it offended their Buddhist principles. Smiley remained unmoved, replying that the cruelty of the Japanese necessitated an action he very much regretted, but which common decency dictated. The Japanese too protested, believing that Smiley was acting out of spite rather than necessity. He explained firmly that the horses were being shot to put them out of their misery, not because the British had won the war. Still, he called in a veterinary surgeon of the Indian army, 'a fine looking Colonel', to inspect the remaining horses. He promptly condemned 400 of the 500 still standing. Phillips had, by now, left Ubon for repatriation, so Smiley was forced to rely on Japanese vets to help with this grim task. He soon discovered, however, that they were inept, taking at least three rounds to kill each horse. Disgusted at their incompetence, Smiley finished this grim task himself, despatching 700 horses with a single shot to the centre of an imaginary diagonal cross drawn between each unfortunate animal's eyes to ears. Only one horse required two bullets. As a cavalryman, Smiley was being decidedly understated when he later wrote, 'I was very thankful when this distressing job was over.'[18] For many years, this harrowing episode clouded his otherwise fond memories of Ubon.

III

Diplomacy had never come easily to Smiley but, due to the nature of his command in Candle, he had to deal with a variety of people with varying agendas to ensure the well-being of prisoners while keeping his 'parish' calm. With their meagre resources, the officers of Force 136 had to depend on the good will of the leadership of Free Siam Movement, which was now moving towards an open accommodation with the United States. Only Pluto and his command offered resolute support for Smiley's mission. But for his authority across the Candle area, Felt would by now have been stymied.

But Smiley now faced a different and altogether more political mission, which indicated the emerging contours of the post-war order in South East Asia. The missions set up by Kemp and Winn lay across the Mekong river, directly opposite a province of French Indo-China that later became Laos. Smiley knew that French officers of Force 136 had been inserted back into the region as a prelude to reasserting colonial rule. While many Laotians remained loyal to France, large parts of the territory bounding the Mekong river were controlled by Annamites, who made no secret of their desire for independence. Many had openly collaborated with the occupying Japanese forces in a marriage of convenience, while the growing influence of Chinese communists added ideological fervour to their nationalist cause. Many had gravitated towards the Viet Minh in neighbouring Vietnam, who already had links with the OSS.[19]

Across the river from Kemp's headquarters in Nakhon Phanom lay the town of Thakhek. Soon after the Japanese surrender, Kemp watched as a low-flying Dakota dropped two parachutists, who turned out to be French officers: Lieutenant François Klotz and his female wireless operator, Lieutenant Edith Fournier, both from 'E' Group, a unit established by Free French Forces attached to SEAC and working closely with Force 136. Although he had

Between Ubon and a Hard Place

not been warned of their arrival, Kemp quickly established a close rapport with his French counterparts. Their mission, it seems, had been arranged in haste for they lacked logistical support and had been dropped in blind, having no contacts with friendly Laotian groups. While the aim of their mission was to fly the Tricouleur, their immediate concern was the fate of French hostages, remnants of a pre-war community who had been captured when the Japanese had overrun Thakhek.

The miserable conditions that Klotz and Fournier had encountered on their insertion – they had lived, for the most part, in a damp and squalid cave – had been alleviated somewhat when Kemp offered them the use of his own headquarters as an interim measure. Meanwhile, Kemp was visited by another French officer of 'E' Force from across the Mekong river, Lieutenant de Fay, who commanded a group of Laotian guerrillas to the south of Thakhek. He brought the alarming news that the survivors of the French community in Thakhek, mainly women and children, were being held hostage by Annamites as insurance against the reimposition of French rule, having been handed over by the Japanese after they had surrendered. Most of the men had been executed by the Japanese during their occupation of the town but a garrison still remained in an ambiguous relationship with the Annamites. By the beginning of September, fears for the safety of the surviving women and children were such that Kemp asked Smiley to intercede, as the French, despite the support of their Laotian soldiers, were too weak to do so.[20]

On 7 September 1945, Smiley, Kemp, Klotz and the governor of Nakhon Phanom (it was felt that a civilian intermediary might lessen tensions) crossed over to Thakhek three-quarters of a mile away on the other side of the river. Smiley hoped that, by dint of rank and as a representative of a victorious power, he could secure the release of the hostages. But while he talked softly, he lacked a big stick, having no troops in support. Like Kemp and Klotz, he carried only a side arm, so guile was clearly going to be their best weapon. The portents at first appeared good. Arriving at a jetty on the opposite bank, they were met by a town official, who took them straight to a convent under Annamite guard, where the hostages were being held. They numbered 23 women (including

5 nuns), a priest, 4 other men, 14 children and 40 orphans of Eurasian parentage. After two hours of threats and cajoling, the Annamites grudgingly agreed to release the hostages into Smiley's care and let them be taken back across the river. But the sudden appearance of a Japanese patrol now scuppered the plan.

Smiley, despite his vehement remonstrations, was now marched with Klotz and Kemp at the point of Japanese bayonets along the main street in Thakhek and into the office of a Japanese officer, Captain Nakajima. A handsome man possessed of almost Latin features, he explained in broken English that he had not received the formal protocols of the Japanese surrender. Until then, he could not release the hostages over to his care. Smiley had no option but to agree to bring Nakajima the written authorisation from the Japanese commander at Ubon. In the mean time, he insisted that Nakajima put his own troops around the convent to safeguard the hostages. Clearly, Smiley did not trust the Annamites.

The three men returned to the convent to explain what would now happen and Kemp recalled the Annamite guerrillas leaving the convent with some docility. By contrast, one of the Japanese guards, most likely drunk, had tried to snatch a wristwatch off one of the nuns. Smiley intervened, causing the soldier to draw his bayonet. Kemp felt for his side arm but a Japanese NCO, seeing the commotion, hit the guard and continued to do so as the wayward soldier was led away under guard. When the incident was reported to Nakajima, the errant guard was again subjected to further blows to the head, Smiley recalling it as an 'interesting piece of Japanese discipline'. He now set off to cover 400 miles in under twenty-four hours to get the necessary authority approved while Kemp volunteered to stay with the hostages. It was a selfless act, his courage suitably fortified by the priest opening two bottles of communion wine in his honour.[21]

Accompanied by Winn and a Japanese officer (later convicted of war crimes) to confirm the orders from Colonel Hosumi, Smiley returned exhausted the next day. Nakajima now complied, ordering the troops under his command to clear Annamite guerrillas from the streets when the hostages were evacuated the following day. On 9 September, all were transported safely across the Mekong river to the hospital in Nakhon Phanom, where they were 'pathetically grateful'. This had been as much a humanitarian enterprise as it was a political mission to shore up French influence. The actions of Smiley and Kemp had actually pre-empted new orders now issued by SEAC that Felt and other SOE missions should do everything in their power to secure the release of all French nationals on the other side of the Mekong.[22] Long after the event, Smiley remained convinced that, but for their timely intervention, all the hostages would have met a bloody end at the hand of the Annamites.

Events unfolding elsewhere soon bore out this view. Klotz and Kemp reported more hostages held close to some tin mines in the village of Boneng, around 50 miles from Thakhek. Smiley realised that fortune had favoured the (very lightly armed) brave in Thakhek and they had ridden their luck. His next foray to rescue hostages would have to be backed up by something more substantial than diplomatic bluster: armed troops. He sent a signal back to SEAC, asking permission to use some of the few remaining British PoWs in Ubon, who had volunteered to cross the Mekong: 'The message came back, "Certainly not. They've been prisoners for three-and-a-half years and you're to get them home as quickly as possible."'[23] But SEAC suggested an alternative. Smiley could rearm a company of Japanese soldiers and use them if necessary to rescue the hostages. It was an unorthodox suggestion, but with Smiley having already led former members of the *Wehrmacht* in action against German and Italian troops in Albania, its logic had a clear appeal.

Smiley quickly assembled a platoon of Japanese troops under the command of a lieutenant who was under strict instructions from Nakajima to obey Smiley. Once on the road, Smiley described how the valley they now drove along in a series of trucks, flanked on either side by mountain tops covered in cloud, filled him with foreboding: 'There was a certain austere beauty in the colours and the shifting light, but to me the whole area felt sinister and oppressive.' His dark mood was because he knew so little about what to expect. He was unsure of the number of hostages, nor did he know the disposition of the Annamite guerrillas or their strength. Smiley again was going in blind, at great risk to himself and colleagues. Nor was he at all sure if his Japanese subordinates would obey him. While they were known for their rigid discipline, Smiley must have wondered if an errant soldier might be tempted to shoot him in the back.

After a few hours, the convoy passed an increasing number of trucks carrying armed Annamites, which were flying the red flag and heading in the opposite direction, towards Thakhek. It was not clear if they were now leaving Boneng, having helped clear the area, and perhaps Smiley was too late. Only when he reached the outskirts of the town did the picture become clearer: a gun battle was in progress, although he was none the wiser as to who was shooting and whose side he should be on. Ordering his Japanese platoon to dismount from their trucks and prepare for action, Smiley, with Kemp alongside, carefully walked towards the centre of the village in what amounted to a two-man reconnaissance. Reaching the centre, Smiley was met by the sight of around a hundred Annamites besieging the village school. Amid the firing, Smiley managed to track down the guerrilla leader, who told him that the men inside were a 'French Robber band', something Smiley instinctively knew to be untrue. He ordered them to cease fire at once. Their truculence – they had, after all, taken casualties – was overcome when Smiley's Japanese troops appeared, looking 'suitably menacing and aggressive'.

It now dawned on Smiley that, if he was not to lose face, he would have to approach the school and attempt to parley with whoever was inside. But the cease-fire had been imposed only on one side. Whoever the defenders of the schoolhouse were, fear and adrenalin made an unhealthy mix for any uninvited and unknown stranger about to walk down the middle of what had been a shooting alley. Yet Smiley felt he had no choice: he was the senior officer in command, he had forced the hand of the Annamites, and if he was not to lose face and the opportunity to prevent further bloodshed, he had to lead by example. Kemp recalled what happened next:

> Telling Klotz and me to stay where we were and ignoring our anxiety for his safety, Smiley broke cover and walked boldly towards the schoolhouse, waving a white handkerchief and calling out at intervals, '*Ne tirez pas, je suis officier anglais.*' With our hearts thumping we

watched him walk slowly up the steps to the barricade across the door. He spoke for a few moments to someone inside and then beckoned to Klotz and me to join him.[24]

It was a singularly brave act and secured the safe passage of the 'Robber band'. The defenders of the schoolhouse turned out to be a French Force 136 officer, Lieutenant Gausset, and ten Lao soldiers under his command. They had initially gone to the tin mines, following reports that French civilians had been taken hostage, only to be ambushed by the Annamites. Seeking sanctuary in the school, they had inflicted casualties. During the continued negotiations for the safe passage of Gausset and his men, as well as for the release of the hostages, the Annamite guerrillas produced the bloodied remains of four of their comrades who had been killed in the exchange of fire. But with the menacing presence of his Japanese troops to hand, Smiley imposed a workable solution: Gausset would return to the jungle with his men, while the hostages – a man, two women and four children, alongside two wounded Lao soldiers – were taken by Smiley back across the Mekong to the safety of Nakhon Phanom.[25]

The luck of these Force 136 officers was not to last. The Annamite guerrillas had no love for Smiley, Winn and Kemp, but their immediate animus was reserved for the increasing number of French officers who were trying to re-establish control over Laos. In the regional capital, Vientiane, fighting between Franco-Laotian forces under one Commandant Fabre and Free Lao forces, supported by the Viet Minh, had broken out. The position of the French was precarious since their government, still reeling from the effects of the war in Europe, was trying to re-establish control over its former colonies with insufficient resources. Fabre was quite clear that only concerted action by the European powers would see off the rising tide of nationalism and the domino effect that would follow. Kemp and Winn agreed, since both were 'deeply committed to the work of imperial restoration, seeing it (the emergence of indigenous national movements) as the context of a global retreat from empire which they resented'.[26] Smiley was sympathetic to the French position but was aware that political sensitivities in SEAC would not condone British involvement with France much beyond immediate humanitarian concerns. The incoming British ambassador to Bangkok, Geoffrey Thompson, was later to warn of too close a British alliance with the French, who, he thought, 'were trying to drag the British into confrontations when they [the British] would rather keep their distance'.[27]

Winn and Kemp had become involved in smuggling arms, ammunition and occasionally French officers to French–Laotian forces on the other side of the Mekong. Some of the arms were Japanese; other heavier weaponry, including mortars, appeared to have been British, dropped with the blessing of SEAC.[28] It was unclear, however, if such support was official British policy, let alone in British interests. The vague nature of operational control at a time of transition allowed orders to be interpreted loosely. Winn and Kemp engaged in this clandestine activity precisely because it had not been expressively forbidden, despite the reservations of some senior officers, who now implored Mountbatten to intervene. They feared that a clash with the Annamite guerrillas who had the backing of the OSS was inevitable, unless British policy was clearly articulated.[29]

The inevitable did happen. On 27 September 1945, Klotz and Kemp crossed the Mekong en route to see Lieutenant Tavernier, another Force 136 officer, south of Thakhek. In mid-September, Smiley became aware that an OSS team had dropped into Candle 'but without reference to me', before it crossed the Mekong and headed to Vientiane. Led by a Major Banks, this team was now in Thakhek when Klotz and Kemp, accompanied by Lieutenant Reese of the OSS, who had presented himself to Kemp earlier that day at Nakon Phanom, arrived. Kemp and Smiley were clear that the purpose of their trip was to arrange the transfer of medical supplies to Tavernier's command. This was no doubt true in this instance, but the Annamites surmised that such humanitarian aid often went hand in hand with arms smuggling. Kemp and Winn were later to survive several attempts on their lives, blamed on agents of the Viet Minh because of their activities in support of the French.[30] On arrival in Thakhek, a tense standoff ensued. The Annamites, with OSS officers looking on, tried to arrest Klotz, citing the French declaration of war against the Viet Minh the previous day as justification for their actions. As Kemp now tried

Between Ubon and a Hard Place

to usher Klotz back to the boat, using his own body to try to shield the Frenchman, an Annamite stepped forward and shot Klotz in the back; he died almost instantly. Kemp had grown close to the young French officer but what shocked him most, and later outraged Smiley, was that none of the OSS officers watching this scene unfold had intervened to protect Klotz. Reese later claimed that their jurisdiction did not extend to intervening in the burgeoning Franco-Annamite conflict. Banks, whose dislike of the French in particular was manifest, agreed.[31] This reflected a wider OSS policy of arming and training some of Ho Chi Minh's forces in northern Vietnam.

Colin Mackenzie was certainly keen to blame the OSS, emphasising that Kemp and Klotz had merely been transferring medical supplies across the Mekong. But his subsequent report of the incident to Mountbatten lacked context. Arms smuggling and support for the French forces struggling to reassert their hegemony in Laos defined much of the Anglo-French liaison efforts across the Mekong, and the Annamites as well as the OSS knew it.[32] Moreover, Mackenzie had allowed the Indo-China section of Force 136 to operate as a self-governing unit with logistical support from SOE but no political direction. It was a dangerous game that was being played, but while Smiley admonished Banks and refused ever to forgive him for his actions, the wider context of Klotz's murder was lost in the moral outrage that Smiley and Kemp felt and recalled so vividly in their later accounts.[33] 'Banks may well have been obeying superior orders to sabotage the French and British Force 136 efforts', Smiley later recalled, 'but to all of us at the time his behaviour was despicable. It was ironic that the Viet Minh, the political organisation of these Annamites, murdered the senior OSS officer in Saigon not long after this incident.'[34]

IV

Winn and Kemp continued to smuggle arms throughout October 1945, the Force 136 diary cryptically referring to it as 'valuable work'. For Smiley, however, his time in Siam was approaching its end, although not before the political situation across the Mekong threatened to become even more toxic. To add to the mix of competing interests hoping to fill the vacuum in Laos before the French could regain control, Smiley discovered that Chinese troops had now entered Vientiane. He had arranged to meet a Chinese colonel who he presumed to be in charge, but after three hours of unproductive talks, Smiley was no better informed as to who this officer owed his allegiance: the communists, the nationalists under Chiang Kai-Shek or just a local warlord. The vying for power in Laos was, for Smiley, 'a very funny set up'. Given his Balkan experiences, he was happy to avoid it if he could:

> There were American OSS, there were communists, then the French themselves with a lot of loyal native [Lao] troops with them. The French SOE officers, Force 136 officers, they had troops. . . . [T]he Chinese were there. It was a real good bugger's muddle altogether, the immediate post-war period.[35]

It also produced some surreal, if macabre, moments. When dining together with Winn at his headquarters in Nong Khai, enjoying brandy and cigars on an upstairs veranda, they were interrupted by Winn's Laotian boatman and *de facto* bodyguard arriving with a Japanese sword dripping with blood. This had been given to the Lao by Smiley as a reward for helping to smuggle arms across the Mekong. The boatman politely reported that he had decapitated a robber he had found pilfering from Winn's stores downstairs. The two men went down to investigate and there, lying in a pool of blood, was the headless body of the ill-fated robber: 'We didn't have any more stores stolen after that,' wrote Smiley.[36]

By mid-October, all the French prisoners rescued by Smiley, Winn and Kemp had been transferred to Bangkok, much to the chagrin of Kemp and Winn, who had employed the more attractive of the Frenchwomen as cipher clerks. With Ubon now emptied of all Allied prisoners and the remnants of the 22nd Division now dispersed to a series of holding camps under the control of the Thai army, there was little for Smiley to do. Pluto was responsible for disbanding the Free Siam Movement

Fig. 8.3 From left to right: Rowland Winn, unknown Chinese colonel, Smiley and Peter Kemp.

in Candle, but before this happened, Smiley made sure that he toured the entire area to offer his thanks to these units for the support they had given to the Felt mission. These visits inevitably culminated in a 'great feast, followed by singing and dancing, and seldom to bed alone'. Smiley let his hair down, expressing the sheer joy of having survived a war when, at times, the odds had been stacked against him. But even now, his luck almost ran out. Flying down to Bangkok with Kemp to confer with Jacques, his Mitsubishi aircraft had to make a forced landing with engine trouble and its undercarriage collapsed.[37] All emerged unscathed but the plane was a write-off. On the way back from Bangkok, Smiley was offered the chance to refresh his own piloting skills, last practised before the war, when he was loaned another Mitsubishi by the Thai air force. On this occasion, again with Kemp as his passenger, a vulture slammed into his port wing soon after taking off, damaging the aileron wires that controlled the aircraft flaps. It says something for either his luck or his latent skills as a pilot that he managed to nurse the aircraft back to the airfield. Whether he should have been flying the aircraft in the first place is, of course, another matter.

The end of October saw Smiley back in Bangkok, writing up post-operational reports, a routine familiar from his time in Cairo and Bari. He was in no hurry to get back to England, partly because he knew that Lord Wavell had nominated him for the staff college at Camberley and the next course did not begin until the end of February, and partly because he was enjoying the social scene in Bangkok. Old friends and colleagues from Ceylon and Calcutta pitched up, including Alan Hare and Billy Moss, who had been dropped by Force 136 on the Kra Isthmus near Malaya the previous May. He also flew to Saigon with Winn, to be greeted by General Philippe Leclerc, a Gaullist in command of the French Far East Expeditionary Force, who had just broken the Viet Minh blockade of the capital. Even so, Leclerc was a realist and saw that France would have to cede some political power to the Vietnamese. But in the mean time, he was keen to honour the efforts of Smiley, Winn and Kemp in supporting his officers: all three were awarded the Croix de Guerre to recognise their role in rescuing the French hostages.

But these awards were nullified by the Foreign Office: the rescues had occurred after the official end of the war, when hostilities were deemed to have ended. Smiley was decidedly understated when he wrote that this was a 'bit mean'. Even more galling, the same perverse logic now denied him the DSO, for which he had been recommended for his leadership of Felt. This was not the first time Smiley was denied an award, nor would it be the last. His service in Siam was eventually recognised with the award of an Order of the British Empire (OBE; Military Division, gazetted in November 1946) but, as Smiley noted ruefully, this could have been earned by a staff officer sitting behind a desk. It gave no formal acknowledgement to the risks he had taken, the lives he had saved or the near-fatal injuries he had suffered during his service in Thailand.[38]

In December 1945, Smiley boarded a troopship in Bombay, which, three weeks later, docked at Tilbury in the Thames estuary. Still only twenty-nine, he had proved himself a brave and resourceful special forces officer and an effective commander in the field, operating in that grey area of 'peaceful belligerence' that defined so many areas of the immediate post-war world. While his diplomatic skills had been found wanting in his dealings with the partisans in Albania, he had acquitted himself well amid the political rivalry and intrigue of South East Asia. He had balanced measured support for the French with a light British footprint on the banks of the Mekong. This was partly by default, since the British presence in the Candle area was always small and the risks taken in the smuggling operations had to be carefully calibrated.[39] Even so, his crowning achievement, requiring diplomacy, political brio and physical courage in leading from the front, was the rescue of the French hostages.

But it was the liberation of the PoW camp at Ubon and the repatriation of those 'poor wretches in their ball-bags' that gave him most satisfaction and remained uppermost in his memory of Thailand. Smiley's prescient action at Ubon saved the lives of many, while ensuring that justice was eventually administered to the necessary few. With staff college beckoning and with SOE falling victim to a Whitehall turf war that would see a hostile take-over by MI6, a return to more orthodox soldiering beckoned. As it turned out, old friends and events elsewhere in the coming years determined otherwise.

Notes

1. Aldrich, *Intelligence and the War against Japan*, p. 323.
2. Cruickshank, *SOE: Special Operations Executive in the Far East*, p. 121.
3. Kemp, *The Thorns of Memory*, pp. 275–6.
4. TNA HS1/68, Siam: Operations War Diary 27/11/43–12/10/45. Entry 1 September 1945.
5. Julie Summers, *The Colonel of Tamarkan: Philip Toosey and the Bridge on the River Kwai* (London: Simon & Schuster, 2005), p. 296.
6. IWM, Accession No: 10340/6 Transcript of Interview with Colonel D. Smiley, Recorded 1989, p. 55.

7. Interview with Colonel David Smiley, London, 22 February 2006; Summers, *The Colonel of Tamarkan*, p. 298.
8. Interview with Colonel David Smiley, London, 22 February 2006.
9. TNA HS1/68, Siam: Operations War Diary 27/11/43–12/10/45. Entry 1 September 1945.
10. O'Brien, *The Moonlight War*, p. 285.
11. Interview with Colonel David Smiley, London, 22 February 2006.
12. Interview with Colonel David Smiley, London, 22 February 2006.
13. Summers, *The Colonel of Tamarkan*, p. 299.
14. Smiley, *Irregular Regular*, pp. 165–6.
15. Interview with Colonel David Smiley, London, 22 February 2006.
16. Smiley, *Irregular Regular*, p. 167.
17. Interview with Colonel David Smiley, London, 22 February 2006.
18. Smiley, *Irregular Regular*, p. 167.
19. Tom Noon, *This Grim and Savage Game: OSS and the Beginning of US Covert Operations in WWII* (Los Angeles: Burning Gate, 1991), pp. 312–17.
20. Interview with Colonel David Smiley, London, 22 February 2006; Kemp, *The Thorns of Memory*, p. 284.
21. Kemp, *The Thorns of Memory*, p. 284; TNA HS1/68, Siam: Operations War Diary 27/11/43–12/10/45. Entry 8 September 1945.
22. Interview with Colonel David Smiley, London, 22 February 2006; TNA HS1/68, Siam: Operations War Diary 27/11/43–12/10/45. Sitrep to 15 Sept.
23. IWM, Accession No: 10340/6 Transcript of Interview with Colonel D. Smiley, Recorded 1989, p. 54.
24. Kemp, *The Thorns of Memory*, p. 293.
25. Interview with Colonel David Smiley, London, 22 February 2006.
26. Aldrich, *Intelligence and the War Against Japan*, p. 354.
27. Quoted in Aldrich, *Intelligence and the War Against Japan*, p. 354.
28. Kemp, *The Thorns of Memory*, p. 295.
29. Aldrich, *Intelligence and the War Against Japan*, p. 352; Interview with Colonel David Smiley, London, 22 February 2006.
30. Smiley, *Irregular Regular*, p. 176.
31. Kemp, *The Thorns of Memory*, pp. 297–301; Interview with Colonel David Smiley, London, 22 February 2006.
32. Aldrich, *Intelligence and the War Against Japan*, p. 353.
33. IWM, Accession No: 10340/6 Transcript of Interview with Colonel D. Smiley, Recorded 1989, p. 55.
34. Smiley, *Irregular Regular*, p. 176.

35. IWM, Accession No: 10340/6 Transcript of Interview with Colonel D. Smiley, Recorded 1989, p. 57.
36. Interview with Colonel David Smiley, London, 22 February 2006.
37. TNA HS1/68, Siam: Operations War Diary 27/11/43–12/10/45. Sitrep to 30 October 1945.
38. Interview with Colonel David Smiley, London, 22 February 2006.
39. Interview with Colonel David Smiley, London, 22 February 2006.

9 From Espionage to Sabotage

I

All officers who hoped one day to command a regiment required the abbreviation PSC – passed staff college – after their name and rank. Smiley was no different, but by his own admission, he did not consider himself particularly gifted academically. If there had been an entrance exam he believed, rather self-deprecatingly, he would have failed. But sponsored by Lord Wavell, he was determined to graduate from the British army staff college at Camberley. He did so while burning the candle at both ends. In March 1946, he had started the six-month course, designed to groom officers for battalion command and above in the intricacies of staff work after returning from six weeks' leave spent enjoying winter sports in Switzerland. He was once again a major; it was not unusual for officers who, because of the exigencies of war, had been promoted in the field to drop down a rank once the fighting was over. Just before he started his course, he was invited to a dinner party in London at 18 Carlton Terrace, hosted by Gavin Astor, later Lord Astor of Hever and Chairman of *The Times*, whom Smiley had known as a captain in the Life Guards. At the table, he found himself seated next to an elegant woman of striking beauty who was Astor's first cousin.

Moyra Tweedie was a widow of twenty-seven, whose husband, Major Hugo Tweedie of the Scots Guards, had been killed in the last month of the war in Europe, leaving two small children. Her father was Lord Francis Scott KCMG DSO, youngest son of the 6th Duke of Buccleuch, who had been the elected leader of Kenya's settlers for most of the decade before the war. His

From Espionage to Sabotage

wife, Eileen, was the daughter of the 4th Earl of Minto, Viceroy of India. Moyra had been brought up in Kenya before being sent to England as a teenager. Her colonial background helped foster an independent spirit, which she felt set her apart from her contemporaries in the world of London debutantes. Her aunt had married the first Lord Astor of Hever and, in London, Carlton House Terrace became her second home. The theatre, however, was her great love and before the war she trained as an actress at the Webber Douglas School of Dramatic Art before winning a place at the Liverpool Repertory Theatre. But the war intervened and, aged nineteen, she volunteered for the First Aid Nursing Yeomanry (FANY), becoming an ambulance driver in Dover. Her father, however, persuaded her to return to Kenya, where she entered the world of intelligence, decoding ciphers as the war spread to East Africa. Intelligent and charming, she excelled at her work. She was promoted rapidly to the rank of sergeant, and in 1941, she was mentioned in dispatches in the same list as her father and, by a twist of fate, one Lieutenant David Smiley, who had been cited for his actions at Palmyra.[1]

Moy, as she was always known, had married Hugo Tweedie in Kenya in 1942 after meeting him while he was competing in a car rally. With her own independent streak, she recognised a kindred spirit in a young officer she later described as 'very wild'. Their daughter Anna was born later that year, Gavin arriving in 1944. With her husband on active service, Moy sailed back to Britain and stayed in the Scottish Borders. It was here that she received the news that her husband had been killed in action in Germany. With two small children to bring up on her own, she now decided to move south to a cottage in Knebworth in Hertfordshire, lent to her by the Lytton family, who were friends of her parents. With money tight, she joined the BBC, the salary being such that she found she could afford a cook and a nanny to care for the children while she was in London.

Moy soon worked her way up at the BBC, becoming a studio manager with the East European section of the World Service at Bush House, and even making announcements on air. It was while working here that she met Smiley. Moy later recalled that this meeting and her eventual marriage to Smiley was all 'arranged'.[2]

Fig. 9.1 Moy Smiley in the uniform of a FANY.

Given the social milieu in which they circulated, this tongue-in-cheek observation did carry an element of truth, but it was to mark the start of a happy and loving partnership that lasted over the next six decades. Still, the courtship took its toll on Smiley, for the staff college course was demanding and exams had to be passed in a syllabus crammed into six months. He would often return in the early hours to Camberley from visits to nightclubs in London with Moy, grabbing just a few hours' rest before he had to be back in the classroom. As he later admitted, 'I was perhaps lucky to pass out.'[3]

But pass staff college he did at the end of September 1946, hoping eventually to command his regiment, the bulk of which had remained to enforce the British occupation in northern Germany. In the mean time, his first staff appointment was to prove not only challenging but rather short-lived. In October, he was posted as assistant military attaché to the British embassy in Warsaw, whose ambassador, Victor Cavendish-Bentinck, 9th Duke of Portland, had been Chairman of the Joint Intelligence Committee during the Second World War.

This was a diplomatic appointment directly under the authority of the Foreign Office and designed to further liaison with the armed forces of a foreign power. The role of military attaché was (and remains) supposedly overt, the information gathered being largely culled from open sources. Yet sending Smiley to Warsaw might, on the face of it, have seemed odd: he spoke no Polish and, other than his association with Polish officers in Cairo, Sophie Tarnowska and Michael Lis, a BLO in Albania, he knew nothing about Poland or its people. French, however, remained the language of diplomacy and Smiley's command of the language, which he had used during his time in Albania, was considered equal to the task at hand. Moreover, his experience of intelligence gathering in the field, not least in identifying the enemy order of battle, was deemed invaluable at a time when Poland and its armed forces were being rebuilt under Soviet tutelage as Moscow looked to expand its control across Central and Eastern Europe.

There was certainly a clandestine aspect to Smiley's mission. Colonel Harold Perkins, who had overseen SOE in Poland during the war, had managed to keep open a handful of radio networks across the country. Joining MI6 after the war, he was now responsible for operations in Poland and Czechoslovakia, his old stamping grounds, where he had kept many of his agents 'warm'. This was anathema to the Foreign Office, whose mandarins assured the Soviets that these wartime networks had been dismantled.[4] One former SOE and MI6 officer, Tony Northrop, described Perkins – or Perks, as he was widely known in 'the firm' – as a physically imposing figure, as well as an avowed anti-communist who was 'a very good boss, forceful and difficult, but ebullient and well intentioned'.[5] Perkins knew of Smiley's wartime record through a mutual friend, Peter Kemp, and so had played a hand in getting Smiley posted to Warsaw. Several of the other British diplomats in Warsaw had a background in intelligence, notably Patrick Howarth and Lewis Massey, so the shift towards the more covert side of gathering information was perhaps not surprising.[6]

II

At the end of October 1946, Smiley arrived in Warsaw. Before leaving London, he had become engaged to Moy, but his personal happiness stood in marked contrast to the devastation that greeted him on his arrival in Poland. Most of Warsaw lay in ruins and, of the buildings remaining, few did not bear the scars of war. From the moment he arrived, Smiley found himself under constant surveillance, mainly from the *Urzad Bezpiecznstwa*, the Polish security service. His hotel room and, later, his flat were searched almost every day, which he knew because 'you left little tell-tale things to see whether things had been moved or not'.[7] Under such conditions, gathering useful intelligence was hard, even though, in the immediate post-war years, a pluralism of a sort was discernible across the Polish political landscape. This was short-lived however. The Peasant Party, the main opposition to the slew of communist candidates, suffered widespread intimidation and violence in the run-up to elections for the national legislature in January 1947. In Lublin alone, Smiley counted eighteen bodies in the street, who he believed to have been murdered by communists with the clear connivance of the Russians. That the communists claimed victory with 99.9 per cent of the vote was no surprise to a man who had experienced communist tactics in the mountains of Albania.

Smiley's main task, though, was to produce military intelligence by monitoring the sites of the main Polish and Soviet units, the state of repair of communications, the location of stores and supplies, the whereabouts of airfields, and any new weaponry. Some of this information could be gleaned from open sources and Smiley had invaluable help from a Polish countess, Maria Marinowska, who worked in the press section of the British embassy, helping to translate newspapers, journals and technical periodicals. But such information could reveal only so much and Smiley preferred to be out in the field, where his own experience could be put to good use. In many ways, his activities were the forerunner of the British army's missions of the British Commanders in Chief Mission to the Soviet Forces in Germany (BRIXMIS), units of specially trained troops operating from West Berlin who would scour the

From Espionage to Sabotage

East German countryside collecting military intelligence, often by nefarious means that included stealing Soviet kit and using subterfuge to photograph new weapon systems; the Soviet SOXMIS (Soviet mission), through a reciprocal arrangement with the North Atlantic Treaty Organisation (NATO), performed exactly the same function in West Germany.[8] In the harsh winter of 1946–7, however, Smiley had neither the technology nor the wider human resources on which to draw. While he took notes and surreptitiously photographed armoured formations and artillery, he had no contact with Poles outside the diplomatic community who might be brave enough to corroborate what little information he had managed to glean.

However, the Poles soon grew tired at Smiley's activities, for he was increasingly interested in Soviet and Polish troop movements in and around the Carpathian mountains, where remnants of the Polish Home Army had formed themselves into small groups of anti-communist partisans. Some have argued that the concern of MI6, and of Perkins in particular, over the fate of these former Home Army members undermined attempts to set up new stay-behind networks in case of a future war with the Soviet Union.[9] Certainly, Smiley's presence in the Carpathian town of Przemysl in February 1947 was unwelcome to the communist authorities. Though he had the permission of the Polish Ministry of Interior to be there and was travelling on a diplomatic passport, Smiley was arrested by Polish troops and held in solitary confinement for three days of interrogation. During this time, he was prevented from contacting the British embassy, a clear breach of protocol, and 'was roughed up', including being hit by the butt of a gun.

> They didn't pull out my toe nails or anything like that. The very extraordinary thing was the War Office [in London] and Foreign Office didn't know I had been arrested and Moy was working in the European service of Bush house and she heard [I had been arrested] through the Polish underground, there was a big Polish section in Bush house . . . she heard before anyone else.[10]

Whatever the level of physical abuse (and Smiley later brushed this aside), it was a sobering introduction to the realities of the

Cold War in Europe. Smiley had undoubtedly extended his activities into the realm of covert intelligence gathering and this was enough for the Polish authorities to declare him *persona non grata* and expel him after his short incarceration. His interpreter, Maria Marinowska, had already been found guilty of spying for the British by a Polish military tribunal in December 1946, a verdict that had everything to do with guilt by association in a climate of increasing paranoia. She was sentenced to twelve years' hard labour. Already in her sixties, this was tantamount to a prolonged death sentence.

Smiley was not sad to leave Poland and at least his enforced departure allowed him to arrange his wedding, which took place at St Margaret's, Westminster, on 28 April 1947, followed by a honeymoon in Spain. His return to the Blues none the less was put on hold. On arriving back in London from Warsaw at the beginning of March 1947, he discovered that his next appointment was a secondment to MI6 at its headquarters in Broadway, opposite St James's tube station. 'Why they chose me I do not know, though I suppose my SOE background had something to do with it. And of course I knew a number of people in the "firm" personally,' he later remarked.[11] Much to the chagrin of MI6, during the Second World War special operations and covert action had been mainly the preserve of SOE. Antipathy between the two organisations has been well documented but it derived from differing philosophies over the nature and scope of secret warfare. For MI6, the sabotage activities of SOE officers and agents, often working with partisan and resistance groups, was the antithesis of the patient accumulation of information by secret intelligence. This sometimes played down the importance of operational intelligence that SOE officers – such as Smiley – did produce but this was to little avail. The head of SOE, Major General Sir Colin Gubbins, did his best to ensure its survival at the end of the war by arguing for a merger of equals with MI6 to produce a new global intelligence service. But by the summer of 1946, SOE had, in the words of Robert Cecil, been 'liquidated with almost indecent haste'.[12]

MI6 did, however, absorb selected individuals from SOE, whose skills in irregular warfare were deemed valuable. Some of them, including Harold Perkins, now worked under the Special Political Action Section and the Directorate of War Planning. This was responsible for preparing 'stay-behind networks and sabotage and subversion cells', to be activated in the event of hostilities with the Soviet Union. Such activities had largely defined the role of SOE in Europe and South East Asia during the war. The Directorate of War Planning now looked to delegate such activities to a reprised SAS, whose future was clouded in doubt until its re-emergence as a special forces unit in the Malayan emergency.[13] It was to the Directorate of War Planning that Smiley now reported as a GII Staff Officer, liaising closely with Colonel Brian Franks, a former commander of the wartime 2nd SAS Regiment. Like its SOE counterpart, the SAS too had been disbanded at the end of the war, but despite resistance from some in the War Office, Franks had lobbied hard for a territorial regiment to take on some of the functions and capabilities of the wartime SAS. His efforts bore fruit. By 1947, a territorial unit, the Artists Rifles, had been redesignated 21 SAS and tasked to conduct SOE-type operations in support of guerrilla groups behind enemy lines. Working with Franks, Smiley discovered that his main task was to develop a series of operational plans that would determine how, in any future conflict, 21 SAS would actually be used.[14]

The secret contingency plans for MI6 which Smiley and Franks collaborated on are still classified but drew heavily on the post-operational reports that Smiley wrote in SOE. They covered all aspects of irregular warfare, from the training of guerrillas to radio communication, signals, logistics, demolitions and field security.[15] From these discussions evolved the idea of the four-man SAS patrol, consisting of commander, demolitions expert, signaller and medic, which could be inserted behind enemy lines, either to fight on its own or to train guerrillas. For a man more used to field operations, Smiley found this type of staff work surprisingly enjoyable. His attachment to MI6 had the added attraction of being paid a diplomat's salary while living in London. Wartime antipathies still festered, however, among some of the occupants in Broadway, as Smiley later recalled: 'Many old SOE hands got the impression that they [some MI6 officers] regarded us as a bunch of bungling amateurs.'[16]

These 'bungling amateurs' were none the less now much in demand and in a part of the world that Smiley knew well: Palestine. He had been approached on his return from Poland by Brigadier Bernard Fergusson, who had served with distinction under Orde Wingate as a Chindit in Burma, to help train selected members of the Palestine Police in paramilitary methods to counter the growing Jewish insurgency and, in particular, the *Irgun Zvai Leumi*. Smiley had known of Fergusson from his previous service in Palestine and had been tempted by the assignment, but on discovering that wives would not be allowed to accompany their husbands, he declined the offer. A former wartime SAS officer, Roy Farran, was recruited by Fergusson, only for his service to end in controversy when he was tried for, but found not guilty of, abducting and murdering a Jewish youth, Alexander Rubowitz, suspected of working for the *Irgun*. Although the body of Rubowitz was never found, Farran's hat with his name stencilled on the inside was found at the scene of the abduction. Most observers, including some senior officers of the Palestine Police, considered the subsequent trial a miscarriage of justice, not least when Fergusson refused to testify on the grounds of self-incrimination. The *Irgun* sought revenge. Soon after Farran returned to Britain, members of an *Irgun* cell addressed a parcel bomb to 'R. Farran' at his parents' home in Wolverhampton. His brother Rex, however, opened the parcel and was killed instantly.[17] The episode is worth recalling because, despite his later collaboration with officials from the Israel Defence Forces and the *Mossad*, Smiley refused to divulge until his final years his involvement in the sabotage by MI6 of Jewish refugee ships seeking to run the British naval blockade in the eastern Mediterranean. The strictures of the Official Secrets Act offer one explanation for his reticence, although, by the early 1980s, he was quite open regarding his involvement in another clandestine mission, Operation Valuable, the joint MI6–CIA attempt to undermine the regime of Enver Hoxha. Rather, it was the fate of Rex Farran and the fear that some in Israel still had long memories that led Smiley to remain tight-lipped about his involvement in Operation Embarrass.[18]

III

By 1947, Palestine was racked by violence as Jews and Arabs realised that the British increasingly lacked the military means, political will and financial wherewithal to enforce the British Mandate. Moreover, in the aftermath of the Holocaust, moral and political pressure mounted, especially among the Jewish survivors of the extermination camps and their sympathisers in the United States, for Britain to abandon its strict migration quota, outlined in the 1939 White Paper, of allowing only 75,000 Jews into Palestine over the next decade. An uneasy truce had existed between the main Jewish militias and the British Mandate authorities during the war. Indeed, cooperation between the *Haganah*, MI6 and SOE had been close and extensive.[19] But by the end of 1946, attacks on British targets and institutions, particularly from the right-wing *Irgun* led by Menachem Begin, had become frequent. These reached a bloody climax with the bombing of the King David Hotel in Jerusalem in July 1946, killing 91 people, among them 28 British, 41 Arabs and 17 Jews who worked for the Mandate authorities.[20] The *Irgun* was behind the attack, although it later claimed its telephoned warnings had been ignored by the British.

This outrage did little to sway international opinion in the favour of the British when faced with the pitiful sight of thousands of Jews, survivors of the death camps, willing to risk crossing the Mediterranean in decrepit vessels to reach the shores of Palestine. But Ernest Bevin, the Labour Foreign Secretary, was having none of this and determined to stop this human traffic from leaving Europe. Having come to power in the July 1945 general election, the Labour government had inherited a bankrupt economy and therefore was more dependent than ever on Britain securing its oil in the Middle East. Anything that might inflame Arab opinion was to be avoided. Moreover, many British officials opposed Zionist demands for a state in Palestine. Not only was the demographic balance still overwhelmingly in favour of the Arabs but also British officials in Palestine were at a loss to explain why the proposed establishment of a Jewish state on Arab land should be the price paid by the Arabs for the sin of European anti-Semitism and genocide. It was summed up in Bevin's ill-judged, if not insensitive, statement to a press conference: '[I]f the Jews with all their sufferings, want to get too much to the head of the queue you have the danger of another anti-Semitic reaction.'[21]

British intelligence was well informed about the activities of Zionist groups behind the secret emigration of Jews from Europe hoping to reach Palestine. Much of this activity was organised by the *Mossad Le'Aliyah Beth*, whose members were invariably drawn from the *Haganah* and were working under the direction of the Jewish Agency: in effect, the government of the Jewish *Yishuv* in Palestine.[22] It was aided and abetted by the American Joint Distribution Committee, which the British suspected of using its humanitarian efforts in providing relief to the thousands of Jewish refugees as a cover to help the *Mossad Le'Aliyah Beth* evade the blockade. In the summer of 1947, the British Cabinet were reading reports prepared by the Joint Intelligence Committee, detailing the numbers likely to risk the sea journey to reach Palestine. Up to 40,000 were 'at present estimated to be waiting to be taken to ports and embarked illegally for Palestine'.[23]

But guarding borders was nigh on impossible, as many European countries had to rebuild virtually from scratch the shattered infrastructure and state institutions that would allow those borders to be controlled. Corruption was rife and when this was combined with the undoubted sympathy (as well as lingering anti-Semitism) for the remnants of European Jewry across much of the continent, British authorities were unable to persuade France, Italy and Greece to prevent their ports from being used to embark Jewish refugees for Palestine.[24] The French, who reckoned that Britain had exploited nationalist movements in Syria and Lebanon at the end of the war to oust them from the Levant, adopted a decidedly pro-Zionist position. If revenge is a dish best served cold, the French authorities now served up a veritable smorgasbord of retribution, ranging from support for the various Jewish militias to benign indifference to their ports being used to embark refugees for Palestine.[25] It was far removed from the Anglo-French cooperation that Smiley had enjoyed across the Mekong river.

Most of the ships used by the *Mossad Le'Aliyah Beth* were bought through what the British referred to as 'non-Jewish confederates' or shipping agents. Many of these vessels were unseaworthy, but these shipping agents formed 'mushroom' companies to have them converted to *Haganah* specifications and then delivered to a particular port at a set date. According to a British intelligence report:

> There is reason to believe that secret contracts are made between HAGANA [sic] and its confederate shipping agents whereby the latter are not paid for ships until they deliver them at the particular ports specified. Thus, the immobilisation of a ship at an early stage is likely to involve the shipping agent in financial loss and may – if prolonged and repeated – even put him out of business.[26]

This is important because what now followed has often been understood purely in terms of preventing the physical departure of ships destined for Palestine from leaving port. Instead, the longer-term aim of Operation Embarrass was to dissuade ship owners from selling vessels to the *Mossad Le'Aliyah Beth*, knowing that they might never get paid. Given that London could do little to disrupt the flow of refugees from across Europe to ports in the southern Mediterranean, it was hoped that sabotage, coupled with the financial loss to the ship owners, might be enough to prevent mass Jewish migration into Palestine. This more robust attitude towards curtailing Jewish emigration was approved at the very top. In the spring of 1947, the Prime Minister, Clement Attlee, sent a memorandum to Hector McNeil, Secretary of State at the Foreign Office, which read: 'It is essential that we should take all possible steps to stop this traffic at source and we ought not to confine ourselves to making general protests to the foreign governments concerned.'[27]

MI6 had been approached at the end of 1946 to see what more aggressive measures it could take to thwart Jewish emigration. Its officers had already been gathering information on refugee flows from Europe in an operation code-named Trespass.[28] The historian Keith Jeffrey has noted that MI6 officials in Broadway believed that, for any intimidation to be successful, the ship's crew would have to suffer 'unpleasant consequences'. The measures considered ranged from tampering with a target ship's water supply and the poisoning of food, all the way to arson. At a meeting held on 14 February 1947, representatives of MI6, the Foreign Office, the Colonial Office and the armed forces decided that a sabotage team should now be formed to act on Trespass intelligence, and to target ships clearly involved with illegal emigration from ports in France and Italy.

It was deemed essential that, if the sabotage team was caught, no connection could ever be made between them and the British government. Their cover story was that the saboteurs had been tasked by an anti-communist organisation based in New York, whose members, all industrialists with Middle East business concerns, feared that the Soviets had infiltrated their own agents among the refugees to undermine Western interests in Palestine. MI6 was effectively playing an early Cold War card for the purposes of deception. In an effort to add credibility to the operation, responsibility for any sabotage was to be claimed by a fictitious organisation called 'The Defenders of Arab Palestine'. Letters sent from Paris and elsewhere in Europe to the British Foreign Secretary and the Prime Minister would claim that such acts of sabotage were designed to thwart a wave of emigration that served only the interests of Moscow. Whether anyone would have believed this cover story had the saboteurs, all British, been caught is doubtful. Even with the benefit of several decades of hindsight, it still all looks rather flimsy.[29]

This underscores the risks that those recruited to 'Operation Embarrass' were taking. All were told that, if captured, tried and imprisoned, they could expect no help from the British authorities; it was an entirely deniable operation. But when Harold Perkins approached him to join the operation, Smiley needed no prompting. While he had enjoyed his work with the Directorate of War Planning, the chance of returning to active operations proved irresistible. He was delighted to be working once again with Perkins, a man he had come to admire greatly from his short time in Poland. Perks now worked for the Operational Production Directorate in MI6 (part of Special Political Action), which looked to retain some SOE capability in the realm of sabotage and subversion. Not a man to be bound to a desk, Smiley noted somewhat cryptically in his own memoir,

From Espionage to Sabotage

I had not only been under the orders of 'Perks' for certain operations (after the war) but he insisted on joining me for the more hazardous and exciting missions. Perks was a big man, full of fun, and not only a brave and congenial companion on operations, but a leader for whom it was a pleasure to work.[30]

A final attraction was that the job would be relatively quick, and as a newly married man, Smiley would soon be back with his wife in London.

IV

Operation Embarrass was largely coordinated from the British embassy in Rome by Frederick Vanden Heuvel, a count of the Holy Roman Empire and former MI6 station chief in Berne. He was assisted by Wing Commander Derek Verschoyle, who, prior to the outbreak of war, had been literary editor of *The Spectator*. He had served with Bomber Command in the Mediterranean before joining MI6 towards the end of the conflict. His diplomatic cover was First Secretary in the British embassy. Contrary to some accounts, Verschoyle never took part in the actual sabotage; his role was to gather intelligence from sources across Europe and to identify those ships suspected of being fitted out for taking Jewish refugees.[31]

The actual team of saboteurs consisted of Perkins, Smiley, a wireless operator of academic bearing, Don Bevers, and a highly decorated RAF officer, Wing Commander James (Jimmy) Blackburn. Renowned for his ability to drop missions with great accuracy, Blackburn had piloted the Halifax that had dropped Concensus I into the mountains of northern Greece in April 1943 before going on to fly Liberators dropping SOE missions and supplies into South East Asia. Fluent in French, he was posted after the war as an assistant air attaché at the British embassy in Paris and a glittering career in the RAF seemed to lie ahead. But Blackburn was a loner and a maverick. He had transferred to the RAF special duties squadron because he had come to disapprove of the Allies' saturation bombing of cities in Europe, which he regarded as a war crime.[32] His real passion, though, was sailing. He had already decided to leave the RAF and fulfil a long-held dream of sailing his own yacht, the *Valfrere*, from England to the Mediterranean. But just before he was due to be demobbed, he was approached by MI6 in Paris. Would he join a venture continuing to serve his country that involved sailing while still being paid a salary by the British government?[33] It is likely that the initial approach was suggested by Verschoyle, who knew Blackburn from their time together with Bomber Command in the Mediterranean. Blackburn's agreement to join the team bolstered the cover story to explain the presence of four Britons on the *Valfrere*, sailing in and out of ports in the western half of the Mediterranean: cigarette smuggling.[34]

This cover was entirely plausible, for cigarettes were the currency of choice in swathes of southern Europe before currency stability had returned, particularly in Italy, whose ports were the key embarkation points for Jewish refugees. Blackburn's yacht could also shadow suspicious ships out at sea, with Bevers relaying this information back to Rome via 'Ocean', an encrypted signals network dealing with Embarrass radio traffic.

In May 1947, Blackburn left England and set sail for Malta, still an important British naval base, where he was joined a month later by the rest of the team. While Perkins was an experienced sailor who held a master mariner's certificate, only Smiley had practical experience of underwater demolitions from his time at STS 102 in Haifa, planting dummy mines on the abandoned hull of Jewish refugee ship, the *Patria*. He now took a brief refresher course in limpet mines at the Royal Navy Diving School in Malta, with Perkins a willing pupil alongside him. Security was tight and the instructors were never told of the intended targets, although many would have surmised what was likely. By the end of June, the mission was ready to depart for southern France and Italy, where the *Mossad Le'Aliyah Beth* was now preparing several ships to run the British naval blockade of Palestine.

The operation was given added urgency by the international publicity surrounding the refugee ship, *President Warfield*, better known as *Exodus 1947*. A former pleasure steamer, it had once ploughed the waters of Chesapeake Bay in the United States before

From Espionage to Sabotage

Fig. 9.2 The 'cigarette smugglers' for Operation Embarrass. Clockwise: Jimmy Blackburn, Smiley, Don Bevers, Harold Perkins. The pictures were taken during 'Embarrass'.

it was bought by the *Mossad Le'Aliyah Beth*. It was already dilapidated, but after a rudimentary refit, it had left the French port of Sète on 9 July 1947, packed with 4,500 refugees. The likelihood that the *Exodus 1947* would be able to run the British naval blockade of the Palestine coast was fanciful. But this belied the true nature of the voyage: its propaganda value. The violence when the Royal Navy boarded the ship on the morning of 18 July, the disembarkation of the refugees at Haifa, and their subsequent journeys back to internment camps in Cyprus and then onwards to displaced persons camps back in Germany prompted a huge international outcry, especially in the United States.[35] MI6 had wanted to sabotage the *Exodus* in Sète before it could embark its human cargo but had been overruled. The British could have done so, for the *Valfrere* monitored the *President Warfield* as it prepared for its historic voyage. Perkins and Smiley had limpet mines with time-delay fuses of up to four days that would have enabled them to be well away from the target area and inside Italian waters before the mines detonated.[36]

Perkins, who was keen to press home the attack, was overruled. He was under strict orders that any refugee ships should be sabotaged in port with no one on board. Such strictures had made sabotage of the *Exodus* impossible: in port, people were always on board, and out at sea, mass deaths would have ensued. Still, one MI6 officer opined that an opportunity had been lost in Sète, for even though the risk of detection was much greater, the failure to sabotage the *Exodus* meant that the Zionists had won an international propaganda coup, whereas the British were castigated. '[I]f the FO had permitted the Secret Service (MI6) to take the appropriate action against the *President Warfield* when they (MI6) suggested doing so', this could have been avoided, he argued. He lambasted the inability of the Foreign Office to appreciate fully the capabilities of MI6, capabilities that could have brought some political gain without the ignominy now heaped upon Britain in the court of world opinion.[37]

Meanwhile, the *Mossad Le'Aliyah Beth* capitalised on this international reaction to the *Exodus* affair. It now intended to run the British blockade in two larger ships, the *Pan Crescent* and the *Pan York*, crammed with refugees. The capacity of both ships was far in excess of that of the *Exodus* and Britain realised that the volume of refugees involved would swamp the internment camps in Cyprus. Yet London could not risk international condemnation again by sending refugees back to Germany. Sabotage was reckoned by many to be the only answer. MI6

From Espionage to Sabotage

Fig. 9.3 A secret MI6 reconnaissance photo of a ship suspected of being used by *Mossad Le'aliyah Beth* for taking Jewish refugees to Palestine, lying in Genoa harbour.

had suborned a Greek shipping magnate to provide information on some of the activities of the *Mossad Le'Aliyah Beth* and on the location of the ships it was looking to buy and refit for the voyage to Palestine.[38]

To keep their strict cover as cigarette smugglers, the Embarrass team on board *Valfrere* made sure that they were seen in a series of ports along the Italian coast, including Portovenere and the small island of Ponza, dealing in their contraband as they sailed along and gathering intelligence where they could. In larger ports such as Genoa, they took several close reconnaissance photographs of suspected immigrant ships, including some whose profile closely matched the *Pan Crescent* and *Pan York*. The *Pan Crescent* eventually made for Venice for refit work before sailing on to the Black Sea, where it was to take on refugees from the Romanian port of Constanza. With Blackburn at the helm, the Embarrass team followed discreetly in its wake. One night in August 1947, it was rocked by an explosion below the waterline while in Venice harbour. Under cover of darkness, Smiley and Perkins had paddled a dinghy the short distance from their yacht and attached limpet mines below the hold of the ship. The timers were set to allow the two cigarette smugglers and the *Valfrere* time to clear the harbour before the mines detonated, causing the ship to list badly. Though a member of the crew was later said to

215

have been killed, there was no proof of any fatalities. It had been, to all intents and purposes, a 'clean' operation'.[39]

In the coming months, these feats of sabotage were repeated in various Italian ports. Five suspected refugee ships were sabotaged by Smiley and his team. One was described as a total loss; two others, presumably including the *Pan Crescent*, were damaged; and the mines on the remaining pair were dislodged and later discovered by divers. Even though the mines were clearly of British manufacture, it was felt that this would leave few clues as to the saboteurs' identity because so many were available as war surplus across Europe.

But the activities of the Embarrass team were never discovered and were later held up by MI6 as an example of how clandestine operations could achieve results at relatively little cost. Keith Jeffrey noted that

> In September 1947 SIS (MI6) claimed that the deterrent effect of the ship attacks has caused a complete cessation of sailing from Italy. The following spring they noted that a number of potential emigrant vessels had left Italian waters and that the Jewish organisers of the illegal immigration had lost confidence in the chief provider of ships.[40]

The discovery of limpet mines on ships yet to be paid for by the *Mossad Le'Aliyah Beth* rattled the ships' agents in Italian ports, who feared sabotage would prevent payment from the Jewish Agency as well as invalidating any insurance claim. Responsibility for the attacks by the shadowy 'Defenders of Arab Palestine' may or may not have been entirely convincing, but it helped to muddy the waters even more.[41]

But events on the ground in Palestine itself ultimately determined the fate of the British Mandate. In the face of increased terrorism and despite some 100,000 British soldiers and police, the internecine violence between Arabs and Jews forced the British to hand the problem of Palestine over to the United Nations. In November 1947, the General Assembly voted for the partition of Palestine into separate Jewish and Arab states. Britain abstained but it marked an ignominious end to the Mandate. It withdrew the last of its troops from Palestine soon after Israel declared independence on 14 May 1948. The Embarrass team had been stood down from operations at the end of January, its role following the partition vote restricted to reconnaissance and intelligence gathering along the coast of Italy. Blackburn recalled that he continued to sail around the Mediterranean with limpet mines that Perkins and Smiley had never used and MI6 had forgotten to reclaim.[42] With his love of the open sea and a newly acquired taste for smuggling (gained at the expense of the British government), this was not to be his last involvement with MI6.

Of all the episodes in Smiley's secret service, this was the one that remained most firmly in the shadows, with just the odd comment in later life hinting at an operation whose legacy Smiley deemed too sensitive to expose to the wider public gaze, let alone academic scrutiny.[43] Because of his service with both SOE and the Directorate of War Planning, several authors did link him to the sabotage of Jewish refugee ships, although Operation Embarrass was disclosed only with the publication of the official history of MI6 in 2010 soon after his death.[44] He confirmed his participation after much reflection and a realisation that the enmities surrounding the British counter-terror campaign in Palestine had long abated. Nor, Smiley reasoned, was he disclosing any great secrets that might compromise individuals or tradecraft. All involved had long passed away and the placing of limpet mines was hardly a technical innovation known to just a few. His conscience remained clear: Operation Embarrass was intended to protect British interests in the Middle East and he was emphatic that his actions against the ships had been 'clean'. Later reports published in *The Observer* and *The Guardian* four decades later, that suggested fatalities had been inflicted, therefore upset him greatly. He knew, however, that political sensitivities, even in the late 1980s, would prevent him from speaking out. As such, acknowledging and explaining his involvement in Operation Embarrass was about setting straight a record that he felt had long been sullied by erroneous and poorly sourced reporting.[45]

His next involvement with MI6 was less politically sensitive but was to end in death, recrimination and allegations of betrayal among those involved. It was an operation that drew its protagonists deep into the heart of Albanian affairs and epitomised the early exchanges of the Cold War. It was an operation whose shortcomings were occasioned by many adverse circumstances, but whose ultimate fate was attributed to the actions of one individual who Smiley referred to for the rest of his life as 'that bloody man Philby'.[46]

Notes

1. Interview with Moyra Smiley, London, 22 February 2006.
2. Interview with Moyra Smiley, London, 22 February 2006.
3. Interview with David Smiley, London, 21 October 2005.
4. Stephen Dorril, *MI6: Fifty Years of Special Operations* (London: Fourth Estate, 2000), pp. 255–6.
5. Nicholas Bethell (2016), 'Interview with Anthony Northrop, March/April 1984', in Robert Elsie and Bejtullah Destani (eds), *The Albanian Operation of the CIA and MI6, 1949–1953: Conversations with Participants in a Venture Betrayed* (Jefferson, NC: McFarland, 2016), p. 132.
6. Dorril, *MI6: Fifty Years of Special Operations*, pp. 255–6.
7. IWM, Accession No: 10340/6 Transcript of Interview with Colonel D. Smiley, Recorded 1989, p. 58.
8. For the work of BRIXMIS, see Tony Geraghty, *Beyond the Front Line: The Untold Exploits of Britain's Most Daring Cold War Spy Mission* (London: HarperCollins, 1996).
9. Dorril, *MI6: Fifty Years of Special Operations*, p. 258.
10. Interview with David Smiley, London, 21 October 2005.
11. Bethell, 'Interview with Colonel David Smiley 12 February 1981', p. 151.
12. Robert Cecil, '"C's" war', *Intelligence and National Security*, 1/2 (1986), p. 182.
13. See Philip H. J. Davies, 'From Special Operations to Special Political Action: The "Rump SOE" and SIS Post-War Covert Action Capability 1945–1977', *Intelligence and National Security*, 15/3 (2000), p. 59.
14. Interview with David Smiley, London, 21 October 2005.
15. Smiley condensed these lessons in a small booklet that he wrote for Harold Perkins on the role of BLOs working with resistance networks. Perkins eventually returned this booklet to Smiley in 1952 but urged him to keep it safe in the event it might be needed

in an emergency. Letter from Harold Perkins to David Smiley, 14 January 1952. IWM Archives.
16. Smiley, *Albanian Assignment*, p. 158.
17. See Cesarani, *Major Farran's Hat*.
18. Interview with David Smiley, London, 20 October 2008.
19. On British intelligence collaboration with the *Yishuv* during the Second World War, see Clive Jones, 'Good Friends in Low Places: The British Secret Intelligence Service and the Jewish Agency 1940–1945', *Middle Eastern Studies*, 48/3 (2012), pp. 413–28.
20. For detailed descriptions of the Jewish insurgency and the end of the British Mandate in Palestine, see Motti Golani, *Palestine between Politics and Terror 1945–1947* (Lebanon, NH: Brandeis University Press/University Press of New England, 2013); Norman Rose, '*A Senseless Squalid War*': *Voices from Palestine 1945–1948* (London: Bodley Head, 2009).
21. Golani, *Palestine between Politics and Terror 1945–1947*, p. 83.
22. TNA KV 3/56, Top Secret. Illegal Immigration Review No. 2 Period 16 June–15 July 1947. For a wider appreciation of the British intelligence against illegal immigration, see Steven Wagner, 'British Intelligence and the "Fifth" Occupying Power: The Secret Struggle to Prevent Jewish Illegal Immigration to Palestine', *Intelligence and National Security* (2013), available at <http://dx.doi.org/10.1080/02684527.2013.846730>.
23. TNA CAB 158/1 JIC, Report (47) 28(0): Top Secret. Subject: Illegal Immigration to Palestine – Complicity of Certain Organisations, 11 June 1947.
24. TNA PREM 8/624, Top Secret: From Hector McNeil to Prime Minister. Subject: Illegal Immigration into Palestine (undated).
25. See, for example, Meir Zamir, *The Secret Anglo-French War in the Middle East: Intelligence and Decolonization* (London: Routledge, 2014).
26. TNA KV 3/56, Top Secret. Illegal Immigration Review No. 2 Period 16 June–15 July 1947, para. 37.
27. TNA PREM8/624, From Attlee to Minister of State Foreign Office Hector McNeil, 23 April 1947.
28. Keith Jeffrey, *MI6: The History of the Secret Intelligence Service 1909–1949* (London: Bloomsbury, 2010), p. 691.
29. Interview with David Smiley, London, 20 October 2008.
30. Smiley, *Albanian Assignment*, p. 158.
31. The most reliable, although incomplete, account of those who participated in Operation Embarrass is to be found in Nigel West,

The Friends: Britain's Post-War Secret Intelligence Operations (London: Weidenfeld & Nicholson, 1988), p. 33. A more sensationalist account is to be found in Gordon Thomas, *Operation Exodus* (London: JR Books, 2010), p. 157.
32. IWM 12/19/1 Wing Commander J. Blackburn DSO, DFC. Transcript of Conversations – Wartime Reminiscences, 30 September 1992; Nicolas Bethell, 'Interview with Kevin Walton, 29 November 1984', in Elsie and Destani (eds), *The Albanian Operation of the CIA and MI6, 1949–1953*, pp. 163–4.
33. IWM 12/19/1 Wing Commander J. Blackburn DSO, DFC. Transcript of Conversations – Wartime Reminiscences, 30 September 1992.
34. Interview with David Smiley, London, 20 October 2008.
35. André Gerolymatos, *Castles Made of Sand: A Century of Anglo-American Espionage and Intervention in the Middle East* (New York: St Martin's/Thomas Dunne, 2010), pp. 101–3.
36. Jeffrey, *MI6*, p .694.
37. Jeffrey, *MI6*, p. 694.
38. Interview with David Smiley, London, 20 October 2008.
39. Interview with David Smiley, London, 20 October 2008; Dorril, *MI6: Fifty Years of Special Operations*, p. 548.
40. Jeffrey, *MI6*, p. 694.
41. Interview with David Smiley, London, 20 October 2008.
42. IWM 12/19/1 Wing Commander J. Blackburn DSO, DFC. Transcript of Conversations Wartime Reminiscences, 30 September 1992.
43. Nicholas Bethell, 'Interview with Colonel David Smiley 12 February 1981', in Elsie and Destani (eds), *The Albanian Operation of the CIA and MI6*, p. 151.
44. Davies, 'From Special Operations to Special Political Action', p. 59. See also Nigel West, *The A–Z of British Intelligence* (Plymouth: Scarecrow, 2009), p. 499.
45. Interview with David Smiley, London, 20 October 2008.
46. IWM, Accession No: 10340/6 Transcript of Interview with Colonel D. Smiley, Recorded 1989, p. 59.

10   Subversion and the Ceremonial

I

In May 1948, Smiley returned to his parent unit, the Royal Horse Guards, as second in command of the regiment. Since the end of the war, the Blues had been stationed at Wesendorf, near Hanover, as part of a British army now occupying much of northern Germany, and became one of the first armoured regiments to be incorporated into the British Army of the Rhine (BAOR). Smiley was a step closer to fulfilling his ambition of commanding his regiment but it was not an easy time. Demobilisation of soldiers who had contributed to an *esprit de corps* during the fighting in northern Europe inevitably hurt morale. This could not easily be replicated by the influx of national servicemen, many reluctant warriors, whose standards of soldiering were often mocked by regular soldiers and NCOs alike.[1] While Smiley was happy to be back with his regiment, his return was tinged with some frustration.

He had hoped to be given command of the regiment as a lieutenant colonel, given his wealth of experience in conventional and unconventional warfare, underpinned by being a recent graduate of staff college. But when the commanding officer of the Blues stood down soon after Smiley's arrival, the promotion of an outsider to take over was a setback. Smiley was still considered too young at thirty-two to command the most senior regiment in the British army. The accelerated promotion in times of war now no longer applied and Smiley would have to wait his turn. He found being second in command 'a very boring job', not helped by the routine of garrison duties. Fraternisation with the German population was still officially discouraged and BAOR, while not quite an army of occupation, was yet to enjoy wider appreciation across Germany as a necessary bulwark against the Soviet Union.[2]

Smiley did, however, enjoy his new-found family life. With Moy and his two stepchildren, Gavin and Anna, in tow, he moved first to Menden near Dortmund, then to Hanover, where their older son, Xan de Crespigny, was born in May 1949. But any thoughts of a longer stay in Germany were put aside when, in the spring of that year, Smiley was visited in Wesendorf by two MI6 officers, one of whom was 'Perks': would he be prepared to rejoin 'the firm' as part of a wider mission to destabilise the communist regime in Albania?[3] He again accepted without hesitation. For one thing, it would be a chance to repay a debt to those Albanians he believed had been so badly let down in the summer of 1944 by a combination of communist influence in SOE and misplaced strategic opportunism on the part of senior British officers. Moreover, he was assured that his family would be able to accompany him on his new assignment, which would take him back to the Mediterranean and Malta; indeed, Moy would play a part in the drama that now unfolded.

The genesis of what became known as MI6's Operation Valuable was largely the result of the efforts of one man. Julian Amery had never wavered in his belief that Albania had been unnecessarily sacrificed to Enver Hoxha and his communist cohorts. After the war, he was elected to the House of Commons in 1950 as the Conservative member for Preston North. He had married Catherine Macmillan, daughter of the future Prime Minister, Harold Macmillan, but continued to lobby ministers in the Attlee government against the dangers of Soviet expansionism in the Balkans. Greece was racked by civil war and threatened by the communist insurgents of ELAS, who were receiving supplies and sanctuary from their comrades in Yugoslavia and Albania.

But while wrapped in the logic of a *Realpolitik*, his view of the threat posed by Moscow to British interests in the eastern Mediterranean could not disguise what he saw as the moral debt owed by Britain to the peoples of the Balkans, and of Albania in particular. In 1948, he published his memoirs of his time with the Concensus II mission, *The Sons of the Eagle*. In many ways, the book was a call to arms. Its epilogue claimed that the tribal nature of Albania was already proving anathema to the central control of a dictator whose attempts to crush all opposition had sown the seeds of a new resistance movement that 'will ripen with the perennial struggle of the Powers and sooner or later the harvest of hate must be reaped'.[4] In May 1946, two British cruisers sailing the narrow waters between the Greek island of Corfu and the Albanian mainland were shelled. More seriously, six months later, mines in the same stretch of water hit two Royal Navy destroyers, HMS *Saumarez* and HMS *Volage*, killing forty-four sailors. Britain now had a motive to reap this harvest.[5] With his strong political connections, Amery continued to lobby for tougher measures to be taken against Albania. Throughout 1948, he underscored the message of his book with a series of articles warning against Moscow's increasing reach across the Balkans.

Despite his Conservative pedigree, Amery's views on Albania resonated with Clement Attlee and his Foreign Secretary, Ernest Bevin, whose own grounding in the socialist milieu of the trade union movement had instilled in him a loathing of communism. Both now gave their assent for plans to be drawn up to subvert Hoxha and his regime.[6] By February 1949, MI6 had fleshed out the detail, their recommendations circulated for discussion in Whitehall by the chairman of the Joint Intelligence Committee, William Hayter. The MI6 paper made three recommendations: to disrupt Greek communist rebel bases and their communications by infiltrating guerrillas into Albania by sea and air; to foment insurrection and unrest in the north of the country to draw troops away from the south; and to organise raids across the border from Greece itself.[7]

Over the coming weeks, a more refined plan was drawn up comprising two distinct but interlinked phases, movement between them being contingent upon clear objectives being met in the initial phase. The first was to find out whether, in fact, there existed enough popular discontent in Albania towards the Hoxha regime by setting up a series of intelligence networks. Once these were established, the next phase would be to use these networks to help instigate an insurrection and, eventually, to detach Albania from the rest of the Soviet bloc. The chief of MI6, Sir Stewart Menzies, cautioned, though, against overreach.

He endorsed Valuable but made clear that its scope should be restricted at first to southern Albania and be treated 'as a test'. '[I]n the light of experience gained there I would then consider whether it would be worthwhile to undertake similar possibilities in the North.'[8]

The north, however, soon became an American responsibility, as Washington also viewed Albania as an attractive target, especially following Tito's break with Stalin in June 1948, which isolated Albania geographically from the rest of the Soviet bloc. It meant that Britain could share the financial burden of the operation with Washington amid the post-war austerity. Between 20 and 26 May 1949, representatives of MI6, the Foreign Office and the Office of Policy Coordination (OPC) of the US State Department met in Washington to discuss a plan of joint action. Washington's proposed subversion of Albania, code-named BGFIEND, was on an altogether larger scale than Valuable but its essence was the same: to infiltrate, mostly by parachute, teams of Albanian exiles into the mainly tribal centre and north of the country, establish the relevant networks and, eventually, organise the overthrow of Hoxha. Like their British counterparts, many of the American officials involved had cut their intelligence teeth during the war. This included Robert Low from the Office of Special Operations (OSO) of the newly formed CIA, who headed up the operational element of BGFIEND, and the head of the OPC, Frank Wisner, who had served with the OSS in Egypt and Turkey.

The need to coordinate Anglo-American clandestine activity in the same operational theatre was evident and was realised in the establishment of the Special Policy Committee. But wider political concerns drove this bureaucratic union: the suspicion in Washington that the British hoped to leverage any success achieved in Albania to expand their influence in other parts of the eastern Mediterranean and probably at the expense of the United States. What Washington now labelled Operation 'Valuable-Fiend' therefore had a subplot: to exercise control over British ambitions in the Mediterranean. As in Siam, suspicions of its imperial reach still influenced American views of British foreign policy. Still, Britain had more recent operational experience in Albania, and the Americans knew that, without close cooperation, separate

Subversion and the Ceremonial

missions would do little to unify a fractious Albanian diaspora, from which London and Washington hoped a new political order would emerge.[9]

While planning to coordinate the insertion back into Albania of trained guerrillas recruited mainly from displaced persons camps in Italy and Germany, Britain and the United States set up the Free Albanian Committee, also known as the Albanian National Committee. The Free Albanian Committee was an uneasy mix of exiled Zogists, led by Abas Kupi, whose political fortunes the British hoped to resurrect, and members of the *Balli Kombetar*, led by Mithat Frashëri. Other senior members of the committee included Said Kryeziu, to represent the tribal leaders who had no party affiliation. But aside from a shared hatred of Hoxha, little united the Zogists, who enjoyed British patronage, and the *Balli Kombetar*, whose staunch republican credentials appealed more to Washington. On 14 July 1949, it fell to Amery, Billy McLean and Robert Low to win the acquiescence, if not the assent, of the exiled King Zog, now ensconced in Cairo, to the activities of the Free Albanian Committee. Without it, they knew, Kupi and his Zogists would walk away, the fragile unity presented by the Free Albanian Committee would dissipate and covert action of any type would be impossible to mount. The exiled monarch blustered, claiming he was still the legal sovereign responsible for endorsing any government. After Amery promised a referendum on the future of his dynasty once Hoxha was overthrown, Zog relented. He would not support the Free Albanian Committee openly but neither would he oppose it. Amery had no authority to offer this political sweetener but, for Low, it saved the Free Albanian Committee and the entire enterprise to unseat Hoxha. Low later recalled it as 'The most dazzling display of verbal diplomacy I have ever witnessed'.[10]

II

On 7 July 1949, Smiley entered the somewhat austere headquarters of MI6 Broadway in St James's, London, and was directed to an office where Perkins awaited his arrival. After a day-long briefing, his role became clearer: to train a group of Albanian exiles, plucked from displaced persons camps in Italy, in guerrilla warfare. It was a condensed SOE-type syllabus but one that stressed intelligence gathering rather than sabotage. The students would be trained in the use of a range of small arms and explosives but would not at this stage attack Albanian security forces and infrastructure. This would come later in phase two of the operation, once solid networks had been established. The training had to be fitted into just six weeks, beginning in September. Albanian winters, as many of the old SOE hands involved in the operation pointed out, were savage. The grim fate of the Spillway mission under Brigadier Trotsky Davies was fresh in the memory and the men needed to be infiltrated before the seasons turned.

After some debate, a training base for Smiley and his team had been selected in a secluded part of Malta, away from the 'flesh pots' of the capital, Valetta. Located in the south-western corner of the island and dating from the Napoleonic wars, Fort Benjimma was about as remote a structure as could be found on Malta, access being possible only up a hidden track. With thick outer walls, a moat and a drawbridge, it offered secure accommodation for the training staff and students, and ample space for stores and classrooms. All activity at the fort was to be closely coordinated with the Special Policy Committee in Washington via London. The Americans' own teams were to be trained in southern Germany for parachuting into northern and central Albania; the British preferred sending in their teams more quietly by sea. Once the bulk of the exiles in Malta had been trained and sent secretly to southern Albania, Smiley would move with a small staff to Greece to monitor progress, with a modest signals station set up in Corfu to manage the radio traffic and liaise with London.[11]

The operation had been sold to Ernest Bevin as an adjunct to resolving the troublesome civil war in Greece.[12] But Smiley reckoned that the main purpose of the operation was not, as Amery once suggested, to relieve the pressure on Greece by disrupting insurgent activity just across the border in Albania that was fuelling the Greek civil war. He was only too aware of the mutual loathing that marked the ties between Greeks and Albanians, a loathing grounded in rival territorial and ethnic claims across their shared border. The crisis in Greece was, to him, incidental.

> I think the idea was to topple Hoxha and to get a friendly government in his place. . . . I would hate my Albanian friends to think I did what I did merely to help the Greeks. They would have objected strongly to being used as cat's paws or pawns in some Balkan game. If it had been put to me in that way, I don't think I would have taken the job on. I was a soldier. It was not for me to ask political questions. On the other hand, I could have turned the job down. The question put to me was, 'Would you like to help your Albanian friends to kick out Enver Hoxha?'[13]

Just twenty-four hours after his arrival in London, Smiley flew to Malta to begin preparations for training his first batch of Albanians. As cover, he had been promoted to lieutenant colonel, appointed Deputy Chief of Staff to the British garrison headquarters in Valetta and given a spacious office in the Castille, a majestic building once owned by the Knights of St John. His real job was known only to three people outside Fort Benjimma: the Commander in Chief, Admiral Sir John Power; his chief intelligence officer, Captain (later Vice Admiral) John Inglis; and the island's senior intelligence officer, Major Bill Major of MI5. Although overseas intelligence postings were normally under MI6, Malta was a Crown Colony, and as such, it fell under the domain of their domestic counterpart, a pattern repeated across most of the British empire. Major Major, whose combination of rank and name caused much confusion and hilarity, oversaw security around the fort. He made sure that the small arms, explosives and equipment needed for training passed through Maltese customs with few questions asked, something for which Smiley was particularly grateful.[14]

The curriculum was taught by an eclectic staff, whose skills in the art of guerrilla warfare were more than matched by individual eccentricity or emotional crises. The strangest appointment was Dr Robert Zaehner, an Oxford don in classical Persian, who had served in MI6 during the war, using his cover as press attaché in Tehran to help set up agent networks across the Iranian border in

Soviet Central Asia as the war drew to a close. A brilliant linguist, he was assigned to Valuable as it was claimed he learned fluent Albanian quickly.[15] This seems unlikely because the Valuable team was put together at relatively short notice and Zaehner had no previous contact with Albania or Albanians. However talented a linguist, given the time available to train the guerrillas, Zaehner could be expected to do no more than pick up a basic understanding of Albanian. This he may well have acquired but, as Smiley recalled, 'his own speciality and Albanian had little in common'. Even so, 'he was a most useful and entertaining member of the staff'. His true value was realised by drawing on his own experience in Persia to teach his students how best to set up intelligence networks, key to the success of the first phase of the operation.[16]

With his horn-rimmed glasses and crumpled tweed jacket, Zaehner looked like the archetypal Oxbridge don and the antithesis of an army officer, even though he held the rank of captain. By contrast, Major Alfred Howard of the Scot Guards was, in Smiley's words, a typical 'guards type'; as a former quartermaster who had been commissioned from the ranks, he acquired the name 'Q'. He provided instruction in navigation and map reading while his MI6 colleague, Captain Alistair Grant, oversaw weapons training. Grant, however, was somewhat diffident towards his responsibilities for he had become involved in a torrid affair that put him 'a bit off balance'.[17] While Grant eventually found love elsewhere, he was released by MI6 once Operation Valuable was over. Ihsan Toptani, who had helped found the Free Albania Committee, was brought over to Malta as an interpreter, aided by Abdyl Sino, a former member of the *Balli Kombetar*, and Jani Dilo. To help their cover, both were given temporary commissions in the British army, although Dilo, who spoke French but no English, had to pass himself off as a French Canadian. As these men represented various wings of the Albanian opposition in exile, their recruitment was as much about preventing internecine disputes between their students as it was to smooth liaison and translation.

Signalling, encryption and deciphering were perhaps the most important parts of the curriculum. Here Smiley was well served by the recruitment of Jeffrey (John) Kelly, a young MI6 wireless

Fig. 10.1 The MI6 Training Team, Fort Benjimma, Malta, 1949. From left to right: Alistair Grant, 'Q' Howard, John Kelly, Smiley, Gunner Collins, Doc Zaehner.

operator who trained the Albanians in radio security. Equally, Broadway needed to be kept informed of progress and, here, Gunner Collins ensured that communications with London were reliable and secure. Smiley's admiration for Gunner remained unbounded, not least from his time in Siam, where his quick thinking had saved Smiley's life. Moreover, Gunner understood the Albanian mind-set from his own service behind the lines in the Balkans, and his experience was invaluable, Smiley felt, in coaxing the best out of volunteers whose enthusiasm for the cause might wane as the enormity of their undertaking steadily became apparent.

Finally, Moy was brought on board as a cipher clerk following a quick refresher course in London. Not only had she proved extremely skilful in this line of work during the war, but being the wife of the Deputy Chief of Staff to Garrison HQ provided the perfect cover because, in this case, it happened to be true.[18] Two former Royal Marine sergeants, Terence Cooling and Derby Allen, taught basic boat-handling skills and oversaw a physical fitness regime, while a third NCO, Sergeant George Odey, ran the armoury.[19] Smiley's own contribution to the curriculum lay in the realm of explosives. He later remembered the fun that was had by his Albanians detonating small charges in the moat at Fort Benjimma. Indeed, Smiley tried to foster a relaxed atmosphere among staff and students alike, believing that this would help the Albanians learn more easily and gain confidence in being able to operate effectively once in the field. This reflected his own experience of SOE teaching methods and certainly resonated among the Albanians. Many later recalled with fondness their instructors and the quality of the training they received. During his time at the fort, Smiley became close to his charges and nurtured an almost paternalistic concern for their welfare, feelings that were reciprocated. Years after the event, many of the survivors still remembered 'the Colonel with particular affection'.[20]

The first of the forty-eight Albanians recruited to Operation Valuable arrived at Fort Benjimma in the late summer of 1949. Most were recruited from camps close to Naples by Abas Kupi and Abas Ermenji of the *Balli Kombetar*, the latter an avowed anti-communist who was close to Amery. The diminutive stature of these recruits earned them the nickname 'Pixies' from the training staff. While meant affectionately, it also captured a sense of their physical fragility. Because these men had been poorly fed in their post-war camps, the training staff worried as to how they would cope, physically and mentally, in a hostile environment.[21] Even so, all admired their courage and patriotism, not least Smiley, who made sure he got to know each individual under his care: 'Most of these men had been in camps in Germany and Italy and they had, poor chaps, no country, no future – they volunteered because they wanted to get back to their own country.'[22]

As well as small-arms and basic demolition training, the Pixies learned, under Kelly's keen eye, to work the B2 wireless set, previously used by SOE missions across Europe. Rather than being given heavy batteries to power the sets, they were issued with bicycle generators, requiring one man to pedal continuously to ensure a consistent current for wireless transmission. These frames were unwieldy, however, and when combined with the weight of the wireless set, food, spare clothing and ammunition

Subversion and the Ceremonial

Fig. 10.2 Four of the 'Pixies' in training, Malta, summer 1949.

that made up the bulk of the Pixies' equipment, it only added to the considerable burden to be carried by small men over very harsh terrain.[23] Most of the Pixies had no experience of boats but were now introduced to the rudiments of transferring from one vessel to another at sea. The plan was to take them in a reconditioned fishing boat from Malta to a point just off Otranto on the Adriatic coast of southern Italy, where they would then be transferred to a Greek sailing *caique* for the final journey to the Albanian coast.

While keeping a close eye on their training, Smiley still had to maintain appearances and ensure that his face was seen at the Castille and the expected social engagements in his role as Deputy Chief of Staff. The hot summer in Malta meant that garrison duties finished at around midday, so the afternoons were spent either escaping the heat or playing sport. This meant Smiley could again take up polo, which he had last played before the outbreak of the war. His fellow players included Lord Mountbatten, now a vice admiral in the Mediterranean fleet, and his nephew, Prince Philip, whose young wife, Princess Elizabeth, had given birth nine months previously to her first child, Prince Charles.[24]

Smiley's double life meant that they needed a reliable nanny to look after the children. Throughout the later summer, Moy worked closely with Gunner in 'enciphering and deciphering radio traffic to London, reporting on the Pixies' progress. Smiley was encouraged by what he saw, although he realised that they could not reach a high standard in so short a time. Still, he believed they had become proficient enough to undertake phase one, reconnaissance and the setting up of clandestine networks. To this end, the Pixies self-selected themselves into groups, determined by political allegiance, or tribal or family ties, or a combination of all three, choosing the areas of southern Albania they knew best in which to operate.[25]

In late August and under the watchful eyes of their instructors, the Pixies held a full dress rehearsal off the coast of Malta, codenamed Operation RAKI, to test their proficiency in the skills taught at Fort Benjimma.[26] Given the rather rushed circumstances of their training, those present felt that the Pixies acquitted themselves well. Smiley, for one, reckoned that 'we had trained them pretty thoroughly', although his MI6 successor in Malta and former SOE hand with Albanian experience, Tony Northrop, later expressed profound misgivings. He feared that the training was inadequate, given the timetable, but more importantly, that the teams lacked leaders of real calibre to make a success of the operation.[27]

By mid-September, the first thirty Pixies were readied for infiltration. Over the next six weeks, six groups of five men each embarked at night on an old motor fishing vessel off the Maltese coast manned by the Royal Navy, then made a rendezvous with a Greek sailing *caique*, the *Stormie Seas*, crewed by two former naval officers, Sam Barclay and John Latham, who had run similar operations on behalf of SOE in the Aegean. While nominally a sailing boat, the *Stormie Seas* had been adapted for secret landings and fitted with powerful engines paid for by MI6. This gave it the range and ability to cover the distance between the Italian

Subversion and the Ceremonial

coast and southern Albania under the cover of darkness and to be gone by daylight.

The Pixies were then transferred to a small dinghy and rowed ashore by Cooling and Allen to begin their trek into the interior of their homeland.[28] One of the first groups to be dropped made landfall at Seaview, the cove used by the Concensus I and other SOE missions in 1943. Air reconnaissance confirmed that the area remained sparsely inhabited and still appeared suitable for landing teams earmarked for the area around Dukati and Gjinokaster. Other teams were dropped further up the coast, north of the mouth of the Sermani river, and headed for the area around Korcë. With some Pixies now landed in Albania and the rest on their way, Smiley's involvement in the training phase of Operation Valuable was over, so he prepared to move with his family to Greece. As expectations mounted, he would now monitor the progress of the men who, he firmly believed, would determine the fate of Albania.

III

A new country required a new cover for Smiley, so he was now appointed a senior staff officer, GI (Operations and Intelligence), to the British Military Mission responsible for training and liaison with the Greek armed forces fighting the communist insurgency. Only two people at the British embassy in Athens knew of Smiley's real mission: the head of the mission, General Nigel Poett, and the resident MI6 station chief, Pat Whinney. To add lustre to his cover, Smiley and his family were housed in a spacious villa in the coastal town of Glyfada, just outside the Greek capital. But he also ran a safe house in the Athenian suburb of Kifissia, where he expected to debrief the Pixies after they had crossed the border back to Greece.[29] At the same time, without the knowledge of the Greek authorities, MI6 set up a radio station in the Villa Bimbelli on Corfu. Lying only three miles off the Albanian coast, Corfu seemed the ideal spot from which to monitor the Pixies' progress as they made their way inland from their various drop-off points along the coast. Overseen by another old Albania hand, Alan Hare, who had joined 'the firm' after the war, the staff at Bimbelli now waited expectantly throughout early September for the first of the teams to come up on air. It was a forlorn wait.

Of the six teams trained by Smiley and landed along the southern coast of Albania between early September and early October 1949, none was able to establish anything akin to an intelligence network in their designated areas. Having landed at Seaview on 16 September, one four-man team, led by Sami Lepenica, was ambushed near the village of Dukati as they headed towards the coastal town of Vlora. All were killed. Another group, led by Ramiz Hataj, suffered a similar fate close to Nivica, not far from the Greek border, on 4 October. Hataj was killed, while the other members split up, believing this would make it harder for the pursuing Albanian security forces to track them down. They eventually crossed the Greek border on 16 October. The final batch of Pixies that landed on 6 October did reach their designated areas close to Gjinokaster and Korcë, but tentative contacts with local villagers soon made it clear that few were prepared to help them, amid widespread security sweeps across southern Albania. One team, led by Xhemal Asllani, crossed back into Greece on 27 October, while heavy snow in the Kolonja region close to Korcë ended the mission of the group led by Sefer Luarasi, who entered Greece two days later.[30]

The fact that so few of the teams made radio contact with Corfu when first infiltrated did not at first seem to worry MI6. On 11 October, a Foreign Office briefing paper prepared for Sir Anthony Rumbold, head of the Southern Europe Department, noted that the 'pre-winter reconnaissance parties have now been successfully infiltrated as planned and without loss' and that the Malta base, having largely served its purpose, would be closed down by December.[31] But as October progressed, a sense of foreboding began to shroud the mood in the Villa Bimbelli. The brief signals received from the Pixies strongly suggested that some had been compromised, while others had clearly failed to establish anything like a firm operational base from which to gather intelligence. News of the Lepenica team had filtered out, leading Smiley now to wonder if a security breach in Malta had led to their deaths. But while these initial infiltrations could not be considered a success, the authorities in London did not see them as an unmitigated disaster either. The rate of attrition was 20 per cent, which some considered a reasonable price to pay for the initial intelligence gathered. In a report on 'Operation Valuable' up to the middle of November 1949, Rumbold was decidedly upbeat:

> The first phase [of Valuable] has now been partially completed with the infiltration of six reconnaissance parties into Southern Albania and preparations are in hand for the infiltration of further parties into Central and Northern Albania at a later date. The results of the operation are to date *encouraging* [my emphasis]. Bearing in mind that the area of Southern Albania in which we are operating is particularly unsuitable and difficult for these activities, being the back area to the Greek rebel forces based in Albania and consequently subject to more intense security policing and controls than elsewhere, it is remarkable that three of our parties have traversed the country from the coast north of VALONA to the Greek frontier without casualties.[32]

It is not clear what sources informed this rather buoyant assessment: the intermittent nature of the wireless traffic with Corfu concerned Hare, and what little was received suggested that most of the missions had been 'bumped' almost as soon as they landed. The situation was further complicated by the Greeks, who, completely ignorant of the operation, suspected the Pixies of activities related to irredentist Albanian claims on Greek territory. MI6 therefore had to divulge the nature of its work to a select few Greek military officers after two Pixies, Turham Aliko and Ahmet Kuka, who crossed back into Greece on 21 October, confessed their true mission to officers from Greek military intelligence. All those who reached the frontier were picked up by the Greek gendarmerie and eventually released into Smiley's care and a more detailed debriefing.

A more sober appreciation of what was meant by 'encouraging' soon began to inform Smiley's assessment of Operation Valuable as the losses incurred began to weigh heavily on his mind. The survivors did indeed bring back useful intelligence on conditions in southern Albania. But all those who returned reported that they had been expected, suggesting that the whole mission had in fact been exposed. In 1984, Nicholas Bethell published *The Great Betrayal*, his account of Operation Valuable, which, while pointing to a lack of security among those Albanians recruited from the camps in Italy, firmly pointed the finger at Harold 'Kim' Philby, the British double agent who had been in the service of Moscow since being talent-spotted by Soviet intelligence at Cambridge in the 1930s. It was a compelling case. In his own self-serving autobiography, Philby suggested (without revealing any details) that he had indeed passed material to his Soviet handlers that had scuppered several British secret operations in Eastern Europe and the Caucasus.[33]

The role of the individual as the cause of a wider misfortune has a powerful explanatory pull. It can obviate or, indeed, remove altogether the need to explore other contributing factors, including poor planning and coordination, inadequate field security and simple bad luck, multiple causes that, individually or taken together, can offer more prosaic, if equally compelling, explanations for the failure of a mission. Bethell did acknowledge that field security was lax: Italian intelligence officers witnessed the transfer of the Pixies from their fishing boat to the *Stormie Seas* on 2 October, which they quickly reported to James Angleton of the OSO, who, based in Rome, oversaw the security of Operation Valuable-Fiend from the American end. Angleton had long held doubts about its viability for precisely this reason and apparently, with some glee, informed Wisner of this security breach.[34] Bethell, however, laid the blame firmly on Philby's treachery. He had the motive – ideological fidelity to the Soviet Union – and the means – he was the newly anointed MI6 station chief in Washington – to pass on highly classified information to Moscow. It was an explanation that, four decades after the event, Smiley continued to champion:

> The Americans had to tell us what they were doing. I had to tell the Americans what we were doing. This was all done through Washington (the Special Policy Committee) . The go-between was this fellow Philby who was told by the Americans what to tell the British,

told by the British what to tell the Americans and told the Russians as well. So it was a disaster.³⁵

Philby unquestionably knew about Valuable, but the precise nature of that knowledge and its timing cast doubt on the argument made by Bethell and others.³⁶

Until the end of August 1949, Philby was the MI6 station chief in Ankara. His subsequent posting to the United States marked him out as the rising star of the British secret service; some even suggested that, but for the defection of his fellow Cambridge spies, Donald Maclean and Guy Burgess, in 1951, he might well have risen to the very top of MI6.³⁷ But his knowledge of Valuable would have been circumscribed: compartmentalisation would have meant that little detailed information would have crossed his desk in Ankara. By the time he passed through London on his way to Washington in September 1949, the training of the Pixies was largely complete; around twenty had already been landed on the Albanian coast. Staff in Broadway would have briefed Philby on the goals of the mission as he was taking over as MI6 representative on the Special Policy Committee in Washington, but it is unlikely that this briefing would have included the precise landing sites and the chosen routes across Albania. Finally, some authors have suggested the extent to which British and American cryptographers had managed to break Soviet cipher traffic – code-named Venona – between Moscow and their stations in Washington and New York was a far more urgent task for Philby to familiarise himself with in the brief time he was in London. He needed to assess the likely damage to Soviet intelligence operations and report this back to Moscow. In short, events in Albania were not his intelligence priority.³⁸

For Smiley, the 'penny dropped' in 1963, when Philby fled to the Soviet Union while working as journalist for *The Observer* in Beirut. Convinced that operational security in Malta had been tight, he found it easy to blame Philby, despite the rushed timeline and the extent to which he would have known about the detail of Operation Valuable. But there is a sense too that Philby's treachery was of a piece with the pro-communist sympathies that Smiley, McLean and Amery believed had permeated SOE headquarters in

Bari: yet again, British interests and brave Albanians had been sold out by the enemy within. It was a belief and conviction that Smiley held for many years. But more recent evidence suggests that there are several reasons to explain the failure of Operation Valuable. Indeed, in the winter of 1949, Smiley himself was made aware by Greek intelligence officers of a serious security leak and its likely culprit.

An internal memorandum dated 21 October from the OSO claimed that 'Valuable-Fiend' was widely known to the Italians and Greeks, both of whom were also trying to run intelligence operations into Albania throughout the summer and autumn of 1949. Their knowledge of the operation extended to the use of Malta as the training base, the identities of the officers involved, and MI6's radio base on Corfu. The lack of signals security here alarmed the Americans: 'The British teams have been using short wave radio-telephone, which has undoubtedly been monitored and DF'd [Direction Found] by now.'[39] This lack of security had been acknowledged in London. An intelligence summary circulated among the relevant Whitehall players on 16 November 1949 noted:

> It appears that Enver Hoxha was aware of the names of the thirty Albanians who left Italy with a view to entering Albania some two months before they did in fact arrive. These names corresponded with those of our six reconnaissance parties who were therefore 'expected'. In the case of the leakage about our six parties it is evident that the leakage took place in Italy.[40]

The Yugoslav government too was sending Albanian exiles across their frontier in an effort to destabilise Hoxha; like their Anglo-American counterparts, these missions also suffered casualties as local communities, afraid of government reprisals, refused to offer shelter and support.[41]

The Americans soon begun to suspect that the Albanian diaspora in camps across Italy had been heavily penetrated by the Albanian intelligence service, the *Sigurimi*, whose agents sought, even before the creation of the Free Albanian Committee, to compromise the main opposition groups, which included the pro-Italian *Blloku Kombëtar Indipendent* as well as the *Balli Kombetar* and the *Legaliteti*, the political party of the Zogists. If discovered, such agents were shown no mercy. One informer suspected of being in the pay of the *Sigurimi* met a very Romanesque end: he was strangled, shot and his body dumped in the Tiber.[42] Moreover, at a time when southern Albania was on high alert and thick with security personnel precisely because of the Greek civil war, some questioned the wisdom of using known landing areas such as Seaview, however secure it may have appeared on aerial reconnaissance photographs. It was certainly known to Albanians who had fought with the partisans and, as it turned out, it was not just the British who used it as a point of infiltration. Over several days in September, the Greek and Italian intelligence services had also landed their own agents at the cove without the knowledge of, or any coordination with, the British or Americans.

It also transpired that the bloody fate of the Lepenica team was sealed even before they left Malta, victims of an efficient double-cross operation run by the *Sigurimi*. In July, they had intercepted and captured a team run jointly by the Italians and Americans, who had been dropped into the Kurvelehi mountains 40 miles south-east of Vlora. One was killed and the other three captured. Under threat of execution, one of its members, Ethem Çako, was turned and, for over a year, fed false messages and reports back to his handlers in Rome. It was reminiscent of *Das Englandspiel* during the Second World War, when captured SOE agents in the Netherlands were turned under threat of death by their German captors. As part of their briefing before leaving Malta, Smiley had told the Lepenica team to contact Çako, believing him to be operating effectively in the area between Vlora and Dukati. Only in May 1950, when Çako was deemed to have served his purpose, did Tirana reveal his fate and that of his colleagues. In November 1949, Smiley, operating from the British embassy under the cover name of 'Mr Bennett', was told by a Greek military intelligence officer that Athens believed Çako was operating under the control of the *Sigurimi*. Smiley forwarded these concerns to London, where they were passed on to the Special Policy Committee. But because the intelligence on which the Greeks had based their assessment could not be verified, London saw no reason to take further action.⁴³

Despite these leaks and the widely known purpose of the Malta base in European intelligence circles, by the spring of 1950, a new batch of Pixies was being trained at Fort Benjimma. They were still being sent by sea into southern Albania, with Jimmy Blackburn handling some of the landings for MI6 in a reconditioned German rescue launch, the *Henrietta*, whose upkeep was paid for by the CIA.⁴⁴ But British enthusiasm for Valuable Fiend had begun to flag.⁴⁵ This was not just because of mounting security concerns. Rather, the communists had been crushed in the Greek civil war, removing at a stroke a key motive for the operation. Furthermore, the growing ideological hostility between Tito and Hoxha, a hostility underscored by simmering ethno-national tensions in Kosovo, meant that Albania was effectively isolated.

Smiley's own involvement in the operation was now all but over. He continued to debrief Pixies who managed to escape back into Greece and, more than once, had to mollify suspicious Greek gendarmes who doubted the intentions of Albanians arrested at the frontier. By the time Smiley's attachment under cover to the British Military Mission had ended in the summer of 1950, it had become clear to him that the premise on which Valuable had been based was flawed: there was no real indigenous resistance on which to build. By 1951, the operation was very much an American concern, with Washington continuing to believe, despite its own evidence, that Albania remained a 'low-hanging' fruit ready to drop into its hands.⁴⁶ Only in 1953, after further heavy casualties, did the United States finally cut its losses.⁴⁷

Smiley remained proud of his role in Valuable but his reflections were tinged with deep sadness. He saw it as a means to right a wrong brought about by what he, McLean and Amery had regarded as short-term expediency over longer-term gain. This can be criticised for ignoring wider realities on the ground in Albania in the pursuit of vengeance but it was heartfelt none the less. The failure of Valuable and the belief that it had been betrayed by Philby added to a deeply felt sense of loss and, indeed, guilt. Interviewed in 1984 for a BBC documentary, he spoke movingly about this:

I feel very sad, to be quite frank. I mean, looking back on it knowing the result, it was just heart-breaking. I can't think of any other words to describe it really ... if you were in a responsible position and – I didn't know it then – you were sending men to their death, it's a pretty horrible feeling to say the least in retrospect.[48]

But it was a false premise that had led politicians in London to sanction 'Operation Valuable' in the first place. Those promoting it, notably Amery, misjudged the mood and conditions in Albania, which, under Hoxha, had quickly become a republic of fear. Smiley conceded as much in 1989, when he was asked, with the benefit of hindsight, if the Albanian population could have been roused. 'I think', he replied, 'with hindsight now the answer's very little hope. Because the communists had got such a grip on the country with their security forces.'[49]

IV

In August 1950, Smiley returned to Wolfenbüttel in Germany and once again took up his post as second-in-command of the Blues with the rank of major. It was undemanding but was made more palatable by knowing that he would be the next commanding officer of the Royal Horse Guards. He concentrated on reacquainting himself with the regiment's armoured reconnaissance role while trying to enthuse national servicemen and regulars alike in the routine of garrison duties and patrolling the border with East Germany. During this time, his second son, Philip David, was born in August 1951 and christened at St George's Chapel in Windsor. Finally, at the end of November, aged thirty-five, he was promoted to lieutenant colonel in command of the Royal Horse Guards

As a regular soldier devoted to his regiment, it was the apogee of his career and he took great pride in the ceremonial duties performed by the Blues. One of his first tasks in command was, none the less, a more sombre affair. Returning to London in February 1952, he rode escort at the funeral of King George VI as the cortège passed through the grey, damp streets of a capital still

Fig. 10.3 On ceremonial duty with 'the Blues', Windsor, 1953.

recovering from the Blitz. A month later, again with great pride tinged with emotion, Smiley brought the Blues back to England after almost thirteen years of continuous service overseas. As they approached Combermere barracks in Windsor, Smiley reflected on the fact that he was one of only two officers and thirteen men remaining from the regiment's original complement that had set out for Palestine in 1940.[50]

For the next three years, Smiley thoroughly enjoyed his command, mixing the ceremonial with the civic amid bouts of armoured reconnaissance training on Salisbury Plain or the battle ranges around Thetford, seemingly a far cry from the secret lives he had led for most of the last nine years. During this time, the Blues were increasingly called upon to perform duties in support of the civil authorities. These included helping victims of the great North Sea flood of January 1953, when a high spring tide and a severe storm combined to flood the low-lying areas of East Anglia and Lincolnshire, killing over 100 people and forcing

Subversion and the Ceremonial

30,000 to be evacuated. With the army mobilised to help shore up existing flood defences and repair storm damage, the Blues spent much of their time next to the town of Maldon, from where Smiley's maternal grandfather, Claude de Crespigny, had set out in a hot-air balloon across the North Sea. Filling sandbags might not have been the most glamorous of jobs but other civic duties brought financial rewards for the enterprising. A series of petrol-tanker strikes had begun to bite and at a time of economic hardship – rationing was still ongoing- the new Conservative government under Winston Churchill deployed the army to maintain fuel supplies to garages. The efficiency of the troopers from the Blues who drove the tankers was such that many earned huge tips from grateful garage owners, a welcome addition to their meagre army pay. The Blues were also employed to unload cargo during the London dockers' strike; once again, grateful ship owners were more than happy to reward soldiers who proved more efficient than the dockers in handling the cargo.[51]

Riding Sovereign's Escort for the Queen's Coronation on 2 June 1953, however, remained the highlight of Smiley's four years in command of the Blues. Riding by the back right wheel of the gold state coach, he recalled with pride giving the order 'Sovereign's Escort, Walk March', a command that started the procession from Buckingham Palace to Westminster Abbey. The noise from the crowds was tremendous, with thousands of schoolchildren lining the streets from Embankment to Parliament Square. The spectacle passed off with a precision admired across the globe, although he recalled with a smile one senior officer shouting above the noise of the crowd, admonishing a military band for playing the national anthem before the gold state coach had passed by and then, in a stentorian voice, ordering the hapless bandsmen to 'play that bloody thing again'. He always wondered if the Queen heard.[52]

On 30 November 1954, Smiley issued his last set of orders to the Blues before stepping down as commanding officer. He noted that the regiment had undertaken its varied duties with great professionalism and keenness, and concluded his message by adding that 'The standard of discipline and efficiency in the regiment is one of which we can all be proud, and this is due to the loyalty and keenness of all ranks, for whose support I am extremely grateful.' He was certainly a popular commanding officer, not always easy when the turnover of national servicemen often made peacetime cohesion difficult. He was well served by some very able NCOs but he was meritocratic, conscious that the Blues had a reputation for accepting some officers on the basis of class rather than ability. His reputation as an exceptionally brave soldier was known across the regiment; he was, after all, the only officer in the Household Cavalry to have been awarded the Military Cross twice. He led from the front and expected all his officers to shoulder responsibility, gaining a lot of credibility from those he commanded because they knew he would never ask of them something he was not prepared to do himself.[53] When he handed over command in 1954, he wrote that his time in charge of the Blues had been the 'most memorable and proudest of his life'. Given the rich, if unorthodox, tapestry of his military career to date, this was some statement.

This career, however, was now at a crossroads. Despite passing staff college and commanding his regiment, it was not clear that he would be given a higher command. He had been offered a staff post in Whitehall as Silver Stick in Waiting, a ceremonial role held by colonels of the Household Cavalry. Smiley turned it down, mainly for financial reasons: he felt the pay of a full colonel, then around £2,500 a year, was not enough both to support his family and to pay for the social engagements the position of Silver Stick entailed. Together with Moy, he had decided that he would soon leave the army and thought of buying a farm in Kenya. Moreover, much of the wealth he had inherited had been lost in some poor investments, and finances had to be carefully managed if their Kenyan idyll was to be realised. But with rank and experience on his side, Smiley now applied in the interim to become a military attaché. This made financial sense: as an accredited diplomat, he would be paid out of the Foreign Office budget, whose pay scales were more generous than those of their military counterparts, and included a substantial housing allowance. When offered a posting to Sweden, Smiley readily accepted.

In April 1955, he arrived in Stockholm. It proved to be a strange experience. With its strict regime of social engagements to attend and the rather stiff rules of Swedish etiquette

Subversion and the Ceremonial

to be followed, he often found the posting rather taxing. It was also very different from his previous experience as an attaché. Whereas in Poland the authorities had deliberately stymied his efforts at liaison, let alone intelligence gathering, the Swedish armed forces operated a virtual open-door policy, allowing Smiley to visit most units and bases across the length and breadth of the country. He joined army units on survival exercises in the Arctic Circle, learned to construct igloos, and marvelled at the ability of Swedish armour to cross frozen lakes without even cracking the ice. He was aware, however, that, with its long history of neutrality, the Swedish army had little combat experience beyond peace-keeping operations, although its doctrine and organisation had been heavily influenced by its close association with the Prussian military. Indeed, the army had been largely pro-German during the war, whereas the sympathies of the navy and air force had lain squarely with the Allies. Even so, Smiley never experienced any hostility from the army; indeed, several officers, such as General Carl von Horn, became close friends. Swedish troops that were posted overseas invariably went under the flag of the United Nations, leading to what Smiley remembered as some rather naïve questions. He often lectured these troops on his own experience of war. After one such talk to a unit about to deploy as cease-fire monitors on the Israeli–Jordanian border, he was taken aback by a young officer asking how many refrigerators his unit should take with them.[54]

While Smiley could gather information almost at will from his Swedish military contacts, he conducted one intelligence activity where subterfuge was required. Britain and its NATO allies were not at all sure that, if the Cold War became hot and Sweden was invaded, its armed forces could hold out for any extensive period in the face of a Soviet advance. Smiley therefore reconnoitred over forty roads and bridges deemed likely to be of strategic importance to any Soviet invasion force. These would have been targets for SOE-type demolition teams in any future war. It was a sensitive task; if discovered, it could be construed as an infringement of Swedish diplomatic hospitality and a violation of Swedish neutrality if the authorities in Stockholm concluded that Britain

Fig. 10.4   Military attaché, Sweden, 1957.

and her NATO allies had earmarked such sites for destruction. To circumvent this problem, Smiley asked Moy to pose on a series of bridges, the family snaps helping to disguise this particular intelligence-gathering activity. Given his own bridge-blowing exploits during the war, Smiley brought a particularly critical eye to bear.[55]

While he tired of the frequent rounds of social engagements, they occasionally produced some rather surreal moments. At a gathering in the aftermath of the Anglo-French invasion of Suez, the British delegation was generally snubbed by the other diplomats. But his opposite number in the Turkish embassy broke ranks, urging on the British with 'I hope you give them [the Egyptians] hell.' Similarly, the British and other European delegations snubbed their Soviet counterparts at another cocktail party after Moscow's intervention in Hungary. It was all part of a diplomatic game, which often hid more intimate associations. A keen tennis player, Smiley made close friends on court with the

Subversion and the Ceremonial

Fig. 10.5   Moy on a 'bridge of interest', Jokkmokk, Sweden, 1957.

Polish military attaché, both conversing in French. This officer was discreetly but decidedly anti-Soviet and Smiley sensed that, if handled with care, he could be persuaded to defect. The Warsaw Pact had only just been formed and, while not a senior ranking officer, the Polish attaché would have brought useful insights into Polish and Soviet operational planning.

Before he could land this catch, however, Smiley's posting came to an end and, despite briefing his successor as to the prize to be had, the possibility was never developed. More than most aspects of intelligence, the handling of an agent, or in this case a potential defector, is extremely delicate, and dependent as much on personal chemistry as any political or ideological affinity. Even so, Smiley felt strongly that an opportunity had been missed. There was, however, a further twist in this saga of diplomatic and intelligence subterfuge on the Swedish tennis courts. At the same time that Smiley was trying to encourage his Polish tennis partner to come over to the British, he also played with and against Colonel Stig Wennerström, a mid-ranking officer in the Swedish air force. In 1963, Wennerström was arrested, convicted of spying for the Soviet Union and sentenced to fifteen years. It sent shock waves across Sweden's political and military elite at the time and surprised Smiley, who had regarded Wennerström as a dedicated if rather aloof officer. To his relief, his own conversations with Wennerström never strayed beyond discussing the generalities of their respective positions.[56]

After two years in Sweden, however, Smiley had begun to tire of Swedish social life. Having 'always been a small wiry sort of chap', his son Xan recalled, he now began to put on weight. 'Actually, it was the first time he got fat.'[57] He now looked forward to the end of his posting, as he had bought a small farm in Kenya and intended to leave the army on his return to London in April 1958. However, at the end of February, while on a short trip to London, Smiley received a phone call from his old friend, Julian Amery. Having been elected a Conservative MP in 1950, Amery had quickly risen through the party ranks. By 1957, he was Undersecretary of State for War in the government of his father-in-law, Harold Macmillan. Now, he approached Smiley about a job back in the Middle East, in a country of which Smiley readily admitted he knew little but which, it turned out, was to be the scene of his greatest military triumph.

Notes

1. White-Spunner, *Horse Guards*, p. 555.
2. Interview with David Smiley, London, 21 October 2005.
3. Nicholas Bethell, 'Interview with Colonel David Smiley 12 February 1981', in Elsie and Destani (eds), *The Albanian Operation of the CIA and MI6*, p. 147.
4. Amery, *Sons of the Eagle*, p. 340.
5. It was later asserted that the mines were most likely laid by the Yugoslav navy, but no matter: on 9 April 1949, the International Court of Justice in The Hague held Tirana responsible and ordered compensation to be paid. Tirana refused. See Albert Lulushi, *Operation Valuable Fiend: The CIA's First Paramilitary Strike Against the Iron Curtain* (New York: Arcade, 2014), p. 31.
6. Richard J. Aldrich and Rory Cormac, *The Black Door: Spies, Secret Intelligence and British Prime Ministers* (London: HarperCollins, 2016), pp. 154–5.

7. TNA FO 1093/452, Top Secret: Communist Action in Albania, 3 February 1949.
8. TNA FO 1093/452, Top Secret: From 'C' to Sir William Strang, 4 March 1949.
9. Lulushi, *Operation Valuable Fiend*, p. 55.
10. Bassett, *Last Imperialist*, p. 139; 'The Cost of Treachery', Producer Adam Curtis, BBC1 TV, Broadcast 30 October 1984.
11. Interview with David Smiley, London, 21 October 2005; Smiley, *Albanian Assignment*, p. 160.
12. Giselle Gwinnett, 'Attlee, Bevin and Political Warfare: Labour's Secret Anti-Communist Campaign in Europe, 1948–51', *The International History Review*, 39/3 (2017), pp. 426–9.
13. Nicolas Bethell, 'Transcript of interview with Colonel David Smiley 12 February 1981', in Elsie and Destani (eds), *The Albanian Operation of the CIA and MI6*, p. 154.
14. Interview with David Smiley, London, 21 October 2005; Smiley, *Albanian Assignment*, p. 160.
15. See the biographical entry for Robert Zaehner in Nigel West, *The A–Z of British Intelligence* (Plymouth: Scarecrow, 2009), pp. 598–9. Bethell, *The Great Betrayal*, p. 67.
16. Zaehner later became involved in the early MI6 campaign to besmirch the Prime Minister, Muhammed Mossadeq, in Iran, where the nationalisation of British oil interests eventually prompted his overthrow in 1953 in a joint CIA/MI6 coup. See Aldrich and Cormac, *The Black Door*, pp. 156–7.
17. Nicolas Bethell, 'Interview with Colonel David Smiley, 12 February 1981', in Elsie and Destani (eds), *The Albanian Operation of the CIA and MI6*, p. 148.
18. Interview with Moyra Smiley, London, 22 February 2006; Interview with David Smiley, London, 21 October 2005.
19. Peter Harclerode, *Fighting Dirty: The Inside Story of Covert Operations from Ho Chi Minh to Osama bin Laden* (London: Cassell, 2002), p. 52.
20. Bethell, *The Great Betrayal*, p. 71.
21. Nicholas Bethell, 'Transcript of interview with Terence Cooling, 25 August 1984', in Elsie and Destani (eds), *The Albanian Operation of the CIA and MI6*, p. 53.
22. 'The Cost of Treachery'.
23. Smiley, *Irregular Regular*, p. 190.
24. Smiley, *Albanian Assignment*, p. 162.
25. Interview with David Smiley, London, 21 October 2005; Nicholas

Bethell, 'Interview with Colonel David Smiley 12 February 1981', in Elsie and Destani (eds), *The Albanian Operation of the CIA and MI6*, p. 149.
26. Lulushi, *Operation Valuable Fiend*, p. 80.
27. Nicholas Bethell, 'Transcript of Interview with David Smiley, 12 February 1981', in Elsie and Destani (eds), *The Albanian Operation of the CIA and MI6*, p. 149; Nicholas Bethell, 'Transcript of Interview with Anthony Northrop, March–April 1984', in Elsie and Destani (eds), *The Albanian Operation of the CIA and MI6*, pp. 132–9.
28. Nicholas Bethell, 'Transcript of Interview with Sam Barclay, 1 April 1981', in Elsie and Destani (eds), *The Albanian Operation of the CIA and MI6*, pp. 26–31.
29. Interview with David Smiley, London, 21 October 2005.
30. Lulushi, *Operation Valuable Fiend*, pp. 80–2.
31. TNA FO 1093/452, Top Secret: From Nigel Bicknell to Sir A. Rumbold , 'The Present Position of Operation Valuable', 11 October 1949.
32. TNA FO 1093/453, Top Secret: Albania, 15 November 1949.
33. Kim Philby, *My Silent War: The Autobiography of a Spy* (New York: Modern Library, 2002).
34. Bethell, *The Great Betrayal*, p. 99; Bethell, 'Interview with James Angleton, 4 April 1984', p. 26, in Elsie and Destani (eds), *The Albanian Operation of the CIA and MI6*, p. 149; Robin W. Winks, *Cloak and Gown: Scholars in the Secret War 1939–1961* (New Haven, CT/London: Yale University Press, 1987), p. 398.
35. IWM, Accession No: 10340/6 Transcript of Interview with Colonel D. Smiley, Recorded 1989, p. 59.
36. See, for example, Michael W. Dravis, 'Storming Fortress Albania: American Covert Operations in Microcosm, 1949–54', *Intelligence and National Security*, 7/4 (1992), p. 434; Thomas Rees, 'Blunder and Betrayal in the Balkans', *The Guardian Weekend*, 10 October 1998, pp. 20–6.
37. Gordon Corera, *The Art of Betrayal: Life and Death in the British Secret Service* (London: Weidenfeld & Nicolson, 2011), p. 74.
38. Tom Winnifrith, 'A Betrayal Betrayed: Kim Philby and Albania', in James Pettifer (ed.), *Albania and the Balkans*, pp. 96–118; Lulushi, *Operation Valuable Fiend*, pp. 85–6.
39. Secret Draft Memorandum. Subject: Factors Affecting Continuation of Operations in Malta 21 October 1949, available at <https://www.cia.gov/library/readingroom/docs/OBOPUS%20BGFIEND%20%

20%20VOL.%2014%20%20%28BGFIEND%20OPERATIONS%29_0098.pdf> (last accessed 29 October 2017).
40. TNA FO 1093/452, Top Secret: Albania – Intelligence Summary, 16 November 1949.
41. CIA-RDP82–00457R003600100001–4: Confidential. Subject: Alleged Yugoslav Operations into Albania, 24 October 1949. US–Yugoslav intelligence collaboration over Albania was the subject of a BBC Radio 4 Documentary. Presented by Gordon Corera, 'The Albanian Operation', *Document*, BBC Radio 4, Broadcast 5 July 2016, available at <http://www.bbc.co.uk/programmes/b07j4ppw> (last accessed 6 December 2018).
42. Lulushi, *Operation Valuable Fiend*, p. 86.
43. Top Secret. Report of Interview between Colonel Smiley and Zotos, available at <https://www.cia.gov/library/readingroom/docs/OBOPUS%20BGFIEND%20%20%20VOL.%2014%20%20%28BGFIEND%20OPERATIONS%29_0098.pdf> (last accessed 29 October 2017).
44. Bethell, *The Great Betrayal*, p. 143.
45. TNA FO 1093/453, Secret and Personal to Frederick Hoyer-Millar, KCMG CVP Washington from Foreign Office, 2 January 1950.
46. Richard J. Aldrich, *The Hidden Hand: Britain, America and Cold War Secret Intelligence* (London: John Murray, 2001), p. 164.
47. Corera, 'The Albanian Operation'.
48. 'The Cost of Treachery'.
49. IWM, Accession No: 10340/6 Transcript of Interview with Colonel D. Smiley, Recorded 1989, p. 60. The value of Philby's treachery in the eyes of Moscow and Tirana was perhaps in corroborating what they already knew. See Stephen Grey, *The New Spymasters: Inside Espionage from the Cold War to Global Terror* (London: Penguin/Viking, 2015), pp. 46–7.
50. The other officer was Valerian Wellesley, later the Duke of Wellington, who succeeded Smiley in command of the Blues.
51. Interview with David Smiley, London, 21 October 2005.
52. David Smiley, interviewed on 'Time Watch – The People's Coronation', BBC2, 18 May 2007; 'Crowning Glory: Interview with a Ceremonial Escort', *Royal Insight*, May 2003, available at <www.royal.gov.uk/output/Page2285.asp> (last accessed 20 May 2006).
53. Interview with Xan Smiley, Taston, Oxfordshire, 30 June 2006.

54. Interview with David Smiley, London, 21 October 2005.
55. Interview with David Smiley, London, 21 October 2005.
56. Interview with Moy Smiley, 22 February 2006.
57. Interview with Xan Smiley, Taston, Oxfordshire, 30 June 2006.

11 As Tough as Teak

I

It was only Julian Amery who could have persuaded Smiley to put his Kenyan plans on hold. The terms of his departure from the army had already been approved. He had decided to forgo his army pension and instead to accept a one-off payment of £8,000 known as a 'golden bowler' (which he later regretted), and looked to enrol at the Egerton Agricultural College, near the Kenyan town of Nakuru, to learn to farm in Kenya.[1] Instead, Amery persuaded Smiley to consider one final post, arguing that he was the most qualified to take on the role he had in mind: commanding officer of the Muscat and Oman Field Force. Smiley later referred to it as his Albanian past catching up with him, but even so, he hardly knew where Oman was and even less about its politics. But Amery was convinced he was the right man for the job. It required pluck, tenacity, courage and not a little diplomatic nous. Smiley would very much become poacher turned gamekeeper.

In 1958, the Sultan of Muscat and Oman faced a serious rebellion. Poverty-stricken and ruled as an absolute monarchy under Sultan Said Bin Taimur al-Said, Oman was a little-known corner of Arabia, framed by the Arabian sea to the south and the Persian Gulf to the north-east, and bordered inland by the great sand sea of the Empty Quarter, the Rub al-Khali. Its ties to Britain could be traced back to the seventeenth century and the East India Company. Subsequent treaties recognised the independence of the Sultan but Oman was, in effect, a fiefdom of Britain, which offered defence guarantees that helped secure its trade routes to India and other far-flung outposts of empire. The discovery of

The Clandestine Lives of Colonel David Smiley

Fig. 11.1 Map of Oman.

oil in the Arabian Peninsula and the prospect that commercial quantities might be found in Oman's arid interior inflated the country's economic and strategic importance.

Said Bin Taimur had inherited a husk of a country when he ascended to the throne in 1932. His granting of a concession to explore for oil to Petroleum Development Oman and Dhofar Ltd (PD(O)), whose shareholders included Shell and the Anglo-Persian Oil company (later British Petroleum), was the only modern development he had allowed. In the 1950s, around three-quarters of all babies born were reckoned to die: trachoma and malnutrition were widespread. There were only three schools and a single hospital in Muscat, run by American missionaries. Some have explained Bin Taimur's extreme parsimony by him having inherited a bankrupt state from his profligate father. Whatever the cause, by the 1950s, discontent had spread across a predominantly tribal society, discontent that others were now ready to exploit.[2]

A rebellion had broken out in the interior, concentrated in and around the oasis town of Nizwa at the foot of the massif that is the Jebel Akhdar. Led by Imam Ghalib bin Ali and his brother Talib, and enjoying the support of Sheikh Suleiman bin Himyar of the Beni Riyam, whose tribe dominated the Jebel, the rebellion had religious overtones that challenged the legitimacy of the Sultan among the tribes who piously followed a strict *Ibadhi* interpretation of Islam. The rebels also enjoyed powerful foreign sponsors in Egypt and, importantly, Saudi Arabia. It was an uneasy alliance, for President Nasser regarded dynastic regimes as antediluvian, but both Cairo and Riyadh saw an advantage in challenging the last vestiges of British colonial rule in the Middle East. Nasser, in particular, resented the Sultan's reliance on British protection as the epitome of a nefarious imperial power defending a regressive potentate, the very antithesis of the Arab pride and social progress that he claimed to represent. But it was Saudi Arabia and the United States that offered the more potent challenge to British interests in Oman.

Competing claims to territory thought to contain oil had long soured relations between Riyadh and Muscat, and complicated those with London. The Buraimi Oasis was contested by Saudi

Arabia on the one hand, and the Trucial State of Abu Dhabi and the Sultanate of Muscat and Oman on the other. Diplomatic ties between Britain and Saudi Arabia had been broken when the Trucial Oman Scouts, led and officered by the British, evicted a Saudi police contingent in 1955 after the failure of international arbitration over the contested oasis. London blamed Riyadh, as it had evidence that the Saudis had been trying to bribe members of the International Court of Justice.[3] The British also suspected that the Arabian–American Oil Company (ARAMCO) had a hand in the Saudi intrigue, as it sought to expand its oil interests at the expense of rival companies under British patronage. The crisis over Buraimi therefore had more than just a symbolic value for the British: it was a test case regarding how far London was prepared to defend its energy security in the face of the Saudi state and its Omani protégés, who had close ties with Washington.

In the aftermath of the Suez crisis and the humiliating British climbdown under pressure from the Eisenhower administration, the British government was keen that further military engagements in the Middle East remain discreet. The Foreign Office wanted to avoid overt displays of British martial prowess that might inflame Arab nationalist sentiment or provide Washington and its proxies with the opportunity to gain influence at the expense of the Sultan. But Saudi Arabia saw an advantage to be had in arming the forces of Ghalib bin Ali, whose opposition to the Sultan was bolstered by two powerful tribes, the Beni Riyam and the Beni Hinna in the region of the Jebel Akhdar. Based on this vast mountain and supplied with weapons and mines smuggled from a Saudi military base at Dahran, the rebels (later to be called the Oman Rebel Army, or ORA) laid landmines on the few passable roads linking Muscat to the north and east of the sultanate. Crucially, this endangered travel and oil exploration as the rebels attacked the few viable communication routes between Muscat and the interior. This was brought home to Whitehall when, in July 1957, rebel forces virtually annihilated a column of the British-led Muscat and Oman Field Force on the approaches to Nizwa. While a contingent of British troops eventually pushed the rebels back to the sanctuary of the Jebel Akhdar, they were too few to inflict any real punishment on the insurgents. Moreover, the Foreign Office, mindful of international opprobrium from other Arab states at the United Nations over accusations of British imperialism, was unwilling to increase the extent of British military involvement any further.[4]

It was against this background that, at the end of December 1957, Amery arrived in the Sultanate. He was dismayed by what he saw: the Muscat and Oman Field Force lacked not just the necessary men and equipment, but also, above all else, decisive leadership. They had been led by Brigadier Patrick Waterfield, a former gunner in the Indian army, whose military limitations had been cruelly exposed outside Nizwa. Amery later noted that 'the Muscat Officers are mostly poor – not on top of the job – they do not demonstrate any leadership'. He described Waterfield as 'essentially a staff officer'.[5]

Confident of his diplomatic wiles, Amery now persuaded the otherwise recalcitrant Sultan to accept that his armed forces be reorganised as a matter of urgency to counter the rebellion. He also agreed, albeit reluctantly, to a civil development programme to address the social (if not political) grievances that Amery knew underpinned tribal support for the rebel leadership. Britain would have to foot the initial bill, estimated at around £540,000 in capital expenditure and £374,000 in recurrent expenditure, an amount the British government clearly hoped to recoup if oil was struck in commercial quantities.[6] But most pressing for Amery was instilling a fighting spirit in a revamped Omani military that could not only defeat the rebels on the Jebel Akhdar, but equally prevent further Saudi (and suspected American) support for the rebels.

On his return to London, it was clear that Amery only ever had one candidate in mind to rebuild and lead the Muscat and Oman Field Force: Smiley. On 22 February 1958, he wrote to the Sultan:

> Smiley has been one of my closest friends for years. We served together with the Albanian guerrillas during the war and I know of no one with whom I would rather go 'tiger shooting'. Your highness will find him brave, honourable and imperturbable. As an officer who has served in the Queen's Household Regiments he knows the highest standards of service. As a successful guerrilla leader he also knows how to organise

and lead less experienced troops. I have every confidence that your highness will be well and faithfully served by this officer.[7]

But Smiley would have to serve two masters: his appointment needed to be cleared with the headquarters of Land Forces Persian Gulf in Bahrain, whose parish and commitments in terms of manpower and equipment included Muscat and Oman. While this fell under the newly formed Middle East Command in Aden, it was to Bahrain that the commander of the Sultan's forces was, in the first instance, to refer in matters of military support. The War Office cable recommending Smiley's appointment to Land Forces Persian Gulf was fulsome in its praise, noting that his experience and style of leadership were particularly suited for the conditions in Oman:

> He is essentially a commander with a bent for guerrilla warfare and one who get results by precept and example rather than by coercion. He draws wholehearted co-operation from his subordinates by reason of the confidence that he inspires in them. He is resourceful, determined and has good powers of command.[8]

But despite these glowing references, Smiley questioned his own suitability. He neither spoke Arabic nor had served alongside Arab troops. Amery's reply was unequivocal: he had more experience of guerrilla warfare than almost any serving officer in the British army, while his three years in Stockholm had given him experience of the many ways of kings, diplomats and courtesans.[9] Still, Smiley's final acceptance of the post was conditional on his wife's agreement and on knowing the terms and conditions of his service. Moy was decidedly enthusiastic, easing his decision to accept a post that meant putting a new life in Kenya on hold. He would become the commander of the Muscat and Oman Field Force with the rank of full colonel, with the remit, first, to reorganise and retrain the armed forces, and second, to prosecute a successful campaign against the rebels on the Jebel Akhdar.

This had now become more urgent because, from their mountain sanctuary, they were now making regular forays to lay mines. Meanwhile, the smuggling of arms by dhow and camel from

As Tough as Teak

Saudi Arabia was becoming more blatant as the rebels sensed the weakness of the Sultan's ability to respond.[10] Indeed, despite being owed six weeks' leave after returning from Sweden, Smiley was given only ten days of what he recalled 'frantic preparation' before he finally arrived at Beit al-Falaj, the headquarters of the Muscat and Oman Field Force just outside Muscat, on 18 April 1958. What he discovered on arrival appalled and infuriated him in equal measure.

II

Smiley knew from his official briefings and discussions with Amery that conditions in Oman would be tough. His total force consisted of 23 contract officers (12 British, 6 Pakistani and 5 Arabs) and 848 men, the bulk of whom were divided between two undermanned regiments comprising less than a battalion each – the Muscat Regiment and the Northern Frontier Regiment (NFR) – while artillery was limited to two 5.5 inch guns. This meagre force was supplemented by two squadrons of the Trucial Oman Scouts, two troops of the 13/18 Hussars with four Ferret armoured cars each, and eight Royal Marines attached as instructors to the NFR. The navy was almost non-existent, save for a few dhows pressed into half-hearted anti-smuggling operations, while the air force consisted of two small Pioneer reconnaissance aircraft, plus a smattering of RAF signalmen based at Beit al-Falaj, who provided communications links to Bahrain. The soldiers of the Muscat Regiment and NFR were a mix of Arabs and Baluchis from the Omani coastal enclave of Gwadur and beyond that had only recently been returned to Pakistan. The quality of these troops varied but morale was decidedly low. The NFR was still licking its wounds after the debacle around Nizwa, while the need to man various positions in and around the capital meant that the Muscat Regiment was unable to operate as a coherent unit against the rebels. Adding to his woes, Smiley had no in-house intelligence, while the Sultan showed no serious desire to acquire it, much beyond the ad hoc efforts of individuals who reported to him directly.[11]

His problems were further compounded by the quality of the contract officers nominally under his command. The presence of contract officers in the Muscat and Oman Field Force was deliberate, an expression of the Sultan's distrust of developing an indigenous officer corps. He reckoned that the spate of coups across the Middle East in the 1950s had been the work of mid-ranking Arab officers.[12] Contract officers – mercenaries by any other name – were unlikely to bite the hand that fed them. But Smiley found them a 'very mixed bag'; some were 'high grade although the general average was poor'. Because such officers were employed by the Sultan, their dismissal lay within his gift. Smiley could only recommend their removal and on several occasions this occurred, mainly for drunkenness and dishonesty, but blatant acts of homosexuality that could not be covered up also resulted in contracts being terminated.[13]

Those few contract officers that Smiley regarded as 'high grade' were, however, very good indeed. He found Lieutenant Colonel Colin Maxwell, late of the Royal Scots Fusiliers, who became his deputy commander, to be of inestimable value. His local knowledge of Oman and Omanis, born of his time commanding the NFR, was more than equalled by the affection in which he was held by his troops. Major Malcolm Dennison, a former wartime RAF officer, was the effective embodiment of the total Muscat and Oman Field Force intelligence capability. He had an anthropologist's eye, understood full well the tribal landscape and was fluent in Arabic. He gently cajoled, rather than forced, information from informants and captured enemy alike, and gave Smiley at least the kernel of expertise around which a better, more professional intelligence organisation could be built. Even so, he soon discovered that, in the Sultan's mind, intelligence was akin to subversion. Moreover, the Sultan had a particular dislike for Dennison, having taken umbrage over a previous slight, and had expressly forbidden his intelligence-gathering activities among the tribes. Smiley cunningly overcame this by making Dennison a 'recruiting officer', the perfect cover that allowed him to continue his intelligence work unhindered by the Sultan's diktat.[14]

Still, contract officers were often wont to discuss and debate the wisdom of Smiley's orders, rather than instantly obey his commands, as normally befits a military hierarchy. Breaking the grip of the 'contract officer's mess' if the Muscat and Oman Field Force was to operate effectively was clearly necessary but could not be achieved by admonishing individuals. Smiley's ability to lead by 'precept and example' was sorely needed throughout his three years in Oman, and at times he felt that even this was insufficient. But after the defeats around Nizwa, many of the contract officers found him a breath of fresh air. One, Philip Allfree, wrote:

> David Smiley was an exceptional man. He was short, with unblinking eyes and a flat mild face like a parson. He was as tough as teak. . . . He had friends in the most lofty of places, an unslakable thirst for danger. . . . Whoever chose him for us was a genius, for Smiley's combination of guerrilla pugnacity and Guards punctilio was really what we had been needing for a long time.[15]

Change was clearly needed – and fast. Smiley looked to bring in regular British army officers on secondment as staff officers and in combat roles. Accompanying him to Muscat had been Major John Goddard, a Royal Engineer, who would serve as a staff officer overseeing and implementing Smiley's plans for the restructuring and retraining of the Muscat and Oman Field Force. Conscientious and efficient, he was somewhat deferential to regulations but Smiley found him invaluable. The same could not be said of Waterfield. His disastrous leadership of the Muscat and Oman Field Force had prompted calls for his removal in Whitehall but the Sultan would have none of it. Instead, he made him Military Secretary – in effect, his Minister of Defence – which allowed him considerable influence over who, what and when was allowed access to the Sultan. Even though Smiley's terms of service supposedly gave him right of access, the reality was often decidedly different: Smiley had to negotiate meetings or rely on Waterfield to pass on messages, pending a decision from the Sultan. On more than one occasion, Smiley discovered that Waterfield made policy decisions without even passing on such requests, despite having claimed to have done so. Always a somewhat testy relationship, it had decidedly soured by the time Smiley left Oman three years later.[16]

But domestic issues of an altogether different nature almost ended Smiley's service in Oman before it began. In London, he had been assured that accommodation in Beit al-Falaj would be of a standard and size that would allow his family to stay for extended periods during the cooler months of the year. What was presented to him by Waterfield on his arrival left him aghast: a squat bungalow of just three rooms, no air conditioning, little furniture and a complete absence of ablutions, save for the use of old four-gallon oil drums filled with water and a 'thunder box' left in one bedroom to answer the call of nature. Quite reasonably, Smiley felt he had been tricked: Waterfield was the author of the original signal to London that promised a house with thirteen rooms and adequate ventilation that awaited his arrival. It had helped sway Smiley into accepting the posting. These living quarters were clearly inadequate and 'I was damned if I would impose it [the accommodation] on Moy.' To add insult to injury, he had to pay for his accommodation out of his own salary. He almost resigned on the spot. But as a child of the Kenyan bush, Moy was forthright: 'Nonsense: You stick it out and I'll join you there in the autumn. Just put up with it till then.' Smiley was not the only one as 'tough as teak'.[17]

Stiffened by his wife's resolve, he now set about shaking the forces under his command out of their defensive mind-set. To do this, he needed the backing of the Commander Land Forces Persian Gulf in Bahrain, Brigadier Edward Tinker, and the political resident, Sir Bernard Burrows, whose political masters in the Foreign Office remained wary of any brazen use of military force. At the same time, Smiley remained under the command of the Sultan, unless the orders he received from him clashed directly with British interests, in which case he was to refer to the Foreign Office. Smiley knew he required his approval if his overhaul, retraining and expansion of the armed forces was to win the ultimate dividend: the defeat of the rebel forces. He soon learned, however, that Sultan Said Bin Taimur spent as little time as he possibly could in Muscat, much preferring the isolation of his palace on the shoreline in Salalah, over 500 miles away to the south in Dhofar.

At their first meeting, a week after his arrival in Oman, Smiley was left in little doubt as to the Sultan's intent. While determined

Fig. 11.2 Smiley with Sultan Said bin Taimur, Salalah, 1958.

to see the back of the rebels, he was unwilling to release the funds to do so, either to support the modernisation and expansion of his own armed forces or to invest in the infrastructure of his country – roads, schools, hospitals – whose paucity had help stir up the rebellion in the first instance. Schools, the Sultan feared, were vassals for spreading 'Nasser's seditious ideas'; hospitals were not needed because the country could not sustain a large population. This attitude often led Smiley to ponder whether he was fighting for the wrong side; faced with such social and economic injustice, he fully appreciated why so many Omanis, especially in the interior, supported the forces of Ghalib bin Ali.[18]

The one concrete result of the meeting was that the Sultan announced that Smiley would be appointed as Commander, rather than Chief of Staff, of what would now be known as the Sultan's Armed Forces (SAF), and that it would reorganised along the lines of a regular British army brigade. This was to be a rare example of a clear, positive decision taken by an individual that, in his private correspondence with friends and family, Smiley increasingly referred to as his 'lord and master'. Future requests for resources – be it men or matériel – were, more often than not, met by the Sultan's standard refrain, 'I see Colonel Smiley, I see. I will think about it.'

This meant that Smiley had to rely on Brigadier Tinker, Middle East Command in Aden, and his own bloody-mindedness to get the SAF in anything like a fit state to fight the rebels. His bloody-mindedness he could rely on; the other two, less so. He did enjoy good relations, initially at least, with Tinker but subsequent communications with him and the political resident in Bahrain, Sir Bernard Burrows, made it clear that his hands were tied by a combination of financial constraints and what Smiley regarded as a rather supine attitude to political risk. Given the rugged mountain terrain of northern Oman around the Jebel Akhdar, he saw a clear need for at least five key elements if, as the newly appoint *al-Qaid* (commander) of the SAF, he was to defeat the rebels: up to twenty-five seconded officers from the British army directly under his command; the expansion and deepening of the intelligence capabilities of the SAF; the introduction of assault pioneers to help with road construction, demolitions, mine clearance and the provision of basic infrastructure; the supply of donkeys or mules to carry food, water and heavier weaponry in mountainous terrain; and the expansion of the Omani air force beyond its puny collection of two Pioneer aircraft.[19]

These proposals inevitably met with resistance. The Foreign Office, mindful that the British government would have to 'foot the bill', disputed the numbers of assault pioneers requested, as well as the cost of importing donkeys from Somalia. The real stumbling block, however, was the Foreign Office insistence that, before the proposals were agreed by the Sultan, they be submitted to Waterfield's scrutiny, in effect giving him a veto over Smiley's plans.

This is precisely what happened. Waterfield raised objections with the Foreign Office that Smiley's proposals 'would add considerably to the already increasing costs of the reorganisation'.[20] Such penny-pinching by Whitehall and Waterfield, the latter with the apparent blessing of the Sultan, constantly worried and frustrated Smiley throughout his tenure as CSAF. It proved equally exasperating for his colleague, Colonel Hugh Boustead, who, as an old Arabian hand of immense experience, had been appointed to oversee civil development across the sultanate. In a private letter to Amery written while on leave in the summer of 1959, Smiley vented his spleen over British parsimony: 'My views on the political future of Oman can be briefly summed up by that homely American proverb: "Either piss or get off the pot".'[21]

Some progress was made: he did, for example, reach a compromise over the recruitment of assault pioneers. He was allowed to raise a platoon attached to SAF headquarters, the view being that, over time, their skills would cascade down to regular infantry companies. Progress too was made in seconding officers from the British army, although never in the numbers Smiley felt were needed to make up for the poor leadership of many of the contract officers. He desperately needed more time and resources at a time when the rebels on Jebel Akhdar were becoming more active and daring in their mining activities. Just how daring, he was soon to discover.

It was not until he made his own forays into the interior of Oman that Smiley fully understood the magnitude of the task before him. Throughout May and June 1958, he toured the base of the Jebel Akhdar, accompanied by Sayyid Tariq, the Sultan's half-brother and Minister of the Interior. Unlike the semi-reclusive Sultan, Sayyid Tariq not only was well educated, having attended the University of Heidelberg, but also was popular among many of the tribes of the interior. Because of this, the Sultan was 'jealous and afraid' of him and used his control over the meagre state coffers to curb the activities of his sibling by threatening to withhold his stipend. Tariq, however, proved instrumental in allowing Smiley a glimpse of the tribal eddies and rivalries that defined the Omani political landscape and helped fan the Imam's rebellion. Outside Nizwa, the writ of the government was largely unknown and Smiley had to proceed with care through villages known to be sympathetic to the rebels. The ever-present threat of a sniper attack, combined with travel on rough tracks, made progress difficult. The overwhelming concern, however, was mines. The rebels' widespread use of mines – very much akin to the Improvised Explosive Devices that caused such mayhem in Iraq and Afghanistan – was meant not only to disrupt SAF columns and undermine the Sultan's authority, but also to deny access to the PD(O) in their search for oil, on which the future viability of the Sultanate largely rested. These mines, mainly of American manufacture, were relatively small and designed to blow a wheel off a Land Rover or armoured car. Later, larger plastic mines that were harder to detect were smuggled in from Saudi Arabia, some overland, others by sea along the Batinah coast. Despite protests by London, the Americans claimed they had no control over how the Saudis used such military supplies, though Smiley felt this was little more than a ruse. It was alleged that ARAMCO, with its intimate ties to Washington and Riyadh, had let the smugglers use their fuel dumps before crossing the almost invisible frontier that separated the Sultanate from the Kingdom. Some commentators, notably the historian of the Arabian Gulf, J. B. Kelly, went further: 'The rebels were', he argued, 'in regular wireless communication with both the Saudis and the Central Intelligence Agency,' although the actual source of this claim is unclear.[22]

Still, almost all officers and men of the SAF and many employees of the PD(O) had been blown up or had several near-misses with mines around Nizwa and below the Jebel Akhdar. They almost visited personal tragedy on Smiley. During the course of a later visit to the Omani interior, a Land Rover carrying Moy and their young son, Philip, ran over a mine that failed to detonate. Others were not so lucky. When SAF men were killed, Smiley thought that convicted minelayers should be shot rather than sent to prison. Given his own experience of guerrilla war, he had little sympathy for the methods of the rebels, as opposed to their wider cause.[23] At the very least, he believed harsh measures, including house demolitions, should be meted out to villages suspected of aiding and abetting those laying mines. He acknowledged that, having laid his own fair share of these explosive devices during his time in Albania, it was 'galling to find himself at the receiving end'.[24] As the fate that befell the village of Muti showed, he had little hesitation in practising what he preached if, as a professional soldier, he thought it served the purpose of deterrence.

If the morale of the SAF was to improve, Smiley knew it could not wait upon the requested military manna he had asked for from Bahrain and the Foreign Office. He urged the SAF to be more aggressive with patrols around the base of the Jebel Akhdar and to try to impede the supply routes used by Ghalib and his tribal supporters to reach the plateau. Smiley led some of these patrols himself, with Tariq often in tow; others were led by the handful of Royal Marine NCOs attached to the Muscat Regiment and NFR, whose aggressive leadership Smiley greatly valued. On 17 June 1958, one of the NCOs leading these patrols was killed in a well-prepared ambush close to the village of Muti. The SAF men with him assumed that the perpetrators had been helped by the villagers, many of whom had already been suspected of harbouring mines and small arms for the rebels. It determined Sayyid Tariq to rid Muti once and for all of its insurgents. A force of SAF and Tariq's own tribal militia (*askers*) were assembled and, under the command of Smiley and Tariq, burned the village to the ground. Perhaps knowing its fate, the village had been completely emptied of all its inhabitants before this act of vengeance was wrought.[25]

III

The challenge of conquering the Jebel Akhdar was as much psychological as it was physical. Rising from the coastal plain, the Jebel is nearly 50 miles in length and 20 miles wide. On top is a large, undulating plateau, punctuated by hills and surrounded by jagged peaks, some rising to 10,000 feet on its northern flank, thereby creating a natural fortress. Snow on the higher peaks in winter is not unknown. In 1958, this plateau, itself 20 miles long and 10 miles across at its widest point, housed a cluster of villages such as Saiq and Sharaijah, which were self-sufficient in food and water, and steadfast in their allegiance to Sheikh Suleiman. Together with Ghalib and Talib, Suleiman sheltered in a string of caves across the plateau, almost impervious to aerial attack, despite the best efforts of RAF Shackletons and rocket-firing Venoms that had bombed and strafed the plateau at intervals from 1957 onwards. The exact number of the rebels was hard to assess with any degree of accuracy: some estimates suggested 60–100 of the Beni Riyam trained by the Saudis, and able to call perhaps on another 400–500 tribesmen, some from the Beni Hinna, who formed defensive pickets along the main routes leading up to the plateau.[26] Smiley had spent much of May and early June 1958 visiting various *walis* (in effect, government representatives) in villages to the south and west of the Jebel, where he would 'fuddle', a corruption of the Arabic *Fadel*, meaning to eat or drink, with the local inhabitants. It not only was a matter of courtesy but also occasionally allowed the odd nugget of information to surface that could help build up an appreciation of the rebels.

At the end of June, Smiley conducted a more detailed reconnaissance around the whole base circumference of the Jebel Akhdar, covering nearly 900 miles. This impressed on Smiley the sheer number of potential routes up the Jebel, along which the rebels could be resupplied. While he could block the more obvious approaches to Ghalib's redoubt, the forces under his command were 'totally inadequate' to enforce an effective blockade. This point had been brought home most forcefully earlier that month. A 3 ton lorry carrying 4 Browning heavy machine guns, 9 mortars, 13 Bren guns and ammunition, all accompanied by forty tribesmen, managed to drive from Sharjah down the Batinah coast, before turning into the Wadi Beni Kharus, where their cargo was unloaded and transported by donkey up to the top of the Jebel.[27]

Though a more aggressive spirit was slowly being instilled in the patrols of the SAF, Smiley knew they were well below brigade strength and nowhere near capable of defeating Ghalib and his rebels. He had already approached Christopher Soames, son-in-law of Winston Churchill, who, as Secretary of State for War, had been visiting Sharjah, and asked him for a brigade of British troops, preferably paratroopers, Royal Marines or indeed elements of the SAS, to be sent to Oman to help defeat the rebels. Soames, a close friend of Amery, was sympathetic but could not promise anything more than perhaps two battalions of infantry, troops Smiley felt would struggle to cope with the physical demands of soldiering in such an unforgiving environment. Still, Smiley's approach to Soames went over the normal chain of command; by rights, it should have been made through Tinker in Bahrain and Middle East Command in Aden. The RAF, however, oversaw Middle East Command, and while Smiley praised it for

Fig. 11.3 An Omani 'fuddle' with the *Wali* of Buraimi.

the air-to-ground support he got from its Venom fighters in particular, he felt strongly that Aden should never have been an RAF command at all, given the overwhelming ground nature of the war. The limits placed by Aden on how and when RAF transport aircraft could be used in support of the SAF were also a particular irritant.[28] More broadly, though, Smiley believed official policy towards Oman was inhibited by a Foreign Office wary of the regional opprobrium that British ties with Muscat provoked. As a secret SAS briefing paper noted, 'The UK Government is highly sensitive to accusations of meddling in another country's affairs – however justified they may be – and even though [British military] action is [being] taken at the request of the Sultan.'[29]

At the end of September 1958, Smiley returned to Britain for what should have been a period of leave. Instead, he spent time meeting Soames and Amery, arguing forcefully for reinforcements, which, if sent, would allow the SAF to assault the Jebel over the winter months with a fair chance of success. Again, Smiley was circumventing the official chain of command, using personal contacts with ministers to do his bidding with the chiefs of staff in London and the Cabinet. It was unorthodox but he felt he had no choice. He had already been forthright in outlining the consequences of failing to defeat the rebels on Jebel Akhdar. If the SAF then lost Nizwa and Izki to Talib and Ghalib, tribes now sitting on the fence would come over to the rebels, lines of communication could be cut and eventually Muscat would be taken by the rebels as the SAF collapsed. This worst case scenario resonated with Amery, who was keen to see resources pushed Smiley's way. Given his role in persuading his former comrade in arms to go to Oman, he also felt a personal responsibility.[30]

In fact, in the summer of 1958, consideration had been given by the chiefs of staff to a much larger-scale operation to defeat the rebels – Operation Dermot – which would, at its most expansive, have involved an aircraft carrier, two infantry battalions (one of which would have been Gurkhas), two companies from the Parachute Regiment and several batteries of artillery. It was eventually cancelled because of Iraqi threats to the territorial integrity of Kuwait, as well as Foreign Office objections to the 'noise' such an operation would inevitably entail. This forced a radical rethink.[31] A much more modest plan considered was to select five or six specially trained British officers, accompanied by bodyguards and an English-speaking interpreter, who would sally forth into the foothills of the Jebel Akhdar, laden with cash with which to bribe tribesmen of the Beni Riyam and Hinna, and would gradually establish an effective network of informers. Leading rebels would thus be captured, turned or, if circumstances dictated otherwise, ambushed by 'killer squads'.[32] By gaining access to the plateau by subterfuge, they would bring the rebellion to an end.

The architect of this plan, Major Frank Kitson, had cut his counter-insurgency teeth using such methods against the Mau Mau rebellion in Kenya, counter-gangs proving particularly effective in the thick Kenyan forests where many Mau Mau sought refuge.[33] Dennison, however, thought the plan flawed: conditions on the Jebel were far removed from those in the Kenyan bush. There was scant cover, little water and no chance that a British officer, however well versed in Arabic and the local customs, could pass himself off as a native. It was hard enough for a tribesman. Dennison had learned this lesson the hard way. He had managed to procure the services of one member of the Beni Riyam intimately familiar with the Jebel. Briefed in great secrecy, he was assassinated in the village of Qarut before he had got anywhere near his intended area of operations.[34]

Still, the pressure Smiley asserted in Whitehall through Soames and Amery began to take effect. The director of military operations, Lieutenant General Hamilton, now suggested that a squadron from 22 SAS could be spared to help the SAF. The suggestion combined an element of instrumentalism with happenstance: having helped suppress communist insurgents in Malaya in a campaign lasting over a decade, the SAS could now be committed elsewhere where a light footprint or, better still, deniability could be assured. It was also a deployment that could reinforce the importance of retaining a special forces capability at a time when some might question their continued relevance in the British army's order of battle.[35] It also appealed to the Middle East Command, who reckoned the SAS could meet two apparently contradictory demands: to quell the rebellion but without making a diplomatic noise. Timing, too, was important: any operation had to be conducted in winter while the temperature remained tolerable. The Foreign Office, still wary about the deployment of British troops, also remained keen that any operation be concluded by the end of March, as the United Nations was due to discuss colonialism and the Middle East the following month. British military operations in support of an antediluvian potentate would prove politically uncomfortable if fighting was still ongoing and casualties proved heavy.

With the backing of Amery and Soames, Smiley received 'D' Squadron 22 SAS in November 1958. He had also procured the services of a squadron of the Life Guards with Ferret scout cars, ideal for protecting convoys and able to withstand the mine blasts that had proved so costly. He felt strongly, none the less, that the SAS should play a supporting role to the SAF; after all, it had been the soldiers of the NFR and the Muscat Regiment that had incurred the most casualties but were now taking the war to the rebels. Moreover, their knowledge of the Jebel was still much greater than that of the British special forces. They had already occupied the small town of Tanuf and held it against a determined rebel attack, severing the last supply line negotiable by donkeys and camels that had hitherto carried heavy weaponry and supplies to the summit of the Jebel. Amid the acclaim heaped on the SAS for their prowess in eventually conquering the Jebel Akhdar, it was often forgotten that a patrol of the NFR led by a contract officer, Major Tony Hart, had discovered a route to the top of the Jebel – the so-called Hajar track – that was unguarded, a priceless achievement that Smiley was keen to exploit to the full. The increasingly aggressive patrolling of the SAF, combined with an aerial campaign using 1,000 lb bombs that hit what passed for infrastructure on the Jebel – primarily cultivated areas, livestock and water supplies – was also having an effect.[36] Whatever the moral issues involved in using such heavy ordinance – Parliament was informed only well after the bulk of rebels had surrendered or fled – Smiley received growing anecdotal evidence that many of the Beni Riyam had simply had enough.[37]

The commanding officer of 22 SAS, Lieutenant Colonel Anthony Deane-Drummond, saw things differently: the SAF would be the subordinate partner in support of the SAS and would consolidate positions once taken by his troops as they skirmished up towards the plateau. This was supported by the Commander in Chief of Middle East Command, Air Vice-Marshal Maurice Heath. In a kind but pointed missive to Smiley, he made the use of the SAS contingent on the SAF playing a support role and refused his request for a company of infantry to support his own plan for an assault up the Hajar track. The use of regular infantry soldiers, Heath reminded Smiley, had been denied by the British government and he certainly was not prepared to disobey his political master in London over the issue.[38]

This rather missed the point. Smiley had wanted an infantry company sent to Oman to release his own troops, supported by the SAS, to lead the assault. Damaging crossed wires over command responsibility was now a real possibility. Smiley, as commander of the SAF, believed overall leadership and responsibility for any ground operation lay with him. Regarding 'the interference from Aden to be almost intolerable', he now thought of resigning, deeming that the failure to exploit a clear opportunity, coupled with the strictures put in place giving primacy to the SAS over the

SAF, effectively questioned the competence of the latter and, by extension, the viability of his own plans.³⁹

Reason now prevailed. 'D' Squadron had begun to probe various routes up the Jebel from both the north and the south from late November. One half of the squadron managed to secure a toehold on the plateau some 2,500 yards from a feature called the Aqabat al Dhafar, where the SAS battle report later noted 'some spirited engagements were fought with a worthy enemy'. By the end of December, the SAS had the upper hand; but both Smiley and Deane-Drummond realised that another squadron would be required, alongside greater cooperation with elements of the SAF whose local knowledge, Deane-Drummond had now realised, was crucial. While glowing in his appreciation for these SAS operations, Smiley's assessment was blunt: '[I]n their [the SAS] initial appreciation of their task, they greatly underestimated the enemy.'

It remains moot whether an opportunity to wrest the Jebel Akhdar from Ghalib by exploiting the Hajar track was missed in December 1958. But by January 1959, with 'A' Squadron under Major John Cooper now in theatre, Smiley and Deane-Drummond worked together to plan an attack suited to overcoming the physical conditions on the Jebel and the political strictures laid down in Whitehall. Together, the SAS, SAF, the Trucial Oman Scouts and the RAF set up an operational base in Beit al-Falaj, with a forward tactical headquarters located at Nizwa coordinating the actual assault. Smiley was put in overall command, with Deane-Drummond appointed as his deputy. This gave Deane-Drummond operational control where required over all units, which included the SAF and SAS (code-named Vector Force), elements of the Trucial Oman Scouts seconded for the operation, and a squadron of the Life Guards. The battle plan that now unfolded was an expanded version of Smiley's original proposal, but more daring in the innovative use of new approaches up to the plateau that both Smiley and Deane-Drummond had identified through careful aerial reconnaissance. While an SAS presence remained on the Aqabat al Dhafar, it was some distance from the key rebel villages of Habib, Saiq and Sharaijah. Although Smiley knew that the main approaches to the plateau would be heavily guarded, he hoped that diversionary attacks along these routes by the NFR, plus a diversionary thrust from elements of 'D' Squadron SAS from Tanuf, would draw forces away from the main assault by the SAS. This was to advance up a previously unmapped route between two *wadis*, the Wadi Kamah and Wadi Suwaiq, to take the rebel strongholds on the plateau of Saiq and Sharaijah. These diversionary attacks grew in their intensity between 8 and 22 January 1959.[40]

The final assault was set for the end of January, allowing the SAS to make use of a full moon. While absolute secrecy was demanded, Dennison told tribal donkey handlers, pressed into service in support of the operation, that the main assault would be along the Tanuf track. Within twelve hours, news of the supposed route had reached the rebels. It was a brilliant act of deception, drawing away significant rebel forces from the actual route taken by the SAS, formidable as this was. Though several fierce engagements were fought between 26 and 27 January, casualties among the assault force were remarkably light. Three SAS soldiers were badly wounded when a sniper's bullet hit a grenade in a Bergen rucksack; two died. This loss of life could not, however, detract from what had been a remarkable feat of arms and physical endurance; the last time the Jebel had fallen to an attacking force had been to the Persians, well before the Christian era. The last feature, code-named 'Beercan', was secured just above Saiq in the early hours of 27 January when rebel resistance crumbled, helped by the rebels mistaking a series of much-needed parachute resupply drops as a full-blown airborne assault.[41]

The failure to kill or capture Ghalib, Talib and Suleiman was a disappointment; the trio managed to escape down the Muti ridge and eventually sought sanctuary in Saudi Arabia. But with their flight, the rebellion, at least in the name of the Imamate, had been crushed. Mortars, light machine guns, mines and a range of small arms were recovered while a treasure trove of documents was discovered in a labyrinth of caves used by Suleiman as his headquarters. Letters gave away the names of prominent individuals in Muscat, sheikhs, various *walis* and tribal elders who, despite proclamations of fidelity to the Sultan, had been helping the Imam by providing support for the minelayers and arms smugglers in the interior. Realising that a magnanimous gesture might ensure quiescence on the Jebel and prevent vendettas sowing the seed of future rebellion, Smiley instructed that all rebels who surrendered their arms be pardoned and allowed to return to their villages. It was an astute move: the Jebel Akhdar never again became a major redoubt for rebellion against the Sultan.

IV

The capture of the Jebel Akhdar was, in many ways, the apogee of Smiley's military career. From the near-disasters of 1957, he had retrained and expanded what had been an underfunded, poorly trained force that not only had contained the rebels, but had, from the autumn of 1958, conducted increasingly aggressive operations against their mountain redoubt. He had largely planned the final assault and exercised effective leadership over the disparate forces under his command as the attack worked through its phases. Since the quality of these forces varied and they had no previous experience of working together in combat, this was no mean achievement. Amery, by now Under-Secretary of State in the Colonial Office, wrote to Smiley:

> The conquest of the mountain is one of the best things that has happened since the [Second World] war and one of the few victories we can chalk up to our credit in the Middle East. . . . There has been very little publicity here but the cognoscenti here and in other countries have been suitably impressed.[42]

The cognoscenti in London appeared less so when it came to allocating awards and decorations. With the upcoming UN debate on the Middle East, the Foreign Office was still keen to ensure that the campaign was denied the oxygen of publicity.[43] Inevitably, and despite the order not to disclose details of the campaign to the media, accounts of the fighting were revealed after Deane-Drummond wrote an account in the spring of 1959 in *The Times*. This and other later accounts largely extolled the SAS; the role of the SAF, Trucial Oman Scouts and units such as the Life Guards was downplayed or ignored altogether. Smiley suspected that these leaks had been orchestrated. By basking in the limelight, the SAS helped ensure its survival.

Smiley did not begrudge the SAS its success. Indeed, he recommended Deane-Drummond for his DSO and fully supported the award of the MC to Major John Watts, Captain Peter de la Billière, Captain Rory Walker and Lieutenant Tony Jeapes for their outstanding bravery and leadership fighting up the Jebel.[44] But his efforts to have an Oman campaign medal struck for British troops who had served alongside the SAS came to nought, despite enlisting the help of Gavin Astor, who owned *The Times*. The government argued that British troops such as the Life Guards, who had provided invaluable fire support in the infantry role for the assaulting forces, were engaged in operations against the Sultan's enemies, rather than the Queen's. This arcane Whitehall logic meant they did not meet the criteria for a campaign medal. In light of the decorations given to the SAS, a double standard was glaring. Moreover, Smiley felt strongly that the role of the SAF should have been recognised, along with his own leadership, through the award of a DSO. It remained a deep source of personal grievance well into his old age that this was denied. As he was Commander of the SAF, no senior British officer above him could recommend him for the award, while the same argument over whether, in fact, he was fighting the Queen's enemies was again presented as a reason for withholding the DSO. The Queen herself later questioned why Smiley's role was never properly recognised.[45]

The culprit may have been Brigadier Tinker. While not entirely unsupportive of Smiley, he was unsympathetic towards the Sultan and, indeed, to the SAF, which he saw as a drain on his own resources at a time when the larger threat to British interests in the Gulf came from an increasingly aggressive Iraq with its claims on Kuwait. Tinker was labouring under his own constraints but Smiley suspected too that he was damned by the Brigadier's faint praise. By his own admission, Tinker had opposed Smiley's appointment on the grounds that 'someone who only marginally decided to take it [the role of CSAF] on, was not really in the frame of mind to make a success of it'.[46] Smiley had proved this doubter wrong but this did little to change the mind of an officer who politely chided Smiley for his vexed relationship with Waterfield and for doing little to assuage the strained relations between the contract officers and the Sultan's *éminence grise*. Smiley, in turn, somewhat disparaged Tinker, often referring to him as a 'desk wallah' within earshot of his children when they visited Muscat in their school holidays.[47] Moreover, Smiley's use of personal contacts to lobby for extra resources for the SAF rankled in both Bahrain and Aden because it clearly circumvented the chain of command, much to their embarrassment. His reward from the Sultan for helping to save his throne proved equally meagre: an Arabic coffee pot, made in London. He presented it to Smiley in Salalah with the words, 'Thank you for winning the war for me.'[48]

A sense of disillusion marked the rest of Smiley's time in Oman. On several occasions, he was approached by the Foreign Office to take military attaché posts elsewhere, including Jordan, where he would have held the rank of brigadier overseeing a large British military mission, but the War Office refused to let him go.[49] With the constant support of Moy, he agreed to soldier on until the end of his secondment when, finally, he could take his 'golden bowler' and settle down to farm in Kenya. The security situation in northern Oman remained tense, however, and while the Jebel Akhdar campaign had dealt a decisive blow to Ghalib and his followers, this was far from clear at the time. Mining and arms smuggling, sponsored by both Saudi Arabia and Iraq, continued, yet to Smiley, the Sultan was as remote as ever and his audiences less frequent. Communication was increasingly mediated through Waterfield, who was, in Smiley's eyes, an unreliable interlocutor who used his military rank to obfuscate the key decisions that now needed to be made.

The medieval cruelty of the regime was apparent to anyone who had the unpleasant task of visiting those incarcerated in Jalali prison overlooking Muscat's harbour. Prisoners in shackles were kept in dungeons without access to food or clean water. An arbitrary penal system had hardly moved beyond the Dark Ages. More than once, Smiley remonstrated with Waterfield over the prisoners' lack of clean water for washing and drinking; one political prisoner starved to death while others were fed at irregular intervals. Such interventions rarely improved conditions. For many, being sent to Jalali prison was tantamount to a death sentence.[50]

Jalali was a symptom of the myopia afflicting Anglo-Omani relations. Smiley clearly saw the need for radical political reform but the Foreign Office refused to lean on the Sultan, who now believed his dynasty to be secure. Oil had begun to flow from Omani wells, and while not yet in sufficient quantities to turn the Sultanate into a Nirvana, it none the less promised a handsome dividend that unsettling or unseating the Sultan might threaten. Smiley was not convinced. Saudi subversion continued and failure to address the social and economic malaise across Oman more forcefully threatened what gains had been made. In some secrecy and with the support of a British consul-general in Muscat, William Monteith, Smiley sent a signal to London warning of dire consequences if political reform were not forthcoming and asking for the Sultan to be deposed. The Foreign Office quickly poured cold water on the suggestion, but for a man who had always believed in the loyalty of service and the value of monarchy in any political system, this was a radical departure.[51] Just over a decade later, Said bin Taimur was indeed removed by a coup with the tacit support of Britain and the active involvement of British officials in Muscat.[52]

Improving security remained Smiley's priority, however, although the financial truculence of the Sultan and Waterfield's interference continued to inhibit his more wide-ranging reforms. He persuaded London to fund a limited expansion of the SAF and to help establish a gendarmerie to police Oman's border with the Trucial States and the Batinah coast, areas that needed a permanent security presence if the flow of arms and weapons to the remaining rebels was to be stemmed. He also wanted to expand the numbers of Omani Arabs within the SAF and promote those who had proved themselves on operations. One such soldier, Said Salim al-Wuhaybi, was one of the first Omanis to be commissioned by Smiley from the ranks, an early example of Omanisation, designed over time to train a cadre of officers who would replace foreign contract officers. It was an act of confidence in an individual that was to prove of particular benefit to Smiley in his later years, but at the time it ran very much against the wishes of a Sultan still wary of developing an indigenous officer corps.

The gathering of good intelligence was Smiley's most pressing challenge. The treasure trove of documents discovered in Suleiman's cave, while a godsend, highlighted the complete lack of an effective intelligence capability. Dennison was still the only trained intelligence officer in the SAF and even his abilities could be harnessed only through subterfuge. Through Major Isaacs, an expert in psychological warfare seconded from the Intelligence Corps who interviewed many of the rebels, Smiley had begun to build up the equivalent of a database of the rebels' structure, tribal and political affiliations, and modus operandi. But even here, the Sultan's prejudice impeded his work: Isaacs, who was Jewish, was ordered out of Oman, despite Smiley's protests to the Sultan. All the same, Smiley managed to set up a small intelligence section at the SAF headquarters in Beit al-Falaj, comprising two seconded officers and three NCOs, one of whom was a topographer; the lack of accurate maps had badly hindered military operations. This section was supplemented by the appointment of Desert Intelligence Officers (DIOs) in the main towns, such as Nizwa, Sur and Izki. The Sultan grudgingly agreed to this, on condition that they would be contract officers whose loyalty to the Sultan, by dint of him paying their wages, could be assured. While of varying quality, they at least provided a hub around which the game of cat-and-mouse against Saudi subversion could at least be played out on something approaching an even playing field.[53]

Landmines were still the weapon of choice for what was now called the Oman Rebel Army. Though now devoid of the religious legitimacy once enjoyed by the Imam, the rebels still sought to inflict damage on the SAF, as well as on the installations and oil infrastructure of the PD(O). The Oman Rebel Army, estimated to number around 400 men, was largely made up of Omani expatriates who, having worked as indentured labour in the burgeoning energy fields across the Gulf region, had come under the heady influence of Arab nationalism. That Saudi Arabia was hardly a bastion of republican idealism hardly mattered: it was still willing to supply the training and means by which the Sultanate could be overthrown.[54]

The Oman Rebel Army had cells in several of the Trucial States, whose rulers, out of antipathy towards the Sultan, had often turned a blind eye to their activities.[55] This might have put British DIOs loyal to the Sultan at odds with their counterparts serving in the same capacity for the potentates in such places as Abu Dhabi and Dubai. Such clashes of interest were largely avoided by Norman Darbyshire, MI6 head of station in Bahrain, who helped coordinate intelligence sharing and the running of agents across the Gulf. An old Middle East hand with wartime experience in Persia, Darbyshire oversaw the distribution of cash to recruit informers in Dammam, the main Saudi training centre for rebels, from where mines of varying shapes and lethality were transported to the Trucial States before being smuggled into Oman.[56] Many of these informers were run by the DIOs, with Smiley and Dennison overseeing the collection of intelligence. Darbyshire, however, was not always entirely convinced of the value of such payments. After all, if loyalty was bought by the highest bidder, the value and accuracy of the intelligence could often be skewed to suit a particular customer.

Yet such risks had to be taken, given the lack of alternative information gathering, notably signals intelligence. Darbyshire was concerned, however, that several agents being run by DIOs could be covering the same target and he was keen to avoid duplication of effort, especially when they were operating in other Gulf States. It was a point readily understood by Smiley, who developed a close working relationship with Darbyshire and, later on, his successor, John da Silva. Together with Dennison, Smiley gradually created a network of agents that covered Dubai, Sharjah, Qatar and as far afield as Kuwait.[57]

Results were achieved, partly because rebels who surrendered mines were rewarded. They were paid largely out of the secret vote allocated to MI6 rather than by the Sultan, who knew little of the scope and scale of an intelligence operation run on his behalf. In 1960, for example, intelligence revealed that 32 mines, with detonators sent separately, 19 grenades and several pistols had been trafficked into Oman via the Trucial States, some smuggled in by dhow.⁵⁸ The actual volume of weapons and explosives that got through is hard to gauge; it was enough, though, to sustain a low-level insurgency throughout the early 1960s. By 1963, however, facing the growing challenge of Egypt's intervention in the Yemen civil war that had broken out the previous year, the Saudis had withdrawn their support for the rebels. The intelligence effort had certainly helped contain the Omani insurgents but it was never enough to stem the tide of change that now lapped at the gate of a Sultan increasingly isolated in his coastal retreat in Salalah.

By now, Smiley's tenure as CSAF had drawn to a close. Though he had achieved his greatest military triumph on the Jebel Akhdar, he confessed to feeling tired and not a little disillusioned by his Oman experience. He had won a war, secured British interests for the moment in a strategic corner of Arabia, and left behind the nucleus of an effective, if still pitifully small, armed force. Though asked by the Sultan and Whitehall to extend his service for another year, he refused, later admitting that, by 1961, 'I was utterly cheesed off.' His fractious relationship with Tinker in Bahrain, frustration with Middle East Command in Aden, and finally, his utter disillusion with Waterfield's gatekeeping had taken their toll. With a deep sense of grievance over the lack of recognition for his role in conquering the Jebel Akhdar, he was determined to call time on his tenure as CSAF. Given a last opportunity to vent his spleen at the highest level, he did so. He met with the Cabinet Secretary, Philip de Zulueta, soon after his return to London, an encounter that was minuted to the Prime Minister, Harold Macmillan. Smiley, it was reported, opined that 'The Sultan is impossible to work with and has put his faith in an unreliable Englishman. . . . Smyley [sic] has some hopes of the Sultan's son who is at Sandhurst and he proposes to cultivate the boy which will do no harm.'⁵⁹

Smiley's own future, though, was far from certain. Kenya's push towards independence now called into question his plan to become a farmer amid rising political turmoil and uncertainty surrounding the future of white-owned farms, and with his children being educated privately in England, the cost of air fares to and from Kenya looked increasingly prohibitive. It forced him to reconsider his options, which included perhaps staying in the army. In April 1961, he had been offered command of the three SAS regiments, a post for which his manifold experience of intelligence and guerrilla warfare supremely qualified him. Interested, he insisted that such a command should warrant his promotion to brigadier. The War Office baulked at such a promotion, even though Smiley's responsibilities as a colonel in the SAF encompassed a brigade-sized force. Realising he would not immediately rise above the rank of colonel, Smiley resigned his commission and left the army. He sold his farm in Kenya and now looked to settle into civilian life. Yet he had no clear plan and no real idea of what he wanted to do, let alone could do. His prospects looked uncertain. Yet he was to return to Arabia far sooner than he could have ever envisaged.

Notes

1. St Anthony's College Oxford Middle East Centre: Papers of Colonel David Smiley Accession No: GB165–0336 (hereafter MEC Smiley Papers GB165–0336) 1/2. Report: Confidential from Colonel David Smiley to Brigadier Edward Tinker, 5 December 1959.
2. A somewhat sympathetic portrait of Sultan Said bin Taimur is to be found in Uzi Rabi, *The Emergence of States in a Tribal Society: Oman under Sa'id bin Taymur 1932–1970* (Brighton: Sussex Academic Press, 2007), p. 320.
3. Tore T. Petersen, *The Decline of the Anglo-American Middle East 1961–1969: A Willing Retreat* (Brighton: Sussex Academic Press, 2006), pp. 10–11.
4. Colonel D. de C. Smiley MVO, OBE, MC, 'Muscat and Oman', *The Royal United Services Journal*, 105/616 (1960), pp. 23–4.
5. Bassett, *Last Imperialist*, p. 167.
6. TNA NA PREM 11/4923 338047, Confidential: Sultan of Muscat and Oman, 17 July 1958; PREM 11/4923 338047 Secret: From Mr Selwyn Lloyd to Sir Bernard Burrows (Bahrain) Visit of the Sultan of Muscat and Oman, 20 August 1958.
7. Churchill College Cambridge: Papers of Julian Amery (hereafter Amery Papers), AMEJ 1/1 545/1 Secret: From Julian Amery to His Highness Sultan Sayyid bin Taimur al-Bu-Said, 22 February 1958.
8. Amery Papers, AMEJ 1/1 545/1, Secret: From Foreign Office to

Bahrain Telegram No. 266, 22 February 1958.
9. MEC Smiley Papers GB165–0336 1/2, Draft letter to Brigadier Edward Tinker, 5 December 1959.
10. David Smiley (with Peter Kemp), *Arabian Assignment* (London: Leo Cooper, 1975), pp. 16–17.
11. MEC Smiley Papers GB165–0336 1/1, Report on the Tenure of Command of the SAF by Col D. de C. Smiley from April 1958 to March 1961.
12. Interview with David Smiley, London, 21 October 2005.
13. MEC Smiley Papers GB165–0336 1/1, Report on the Tenure of Command of the SAF by Col D. de C. Smiley from April 1958 to March 1961.
14. Interview with David Smiley, London, 21 October 2005.
15. P. S. Allfree, *Warlords of Oman* (South Brunswick, NJ, and New York: Barnes and Noble, 1968), p. 113.
16. MEC Smiley Papers GB165–0336 1/2, Personal & Confidential. From David Smiley to Pat Waterfield, 21 February 1961.
17. Smiley, *Arabian Assignment*, p. 21.
18. Smiley, *Arabian Assignment*, p. 21; MEC Smiley Papers GB165–0336 1/1, Personal and Secret. Letter from David Smiley to Julian Amery, 11 August 1959.
19. Amery Papers AMEJ 1/1 545/1, Confidential: From Sir Bernard Burrows, Bahrain to Foreign Office, 27 May 1958; Amery Papers AMEJ 1/1 545/1, Secret: CSAF Proposed modifications to SAF Establishment, 27 May 1958.
20. The total cost for military expansion and civil development for 1958 was estimated at £540,200 with a total recurrent cost year on year of £374,000. Amery Papers AMEJ 1/1 545/1, Confidential: Costs likely to be incurred by her Majesty's Government on Muscat subsidy (undated); Secret: From I. T. M. Lucas, Foreign Office to Bahrain. Military Reorganisation in Muscat, 2 June 1958.
21. MEC Smiley Papers GB165–0336 1/2, Personal and Secret: To Julian Amery, 11 August 1959.
22. J. B. Kelly, *Arabia, the Gulf and the West* (New York: Basic Books, 1980), p. 117. A secret SAS assessment suggested that the rebels had had wireless contact with Saudi Arabia but, by November 1958, their one set had become unserviceable. Liddell Hart Centre for Military Archives, Papers of Major General Anthony Deane-Drummond (hereafter LHC: Deane-Drummond Papers), Secret: 'Rebel Forces on Jabal [sic] Akhdar and surrounding area', 17 November 1958.

23. Smiley, *Arabian Assignment*, p. 67.
24. Smiley, *Arabian Assignment*, p. 49.
25. Smiley, *Arabian Assignment*, p. 58.
26. LHC: Deane-Drummond Papers, Secret: 'Rebel Forces on Jabal [sic] Akhdar and surrounding area', 17 November 1958.
27. Smiley, 'Muscat and Oman', p. 37.
28. MEC Smiley Papers GB165–0336 1/2, Letter from David Smiley to Julian Amery, 6 December 1958.
29. LHC: Deane-Drummond Papers, Top Secret: The Enemy, 16 November 1958.
30. MEC Smiley Papers GB165–0336 1/2, Personal and Secret: From David Smiley to Julian Amery, August 1958.
31. J. E. Peterson, *Oman's Insurgencies: The Sultanate's Struggle for Supremacy* (London: Saqi, 2007), pp. 114–15.
32. LHC. Deane-Drummond Papers, Secret: Report on Operations by 22 SAS in the Oman, 18 Nov 1958–29 [sic] Feb 1959.
33. Frank Kitson, *Bunch of Five* (London: Faber & Faber, 1987), p. 168.
34. Deane-Drummond Papers, Letter from Malcolm Dennison to Anthony Deane-Drummond, 29 January 1989.
35. Peter de la Billière, *Looking for Trouble: SAS to Gulf Command* (London: HarperCollins, 1994), p. 128.
36. Peterson, *Oman Insurgencies*, p. 146, note 1.
37. Smiley, *Arabian Assignment*, p. 68. On the role of the RAF, see Sebastian Ritchie, *The RAF, Small Wars and Insurgencies: Later Colonial Operations, 1945–1975* (Air Historical Branch/RAF Centre for Air Power Studies, 2011), p. 53.
38. MEC Smiley Papers GB165–0336 1/2, Secret: From Air Vice-Marshal M. M. Heath to Colonel D. de C. Smiley, 1 December 1958.
39. MEC Smiley Papers GB165–0336 1/2, Personal: From David Smiley to Julian Amery.
40. Smiley, 'Muscat and Oman', p. 43.
41. Smiley, 'Muscat and Oman', pp. 44–5.
42. MEC Smiley Papers GB165–0336 1/2, Private and Secret: From Julian Amery to Colonel David Smiley, 10 March 1959.
43. MEC Smiley Papers GB165–0336 1/2, Letter from Brigadier Edward Tinker HQ Land Forces Persian Gulf to David Smiley, 9 December 1959.
44. Interview with David Smiley, London, 21 October 2006.
45. Interview with Xan Smiley, Taston, Oxfordshire, 30 June 2006.

Amery too raised the issue of awards and appropriate recognition for Smiley's efforts, which Smiley acknowledged. See MEC Smiley Papers GB165–0336 1/2, Confidential and Personally typed: From David Smiley to Julian Amery, 22 November 1959.
46. MEC Smiley Papers GB165–0336 1/2, Letter from Brigadier Edward Tinker HQ Land Forces Persian Gulf to David Smiley, 9 December 1959.
47. Interview with Xan Smiley, Taston, Oxfordshire, 30 June 2006.
48. Interview with Moyra Smiley, London, 22 February 2006.
49. MEC Smiley Papers GB165–0336 1/2, Confidential: From Colonel David de C. Smiley to Brigadier Edward Tinker, 23 November 1959.
50. MEC Smiley Papers GB165–0336 1/2, Letter from David Smiley to Col. Pat Waterfield, 19 June 1960.
51. Interview with David Smiley, London, 20 October 2008.
52. 'Britain's Role in the 1970 Coup in Oman', BBC Radio 4, *Document*, Broadcast 23 November 2009, available at <http://www.bbc.co.uk/iplayer/console/b00ny7nb> (last accessed 7 December 2018).
53. MEC Smiley Papers GB165–0336 1/1, Report on the Tenure of Command of the SAF by Col. D. de C. Smiley from April 1958 to March 1961.
54. TNA WO 337/10 Oman Intelligence Reports, Confidential: Arms Smuggling by Omani Rebels in the Trucial States, 12 July 1961.
55. TNA WO 337/10, Secret: Intelligence Picture as at 1 January 1961, 8 January 1961.
56. MEC Smiley Papers GB165–0336 1/2, Secret: Letter from Norman Darbyshire to Colonel David Smiley, 17 May 1960.
57. MEC Smiley Papers GB165–0336 1/2, Secret: Letter from Norman Darbyshire to Colonel David Smiley, 27 May 1960.
58. TNA WO 337/10, Oman Intelligence Reports, Confidential: Arms Smuggling by Omani Rebels in the Trucial States, 12 July 1961. Appendix A: Known incidents of Weapons Smuggling in the Trucial States.
59. TNA PREM 11/4923, From P de Z to the Prime Minister, 26 June 1961.

12 Our Man in Yemen

I

Finding gainful employment after leaving the army proved more challenging than Smiley ever expected. The disappointment over his failure to be promoted to brigadier and, with it, to command the three SAS regiments, coupled with his decision to forgo a new life in Kenya, meant a very uncertain future. His army pension, some £3,000 per year, barely covered his children's school fees and was far too little to buy a family home. Thanks to the generosity of Moy's first cousin, Walter Buccleuch, the family was able to take up the rent-free tenancy of an ancient keep, Branxholm Castle, in the Scottish Borders near Hawick. But Smiley found little demand for his skills or experience in the Lowlands of Scotland.

His attempts to start his own business were less than successful. A mushroom farming venture soon foundered, a failure Smiley confessed was down to his own inexperience. Only a part-time job as an 'itinerant inspector' for Raymond Postgate's *Good Food Guide* added a little to his income, but it was hardly a career. Having retired as a colonel at the age of forty-five, Smiley knew his prospects hardly looked bright. With his two sons still at Eton, money was tight. He had not taken his 'golden bowler' in full, accepting a half-pension in order to pay school fees, so it was with enthusiasm tinged with relief that, in the spring of 1963, he accepted an offer from Billy McLean to accompany him to Yemen, now in the throes of a civil war. With its familiar mix of tribal politics and regional intrigue, this was a conflict whose dynamics were all too familiar to Smiley from his time in Albania and Oman, and one where his skills in unconventional warfare

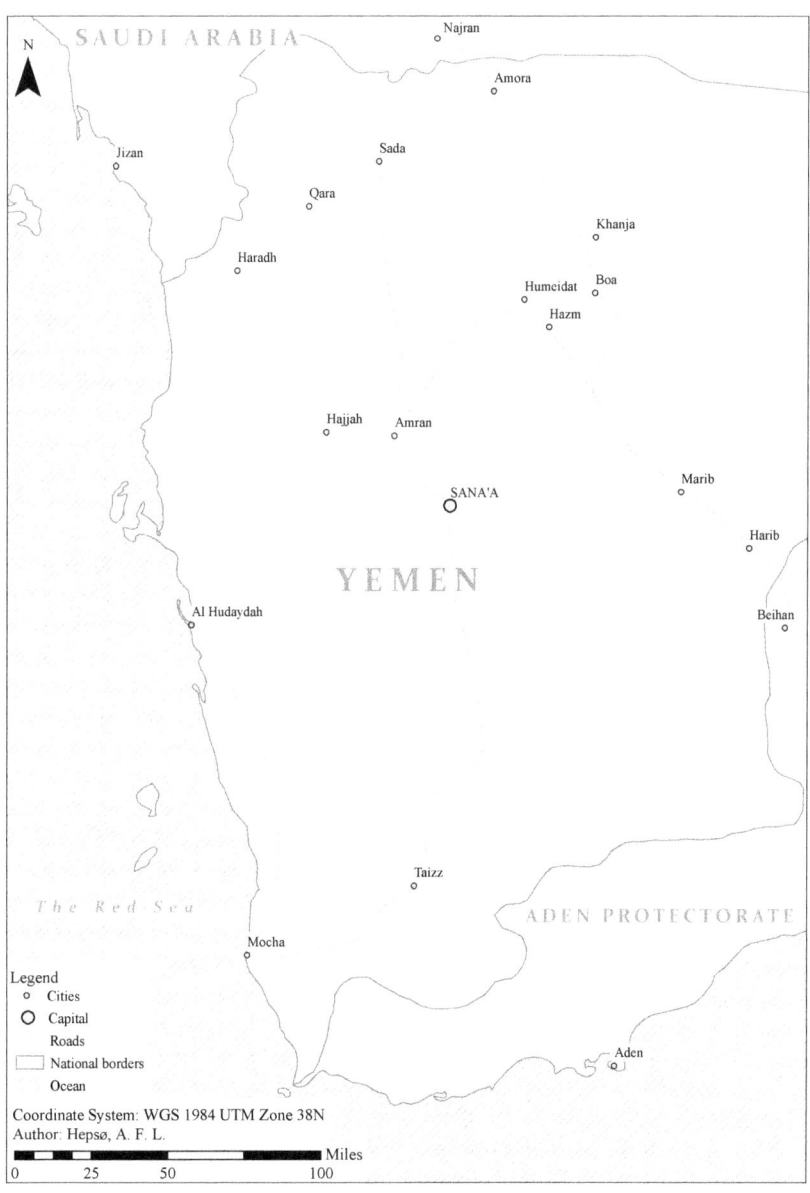

Fig. 12.1 Map of Yemen.

and personal diplomacy, as well as sheer physical endurance, were to be tested to the limit.

On 26 September 1962, a palace coup in Sana'a, the administrative capital of Yemen, overthrew the Imamate, the *Hamid Ud-Din*, and ushered in a new republican government, supported by President Nasser, marking the beginning of eight years of fierce internecine conflict. At its height, some 60,000 Egyptian troops were in Yemen to reinforce a government, led by Brigadier Abdullah Sallal, comprised mainly of representatives drawn from the predominantly Sunni *Shaffei* tribal confederations from the centre and south of the country. The Shia *Zeidi* tribes, located largely in in the mountains to the north and east, remained mostly loyal to the deposed Imam, Mohammed al-Badr. Collectively known as the Royalists, they relied on the largesse of Saudi Arabia, and of Crown Prince, later King, Faisal in particular. Faisal saw Nasser's support for Sallal as an element of a wider attempt to overthrow the House of Saud. As part of an Arab cold war that pitted dynastic regimes against their Republican counterparts, the Saudis tried, throughout the early years of the conflict, to court Western support by playing on the fear that Egypt's role in Yemen would open the door to Soviet penetration of the region.

In London, the Foreign Office advocated recognition of the newly declared Yemen Arab Republic (YAR), both because it viewed the old Imamate as antediluvian and because opposing Arab nationalism would threaten the stability of the newly formed Federation of South Arabia (FSA) and its British military base in Aden. This position enjoyed the support of the Joint Intelligence Committee. In October 1962, its chairman, Sir Hugh Stephenson, produced a report that advocated recognition of the YAR, noting that analysis of recent signals intercepts had revealed the Royalist forces to be weak and controlling less than one-third of Yemen. They were able to carry out sporadic guerrilla attacks only in the mountains to the north and east of the capital, actions that Stephenson believed were poorly coordinated and that made little appreciable impact upon the military superiority of the Republican forces.[1]

This pessimistic view of the Royalist position was shared by the head of MI6, Sir Dick White, who was initially reluctant to commit any of his own officers up country to assess the strengths and weaknesses of Yemen's opposing forces. Only one MI6 officer, Terry O'Bryan Tear, was stationed in Aden at the time of the revolution, and he had yet to travel to the hinterland, compile an up-to-date guide to the tribes and their affiliations, or recruit any reliable agents.[2] However, the Conservative governments of Harold Macmillan and, from October 1963, Sir Alec Douglas-Home refused to act on Foreign Office advice. Officially, the government argued that the Republicans did not command the obedience of a clear majority of the population, a condition if at least *de facto* recognition was to be conferred. Besides, officials in the Colonial Office and the Ministry of Defence felt that recognition of a Republican regime supported by Nasser might undermine the fidelity of tribal groupings and their leaders across South Arabia, on which the political stability and future of the FSA rested.[3]

How to counter Egyptian-backed subversion of the Federation dominated Britain's policy towards the Yemen civil war from the moment the YAR severed diplomatic ties with London in February 1963, precisely over the issue of non-recognition. The debates in the corridors of Whitehall were often acrimonious, with the Foreign Office often feeling itself to be the poor relation in the decision-making. But its diplomats struggled not only against the recommendations of officials in Aden, such as the High Commissioner, Sir Charles Johnston, and later his bullish successor, Sir Kennedy Trevaskis, but also against the interests of a close-knit group of people with direct access to key decision-makers in cabinet.

Sometimes referred to as the Aden Group, they were led by Julian Amery, now holding the junior government portfolio of Minister for Aviation, and Billy McLean, Conservative and Unionist MP for Inverness. They enjoyed discreet support in cabinet from the Colonial Secretary, Duncan Sandys, and the Defence Secretary, Peter Thorneycroft. Collectively, they viewed themselves as guardians of British interests in South Arabia, seeing the Yemen civil war as an opportunity to avenge Britain's humiliation over Suez at the hands of Nasser. Moreover, they regarded the presence of

Egyptian troops in Yemen as a front for Soviet penetration of the region, an assessment that drew them ever closer to Saudi Arabia and Crown Prince Faisal.

Amery, keen as ever on his 'para-diplomacy', used his close family ties in the Middle East to challenge the Foreign Office over recognition. With the support of King Hussein of Jordan, who had every reason to fear Nasser and Arab nationalism, he sponsored a trip by McLean to Yemen in order to assess the true nature of Royalist resistance. Between 21 and 30 October 1962, McLean embarked on a whirlwind tour of the region that took in Jordan, Saudi Arabia and the FSA, from where he crossed into Yemen, leaving from Beihan on the Federation–Yemeni border and arriving in Najran, just over the border in Saudi Arabia, three days later. His reports to cabinet cast sufficient doubt on the assessments of the Joint Intelligence Committee for London to pause for thought over recognising Sallal's regime.[4]

Still, mindful of the sorry international legacy of the Suez affair, Macmillan and Douglas-Home were both reluctant to sanction military action, be it overt or clandestine, on anything like the scale and with the intensity to overthrow the Republican government backed by Egypt. What clandestine activity was carried out against Republican and Egyptian targets was, for the most part, defensive in nature and tightly controlled.[5] This convinced McLean and Amery that only the financial and material largesse of Saudi Arabia could sustain the Royalist cause and thus protect British interests in South Arabia. To this end, they looked to recruit specialists in guerrilla warfare, paid for by the Saudis, to help train and advise the Imam's forces. It was only natural that they would now turn to their old comrade-in-arms: Smiley.

According to his own account in *Arabian Assignment*, Smiley was approached by McLean at the end of May 1963 to go with him on a trip to Yemen to help draft a military appreciation of the Royalists for the Saudis.[6] McLean, by now, had already made four such trips to Yemen, compiling similar reports for the Saudis. But given the brutally rugged mountain terrain where the fighting was taking place and the distances involved, it was physically impossible for McLean to compile reports for Saudi Crown

Prince Faisal that assessed all the various 'fronts' and their needs while continuing to serve as an MP. For Smiley, it was a golden opportunity to earn a lot more than the colonel's salary of £3,000 a year he received before leaving the army. He would now be paid £1,000 per month plus expenses. Given the physical hardships he was to endure over the next five years, he more than earned it.

News of his impending foray to Yemen soon reached MI6, however, and the director of its Middle East operations, John Bruce-Lockhart. In a friendly if pointed missive to Smiley, he wrote, 'HMG's policy is to try and avoid as much as possible being involved in the Yemeni war and that any publicity or widespread knowledge of your presence in the Yemen would be counter-productive to this policy.'[7] Soon, though, the value of Smiley's work in Yemen came to be realised by MI6, as the authorities in Aden struggled to contain a growing wave of violence throughout the Federation. In the absence of diplomatic relations with Sana'a and with no alternative human intelligence assets readily to hand, Smiley, having already worked for 'the firm', would be a dependable source of information, irrespective of his work for the Royalist cause. Bruce-Lockhart's missive may have been of a piece with government policy aimed at avoiding any wider Arabian entanglement, but by October 1963, Smiley had unofficially become 'our man' in Yemen, working, albeit part-time, for MI6.

Journalistic cover to explain his presence in Royalist-held areas of Yemen was now arranged. Originally, this was provided by becoming the 'Special Correspondent' for the *Household Brigade Magazine*. This rather flimsy journalistic credential was stiffened by Amery, who arranged for a press card that accredited him to the *Daily Telegraph*. It was a convivial arrangement for all concerned, though Smiley later noted wryly that he was never paid for any of the articles he wrote for the London daily.[8]

II

Smiley and McLean set off for Yemen via Beirut and Saudi Arabia on 14 June 1963. Two days later, he entered Yemen by truck from the Saudi coastal town of Jizzan on 16 June and made his way to the headquarters of the Imam at al-Qara, high in the mountains of north-west Yemen, about 100 miles from Sana'a. From the eyrie of Imam al-Badr's cave, Smiley made an extensive reconnaissance of the various Royalist 'armies' before finally returning to Jizzan on 11 July. Five days later, he was back in London. It was the first of thirteen trips he made to northern Yemen between 1963 and 1968.

His diary entries indicate the often huge demands that these journeys to Yemen made on him physically. Now in his late forties, he made long treks on foot between the various Royalist camps along precipitous mountain passes that would have taxed the fitness of much younger men. His diary entries for 7, 8, 9 and 10 July 1963 note marches of 5, 6, 15 and 6 hours, respectively, while his account of the climb to the summit of Jebel Ahanoum epitomised the physical trials he endured to fulfil his contract to his Saudi paymasters. On 22 June, he wrote:

> At 6pm we set off as light was failing. I started riding for about half an hour then the track got steeper and it got completely dark so I walked. The climb became a nightmare for the track took the form of huge steps about one foot high. If you can imagine walking upstairs, one foot high steps, in the pitch dark except for the dim light of a hurricane lamp, for three-and-a half hours on end, you can imagine I was wet through with sweat and my legs like jelly.[9]

Adding to such discomfort was the ever-present threat of serious illness in an environment where basic hygiene in the Royalist camps was almost unheard of. The caves where many lived were often flea-infested, while swarms of flies fed off discarded food and human excrement. Attacks of vomiting and diarrhoea became an accepted hazard. Such squalor contrasted with the sheer beauty and grandeur of the Yemeni mountains and their nature. In his diary entry for 29 June, Smiley noted that 'This country would be a delight for botanists and ornithologists. I saw some lovely birds; one with a long yellow beak, head, neck and top half white and bottom half blue/black was making nests like weavers in Kenya.' On another occasion, he noted the profusion of wild flowers that surrounded the mountain village of Magarabah, whose colours were magnified by a wonderful sunset.[10]

Such beauty was a welcome counterpoint to the destruction caused by Egyptian aerial and artillery bombardment that he witnessed in the villages he now passed through with his bodyguards. On 10 July, he entered the village of Kowma, where, he was told, Egyptian aircraft had dropped chemical weapons the previous month. Even after the time that had elapsed, 'evidence of the injuries to children, animals etc' was apparent and he collected samples of bomb fragments and photographed the burns inflicted on the inhabitants. The odour from the bomb crater, 'a sort of geranium smell', was, he recalled, still pungent enough almost to make him faint. Smiley passed the evidence, including shell fragments and soil samples, to the British ambassador in Saudi Arabia, Sir Colin Crowe, for onward despatch to London for further analysis. He also gave samples to the UN representative in Jeddah, Major Birger Schaathun of the Norwegian army, in the hope that similar tests in New York would influence opinion in the Security Council against Nasser.

Smiley suspected that the Egyptians were, in fact, using a form of mustard gas but tests conducted at Porton Down on the various bomb fragments he sent back proved inconclusive. In August 1963, Smiley received a letter from the Ministry of Defence: while traces of tear gas had been found in some samples, the metal casing in others was 'most unlikely to have been used to contain a toxic liquid such as mustard gas or other lethal chemical warfare agents'.[11] He was unconvinced by this technical autopsy. He hoped that a Swiss-based news organisation with whom he had been in touch would expose the Egyptian use of chemical weapons. 'I am convinced that some other type of poison was used,' he wrote. 'How else can one explain the fact that people died from its effects?' Tear gas alone, he concluded, 'could not explain away the sores caused by contamination; it is therefore my view that there must have been some other poisonous chemical substances in the bomb.'[12] It was a view he expressed forcefully in subsequent television and radio interviews throughout the autumn and winter of 1963.[13]

On his return to London, Smiley wrote two detailed reports for

Fig. 12.2   In the Khowlan mountains, Yemen, October 1963.

the Saudi Defence Minister, Prince Sultan bin Abdul Aziz. The first dealt entirely with Egyptian activities in Yemen and illustrated the extent of Cairo's violation of a cease-fire that had been brokered under the auspices of the American envoy, Ellsworth Bunker, in April 1963.[14] The second report dealt solely with the Royalist forces in Yemen. Remarkably perceptive, it identified the problems facing the Royalists, as well as the means by which they could best be addressed. Smiley's reports over the next five years echoed many of the same themes.

Although noting the high morale of the *Zeidi* tribes allied to the Imam, Smiley used his second report to Prince Sultan to expose key deficiencies in the Royalist forces. While these forces were suited in principle to guerrilla warfare, he highlighted the growing shortage of ammunition on all fronts as a result of the Saudis' adherence to the terms of the cease-fire negotiated by Bunker, but whose provisions were ignored by Republicans and Royalists alike. A more pressing deficiency was the lack of a secure, coherent radio network that linked the Royalist fronts. Command and control were haphazard, with instructions issued by the Imam overly reliant on fleet-footed couriers. 'This results in the Imam having little control over his commanders; consequently he cannot co-ordinate his plans,' wrote Smiley. 'From talking to the various commanders I gained the impression that each was fighting his own private war, independently of any commander.' Finally, he derided the tendency of the Royalists to make frontal attacks from their mountain redoubts with the aim of capturing towns and villages. These attacks, for the most part, were wasteful of Royalist lives, as well as ammunition. However, 'Where there had been ambushes on roads, the Egyptians had lost many killed and much equipment, for little or no Royalist losses; these are the obvious tactics the Royalists should pursue.'[15]

His reports also confirmed that Yemen was broadly divided into distinct areas. The *Zeidi* tribes were firmly in control of the mountains in the north and east of the country, while the Egyptians and Republicans controlled the plains, the coastal area and the southern region bordering the Federation, areas where the predominantly *Shaffei* tribes held sway. But in his private notes, which he did not disclose to the Saudis, Smiley was more candid in his criticisms of the Royalists and, in particular, of the tendency of the Imam to inflate the strength of his forces to the point of ridicule. The Imam claimed that each front consisted of an army but Smiley considered them to be more akin to militias, with a small core of trained men supplemented by tribesmen, as circumstances dictated. The distribution of weaponry among the fronts was poor, with a lack of heavy weapons, most notably anti-aircraft guns and heavy mortars, compounded by a shortage of ammunition. Even where arms and ammunition were available, there were too few Royalists qualified to use them effectively against Egyptian and Republican targets. Finally, there were almost no accurate maps, and stocks of medical supplies were hopelessly inadequate.[16]

In view of these deficiencies, it was surprising that a Royalist opposition existed at all, let alone one that had achieved some notable tactical triumphs against the Egyptian army. But it was also an indictment of the weak tactics, poor leadership and overall strategy of the Egyptian forces.[17] With echoes of similar advice

Fig. 12.3 With the Imam, Muhammed al-Badr (centre).

given to the Albanian guerrillas two decades before, Smiley urged the Royalists to play to their strengths as guerrillas and attack the Egyptian lines of communication, especially the main routes linking Sana'a with Hodeidah on the coast and Sada to the north. To help achieve this, Smiley now pressed for the urgent establishment of an integrated radio network with a minimum of six wireless transmitters, along with trained operators to coordinate the various fronts.[18]

In December 1963, Smiley penned another detailed appreciation of the Royalists for the Saudis, this time focusing on their base camp at Khanja, a massive rocky outcrop on the edge of the Rub al-Khali and close to the Saudi border. Here, a rudimentary curriculum in basic guerrilla tactics and weapons training was being taught. On 17 December, he presented a summary of this report directly to the Prime Minister, Douglas-Home, who happened to be a cousin of Moy. This report was more upbeat in its assessment, listing tribes who had come over to the Royalists and adding evidence of those who might defect 'when the time was right'. On the broader political front, he argued that no immediate resolution to the civil war was in sight. The Saudis would not agree to one until the Egyptians had withdrawn, while the Republicans would agree to negotiate only if the Egyptians remained. Smiley estimated that Cairo had lost between 10,000 and 12,000 troops killed and wounded since the start of their intervention.[19] Given his access to the Prime Minister at the same time as the Aden Group were lobbying hard for direct British assistance to the Royalist forces in cabinet, Smiley felt it hardly surprising the Foreign Office viewed his role with barely concealed disdain.[20]

Worse, in the Foreign Office view, was the emergence of a mercenary organisation in which Smiley had become closely involved and in whose hands the fate of the Royalist war effort increasingly came to rest. While Smiley had concentrated on compiling reports for his Saudi benefactors, McLean and Amery had approached the founder of the wartime SAS, Colonel David Stirling, about recruiting mercenaries to advise and train the Royalist forces. Stirling recommended the services of Colonel James (Jim) Johnson, a former commanding officer of 21 SAS. He, in turn, suggested that French military advisors also be recruited. From the outset, the mercenary plan rested on two pillars: money and a secure base. The Saudis supplied the former, funnelling money through the Royalist Foreign Minister at large, Sayid Ahmed Al-Shamy, to purchase military supplies on the open market and to pay the salaries of those recruited. Riyadh, however, would not allow its territory to be used for the mercenary operation because this would violate the Bunker agreement, which limited the use of Saudi territory for supply operations. The only alternative was the Federation itself and, in particular, Beihan state, which bordered Yemen.

This carried its own particular risks. The Foreign Office opposed any activity that stood in contradiction to Britain's declared policy of non-intervention in the civil war. But McLean and Stirling, in the course of separate trips to Aden, carefully courted key individuals in Government House who could facilitate the flow of men and matériel across Federal borders. Protocol demanded that Sir Charles Johnston as Governor and his successor as High Commissioner, Sir Kennedy Trevaskis, avoid direct involvement in supporting the nascent mercenary organisation, although Trevaskis, who knew McLean from Abyssinia, knew of his intent and turned an appropriately blind eye.[21] However, two other men serving in official capacities began to play pivotal roles in the emerging mercenary operation. The first, Flight Lieutenant Anthony (Tony) Boyle, a fast-jet pilot in the RAF, was serving as aide de camp to Johnstone in Aden as part of an obligatory ground tour when he was approached by Stirling in the spring of 1963. He readily agreed to help and, in turn, recruited Major Peter de la Billière, an SAS officer who had won an MC on the Jebel Akhdar and who was now on secondment to the Federal Regular Army.[22] McLean was soon in close liaison with Boyle, holding three meetings with him in London between 23 April and 2 May. Boyle was already well aware that Sharif Hussein of Beihan was used as a conduit for Riyadh's financial and material aid sent to the Royalists. Crown Prince Faisal, his brother Prince Sultan and the head of the Saudi intelligence service, Kemal Atham, brother-in-law of Faisal and an *éminence grise* of the Crown Prince, all maintained that such an arrangement allowed them to support the Royalists without violating the word, if not the spirit, of the Bunker agreement.[23]

With Boyle and de la Billière now establishing a 'rat line' for arms and equipment to be sent from Aden to Beihan without facing the unwelcome attentions of customs officials, the enlistment of the mercenaries gathered momentum. Many, at first, were former French and Belgian soldiers who had fought in Indo-China, Algeria and the Congo, men who Smiley deemed to be of 'a very high class'.[24] However, he preferred those who had a special forces or signals background, although this did not guarantee the qualities of endurance, patience and fortitude needed in Yemen.

An early recruit was Major Rupert France, a wartime SAS officer and an experienced signals operator who had been in the SAF. In October 1963, he was sent to Nequb to set up radio links between Aden and the growing number of field operatives being sent 'up country' to advise the Royalist princes, as well as the Imam. As it was close to the Yemen border, Nequb became the communications hub for what now became the British mercenary organisation (BMO).[25] The British NCOs, most of whom had served in the SAS, Smiley rated highly for their specialist skills but the quality of the officers often left much to be desired. He held only two in particularly high esteem: the veteran Johnny Cooper, whom he had known in Oman, and a later addition, Major Bernard Mills. Like Cooper, Mills had served with the SAS in Malaya and more recently with the SAF in Oman. Linguistic ability was all and, in Smiley's view, 'British officers who proved their worth were those who understood some Arabic' or had previous exposure to the Arab world.[26]

Most supplies and weapons for the Royalist forces were delivered to the various fronts on camel trains crossing the border from Saudi Arabia or, in the case of Nequb in Beihan, from Federal territory. While able to deliver large quantities of arms, ammunition and food, camel trains were slow and often vulnerable to attack by Egyptian and YAR forces. All too often, Royalist fronts were hard pressed to sustain their positions in the face of determined Egyptian assaults, which had become critical by the spring of 1964. The need to alleviate this pressure now led to Smiley's involvement in one of the most intriguing episodes of the whole conflict: Israel's clandestine support for the Royalist forces.

III

In July 1963, McLean held talks with Crown Prince Hassan, the Royalist Prime Minister and the Imam's uncle, who McLean and Smiley regarded as far more capable politically and militarily than his nephew. In his notes, McLean recorded '[t]he desirability of an approach to the Israelis for help, perhaps through Sharif Hussein, or a confidential Israeli Agent or reliable Jew in Aden, or through the French'.[27] Now, in a move condoned by Crown Prince Hassan and by Sharif Hussein of Beihan, who was at the meeting, McLean approached the Israelis over how they could best support the Royalist war effort.

It is unclear exactly when contact was made with Israeli officials. Entries in McLean's notebook point to a preliminary discussion between himself, Amery and the Israeli military attaché in London, Colonel Dan Hiram, in December 1963.[28] This led to a direct meeting at Amery's house at 112 Eaton Square between the Royalist Foreign Minister at large, Ahmed Al-Shamy, and an Israeli diplomat, Ya'acov Herzog, on 10 December. At this meeting, it was agreed that, in return for Israel dropping arms and ammunition directly to the Royalists, they would recognise the Jewish State once victory had been secured and the Imamate restored. While circumspect in his view of the Royalist position, Herzog felt that helping to bleed the Egyptian army dry in the mountains of north Yemen was of sufficient strategic benefit to Israel as to justify the risks involved.[29]

These talks now gathered momentum. On 20 February 1964, Smiley and Johnson left for Tel Aviv under MI6 cover on a Swissair flight via Geneva. In a scene that could have been taken from a spy novel, the pair entered a lift at an airport hotel at a pre-arranged time. Before the doors closed, a man entered, identified himself as their contact, and handed over false passports for their onward journey to Israel.[30] This was to be the first of four trips that Smiley made to Tel Aviv over the next two years to organise covert air drops by the Israeli air force to the Royalists.[31] He recalled:

> I went out several times with MI6 cover [to Israel] with false name and false passport to work on this [covert air drops]. They [the Israelis] gave us a lot of information on the Egyptians and I remember when I was there, I was taken out to a theatre by a chap who had I think been a Squadron Leader in the RAF and who became the head of the Israeli air force.

The officer in question was Major General Ezer Weizman, later to become Israel's Defence Minister and President. The entertainment was twofold: a Yiddish version of 'My Fair Lady', followed by a trip to Mandy's, a nightclub in Tel Aviv established by Mandy Rice-Davies, who, following the Profumo affair, had married an Israeli employee of the national airline, El Al.[32]

That Smiley was now working for MI6 indicates that attitudes among officials in British intelligence had begun to shift towards a more positive view of the mercenary operation. His diary for 15 November 1963 records Smiley meeting with John da Silva in Aden, who had been sent by MI6 to bolster their intelligence efforts in the Federation. Smiley knew and liked da Silva from his Oman days, when, as an MI6 officer based in Bahrain, he had supported Smiley's efforts to interrupt the flow of mines from Saudi Arabia into northern Oman.[33] Later, when Saudi Arabia once more became the main point of entry into Yemen, Smiley formed similar ties of easy familiarity with two other MI6 officers, Paul Paulson and John Christie, who had both had extensive operational experience in the Arab world.[34] Smiley's presence in Yemen certainly helped reduce an intelligence deficit and underscored the value MI6 saw in courting the Israelis, provided this relationship could be kept firmly in the shadows.

Remarkably, Smiley's notes also recall meetings with the Director General of Israel's defence ministry, Shimon Peres; Colonel Eitan Avrahami, a military secretary; Lieutenant Colonel Raphael Ephrat from Israeli military intelligence; Major Ze'ev Liron of the Israeli air force; and Meir Amit, the head of the *Mossad*.[35] Not all the Israelis were convinced that the potential benefits of the operation to Israel were worth the risks entailed. Lieutenant General Mordechai Hod of the Israeli air force was the most senior dissenting voice.[36] The risk to the transport aircraft and its crew from Egyptian fighters was real, while navigation at night over mountains could be treacherous. They all wanted reassurance that the reception committees had experience of planning and receiving air drops. In Smiley and Cooper, the BMO had experience and expertise enough eventually to satisfy the sceptics in Tel Aviv. Indeed, the pilot who flew most of the supply missions from Israel to Yemen, Major Arieh Oz, never had any difficulty in locating the drop zones in the mountains of north Yemen.[37]

Once the Israelis were convinced of the merits of the operation, their commitment proved wholehearted. Overall liaison with the BMO was handled with considerable skill and diplomatic finesse by the *Mossad* station chief in Paris, Nahum Admoni, who developed a lifelong friendship with Johnson and Boyle.[38] Recounting this *liaison dangereuse* four decades later, Smiley remained struck by the sensitive nature of Israel's involvement. He noted:

> The Saudis never knew about the Israeli connection. I think it would have caused a certain amount of trouble if they had known. The

Israelis never received payment – it was in their interests to keep the Egyptians tied down in the Yemen.[39]

But he was also anxious to ensure that his own previous clandestine involvement in Operation Embarrass remained hidden from the Israelis. While the Israelis must have been aware of his service with SOE – after all, they needed to know he had previous experience of organising drop zones – there is no evidence that they knew of his immediate post-war activities in the Mediterranean. If they did, it no longer mattered.

All the clandestine flights from Israel to Yemen were given the code name Operation Mango by the BMO ('Mango' being code for Israel), and Operation Rotev (Gravy) and Dorban (Porcupine) by the Israelis. The first flight took off from outside Eilat in southern Israel on 31 March 1964.[40] Cooper, who received the initial drop, recalled how these flights operated:

> [T]he Stratocruiser flew down the Red Sea with Egypt on the right and Saudi Arabia on the left. They had to come in almost at sea level to avoid detection by Egyptian radar, and when they reached the port of Hodeidha, they swung inland towards the mountains, climbing to 10,000 feet. Our friends had muffled the engines and it was very quiet. Then the huge aircraft came in for the actual drop and as it swept over at about two hundred and fifty feet, sixty parachutes spewed out of the back. It was a beautifully executed professional drop. Abduallah bin Hassan was delighted. He had the mortars and bombs he needed together with a plentiful supply of small arms. . . . Every serial number had been scored out, the parachutes were of Italian origin and even the wood shavings used in the packing had been imported from Cyprus. Even the most expert intelligence analyst would have had a job to unravel that one.[41]

Like Cooper's, Smiley's wartime experience with SOE made him particularly suited to organising drop zones. He controlled two such drops from what he termed 'Mangoland' near Amara and Sada, one on the night of 12–13 June 1965, the other exactly a month later. In total, the Israeli air force flew thirteen such missions between 1964 and 1966, the detailed inventories kept by

Fig. 12.4 Smiley's Land Rover during an Israeli resupply drop. Note the signal fire in the background.

Smiley revealing that he received 'special consignments' numbers 9 and 10. Tony Boyle, who had by now left the RAF, accompanied most of these resupply missions, communicating with Smiley via a 'Eureka VHF' ground-to-air radio set using his old wartime code name, 'Grin'.[42] Boyle and Johnson made sure that home comforts were included in the dropped canisters. These included personal mail, newspapers, and the occasional bottle of Scotch and cans of beer.[43] Smiley noted that the tribesmen receiving the drops became 'exultant', boasting happily that 'With all these new weapons we will drive the British out of Aden,' hardly the purpose for which they were intended.[44]

Israeli support was not just restricted to the delivery of arms supplies. Tel Aviv later furnished Smiley's radio operator and bodyguard, Jimmy Knox, a former member of 22 SAS, with an advanced radio set. It was later returned to the Israelis via the transit hall at Heathrow airport. In return, Smiley briefed the Israeli army on the capabilities of the Egyptian forces, as well as supplying it with samples of shrapnel and shell casing dropped on Yemeni villages, which he believed to have contained chemical agents. His knowledge of Egyptian air operations was also of interest to the Israelis. On one occasion, he was allowed to interrogate an Iraqi pilot who had defected to Israel in a MiG-21 jet fighter, a type used widely in Yemen by the Egyptian air force.[45] On such trips, Smiley took the opportunity to assess the Israel Defence Forces, which impressed him. In a prescient article written in September 1965, he opined:

> Is Nasser really ready or willing to risk an open conflict with the Israelis, especially after the humiliating defeat of his forces by them in 1956? Their unsuccessful showing against the Yemeni Royalists, whose forces are comprised of weakly armed and equipped tribesman lacking in aircraft, armour and discipline does not promise well for any future conflict with the Israeli army. The latter possesses modern arms and equipment, including aircraft, and morale is reputed to be high among its well-disciplined troops.[46]

Whatever the value of Operation Mango in terms of supplies dropped and morale raised, its true effect could be realised only if the tribes loyal to the Royalist cause could play to their strengths and attack Egyptian and Republican lines of communication. On 18 March 1964, Smiley was present at what should have been a coordinated attack against the town of Hajja. An important junction, with roads running south-east to Sana'a, north-east to Amran and west to Hodeidah, these routes had been routinely cut by Royalist forces who dominated the surrounding features. The Egyptians, realising its strategic importance, had kept a company-sized garrison in and around the town. The Royalist plan now was to make a coordinated two-pronged assault from the north and south, removing the Egyptian force for good.

In the event, it was a debacle that Smiley watched with incredulity and growing anger. Though Royalist forces looked down on Hajja, their preliminary bombardment was wildly inaccurate and inflicted little damage on the Egyptians. This military incompetence was matched by the actual assault. Targets in the town had been allocated on a tribal basis, and while those attacking from the north achieved some success, they had to withdraw once it became apparent that no attack whatsoever had materialised from the south.[47] Memories of Albania came flooding back.

Putting aside the protocols of court when addressing the Imam, Smiley was blunt in spelling out the Royalist military failings in the aftermath of Hajja. Planning, supplies, tactics and commanders were all poor. This was aggravated by what Smiley regarded as weaknesses in the Royalist character: ignorance, inefficiency, indolence and incompetence. There was no commander around Hajja, he declared, who had any operational understanding of how best to inflict damage on the Egyptian and Republican force.[48] The Imam took all this with good humour, although Smiley, his ire still raised, felt the Imam had not grasped just how badly his army had performed. Again, Smiley urged that the Royalists play to their strength as guerrillas, attacking lines of communication, ambushing convoys and mining roads rather than directly attacking the towns.

On his return to London, Smiley repeated this advice in a letter to Faisal, by now King of Saudi Arabia. It was a subtle, if inspired, move. While the Imam had a tendency to make light of the Briton's advice, he could hardly do so again if such advice came from his main financial and political benefactor.[49] The need for more advisors was also paramount; by the beginning of 1965, there were only six British, ten French and three Belgians working in the field at any one time. The British were mainly in the Khowlan, with Mills and his radio operator attached to the Royalist 'First Army' under Prince Mohammed bin al-Hussein around al-Jauf. The French and Belgians concentrated upon training Royalist forces at Khanja.[50]

On 3 March 1965, Smiley returned to Yemen on what was his fourth visit; again, the need for proper radio communications dominated his concerns. This fed into his main recommendation concerning the overall organisation of the Royalist forces.

> [Organisation] is one of the weakest points of the Royalists. Each Amir is fighting his own private war. Each is inclined to keep heavy weapons and European specialists to themselves as status symbols. The 12 Belgian/French and 5 [sic] British para-military specialists are not all being put to best use. Co-ordination is necessary, and this can

305

Fig. 12.5 From left to right: 'Nanny', Smiley, Jim Johnson, Bernard Mills, unknown, James Knox (Smiley's bodyguard), Amara, Yemen, 1965.

only be achieved by a commander who is given power to control the heavy weapons, European specialists and the transport. In addition, he must have the right of direct approach to the Amirs, without the usual delays, and the Amir should be urged to listen to, and preferably take, his advice.[51]

It was an assessment the Saudis took to heart. With the blessing of King Faisal, Ahmed al-Shamy and the Saudi Defence Minister, Prince Sultan, offered Smiley overall command of the British mission inside Yemen. Smiley spoke with Jim Johnson, Colonel Roger Falques, who had helped oversee the recruitment of the French mercenaries, and Moy, before agreeing to a contract that let him take a total of four months' leave a year 'to coincide with his children's holidays'.[52] He also consulted McLean, who advised him to take the position but only on condition that 'he had complete control himself and did not [McLean's emphasis] depend on the London office [of the BMO] and that secondly, there was no question of backing the Third Force'.[53] This referred to a group of Republican political dissidents who the Saudis believed could well serve their future political interests in Yemen, even if this meant abandoning support for the Imam.

The fact that Prince Sultan was willing to offer such generous terms to Smiley shows the high regard in which he was held in the Saudi court. It was also a tribute to his powers of leadership that he achieved so much in developing the Royalist military capabilities during what was, in essence, a part-time appointment. Yet the military difficulties facing the Royalists, which had so often been detailed by Smiley himself, could not be resolved by a commander acting, under the terms of his own contract, on a part-time basis. Moreover, tensions within the mercenary organisation, notably between Johnson and Boyle on the one hand, and McLean and David Stirling on the other, over who should deal with the Saudis regarding the late payment of salaries to the mercenaries in the field hardly helped matters. McLean had now begun to feel increasing unease over the direction that Saudi policy was taking, and this was shared by Smiley. He too had begun to suspect an element of Saudi misanthropy in its support of the Royalists:

> My own view was that the Saudis, for their own reasons, were giving the Royalists just enough help to prolong the war but not enough to win it outright; they also suspected, with some justification, that some of the supplies they sent were misappropriated. I had no doubt that the main factor in winning the war was money, because in the last resort most of the tribal Sheikhs would fight for the side who paid them best; so much so that those of the mercenaries who had served in the SAS would say that their old motto 'Who Dares Wins' should be changed to 'Who Pays Wins'.[54]

IV

The most vulnerable point for the Egyptian expeditionary force was still its extended supply routes to its remote garrisons in the north and east of Yemen. Logistical support for these bases had become increasingly tenuous. The distance from Sana'a to the Egyptian garrison at Marib was 80 miles across the Khowlan mountains but Royalist control of this area meant that supplies had to go by a circuitous route that led out from the capital northwards towards Amran and al-Harf. Here, Egyptian convoys had to swing south towards a place called Farah, before turning south-east along a route that followed the Wadi Humeidat and onwards to Marib and Harib. Given its clear vulnerability, a plan was now laid to cut this vulnerable supply artery in the hope that it would force an Egyptian collapse throughout the whole of north-east Yemen.[55] It played to the strengths of the Royalist forces, strengths that hitherto they had only intermittently exploited.

This plan had first been suggested at the beginning of January 1965 but now, under Saudi pressure, Prince Mohammed bin al-Hussein, the twenty-eight-year-old commander of the Royalist First Army in the Khowlan, was told in no uncertain terms by Smiley, Mills and Johnson that unless this particular supply route was attacked, Saudi aid would be withdrawn.[56] The pressure worked. The chosen spot was the Wadi Humeidat, a natural choke-point along the Egyptian supply route between Sana'a and Marib. It had been carefully selected by Mills, who, as the principal liaison officer with the Royalist First Army, brought an operational acumen and aggression to his command that, for Smiley, set it apart from the other Royalist fronts.

The target date of 4 April was postponed by eleven days, but the delay was more than justified by the results. In the most efficient battle fought by the Royalists during the entire civil war, 362 soldiers of the Royalist First Army, backed by 1,290 tribesmen from the Daham and Barat, directed by two British and three French mercenaries, cut this main supply route. Despite several days of determined Egyptian counter-attacks, they held their ground. At the same time, Egyptian positions were attacked at al-Urush north-east of Sana'a, around Sada and throughout the Khowlan. The success of the Humeidat operation meant that this supply route was denied to the Egyptian and Republican forces for the rest of the war. The remaining Egyptian garrisons in eastern Yemen, some 5,000 troops, now had to be supplied by air. Before too long, Nasser allowed these bases to wither on the vine. Faced with such military setbacks and their appalling toll on human life, he decided to consolidate his forces in a defensive triangle whose points were formed by Sana'a, Hodeidah and Taiz.[57] On 25 July 1965, Marib, the last remaining Egyptian garrison of any significance in eastern Yemen, capitulated to Royalist forces led by Prince Mohammed's brother, Abdullah.

The Humeidat operation was the apogee of Royalist military success and showed what could be achieved when disciplined forces, free from tribal politics, had a clearly defined military goal. It also proved the value of an integrated radio network that coordinated diversionary raids. Prince Mohammed proved himself a fine commander, directing his forces with much courage. When Egyptian paratroops threatened to retake the strategic heights of Jebel Ahmar, his leadership was crucial in driving them off the mountain top.[58]

By the summer of 1965, Nasser was on the defensive, and desperately sought a peace deal with King Faisal to let his forces extricate themselves from the Yemeni morass. Records stolen by Royalist sympathisers working at the headquarters of the Egyptian expeditionary force in Sana'a now revealed that, in the period between October 1962 and June 1964 alone, Egypt had lost 15,194 men killed, an average of 24 fatalities a day. Excluding the number of wounded, the rate of attrition on an army of some 60,000 men was unsustainable.[59] With his Republican charges in political disarray, his expeditionary force on the verge of collapse and an economy increasingly distorted by the demands of funding an unwinnable war, Nasser's position in Yemen had never been weaker. When, in August 1965, Nasser reached an agreement with the Saudi monarch in Jeddah for a phased withdrawal of his forces from Yemen, the British looked set to reap the benefits of the Royalist ascendancy in its efforts to turn the Federation into a viable sovereign entity.

But the Saudis now had other ideas. At the beginning of January 1965, King Faisal informed McLean of meetings he had held with those Republican dissidents that comprised the Third Force. Disillusioned with the leadership of Sallal, they now claimed to offer an alternative leadership without Egyptian support, but equally, without the return of the Imam.[60] While recognising that the Third Force had emerged as a result of circumstances inside the Republican government, McLean came to suspect that the Saudis were paying more than just mere lip service to its representatives. He concluded that Smiley, Mills and Johnson had been used by the Saudis to force Prince Mohammed to act precipitously, assuming that the Wadi Humeidat operation would fail. This would then allow the Saudis to disown the Royalists and switch support to a Republican movement that could equally serve Riyadh's interests. Smiley had been unaware of this wider agenda being played out in the Saudi court but he was soon persuaded that McLean was right. In an official report to King Faisal, in which he recalled his own experience in Albania, he wrote:

> It has been my policy to confine myself to military matters. However, as I fear politics may affect the military situation, I consider I must record my view that the support given in SAUDI ARABIA [sic] to the 'Third Party' will result in a weakening of the ROYALIST efforts against the Egyptians. This is because I have already seen signs of the ROYALISTS looking over their shoulders and taking their eyes off the target i.e. the EGYPTIANS. During the last war, when I was serving with guerrillas in Albania, the Royalists and Communists at first both fought the Germans. When it was apparent that the Germans were going to lose the war, both stopped fighting the Germans and fought each other. The result was that the Germans were able to make an unopposed withdrawal from the country. I can visualise a similar state of affairs taking place in the Yemen as I know the Royalist Amirs are already very suspicious that the SAUDI and BRITISH governments may support the 'Third Party' at the expense of the Royalists.[61]

Further doubt over the direction of the Royalist war effort was now cast by politics back in London and by the simmering tensions within the BMO itself. In October 1964, the Labour party under Harold Wilson somewhat surprisingly won a general election. Despite previous assurances to the Federal rulers, a defence white paper published in February 1966 announced that Britain would leave the Federation and abandon the Aden base by 1968. This decision has often been put down to the fragile state of the British economy and the need to defend sterling. But it had as much to do with a loss of political will in a governing party that had never been comfortable defending the last outposts of empire.[62]

The white paper emboldened Nasser not only to freeze the troop withdrawals agreed at Jeddah but also to increase troop numbers in Yemen. Before Britain announced its intended withdrawal, Egyptian forces had been reduced from 40,000 to 20,000. By the summer of 1966, the numbers had increased again to 60,000. Since Egyptian losses in the three years 1962–1965 were between 15,000 and 22,000, the argument that Britain saved Nasser from the folly of his Yemeni venture carries some weight. Mills recalls:

> We (the Royalists and the British mercenary organisation) produced a situation where we'd won, where the Egyptians were prepared to pull out completely from the Yemen. They went to see King Faisal in Jeddah and agreed to go and it was at this time that the new British government announced its intention to leave (South) Arabia. So we'd actually won the game, which is why I got so cross; we'd actually won the game and then it was given away politically because the Labour government was committed to a major defence cut.[63]

The anxieties within the mercenary hierarchy over the future of the BMO began to surface just as Smiley assumed command in the field. Arriving in Jeddah on 17 October 1965 before entering Yemen for the sixth time, he found spirits low among some of the British mercenaries because of simmering tensions between Johnson and McLean. The structure of the BMO as it evolved in the spring of 1963 had seen Johnson assume control of the tactical organisation in the field while McLean, as part of the overarching 'Strategic Planning Committee', had taken responsibility for diplomacy and political liaison with the Saudis. Herein lay the source of disagreement. More sensitive to the Saudi way of doing business, McLean was appalled that Johnson, upset that payment to the mercenaries was continually late or delayed, complained directly to the Saudi Minister of Defence, Prince Sultan. In one fractious encounter, he threatened that, unless salaries were paid forthwith, he would order all mercenaries to be withdrawn from Yemen by December 1965.

McLean was furious, believing that he should have dealt with this matter. Johnson's intervention was, he argued, not only ill-mannered but also an attempt by him, in collusion with Boyle, actually to take over total control of the BMO. A meeting between Prince Sultan, Johnson and Smiley on 18 November over the future of the mercenaries only made matters worse. Smiley confided in his diary that 'Jim's approach was very tactless and obviously resented by Amir Sultan.' McLean now reproached Smiley for failing to control Johnson at this meeting. This criticism took little account of the invidious position Smiley found himself in, caught between the rock of his old friendship with McLean and the hard place of responsibility to ensure that the mercenaries were paid.[64]

Writing to Moy from Jeddah on 2 December, he confessed that he was becoming 'increasingly disillusioned' and 'am seriously considering packing up this whole job out here'. Frustrated at being caught in the middle was only part of the story. His health had suffered from the physical demands of living and travelling with the tribes in the roughest of conditions. He arrived back home to Branxholm just before Christmas, with his return to Yemen planned for late January 1966. Instead, he found himself on the operating table, having cartilage removed from his left knee, which had collapsed under him while out shooting game. Fearful that, in his own words, he be accused of malingering, Smiley returned to Yemen still recovering from the effects of bilharzia and a knee that had not had time to recover fully. A self-portrait he took of himself in the Wadi Harib on his fiftieth birthday shows him cradling a carbine over his heavily bandaged knee. As he later wrote in *Arabian Assignment*, he realised that 'I was no longer fit enough for this kind of physical strain.'[65] His letters to Moy from Yemen had always been filled with love and deep affection, both for her and for the children, but now they increasingly revealed a longing for a more settled home life. But for his generous salary, he confided to her, he would gladly consider 'packing up this job out here. How I wish we were richer and did not have to worry about money so much.'[66]

However reluctantly, Smiley remained on the Saudi payroll for the next three years. Despite the love of his family for Branxholm, the heating costs alone were becoming prohibitive. So Smiley and Moy decided to put the money he had earned into buying

Fig. 12.6 Self-portrait on Smiley's fiftieth birthday, 11 April 1966. Note the heavily bandaged left knee.

a plot of land near to the small town of Jávea, near Alicante in Spain, with the intention of building a villa. But this need to build up his 'nest egg', as well as his loyalty to both McLean and the mercenaries under his command, saw him push to one side any immediate thoughts of resigning and make a further six trips to Yemen between March 1966 and March 1968. These trips were shorter, however, and avoided the period June to September, allowing Smiley to perform his largely unpaid ceremonial duties as a Gentleman at Arms of Her Majesty's Bodyguard, a recent appointment that necessitated his attendance at the royal household during state visits and other high occasions over the summer.

When back in the Middle East, he began to spend increasingly forlorn periods in hotel rooms in Jeddah rather than in the mountains of Khowlan, as the bickering within the hierarchy of the BMO continued. With Britain now bent on withdrawal from South Arabia by 1968, the mercenaries were of diminishing use to MI6. In a report circulated within the organisation by Johnson in the autumn of 1966, he acknowledged the 'stated indifference to our activities by MI6'.[67] Johnson and Boyle now decided to set up an alternative mercenary organisation on a more commercial basis, leading to a final split with McLean, Amery and Stirling in the spring of 1967, when the pair both resigned from the BMO, unable to obtain either the support or the confidence of Prince Sultan or the head of Saudi intelligence, Kemal Atham, in developing their new organisation.[68] In a rare criticism of McLean, Smiley confided to Moy that both 'Billy and Jim . . . are behaving like prima donnas'. Even so, his primary loyalty to his wartime colleagues effectively ended his association with the BMO. While he continued to write summaries of the Royalist war effort for the Saudis, events elsewhere determined the course of the Yemen civil war.[69]

On 5 June 1967, Israel launched a devastating attack on Egypt, which destroyed the Egyptian air force on the ground, smashing its army in Sinai. Within days of this pre-emptive strike, Israeli tanks were on the banks of the Suez Canal with the Sinai Peninsula under its total control. As Smiley had foreseen, the Egyptian army was no match for the Israelis. At the time of this humiliation, which Nasser did much to bring upon himself by becoming prisoner of his own hubris, Egypt still had over 50,000 troops in Yemen.[70] The outcome of the June 1967 war proved a watershed in the Arab–Israeli conflict, but was a catalyst for change too in the Yemen civil war. With his armed forces in ruins, Nasser had little choice but to evacuate the bulk of his army from Yemen, effecting a total withdrawal of all his forces by October 1967, a month before Britain's final withdrawal from Aden. The immediate consequence of the Egyptian departure was the fall of Sallal. Never a popular figure, even among those who supported the Republic, he was overthrown in a bloodless coup. He was replaced by General Hassan al-Amri, whose hostility to the *Hamid Ud-Din* was matched only by his deep loathing for the hapless Sallal. But al-Amri embodied a position that appealed greatly to the Saudis: no return of the Imamate but, equally, independence from Cairo.

Still, by December 1967, al-Amri's grip on power appeared tenuous. Emboldened by the generosity of the Shah of Iran and helped, albeit somewhat begrudgingly, by the Saudis, the Royalists, under their most able commander, Prince Mohammed, looked set to take the capital, Sana'a. Desperate times produced innovative measures, and the new Republican President managed to raise a 10,000–strong popular militia from the mainly *Zeidi* inhabitants of Sana'a to rally to the defence of the capital. At the same time, al-Amri turned to Moscow for help. In January 1968, thirty Soviet-piloted aircraft arrived, allowing the Republic to dominate the skies once again, bombing and strafing the Royalist positions at will. The siege of the city was lifted on 8 February 1968, when a strong force of Republican troops, with Soviet advisers, fought their way up from the port of Hodeidah. Prince Mohammed had lost his best chance to take the capital, win the war and restore his family's dynasty.[71]

The appearance of these Soviet advisers was enough to convince King Faisal that an accommodation with the existing rulers in Sana'a be sought as a matter of urgency. In March 1968, Saudi Arabia finally stopped all aid to the Royalist forces. Without the financial and martial wherewithal to bribe the tribes and to keep their allegiance, the Royalist forces quickly became a shadow of their former selves. When, in December 1968, the last Royalist stronghold at Hajjah fell to the Republicans, a feat achieved more through bribery than martial prowess, the Yemen civil war was effectively over. A coalition government emerged that embraced members of the Third Party. To placate fears of retribution in areas that had been strongly pro-Royalist or pro-Republican, governors of the right hue were appointed. Such magnanimity was not shown to members of the Yemen royal family. All princes were excluded from government, with Prince Mohammed seeking exile in Saudi Arabia. His cousin, Mohammed al-Badr, the last Imam of the *Hamid Ud-Din*, in whose name the Royalist cause was fought, also went into exile, ending his days in obscurity in the English home counties. In their last act of loyalty to him, Smiley, McLean and Amery signed his application for British citizenship.

What had Smiley really achieved in Yemen? Reflecting on his experiences over three decades later, he believed that, after 1966, it had 'all been rather a wasted effort', the defence of

British interests having been superseded by what he considered the unseemly haste of the Wilson government in withdrawing from South Arabia.[72] Once again he drew parallels with the Balkans, writing of 'the enthusiasm, the excitement, the hardship, the danger – the final disappointment; the wheel had turned full circle, back to Albania'.[73]

The parallels with the Balkans do not stop there. As in Albania, Smiley had been subject to forces whose scope and direction he, McLean and others within the BMO could at times influence but never control. Taking the Saudi riyal to protect what he, McLean and others perceived to be Britain's best interests could, given the anti-colonial *Zeitgeist* of the 1960s and 1970s, strike some as arrogant, indeed delusional. Perhaps. But surprisingly enough, testimony to their courage and conviction came from an unlikely source. Given their demonstrated antipathy to the role played by the mercenaries in Yemen, the Joint Intelligence Committee later ran this assessment of their worth:

> Their contribution was out of all proportion to their small number (a maximum of 30 British and 40 French at any one time). If they had not been present, the whole weight of Egyptian air power and modern infantry might have destroyed the Royalist forces as a cohesive body. Had that happened, at a time well before the June [1967] war when Nasser was still resurgent, it would have led to a serious effect on the stability of Saudi Arabia and the Persian Gulf. The threat against the Federation of South Arabia, which eventually became decisive, might have developed far earlier but for the contribution of the mercenaries towards tying down of the Yemeni Republican and Egyptian forces in the Yemen.[74]

Notes

1. TNA: CAB 130/189 GEN 776, The Yemen, Second Meeting, 31 October 1962.
2. Tom Bower, *The Perfect English Spy* (New York: St Martin's Press, 1995), p. 243.
3. For a definitive account of these tribal groupings and the transient

nature of their loyalty to the FSA, see Joseph Kostiner, *The Struggle for South Yemen* (London: Croom Helm, 1984). For a precise account of British policy towards Aden and the Federation, see Karl Pieragostini, *Britain, Aden and South Arabia: Abandoning Empire* (Basingstoke: Macmillan, 1991).
4. Clive Jones, *Britain and the Yemen Civil War 1962–1965: Ministers, Mercenaries and Mandarins – Foreign Policy and the Limits of Covert Action* (Brighton: Sussex Academic Press, 2004/10), pp. 39–45.
5. Jones, *Britain and the Yemen Civil War 1962–1965*, pp. 93–9.
6. Smiley, *Arabian Assignment*, p. 104.
7. DSP: First Trip to the Yemen, 14 June–16 July 1963. Letter from John Bruce-Lockhart to David Smiley, The Reform Club, Pall Mall SW1, 13 March 1963.
8. Interview with Colonel David Smiley, London, 16 September 2002.
9. DSP: First Trip to the Yemen. Diary entry for 22 June 1963.
10. DSP: First Trip to the Yemen. Diary entry for 29 June 1963.
11. DSP: First Trip to the Yemen. Letter from G. W. Wilson, Private Secretary, Secretary of State for War to Colonel D. de C. Smiley, M.V.O., O.B.E., M.C, 26 August 1963; Interview with Colonel David Smiley, London, 6 August 2002.
12. DSP: First Trip to the Yemen. Handwritten letter from David Smiley to Tom Dammann, 10 January 1964; David Smiley, 'Nasser's Air Terror', *The Yorkshire Post*, 5 May 1963.
13. DSP: First Trip to the Yemen. Transcript – BBC Light Programme 'Radio Newsreel' – 'Gas Bomb Attack in Yemen', Broadcast 18 July 1963; 'Focus – The Yemen', Border Television Limited, Broadcast 10 September 1963.
14. DSP: First Trip to the Yemen. Diary entry for 13 July 1963.
15. DSP: First Trip to the Yemen. Military Memorandum on a Visit to the Yemen by Colonel D. de C. Smiley, 14 July 1963.
16. DSP: First Trip to the Yemen. Report on a Visit to Royalist areas of the Yemen by Colonel David Smiley, MVO, OBE MC (handwritten), 14 July 1963; Personal Notebook.
17. See David W. Witty, 'A Regular Army in Counterinsurgency Operations: Egypt in North Yemen 1962–1967', *The Journal of Military History*, 65 (April 2001), pp. 401–39. See also Lt Cdr Youssef Aboul-Enein, 'The Egyptian–Yemeni War (1962–1967): Egyptian Perspectives on Guerilla War', *The US Army Professional Writing Collection*, available at <www.army.mil/professional

writing/volumes/volume2/march_2004/3_04_3.html> (last accessed 17 August 2005).
18. DSP: First Trip to the Yemen. Military Memorandum on a visit to the Yemen by Colonel D. de C. Smiley, 14 July 1963.
19. TNA PREM 11/4928: Note for the Record, 18 December 1963. Meeting between the PM and Colonel David Smiley at 10 Downing Street, Thursday, 17 December 1963. The Foreign Office was informed of the gist of the meeting *after* it had occurred.
20. Smiley, *Arabian Assignment*, p. 166.
21. IWM-NMP, Box 39. According to McLean's diary entry for 2 May 1963, he met Trevaskis, along with Flight Lieutenant Tony Boyle and Bill Allen, and the following day Trevaskis and Julian Amery. Bower, for one, also claims that Trevaskis was more deeply involved in covert support of the Royalist cause. See Bower, *The Perfect English Spy*, p. 248.
22. Peter de la Billière achieved the rank of Lieutenant General, in overall command of British Forces in the Kuwait Theatre of Operations in the 1990/1 Gulf War. He gave a self-censored account of his recruitment by Boyle in his autobiography. See de la Billière, *Looking for Trouble*, pp. 204–5.
23. Smiley, *Arabian Assignment*, pp. 181–2.
24. Dorril, *MI6*, pp. 685–6; IWM Sound Archive 10340/7 Interview with David Smiley.
25. IWM-NMP, Box 39, 'Traffic Passed since Opening the Line at Negub [sic]; DSP: Second Trip to the Yemen. Handwritten Note Listing Personnel; Interview with Colonel David Smiley, London, 16 September 2002; Johnny Cooper, *One of the Originals*, p. 174.
26. DSP: Second Trip to the Yemen. Notebook Entry of 20 November; Smiley, *Arabian Assignment*, pp. 156–7, 162, 187.
27. IWM-NMP, Box 41. Diary of Journey in the Yemen in July 1963. Points discussed with Crown Prince Hassan, 24/25 July.
28. IWM-NMP, Box 20. 'Handwritten note December 1963 – Meeting with Israeli MA'. 'Aluf Megan Hiram Nespach be'London vemakos Givli (Colonel Hiram posted to London to replace Givli', *Yediot Aharanot*, 21 April 1961. Yossi Melman, 'Our Man in Sana'a: Ex-Yemen President was once Trainee Rabbi', *Ha'aretz* (in English), 20 October 2008.
29. Michael Bar-Zohar, *Ya'acov Herzog: A Biography* (London: Halban, 2005), pp. 237–8.
30. IWM Papers of Tony Boyle and Colonel James Johnson Box 64/89/2. Typed Notes: Start of our collaboration.

31. DSP: CV of D. de C. S. (CV of David de Crespigny Smiley) undated; Interview with Colonel David Smiley, London, 1 December 2005; Interview with Colonel David Smiley, 20 October 2008.
32. Interview with Colonel David Smiley, 1 December 2005.
33. DSP: Second Visit to the Yemen. Diary entry for 15 November 1963; Middle East Centre, St Antony's College, Oxford, Accession Smiley GB165–0336 Oman Papers. Secret: Letter from Norman Darbyshire to Col. David Smiley, 12 July 1960; Letter from Norman Darbyshire to Col. David Smiley, 27 May 1960.
34. DSP: Fifth Visit to the Yemen. Diary entry for 26 May 1965.
35. Peres went on to occupy the highest government posts in Israeli politics, including foreign minister, defence minister, prime minister and president. Weizman became defence minister and foreign minister, and later president. DSP: Second Visit to the Yemen, 14 November–8 December 1963. Handwritten note listing Israeli officials and officers; Email correspondence with Colonel David Smiley, Subject: 'Herzog Book', 31st October 2005; Bar-Zohar, *Ya'acov Herzog*, pp. 240–1; Interview with Colonel David Smiley, London, 1 December 2005.
36. IWM Papers of Tony Boyle and Colonel James Johnson Box 64/89/2. Typed Notes: Start of our collaboration.
37. For a detailed account of the air drops from the Israeli side, see Asher Orkaby, 'The 1964 Israeli Airlift to Yemen and the Expansion of Weapons Diplomacy', *Diplomacy & Statecraft*, 26/4 (2015), pp. 659–77. Oz went on to pilot one of the Hercules aircraft as part of the famous Israeli rescue mission to Entebbe in July 1976.
38. Interview with Nahum Admoni and Efraim Halevy, Ramat Aviv, Israel, 30 July 2014. Admoni became director of the *Mossad* between 1982 and 1989; Halevy led the organisation between 1998 and 2002.
39. Interview with Colonel David Smiley, London, 16 September 2002.
40. The code name 'Mango' was chosen because, according to Johnson 'it was the only Egyptian fruit I knew that dropped when ripe'. See Ian Colvin, 'Rhodesia Plane Flew Arms to Yemen Royalists', *Daily Telegraph*, 5 February 1970. See also John Cooper, 'Our Man in the Yemen', *The Elite*, 9/105 (1986), pp. 2081–7.
41. See John Cooper, 'Our Man in the Yemen', pp. 2086–7. Cooper reprised this account in his autobiography, *One of the Originals* (London: Pan/Macmillan, 1991), pp. 177–8. In his description, published four years later, he omitted any direct mention of the Israelis, hinting only at the involvement of a 'friendly air force'.

Ronen Bergman, 'The Officer who Saw Behind the Top-Secret Curtain', *Yediot Aharanot*, 21 June 2015.
42. Interview with Colonel David Smiley, 16 September 2002; Johnny Cooper, *One of the Originals*, p. 178. Boyle described accompanying one such resupply flight on 30 March 1964, turning in across the Red Sea coast with the lights of Hodeidah shinning 40 miles to starboard. See Ian Colvin, 'Rhodesia Plane Flew Iron Curtain Arms to Yemen Royalists', *Daily Telegraph*, 5 February 1970.
43. DSP, Fifth Visit to the Yemen, 25 May–19 July 1965; Special Consignment No. 9, Special Consignment No. 10. Consignment No. 9, for example, consisted of sixteen card boxes that contained 60,000 rounds of .303 ammunition, 200 Lee Enfield .303 rifles, 12 Bren light machine guns, 100 anti-tank mines, 10 Sten sub-machine guns, 5,000 rounds of 9 mm ammunition, 6 bottles of whisky, 2 cases of beer, 2 cases of beef, 2 cases of peas, 1 case each of tinned carrots, pineapple and apricots, 5 gas masks and 100 detonators for anti-tank mines.
44. Smiley, *Arabian*, p. 199.
45. Interview with Colonel David Smiley, London, 6 August 2002, 16 September 2002; Interview with Efraim Halevy and Nahum Admoni, Ramat Aviv, 30 July 2014.
46. Colonel D. de C. Smiley, 'Aden Face-Saver for Yemen Failure', *The Scotsman*, 16 September 1965.
47. DSP: Third Trip to the Yemen. Report on a visit to the Yemen, 7 March–3 April 1964, by Colonel David Smiley. Appendix 'B', The Attack on Hajja.
48. DSP: Third Trip to the Yemen. Report on a visit to the Yemen, 7 March–3 April 1964, by Colonel David Smiley. Appendix 'C', Summary of what I told the Imam.
49. DSP: Third Trip to the Yemen. Letter from Colonel David Smiley to His Royal Highness, the Crown Prince Faisal of Saudi Arabia, 8 April 1964.
50. IWM-NMP Box 36. Personal Diary of visit to the Yemen, January–May 1965 by Lt Colonel Neil McLean; DSP: Fourth Trip to the Yemen, 3 March–9 April 1965.
51. DSP: Fourth Trip to the Yemen. Secret: Report by Colonel David Smiley on 4th Visit to the Yemen 10 March–19April 1965.
52. Smiley, *Arabian Assignment*, p. 191.
53. IWM-NMP Box 36. Personal Diary of Visit to the Yemen: January–May 1965 by Lt Col. Neil McLean DSO. Diary entry for 1 April 1965.

54. Smiley, *Arabian Assignment*, p. 192.
55. Dana Adams Schmidt, *Yemen: The Unknown War* (London: Bodley Head, 1968), pp. 221–2.
56. Smiley, *Arabian Assignment*, pp. 187–8; DSP: Fourth Trip to the Yemen. Diary 3 March–9 April 1965, diary entry for 29 March 1965.
57. DSP: Fourth Trip to the Yemen. Secret: Report by Colonel David Smiley on 4th Visit to the Yemen, March 10–April 5 1965, Appendix 'D'; Schmidt, *Yemen: The Unknown War*, pp. 221–3.
58. Smiley, *Arabian Assignment*, p. 190.
59. Schmidt, *Yemen: The Unknown War*, pp. 234–5. The Egyptian casualty figures were passed over to a Western intelligence agency but Schmidt does not disclose which one.
60. IWM-NMP, Box 9. Notes on Conversation with King Faisal – Jan. 1965.
61. DSP: Fourth Trip to the Yemen, 3 March–9 April 1965: Secret, Report by Colonel David Smiley on Visits to the Yemen March 10–April 5 1965, point 22.
62. DEFE 13/710 77705 Top Secret: Memo from the Chief of Defence Staff, Field Marshal Sir Richard Hull to the Secretary of State for Defence. Subject – The situation in Aden, 25 September 1965. For the breakdown of casualty figures, see Julian Paget, *Last Post – Aden 1964–1967* (London: Faber, 1969), p. 264. See also Petersen, *The Decline of the Anglo-American Middle East 1961–1969*. Petersen argues that it was the anti-colonial sentiment within the Labour party, rather than just Britain's economic malaise, that led to the withdrawal from Aden.
63. Interview with Bernard Mills, recorded as part of 'The Mayfair Set: David Stirling', BBC2, Broadcast 18 July 1999.
64. DSP: Sixth Visit to the Yemen, 13 October–10 December 1965. Diary entries for 18 November and 1 December 1965.
65. Smiley, *Arabian Assignment*, p. 220.
66. DSP: Sixth Visit to the Yemen. Letter to Moy dated 2 December 1965.
67. IWM-NMP, Box Unmarked. 'Report on the Yemen War', by H. J. J. (Jim Johnson), 1 October 1966.
68. DSP: Eighth Trip to the Yemen, 17–27 April 1967. Letter from David Smiley to Moy dated 13 April 1967.
69. DSP: Eighth Trip to the Yemen, 17–27 April 1967. Aide-mémoire (undated).
70. For accounts to the background of the June 1967 'Six Days War',

see Avi Shlaim, *The Iron Wall: Israel and the Arab World* (London: Allen Lane/Penguin, 2000), pp. 218–82; Benny Morris, *Righteous Victims* (London: John Murray, 2000), pp. 302–46.
71. For a more detailed exposition of the siege of the Yemeni capital on which this account is based, see Edgar O'Ballance, *The War in the Yemen* (London: Faber, 1971), pp. 189–202.
72. Interview with David Smiley, 6 August 2002.
73. Smiley, *Arabian Assignment*, p. 237.
74. TNA. CAB 158/69 Secret: The Mercenary Problem – Report by the Joint Intelligence Committee (A) (JIC(68) 9 (Final)), 19 April 1968.

13 An Uncomplicated Patriot

I

Yemen was Smiley's last direct experience of a 'hot war'. He had bought a small plot of land in 1966 with the money he had earned from the Saudis near a village called Jávea, between Alicante and Valencia, in southern Spain. Here, Smiley and Moy built a house they named, appropriately perhaps, 'Tara'. As the tourism industry grew and urbanisation spread along the Spanish coast, they sold Tara and bought a small farm near Beniarbeig, just 5 miles inland from Dénia. Here they built a bigger house and grew almonds, carobs, olives and avocados. It might not have been the agrarian existence Smiley had once envisaged for himself and Moy in Kenya, but he found a peace and contentment, stripped to the waist, pruning or spraying his trees and ploughing his fields as the seasons demanded. The farming was as much a hobby as a commercial enterprise, and harvesting was very much a family affair. Moy often collected the almonds that had fallen to the ground after Smiley had climbed the trees and shaken their branches.[1]

Spain was to be his home for the next two decades. It was cheaper and easier than living in Britain but close enough for family and friends to visit. By now, his own children had begun to spread their wings and the sacrifices he made in taking a half-pension to pay for school fees brought their reward. Smiley's stepson Gavin, educated at Eton and Christ Church, Oxford, was commissioned into Smiley's old regiment, the Blues. His stepdaughter, Anna, became a physiotherapist. Xan followed his stepbrother to Eton and Oxford, reading Russian and history at New College before becoming a foreign correspondent in Africa, the Middle East, the Soviet Union and the United States for *The Times*, *Daily Telegraph* and, longest of all, *The Economist*. Also educated at Eton, Philip graduated from St Andrews University and served as a district officer and then a provincial magistrate in the Solomon Islands before moving to Hong Kong, where he worked for the government before going into business. He was a banker in South Korea and Singapore before heading up operations for Jardine Matheson in South East Asia, based in Thailand. Smiley took great pride in all their achievements, although as Xan noted, his own youthful dalliance with left-wing or liberal causes often used to annoy his father, partly because it challenged his own values and partly because he struggled to articulate his own values of an established order that he had served so faithfully:

> It was the classic sort of clash between an 18 year old youth and a grumpy semi-retired man ... we used to have very long hair which would enrage him and he saw it as an attack on him which it was partly but as I got into my twenties we both came to see the point of each other.[2]

His conservative outlook may have been instinctive rather than being arrived at through reasoned political conviction, but it was no less heartfelt for that. He still maintained a voluminous correspondence with friends, colleagues and associates with whom he had served across the world, including, surprisingly perhaps, Said bin Taimur. In a letter written to the Sultan at the beginning of 1969, thanking him for the gift of a set of first edition stamps celebrating Oman's burgeoning oil industry, he expressed his hope that the Labour government of Wilson would soon fall, helped on its way by the re-election to parliament of Amery, who had lost his seat in the 1964 general election and was now fighting a by-election in Brighton:

> I only wish we had more politicians of his (Amery's) calibre in the Conservative Party. There would then be some hope of getting rid of Wilson and his gang who have done so much harm to our country by forcing on us their socialist policies well knowing that they were against the interests of the country.[3]

Smiley was kept abreast of developments in the Sultanate by friends and former colleagues. At the end of December 1969, O'Bryan Tear, the long-serving MI6 officer he had known in Aden, wrote to Smiley from his latest posting, Bahrain: 'Development in the Sultanate proceeds but at a snail's pace: after a lifetime of pinching and scraping the old man (the Sultan) simply can't bring himself to spending [sic] any money, the only thing that can still save him.'[4] With a full-blown insurgency in the Dhofar region in the south of the country supported by the newly independent People's Democratic Republic of Yemen, fears that a domino effect would see the emergence of left-leaning regimes across the Gulf sympathetic to the Soviet bloc was keenly felt in London. The eventual removal of the Sultan in July 1970 in a palace coup, orchestrated in large part by British contract officers with London's blessing, hardly caught Smiley by surprise. After all, during his tenure commanding the SAF, he had asked the Foreign Office to effect the Sultan's removal and replace him with his son, Qabus bin Said. He knew several of those involved, and it seems likely that O'Bryan Tear used his influence to support a dynastic putsch that eventually saw Said bin Taimur end his days in exile amid the luxury of the Dorchester Hotel in London.[5]

On his Spanish farm, Smiley found time to reflect on his life and pen his memoirs. In 1975, with the help of his wartime comrade, Peter Kemp, he wrote *Arabian Assignment*, an account of his adventures in Oman and Yemen. Written in a clipped, precise style, the book gave an honest account of his travails in both countries. Writing so close to the events, Smiley was guarded in his criticism of Bin Taimur and Waterfield in particular, although his private papers, later deposited at the Middle East Centre at St Antony's College, Oxford, disclose his personal animus towards Waterfield. Similarly, he was loath to describe the extent of the politicking within the BMO as it evolved during the Yemen civil war. Of his association with the Israelis and Operation Mango he gave no hint, out of loyalty to his Saudi employers and Yemeni friends. Nine years later, he published a more open account of his two wartime missions to Albania. Written with a self-deprecation that treads lightly around his own gallantry, *Albanian Assignment* none the less brooked no compromise with the view that Britain had backed the wrong side in eventually favouring Enver Hoxha. The pro-partisan views of left-wing officers in SOE Bari, he still maintained, undermined the true worth of Abas Kupi and the Zogist cause, and sacrificed longer-term British interests in the Balkans for short-term strategic gain.

Smiley's innate political leanings from the outset favoured the Zogist cause. Yet his wartime diaries clearly highlight his misgivings about Kupi, although Smiley continued to admire the Albanian. But *Albanian Assignment* makes scant mention of Kupi's evasions, extolling instead those episodes where Zogist guerrillas did help the Concensus mission to attack the Germans and Italians. Thus the help a Zogist unit gave him in destroying the Gjoles bridge, an act of great individual bravery and daring on Smiley's part, was cited at the time by McLean and Amery to unlock a British supply of arms to Kupi. That it failed to do so nurtured a lingering grievance that, in Kupi, Britain had betrayed a loyal patriot and had handed Albania to a loathsome individual and cause. This feeling intensified, rather than diminished, with the passing of time.

This became the accepted narrative until the publication of Reginald Hibbert's magisterial memoir, *Albania's National Liberation Struggle: The Bitter Victory*, published in 1991. Hibbert enjoyed a successful post-war career in the Foreign Office, becoming ambassador in Paris in 1979. However, a cloud of suspicion hung over him because of his youthful political leanings, which caused a rare moment of turbulence in his otherwise upward diplomatic trajectory. Hibbert's experience of working with the partisans was both sweet and sour, and their eventual triumph produced mixed emotions. Even so, Hibbert maintained it was right to have supported them in light of the Allies' wider strategy in the Balkans. When they were in the field in Albania, he repeated as much to Rowland Winn, later to serve under Smiley in Siam. But after the war, Winn continued to accuse Hibbert of pro-communist leanings, though Hibbert had long been cleared by an MI5 investigation in 1951.[6]

Such ideological sparring persisted in more learned journals. In 1996, Basil Davidson, a centre-left journalist and former SOE officer who had served with Tito's partisans, penned an entertainingly barbed riposte in the *London Review of Books* to those who believed conspirators within SOE had suborned British policy in the Balkans to the communist cause:

> To believe this conspiracy [he wrote], you had to believe that Churchill and his war cabinet, endorsing the British decision to 'switch' their aid [to the Partisans] had allowed themselves to be 'hoodwinked' by junior or very junior officers.[7]

Smiley's allegation that an SOE officer in Bari had deliberately suppressed McLean's signal to Eden requesting the immediate evacuation of Abas Kupi in 1944 now surfaced in an exchange of letters. One questioned Smiley's recall of the same event in *Albanian Assignment* and in his later, fuller memoir, *Irregular Regular*, published in 1994. Smiley was robust in his own defence, noting that *Irregular Regular* merely gave a fuller account of the same event, but added, 'Whether their [left-wing SOE officers'] actions actually affected the outcome of the struggle between communists and non-communists must remain open to debate.'[8]

By the time of this exchange, Smiley and Moy had left Spain and moved back to Britain. Old age and the cumulative effect of so many injuries acquired over the years of active service, combined with those picked up skiing or ice-tobogganing on the Cresta run in St Moritz (for which Smiley held the record for the most consecutive crashes), had taken their toll. In the 1980s, he had a hip replacement and hernia operation, and farming soon proved beyond him. In 1988, aged seventy-two, Smiley returned to London before settling into an old farmhouse near Castle Cary in Somerset. Five years later, he and Moy moved back to London for good, buying a comfortable Edwardian flat in Earls Court, where they could more easily enjoy the company of family and friends.

His life was now more sedate but it still did not deter travel to more exotic corners of the world; nor did it prevent him revisiting old battlegrounds. On one occasion, he even attempted to re-enter Albania as part of a botanical study group. When asked if he had visited the country before and, if so, where he had stayed, he simply replied 'Yes, in a cave'. His application was refused. But as the Cold War ended, the countries of Central and Eastern Europe increasingly opened their borders to the West. Amery, despite his acumen in foreign affairs, never reached his coveted post of foreign secretary, but none the less had maintained an abiding interest in the Balkans. Hoxha had exercised ruthless control over Albania until his death in 1985, ruling what had become, even by Eastern European standards, an impoverished land that modernity had almost passed by. Now, Amery was asked back to Albania by a new generation of politicians almost half a century after he had last set foot on its soil. He gladly accepted, with one proviso: his old comrades should be allowed to go with him. His hosts were only too happy to agree.[9]

Billy McLean had died in 1986, aged sixty-eight. His absence was keenly felt but now, accompanied by Smiley and Hare, and by Nicholas Shakespeare of the *Daily Telegraph*, Amery's party sallied forth for Albania in October 1991. The trip had been organised by the fledgling Democratic Party, who saw, in their veneration of these old SOE hands, a chance to put clear water between the boastful narratives of the old communist order that had sneered at British motives towards Albania during the war and continued to pour scorn on the risks taken by SOE to support the partisans. The Democratic Party, led by Sali Barisha and Gramoz Pashko, proved generous hosts, taking the trio back to their old stamping grounds across a country visibly struggling amid the most acute poverty. Perhaps the most emotional moment, caught on camera, was the reunion of Smiley and Hare with Shaqir Trimi, an old interpreter for the Concensus mission. He had survived twenty years in prison, four in solitary confinement. Smiley was overcome to see him: 'This is one of the happiest days in my life,' Shakespeare recalled him saying, 'To find you when I thought you had been murdered.'[10]

Age proved no barrier to visiting the scene of his more recent exploits too. In October 2002, aged eighty-seven, he was invited by the Yemeni government to visit Sana'a. Hoping to compile an official history of the 1962 revolution, Dr Abdul Karim al-Iryani, the former Prime Minister and Foreign Minister, was anxious to mine Smiley's memory and view his extensive photograph albums from his time with the Royalists. The Foreign Office advised

An Uncomplicated Patriot

against travelling to a country where an *al-Qaida* franchise was active, and close associates worried that Smiley's health would not stand the rigours of travel to a place where good medical care was decidedly limited. By now, he was both lame and hard of hearing. But accompanied by a young assistant, Alex Brittain-Catlin, Smiley set out for Sana'a in February 2003 on a trip lasting just over week. He found the trip fascinating, the sights and sounds of Sana'a, which he had previously seen only with the aid of binoculars, providing a particular enchantment. Still, he was not afraid to voice his opinion. He felt that the representation of the Yemen revolution in the military museum 'was more than a little tendentious'. Promising to furnish the archives in Sana'a with photographs of his time in Yemen – this collection amounted to nearly 700 pictures – he wrote, 'I look back on my week in Sana'a with immense gratitude for the kindness and hospitality which I received there. It was a moving and invigorating experience.'[11]

Frequent trips to Oman gave Moy and himself welcome breaks from the leaden skies of an English winter. He had always received a particularly warm welcome there, not least from Sa'id Salim al-Wuhaybi, whose leadership potential Smiley had first spotted when commanding the SAF; Smiley had recommended him to become the first Omani commissioned from the ranks. As a lieutenant, Sa'id Salim had been party to the planning of the coup that removed the old Sultan, vindication perhaps of Said bin Taimur's antipathy towards having Arab officers in his army. The support and loyalty given by Sa'id Salim to Sultan Qabus was amply rewarded, and he rose to head the royal *diwan*: in effect, the Sultan's cabinet. In the process, he became an extremely wealthy man, as a result of Oman's new-found oil. None the less, he readily acknowledged that, without Smiley's initial benediction, he would not have gained the riches and status he now enjoyed. Taken aback by what he considered to be Smiley's straitened circumstances, Sa'id Salim became a benefactor, lavishing him with perks, and paying for Smiley and Moy to join him in Oman and, on one occasion, to go around the world.[12]

Amid the tranquillity of his retired life in London, however, a new war in the Middle East brought heartfelt family tragedy. Alexander Tweedie, son of Smiley's stepson Gavin and his wife

Philippa, followed family tradition and joined the Blues and Royals. Acting in an armoured reconnaissance role, the regiment had been at the forefront of operations at the beginning of the Iraq war of 2003, and Tweedie had distinguished himself under fire. On 1 April, his Scimitar tank rolled down an embankment during a battle outside the port city of Basra, turning upside down in an irrigation channel and filling fast with water. Despite being evacuated back to the United Kingdom, Alexander Tweedie never regained consciousness and died three weeks later, aged twenty-five. He was buried in Minto church in the Scottish Borders, near an ancestral home of Moy, his paternal grandmother, with full military honours.[13]

II

As he approached his tenth decade, Smiley remained alert and recalled with clarity and precision events dating back to the 1930s and 1940s. He was in great demand and gave freely of his time to a new generation of academics and researchers as official archives opened and new works appeared in which his name and exploits often featured. A talented photographer, who took copious pictures wherever he served (often against official policy), these came to grace a plethora of books dealing with the Second World War and his post-war involvement in Albania and Oman. Realising too the value of much of what he had accumulated, from special equipment acquired during his time with SOE, to documents and photographs from his later service in Oman, he made generous donations to the Imperial War Museum in London and to the Middle East Centre at St Antony's College, Oxford. These remain invaluable resource to any student or academic researching the historiography of Anglo-Omani relations.

His own autobiography, *Irregular Regular*, was published in 1994; it was typically understated in describing actions where his bravery was recognised but circumspect in dealing with his involvement in Operation Embarrass, as well as the more sensitive aspects of his later service in Oman and Yemen. Even so, it offered glimpses into the life of a man whose loyalty to friends

An Uncomplicated Patriot

and to British interests, as he saw them, defined his very essence. What he had to say was treated with respect by those who met him, even if politically on opposite sides. Yevgeny Primakov, later to be head of the Russian foreign intelligence service and foreign minister, came across Smiley in Yemen as an officer of the KGB. Both men were attending the ill-fated cease-fire talks at Harad on the Yemeni–Saudi border at the end of 1965, each using respective press accreditation to justify their presence. Smiley made the point to Primakov that the Egyptian-backed Republicans would never be able to defeat the Royalist tribes, entrenched as they were in their mountain redoubts in the north. The Russian later wrote, 'He knew what he was talking about. As Colonel Smiley, he had been Britain's military attaché in Stockholm. He had also spent more than two years as an adviser to [Imam Mohammed] al-Badr.'[14] Whether Primakov knew or suspected Smiley's wider involvement in special operations and intelligence is unknown.

Smiley's name features in a host of studies, both academic and popular, dealing not only with SOE but with the relationship between intelligence and post-war British foreign policy as it tried to manage imperial decline. He, Amery and McLean sometimes came to be referred to as 'The Three Musketeers', their continued involvement in secret operations post-war being seen as evidence of how a small right-wing coterie used their contacts in the British secret service to try to shape foreign policy.[15] Without doubt, Amery used his political clout to have Smiley appointed to command what became the SAF, although this was not a clandestine role. The influence of Amery and McLean on Smiley's post-war career, and British covert operations post-war more generally, should not, however, be exaggerated. His posting to Poland and, crucially, his involvement in Operation Embarrass were certainly beyond their remit. The compartmentalisation within MI6 restricted knowledge of such operations to the necessary few. It was Perkins, not the other Musketeers, who approached Smiley to train the Pixies in Malta, while other old SOE Albanian hands, Hare and Northrop included, played equally important parts.

Being called a 'Musketeer', with his background in an elite cavalry regiment, influenced other accounts of Smiley in Operation Valuable. In a description bordering on plain caricature, the writer and journalist Ben Macintyre, in his biography of Kim Philby, remarked that 'the Albanian Recruits underwent intensive training under the watchful (if slightly mad eye) of Lieutenant Colonel David de Crespigny Smiley', adding, 'He was imperialist, fearless, romantic and unwary, and in all these respects, he was a neat reflection of Operation Valuable.'[16] Smiley was, however, far from mad, though there is no doubt that he justified British imperialism, on balance believing it to have benefited those whose lives it shaped. But the flaws in Valuable and the selection of recruits were hardly of his making. Moreover, the emphasis on the romantic side of his character was decidedly overplayed. He was first and foremost a professional soldier, doing a job. While he saw Valuable as helping to right what he considered a wrong perpetrated by SOE in 1944, it was an operation driven by the emerging Cold War. As his son Xan later opined,

> Dad is really very unpolitical except for the very basic 'whatever is in British interests'. His whole career was defined by 'were they on our side?' It was as simple as that ... he viewed these secondments or various arrangements with MI6 after the war as a cold war warrior.[17]

It was perhaps inevitable that some wondered if Smiley had inspired Ian Fleming's character, James Bond, or if his activities had, however tangentially, influenced John le Carré to adopt his name for his most famous spy character, George Smiley.[18] Bond was a composite of characters that Fleming had come across while working for naval intelligence in the Second World War. Smiley knew Fleming's elder brother, Peter, from his time in the Far East; there is no evidence, though, despite a conjectured link with Fleming's fascination for agents' gadgetry and the briefcase that blew him up in Siam, that Smiley's secret activities informed Fleming's creation.[19] And the cerebral character of George Smiley was far removed from the more active side of clandestine operations that marked the post-war activities of David Smiley in MI6. After the BBC dramatisation of *Tinker, Tailor, Soldier, Spy* in the autumn of 1979, Smiley wrote to David Cornwell (Le Carré's real name), asking if the use of his surname had been coincidental or inspired by his time as a tutor at Eton, when he might have taught two of his sons or cousins of his family. Cornwell replied he could not quite remember and may have borrowed the name from a school list. But Smiley's sons arrived at Eton after Cornwell had left and there is no evidence he knew the extent of Smiley's own involvement with MI6. Whatever the truth, Smiley saw at least one benefit from the publicity surrounding the book and TV series: people now knew how to spell his surname correctly.[20]

In his last years in Earls Court, Smiley continued to make occasional forays to regimental reunions, or meetings of the Anglo-Thai Society or the Anglo-Albanian Association. It was on one of those visits that he tripped and fell badly. His health gradually deteriorated and he finally succumbed to pneumonia on 9 January 2009. For Moy, his death was a blessed release for a man who had lived a physical life to the full: '[H]e was greatly irked by the infirmities of old age – a battle it always wins – and he was really glad to go.'[21] He was ninety-two.

III

David de Crespigny Smiley was an exceptionally brave man; he was also an exceptionally fortunate soldier. That he lived to such a grand old age was an extraordinary feat in itself. Over the years, he broke virtually every bone in his body, suffered acute bouts of bilharzia, dysentery and malaria, nearly died of typhoid, walked away from numerous air crashes and by chance was evicted from an aircraft that subsequently crashed, killing all on board. This list does not include brushes with death in the Middle East, North Africa, Albania and, of course, Siam.

Moy Smiley died in February 2011, aged ninety-one, two years after her husband. In the years before her death, she used to opine, half in jest that 'David had no imagination and that's why he was so brave.'[22] This chimed with the earlier observation of Smiley, made by Amery, that 'he liked his friends, disliked his enemies but was otherwise more interested in things than in men'. Alan Hare observed affectionately that Smiley 'was not very reflective'. Fair perhaps, but only up to a point. Despite the later portrayals of him as the romantic, he lived very much in the present, and while undoubtedly a risk-taker, the risks that he took were, for the most part, usually calculated. He was conscious that it was not only his own life that was so often on the line.

He was by no means the caricature of a cavalry officer, drawn from the upper class with its rigid social order. From his time as a newly commissioned cornet in the Blues to his time commanding the SAF in Oman, he led from the front, as he did on the Jebel Akhdar. While he believed in military hierarchy, he understood that 'the buck stopped at the top' and that real privilege had to be earned, not given. From all ranks, he enjoyed a great deal of 'street credibility' and this meant a great deal to him. Yet he felt wanting in his formal education, leading perhaps to something of an inferiority complex. He was well read but, next to McLean and in particular Amery, he always felt a political novice. Seeing how they handled diplomacy, not least during the Concensus II mission, he was much influenced by their view of the world. But his wartime diaries also reveal glimpses of an independent mind: for example, his doubts about so completely hitching their efforts to Kupi's wagon. That Smiley stayed the course speaks volumes regarding his loyalty to his friends.

This, and speaking truth to power, be it to politicians, senior officers or Arab princes, was his defining characteristic. It probably cost him his promotion and, most likely, the award of a DSO that was three times denied him. He certainly deserved it for his leadership in Oman. He also knew, however, that winning medals has always been something of a lottery. It has been suggested that this failure to reach a higher rank was because he was not a strategic thinker. There is an element of truth in this. He was certainly a 'doer' rather than a thinker. But it should not be forgotten that he was offered command of the three SAS regiments, an appointment later on realised at the rank of a brigadier. Perhaps his record as a practitioner of irregular warfare and clandestine operations seemed an unsuitable background for higher command. But he had passed out of staff college and commanded a regular brigade-sized formation in containing and defeating an insurgency in Oman, one of the few examples of British success in the Middle East before the triumph of the Dhofar campaign in 1976.

An Uncomplicated Patriot

Fig. 13.1 Earls Court, London, summer 2008, aged 92.

In the realm of special operations he was very much a practical thinker, though not inclined towards the more theoretical aspects of the subject. After his service in Albania, he analysed how future BLOs working with resistance forces should operate behind enemy lines. This recondite document later became a staple of the MI6 curriculum, and influenced how the idea of the four-man team, the basic organisational structure of the SAS, came to develop. Given the plethora of insurgencies faced by Britain after the war, this document's influence should not be lightly dismissed. As Perkins wrote to him of 'his book' in 1952, 'It has been of great value to our trainers in that it has brought BLO theory down to the realms of practical reality.'

Smiley's clandestine lives mirrored Britain's decline as pre-eminent world power. Whether it was wise or right after the war for MI6 to try to maintain an SOE-type capability has been debated. Sir Dick White, later to head both MI5 and MI6, referred to many of the former SOE types who had gravitated towards the secret service as 'being motivated by a nostalgia for lost causes', a barbed comment aimed particularly at Amery and McLean.[23] By the late 1960s, the 'bangs and bullets' ethos of SOE within MI6 had largely played out and the British secret service had returned to its core business of intelligence gathering. Even so, it should be remembered that, until 1966, MI6 retained close links with the mercenaries in Yemen, notably through Smiley and Johnson. Its own efforts to suborn tribal groupings inside Yemen to harm Egyptian intelligence and military assets in and around Taiz, a move away from the cautious approach initially adopted by MI6, had some success by 1965. These operations certainly bore an SOE imprint of sorts.[24]

The mercenary effort in Yemen presaged the controversial emergence of private security firms, notably from the 1990s onwards, as states in the developed world contracted out the provision of security – from protecting humanitarian workers or providing logistical support, through to actual combat operations – to what many critics now regard as little more than mercenaries operating for corporate profit. But it also embodies a more profound observation: that British clandestine operations post-war were largely defensive in their orientation, part of a wider foreign policy repertoire designed mainly to shore up existing British interests, rather than expand or promote new ones. The Directorate of War Planning was about the practical creation of stay-behind networks in the event of renewed conflict with the Soviet Union. Equally, Operation Embarrass was essentially reactive in nature, its ethos reflecting the support Smiley and other members of his Candle mission gave French officers in Indo-China who sought to preserve an empire. Trying to stem anti-colonial nationalism by the use of clandestine methods might have seemed foolhardy. But, for some in Whitehall, SOE poachers of the Second World War seemed well suited to be gamekeepers in its aftermath. Smiley excelled as both.[25]

Intelligence gathering was intrinsic to the clandestine lives led by Smiley, but ultimately, his engagement in secret service was defined by special operations, be it with SOE, MI6 or, later, the mercenaries in Yemen. Smiley enjoyed conventional soldiering and sometimes reckoned that the pinnacle of his career was his three years commanding his regiment, the Blues. But his time as a regular soldier punctuated his irregular activities, rather than the other way around. His career personified the wider struggles of a Britain trying to make sense of its place in a post-war world where its prestige, if not power, counted for a great deal less.

Smiley's funeral was held at Minto parish church on 24 January 2009. At the service, his son Xan gave an oration that was warm and humorous, capturing the character of a man imbued with service to his country. Noting his modesty and his absolute loyalty to friends at home and abroad, as well as his military achievements, he concluded:

> I'm proud that some of my father's exploits may go down in the annals of military history; and of course I'm proud of his bravery. But I think I'm proudest of all of the simpler virtues of his life: his disarming modesty, his uncomplicated patriotism, his down-to-earthness, his instinctive decency, above all his absolute straight-as-a-dye honesty.

It was a fitting tribute.

Notes

1. Interview with David Smiley, London, 21 October 2005.
2. Interview with Xan Smiley, Taston, Oxfordshire, 30 June 2006.
3. MEC Smiley Papers GB165–0336 1/1. Letter from David Smiley to Sultan Said bin Taimur, 15 January 1969.
4. DSP: Thirteenth Trip to the Yemen. Letter from Terry O'Bryan Tear to David Smiley (handwritten), Bahrain, 13 December 1969.
5. The BBC broadcast a detailed exposé of British government collusion in the coup. 'Britain and the Oman Coup', *Document*, BBC Radio 4, Broadcast 23 November 2009, available at <www.bbc.co.uk/programmes/b00ny7nb> (last accessed 1 November 2010).
6. Hibbert, *Albania's National Liberation Struggle*, pp. 242–3.
7. Basil Davidson, 'Goodbye to Some of That', *London Review of Books*, 18/16 (August 1996), p. 20.
8. David Smiley, Letter to the Editor of the *London Review of Books*, dated 12 December 1996, *London Review of Books*, 18/24 (December 1996).

9. Bassett, *Last Imperialist*, p. 243.
10. Nicholas Shakespeare, 'Return to the Land of Zog', *Daily Telegraph Weekend*, 5 October 1991.
11. David Smiley, 'Return to the Yemen', *The British-Yemeni Society Journal*, 11 (2003), p. 23.
12. Interview with David Smiley, London, 21 October 2005.
13. Obituary. 'Lieutenant A. D. Tweedie, Late Blues and Royals, *Household Cavalry Journal*, 2003/4, p. 95; 'The Fallen', BBC2, Broadcast 15 November 2008.
14. Yevgeny Primakov (translated by Paul Gould), *Russia and the Arabs* (New York: Basic Books, 2009), p. 96.
15. Dorril, *MI6*, p. 677; Corera, *The Art of Betrayal*, p. 60.
16. Ben Macintyre, *A Spy Among Friends: Philby and the Great Betrayal* (London: Bloomsbury, 2015), pp. 123–4.
17. Interview with Xan Smiley, Taston, Oxfordshire, 30 June 2006.
18. Steve Doughty, 'Smiley: Gentleman Spy', *The Daily Mail*, 1 July 1997; Obituary: 'Colonel David Smiley', *The Daily Telegraph*, 10 January 2009.
19. Jack Malvern, 'Exhibition pays Tribute to the Spy who Blew Himself Up', *The Times*, 31 August 2013.
20. Adam Sisman, *John le Carré: The Biography* (London: Bloomsbury, 2015), pp. 408–9.
21. Personal letter from Moy Smiley to the author, 2 February 2009.
22. Interview with Xan Smiley, Taston, Oxfordshire, 30 June 2006.
23. Jones, *Britain and the Yemen Civil War*, p. 114.
24. Private information.
25. For an analysis of Britain's use of special operations as a tool of foreign policy, see Rory Cormac, *Disrupt and Deny: Spies, Special Forces and the Secret Pursuit of British Foreign Policy* (Oxford: Oxford University Press, 2018).

Bibliography

Primary Sources

The National Archives
Cabinet Office: Series CAB 130/189; 158/69; 182/49; 182/54.
Colonial Office: Series CO 1015; 1055/2/3/4/5/6/7/10/11/13/29/216.
Foreign Office: Series FO 371/164094; 164156; 168816; 168831–44; 174482; 1746633–39.
MI5: Series KV 3/56.
Ministry of Defence: Series DEFE 7/1304; 13/406; 13/569; 13/570; 13/571; 13/710; 25/128; 25/129; 32/10.
Prime Minister's Office: Series PREM 11/4928, 4929, 4980; 13/1923, 2688.
Special Operations Executive: Series HS1/68; HS7/69.
War Office: Series WO 181/354; 212/191–196; 337/10.

Imperial War Museum, London
Papers of Wing Commander James Blackburn, IWM File 12/19/1.
Papers of Tony Boyle and Colonel James Johnson, IWM Files 64/89/1–4.
Papers of Lieutenant Colonel Neil 'Billy' McLean, IWM Boxes 3,4,6,9,10,19,20,36,39,41.
Papers of Major W. S. Moss, IWM 05/74/1.
Diary of Major D. Smiley, Concensus Mission I, April–October 1943.
Diary of Major D. Smiley, Concensus Mission II, April–November 1944.
Transcript: Accession No: 10340/6 The Middle East in the Second World War; D. Smiley.

Department of Sound Records
Accession No: 8980 Interview with Julian Amery.
Accession No: 10340/6 The Middle East in the Second World War – D. Smiley.

Churchill College, Cambridge University
Julian Amery Papers.
Duncan Sandys Papers.

Middle East Centre, St Anthony's College, Oxford
Papers of Colonel David de Crespigny Smiley – Muscat and Oman 1958–61.

Liddell Hart Centre for Military Archives, King's College London
Papers of Major General Anthony John Deane-Drummond.
Papers of Lieutenant Colonel Count J. A. Dobrski (alias Lt. Col J. A. Dolbey).
Papers of Brigadier E. C. W. Myers.

Private Archives
Papers of Colonel David Smiley, Files for the Yemen 1963–8.

Interviews
Colonel David Smiley (all interviews took place in London), 6 August 2002; 16 September 2002; 18 February 2005; 22 August 2005; 21 October 2005; 1 December 2005; 22 February 2006; 20 October 2008.
Moyra Smiley (née Scott), London, 22 February 2006.
Xan Smiley, Taston, Oxfordshire, 30 June 2006.
Nahum Admoni, Tel Aviv, 14 July 2014.

Microfilm
CIA Research Reports – Middle East 1946–1976 (Bethesda, MD: University of America Publications, 1983). Reel 1 (0214); Reel 2 (0039, 0058, 0064, 0068).

Secondary Sources

Books
Aldrich, Richard J. (2000), *Intelligence and the War Against Japan: Britain, America and the Politics of Secret Service*, Cambridge: Cambridge University Press.
Aldrich, Richard J. (2001), *The Hidden Hand: Britain, America and Cold War Secret Intelligence*, London: John Murray.
Aldrich, Richard J. (2004), *Witness to War*, London: Doubleday.

Bibliography

Aldrich, Richard J. (2010), *GCHQ: The Uncensored Story of Britain's Most Secret Intelligence Agency*, London: HarperCollins.

Aldrich, Richard J. and Rory Cormac (2016), *The Black Door: Spies, Secret Intelligence and British Prime Ministers*, London: HarperCollins.

Aldrich, Richard J., Rory Cormac and Michael S. Goodman (2014), *Spying on the World: The Declassified Documents of the Joint Intelligence Committee*, Edinburgh: Edinburgh University Press.

Allfree, P. S. (1968), *Warlords of Oman*, New York: Barnes and Noble.

Amery, Julian (1948), *Sons of the Eagle: A Study in Guerrilla Warfare*, London: Macmillan.

Amery, Julian (1973), *Approach March*, London: Hutchinson.

Andrew, Christopher (1985), *Secret Service*, London: William Heineman.

Andrew, Christopher (2009), *The Defence of the Realm: The Authorized History of MI5*, London: Allen Lane.

Andrews, Geoff (2015), *The Shadow Man: At the Heart of the Cambridge Spy Circle*, London: I. B. Tauris.

Asher, Michael (1995), *Thesiger*, London: Penguin.

Bailey, Roderick (2008a), *The Wildest Province: SOE in the Land of the Eagle*, London: Vintage/Jonathan Cape.

Bailey, Roderick (2008b), *Forgotten Voices of the Secret War*, London: Ebury/Imperial War Museum.

Bar-Zohar, Michael (2005), *Ya'acov Herzog: A Biography*, London: Halban.

Bassett, Richard (2015), *Last Imperialist: A Portrait of Julian Amery*, York: Stone Trough.

Bauer, Yehuda (1970), *From Diplomacy to Resistance: A History of Jewish Palestine 1939–1945*, Philadelphia: Jewish Publication Society of America.

Beevor, J. G. (1981), *SOE: Recollections and Reflections 1940–45*, London: Bodley Head.

Bethell, Nicholas (1984), *The Great Betrayal: The Untold Story of Kim Philby's Biggest Coup*, London: Hodder and Stoughton.

Bethell, Nicholas (2016), 'Interview with Anthony Northrop, March/April 1984', in Robert Elsie and Bejtullah Destani (eds), *The Albanian Operation of the CIA and MI6, 1949–1953: Conversations with Participants in a Venture Betrayed*, Jefferson, NC: McFarland.

Bloch, Jonathan and Patrick Fitzgerald (1983), *British Intelligence and Covert Action*, Dingle, Co. Derry: Brandon.

Bower, Tom (1995), *The Perfect English Spy*, New York: St Martin's Press.

Boyce, Frederic and Douglas Everett (2003), *SOE: The Scientific Secrets*, Stroud: Sutton.
Bulletin du Comité International d'Histoire de la Deuxième Guerre Mondiale (2000), *The Second World War in XXth Century History – Oslo August 11–12, 2000*, St-Just-la-Pendue: Brochage.
Burrows, Bernard (1990), *Footnotes in the Sand: The Gulf in Transition 1953–1958*, Salisbury: Michael Russell.
Burrows, R. D. (1987), *The Yemen Arab Republic: The Politics of Development, 1962–1986*, Boulder, CO: Westview.
Cavendish, Anthony (1997), *Inside Intelligence: The Revelations of an MI6 Officer*, London: HarperCollins.
Cesarani, David (2009), *Major Farran's Hat*, London: Heinemann.
Cockburn, Andrew and Leslie Cockburn (1992), *Dangerous Liaison: The Inside Story of the US–Israeli Covert Relationship*, London: Bodley Head.
Cooper, Artemis (1989), *Cairo in the War 1939–1945*, London: Hamish Hamilton.
Cooper, Johnny (with Peter Kemp) (1991), *One of the Originals*, London: Pan/Macmillan.
Corera, Gordon (2011), *The Art of Betrayal: Life and Death in the British Secret Service*, London: Weidenfeld & Nicolson.
Cormac, Rory (2014), *Confronting the Colonies: British Intelligence and Counterinsurgency*, London: Hurst.
Cormac, Rory (2018), *Disrupt and Deny: Spies, Special Forces and the Secret Pursuit of British Foreign Policy*, Oxford: Oxford University Press.
Craddock, Percy (2002), *Know Your Enemy: How the Joint Intelligence Committee Saw the World*, London: John Murray.
Cruickshank, Charles (1983), *SOE: Special Operations Executive in the Far East*, Oxford: Oxford University Press.
Davidson, Basil (1980), *Special Operations Europe: Scenes from the Anti-Nazi War*, London: Victor Gollancz.
Davies, Philip H. J. (2004), *MI6 and the Machinery of Spying*, London: Frank Cass.
Davies, 'Trotsky' (1952), *Illyrian Adventure*, London: Bodley Head.
Davis, Wes (2015), *The Ariadne Objective*, London: Corgi/Transworld.
Deakin, F. W. D. (1971), *The Embattled Mountain*, London: Oxford University Press.
De Chair, Somerset (1945), *The Golden Carpet*, New York: Harcourt Brace.

Bibliography

De Crespigny, Claude Champion (1910), *Forty Years of a Sportsman's Life*, London: Mills and Boon.
de la Billière, Peter (1994), *Looking for Trouble: SAS to Gulf Command*, London: HarperCollins, 1994.
Dorril, Stephen (2000), *MI6: Fifty Years of Special Operations*, London: Fourth Estate.
Dresch, Paul (2000), *A History of Modern Yemen*, Cambridge: Cambridge University Press.
Elsie, Robert and Bejtullah Destani (eds), *The Albanian Operation of the CIA and MI6, 1949–1953: Conversations with Participants in a Venture Betrayed*, Jefferson, NC: McFarland.
Fergusson, Bernard (1971), *The Trumpet in the Hall*, London: Collins.
Fielding, Xan (1990), *One Man in his Time: The Life of Lieutenant-Colonel NLD ('Billy') McLean, DSO*, London: Macmillan.
Fischer, Bernd J. (1999), *Albania at War*, London: Hurst.
Foot, M. R. D. (1976), *Resistance: European Resistance to Nazism 1940–45*, London: Eye Methuen.
Foot, M. R. D. (1999), *The Special Operations Executive 1940–46*, London: Pimlico.
Geraghty, Tony (1980), *Who Dares Wins: The Story of the Special Air Service*, London: Book Club Associates.
Geraghty, Tony (1996), *Beyond the Front Line: The Untold Exploits of Britain's Most Daring Cold War Spy Mission*, London: HarperCollins.
Geraghty, Tony (2007), *Guns for Hire: The Inside Story of Freelance Soldiering*, London: Portrait/Piatkus.
Gerber, Haim (1988), *Islam, Guerrilla War and Revolution*, London: Lynne Rienner.
Gerolymatos, André (1992), *Guerrilla Warfare and Espionage in Greece 1940–1944*, New York: Pella.
Gerolymatos, André (2010), *Castles Made of Sand: A Century of Anglo-American Espionage and Intervention in the Middle East* (New York: St Martin's/Thomas Dunne).
Golani, Motti (2013), *Palestine between Politics and Terror 1945–1947*, Lebanon, NH: Brandeis University Press/University Press of New England.
Graham, John (1999), *Ponder Anew: Reflections on the Twentieth Century*, Staplehurst: Spellmount.
Grey, Stephen (2015), *The New Spymasters: Inside Espionage from the Cold War to Global Terror*, London: Penguin/Viking.
Halliday, Fred (1975), *Arabia without the Sultans*, Harmondsworth: Penguin.

Harclerode, Peter (2002), *Fighting Dirty: The Inside Story of Covert Operations from Ho Chi Minh to Osama bin Laden*, London: Cassell.
Hart-Davis, Duff (2011), *The War That Never Was*, London: Century/Random House.
Hastings, Max (2015), *The Secret War: Spies, Codes and Guerrillas 1939–1945*, London: William Collins.
Healey, Denis (1990), *The Time of My Life*, New York: Norton.
Heikal, Mohammed (1996), *Secret Channels: The Inside Story of Arab–Israeli Peace Negotiations*, London: HarperCollins.
Hibbert, Reginald (1991), *Albania's National Liberation Struggle*, London: Pinter.
Hinchcliffe, Peter, John T. Ducker and Maria Holt (2006), *Without Glory in Arabia: The British Retreat from Aden*, London: I. B. Tauris.
Hoe, Alan (1996), *David Stirling*, London: Warner.
Howarth, Patrick (2000), *Undercover: The Men and Women of SOE*, London: Phoenix.
Hudson, Sydney (2003), *Undercover Operator: An SOE Agent's Experiences in France and the Far East*, Barnsley: Pen & Sword.
Innes, Neil NcLeod (1987), *Minister in Oman*, Cambridge: Oleander.
Jackson, Ashley (2006), *The British Empire and the Second World War*, London: Continuum.
Jakub, Jay (1999), *Spies and Saboteurs: Anglo-American Collaboration and Rivalry in Human Intelligence Collection and Special Operations, 1940–45*, Basingstoke: Macmillan.
Jeffrey, Keith (2010), *MI6: The History of the Secret Intelligence Service 1909–1949*, London: Bloomsbury.
Jones, Clive (2004/2010), *Britain and the Yemen Civil War 1962–1965: Ministers, Mercenaries and Mandarins – Foreign Policy and the Limits of Covert Action*, Brighton: Sussex Academic Press.
Kelly, J. B. (1980) *Arabia, the Gulf and the West*, New York: Basic Books.
Kemp, Anthony (1994), *The SAS: Savage Wars of Peace*, London: John Murray.
Kemp, Peter (1990), *The Thorns of Memory*, London: Sinclair-Stevenson.
Kerr, Malcolm (1965), *The Arab Cold War 1958–1964: A Study of Ideology in Politics*, Oxford: Oxford University Press.
Kitson, Frank (1987), *Bunch of Five*, London: Faber & Faber.
Kostiner, Joseph (1984), *The Struggle for South Yemen*, London: Croom Helm.
Kyle, Keith (1991), *Suez*, London: Weidenfeld and Nicolson.
Liddle, Peter (2011), *Captured Memories 1939–1945: Across the*

Threshold of War – The Thirties and the War, Volume II, Barnsley: Pen & Sword.
Lulushi, Albert (2014), *Operation Valuable Fiend: The CIA's First Paramilitary Strike Against the Iron Curtain*, New York: Arcade.
Lyman, Robert (2006), *First Victory: Britain's Forgotten Struggle in the Middle East, 1941*, London: Constable.
Macintyre, Ben (2015), *A Spy Among Friends: Philby and the Great Betrayal*, London: Bloomsbury.
Mackenzie, William (2002), *The Secret History of SOE: Special Operations Executive 1940–1945*, London: St Ermin's.
Maclean, Fitzroy (1991), *Eastern Approaches*, London: Penguin.
McNamara, Robert (2003), *Britain, Nasser and the Balance of Power in the Middle East, 1952–1967*, London: Frank Cass.
Mann, Michael (1994), *The Trucial Oman Scouts: The Story of a Bedouin Force*, Norwich: Michael Russell.
Mawby, Spencer (2005), *British Policy in Aden and the Protectorates 1955–67*, Abingdon: Routledge.
Messenger, Charles (1988), *The Middle East Commandos*, London: William Kimber.
Messenger, Charles (1991), *The Commandos 1940–1946*, London: Grafton.
Mockaitis, Thomas R. (1995), *British Counterinsurgency in the Post-Imperial Era*, Manchester: Manchester University Press.
Morison, John (ed.) (1992), *Eastern Europe and the West*, London: Macmillan/St Martin's Press.
Morris, Benny (2000), *Righteous Victims*, London: John Murray.
Myers, E. C. W. (1955), *Greek Entanglement*, London: Rupert Hart-Davis.
Noon, Tom (1991), *This Grim and Savage Game: OSS and the Beginning of US Covert Operations in WWII*, Los Angeles: Burning Gate.
Nutting, Anthony (1996), *No End of a Lesson: The Story of Suez*, London: Constable.
Oakley-Hill, D. R. (2002), *An Englishman in Albania: Memoires of a British Officer 1929–1955*, London: Centre for Albanian Studies.
O'Ballance, Edgar (1971), *The War in the Yemen*, London: Faber.
O'Brien, Terence (1987), *The Moonlight War: The Story of Clandestine Operations in South-East Asia, 1944–5*, London: William Collins.
Orkaby, Asher (2017), *Beyond the Arab Cold War: The International History of the Yemen Civil War, 1962–68*, Oxford: Oxford University Press.
Ovendale, Ritchie (1996), *Britain, the United States and the Transfer of*

Power in the Middle East, 1945–1962, Leicester: Leicester University Press.
Paget, Julian (1969), *Last Post – Aden 1964–1967*, London: Faber.
Peebles, Curtis (2005), *Twilight Warriors. Covert Air Operations against the USSR*, Annapolis, MD: Naval Institute Press.
Petersen, Tore T. (2006), *The Decline of the Anglo-American Middle East 1961–1969: A Willing Retreat*, Brighton: Sussex Academic Press.
Petersen, Tore T. (ed.) (2010), *Challenging Retrenchment: The United States, Great Britain and the Middle East 1950–1980*, Trondheim: Rostra/Tapir Academic Press.
Peterson, J. E. (2007), *Oman's Insurgencies*, London: Saqi.
Pettifer, James (ed.) (2013), *Albania and the Balkans: Essays in Honour of Sir Reginald Hibbert*, Cornwall: Elbow.
Philby, Kim (2002), *My Silent War: The Autobiography of a Spy*, New York: Modern Library.
Phythian, Mark (2000), *The Politics of British Arms Sales since 1964*, Manchester: Manchester University Press.
Pieragostini, Karl (1991), *Britain, Aden and South Arabia: Abandoning Empire*, Basingstoke: Macmillan.
Podeh, Elie (1999), *The Decline of Arab Unity: The Rise and Fall of the United Arab Republic 1958–1961*, Brighton: Sussex Academic Press.
Primakov, Yevgeny (2009), *Russia and the Arabs*, translated by Paul Gould, New York: Basic Books.
Rabi, Uzi (2007), *The Emergence of States in a Tribal Society: Oman under Sa'id bin Taymur 1932–1970*, Brighton: Sussex Academic Press.
Reynolds, E. Bruce (2005), *Thailand's Secret War: OSS, SOE and the Free Thai Underground during World War II*, Cambridge: Cambridge University Press.
Rigden, Denis (2001), *SOE Syllabus: Lessons in Ungentlemanly Warfare, World War II*, London: Public Record Office.
Ritchie, Sebastian (2011), *The RAF, Small Wars and Insurgencies: Later Colonial Operations, 1945–1975*, Air Historical Branch/RAF Centre for Air Power Studies.
Rose, Norman (2009), *'A Senseless Squalid War': Voices from Palestine 1945–1948*, London: Bodley Head.
Schmidt, Dana Adams (1968), *Yemen: The Unknown War*, London: Bodley Head.
Schwander-Sievers, Stephanie and Bernd J. Fischer (eds) (2002), *Albanian Identities: Myth and History*, London: Hurst.
Seaman, Mark (ed.) (2006), *Special Operations Executive: A New Instrument of War*, London: Routledge.

Bibliography

Shlaim, Avi (2000), *The Iron Wall: Israel and the Arab World*, London: Allen Lane/Penguin.
Sisman, Adam (2015), *John le Carré: The Biography*, London: Bloomsbury.
Smiley, David (with Peter Kemp) (1975), *Arabian Assignment*, London: Leo Cooper.
Smiley, David (1984), *Albanian Assignment*, London: Chatto & Windus.
Smiley, David (1994), *Irregular Regular*, Norwich: Michael Russell.
Souhami, Diana (2000), *Greta and Cecil*, London: Phoenix Press.
Stanley Moss, William (2014), *A War of Shadows*, London: Bene Factum.
Stafford, David (1983), *Britain and European Resistance 1940–1945: A Survey of the Special Operations Executive with Documents*, Toronto: University of Toronto Press.
Stephens, Roger (1978), *Nasser*, Harmondsworth: Penguin.
Stookey, Robert W. (1978), *Yemen: The Politics of the Yemen Arab Republic*, Boulder, CO: Westview.
Summers, Julie (2005), *The Colonel of Tamarkan: Philip Toosey and the Bridge on the River Kwai*, London: Simon & Schuster.
Sweet-Escott, Bickham (1965), *Baker Street Irregular*, London: Methuen.
Thomas, Gordon (2010), *Operation Exodus*, London: JR Books.
Thomas, Martin (2008), *Empires of Intelligence: Security Services and Internal Disorder after 1914*, Berkeley: University of California Press.
Thwaites, Peter (1995), *Muscat Command*, London: Leo Cooper/Pen & Sword.
Trevaskis, Kennedy (1968), *Shades of Amber: A South Arabian Episode*, London: Hutchinson.
Verrier, Anthony (1983), *Through the Looking Glass: British Foreign Policy in the Age of Illusions*, London: Jonathan Cape.
Von Horn, Carl (1966), *Soldiering for Peace*, London: Cassell.
Walker, Jonathan (2005), *Aden Insurgency: The Savage War in South Arabia 1962–67*, Staplehurst: Spellmount.
Walton, Calder (2013), *Empire of Secrets: British Intelligence, the Cold War and the Twilight of Empire*, London: HarperCollins.
West, Nigel (1988), *The Friends: Britain's Post-War Secret Intelligence Operations*, London: Weidenfeld & Nicolson.
West, Nigel (1993), *Secret War: The Story of SOE, Britain's Wartime Sabotage Organisation*, London: Coronet.
West, Nigel (2009), *The A–Z of British Intelligence*, Plymouth: Scarecrow.
White-Spunner, Barney (2006), *Horse Guards*, London: Macmillan.

Wilkinson, Peter (2002), *Foreign Fields: The Story of an SOE Operative*, London: I. B. Tauris.
Wilkinson, Peter with Joan Bright-Astley (1993), *Gubbins and SOE*, Barnsley: Pen & Sword/Leo Cooper.
Williams, Heather (2003), *Parachutes, Patriots and Partisans: The Special Operations Executive and Yugoslavia 1941–1945*, London: Hurst.
Winks, Robin W. (1987), *Cloak and Gown: Scholars in the Secret War 1939–1961*, New Haven, CT, and London: Yale University Press.
Winnifrith, Tom (2013), 'A Betrayal Betrayed: Kim Philby and Albania', in James Pettifer (ed.), *Albania and the Balkans*, Cornwall: Elbow.
Zamir, Meir (2014), *The Secret Anglo-French War in the Middle East: Intelligence and Decolonization*, London: Routledge.

Articles

Abadi, Jacob (1995), 'Britain's Abandonment of South Arabia – A Reassessment', *Journal of Third World Studies*, 12/1, pp. 152–80.
Aboul-Enein, Lt Cdr Youssef (2004), 'The Egyptian–Yemeni War (1962–1967): Egyptian Perspectives on Guerilla War', *The US Army Professional Writing Collection*, available at <www.army.mil/professional writing/volumes/volume2/march_2004/3_04_3.html> (last accessed 17 August 2005).
Al-Albin, A. Z. (1979), 'The Free Yemeni Movement and its Ideas on Reform', *Middle Eastern Studies*, 15/1, pp. 36–48.
'Aluf Megan Hiram Nespach be'London vemakos Givli (Colonel Hiram posted to London to replace Givli', *Yediot Aharanot*, 21 April 1961
Amery, Julian (1987), 'Billy McLean: 1918–1986', *Central Asian Survey*, 6/2, pp .3–6.
Anglim, Simon (2005a), 'Orde Wingate, the Iron Wall and Counter Terrorism in Palestine 1937–39', *The Strategic and Combat Studies Institute*, Occasional Paper No. 49.
Anglim, Simon (2005b), ' MI(R), G(R) and British Covert Operations, 1939–42', *Intelligence and National Security*, 20/4, pp. 631–53.
Bergman, Ronen (2015), 'The Officer who Saw Behind the Top-Secret Curtain', *Yediot Aharanot*, 21 June.
Bishku, Michael B. (1992), 'The Kennedy Administration, the U.N. and the Yemen Civil War', *Middle East Policy*, 1/4, pp. 116–28.
Cecil, Robert (1986), '"C's" War', *Intelligence and National Security*, 1/2, p. 182.
Colvin, Ian (1970), 'Rhodesia Plane Flew Arms to Yemen Royalists', *Daily Telegraph*, 5 February.

Bibliography

Cooper, John (1986), 'Our Man in the Yemen', *The Elite*, 9/105, pp. 2081–7.

Davidson, Basil (1996), 'Goodbye to Some of That', *London Review of Books*, 18/16 (August), p. 20.

Davies, Philip H. J. (2000), 'From Special Operations to Special Political Action: The "Rump" SOE and SIS Post-War Covert Action Capability 1945–1977', *Intelligence and National Security*, 15/3, pp. 55–76.

Doughty, Steve (1997), 'Smiley: Gentleman Spy', *The Daily Mail*, 1 July.

Dravis, Michael W. (1992), 'Storming Fortress Albania: American Covert Operations in Microcosm, 1949–54', *Intelligence and National Security*, 7/4, pp. 425–42.

Fain, W. Taylor (2001), 'Unfortunate Arabia: The United States, Great Britain and Yemen, 1955–63', *Diplomacy and Statecraft*, 12/2, pp. 125–52.

Gandy, Christopher (1998), 'A Mission to Yemen: August 1962–January 1963', *British Journal of Middle East Studies*, 25/2, pp. 247–74.

Gerges, Fawaz A. (1995), 'The Kennedy Administration and the Egyptian–Saudi Conflict in Yemen: Co-opting Arab Nationalism', *Middle East Journal*, 49/2, pp. 292–311.

Gwinnett, Giselle (2017), 'Attlee, Bevin and Political Warfare: Labour's Secret Anti-Communist Campaign in Europe, 1948–51', *The International History Review*, 39/3, pp. 426–9.

Jones, Clive (2004), 'Among Ministers, Mavericks and Mandarins: Britain, Covert Action and the Yemen Civil War 1962–64', *Middle Eastern Studies*, 40/1, pp. 99–126.

Jones, Clive (2006), 'Where the State Feared to Tread: Britain, Britons and the Yemen Civil War', *Intelligence and National Security*, 21/5, pp. 717–37.

Jones, Clive (2012), 'Good Friends in Low Places: The British Secret Intelligence Service and the Jewish Agency 1940–1945', *Middle Eastern Studies*, 48/3, pp. 413–28.

Jones, Clive and John Stone (1997), 'Britain and the Arabian Gulf: New Perspectives on Strategic Influence', *International Relations*, 13/4, pp. 1–24.

Kostiner, Joseph (1981), 'Arab Radical Politics: Al-Qawmiyyun al-Arab and the Marxists in the Turmoil of South Yemen, 1963–1967', *Middle Eastern Studies*, 17/1, pp. 454–76.

Malvern, Jack (2013), 'Exhibition pays Tribute to the Spy who Blew Himself Up', *The Times*, 31 August.

Melman, Yossi (2008), 'Our Man in Sana'a: Ex-Yemen President was once Trainee Rabbi', *Ha'aretz* (in English), 20 October.

Mawby, Spencer (2002), 'The Clandestine Defence of Empire: British Special Operations in Yemen 1951–1964', *Intelligence and National Security*, 17/3, pp. 105–30.

Obituary (2008). 'Lieutenant A. D. Tweedie, Late Blues and Royals, *Household Cavalry Journal*, 2003/4, p. 95; 'The Fallen', BBC2, Broadcast 15 November.

Orkaby, Asher (2015), 'The 1964 Israeli Airlift to Yemen and the Expansion of Weapons Diplomacy', *Diplomacy & Statecraft*, 26/4, pp. 659–77.

Petersen, Tore Tingvold Petersen (1992), 'Anglo-American Rivalry in the Middle East: The Struggle for the Buraimi Oasis, 1952–1957', *International History Review*, 14/1, pp. 71–91.

Rees, Thomas (1998), 'Blunder and Betrayal in the Balkans', *The Guardian Weekend*, 10 October, pp. 20–6.

Shakespeare, Nicholas (1991), 'Return to the Land of Zog', *Daily Telegraph Weekend*, 5 October.

Singer, P. W. (2001/2), 'Corporate Warriors: The Rise of the Privatized Military Industry and its Ramifications for International Security', *International Security*, 26/3, pp. 186–220.

Smiley, Col. D. de C. (1960), 'Muscat and Oman', *The Royal United Services Journal*, 105/616, pp. 23–4.

Smiley, David (1963), 'Nasser's Air Terror', *The Yorkshire Post*, 5 May.

Smiley, Colonel D. de C. (1965), 'Aden Face-Saver for Yemen Failure', *The Scotsman*, 16 September.

Smiley, David (1996), Letter to the Editor of the *London Review of Books*, dated 12 December 1996, *London Review of Books*, 18/24 (December).

Smiley, David (2003), 'Return to the Yemen', *The British-Yemeni Society Journal*, 11, p. 23.

Smith, Simon C. (1995), 'Rulers and Residents: British Relations in the Aden Protectorate 1937–59', *Middle Eastern Studies*, 31/3, pp. 509–23.

Taulbee, James Larry (1998), 'Reflections on the Mercenary Option', *Small Wars and Insurgencies*, 9/2, pp. 145–63.

Wagner, Steven (2013), 'British Intelligence and the "Fifth" Occupying Power: The Secret Struggle to Prevent Jewish Illegal Immigration to Palestine', *Intelligence and National Security*, available at <http://dx.doi.org/10.1080/02684527.2013.846730> (last accessed 5 December 2018).

Witty, David W. (2001), 'A Regular Army in Counterinsurgency Operations: Egypt in North Yemen 1962–1967', *The Journal of Military History*, 65 (April), pp. 401–39.

Verrier, Anthony (1967), 'British Military Policy on Arabia', *Royal United Services Institute Journal*, CXII/648, pp. 349–55.

Zamir, Meir (2010), 'The "Missing Dimension": Britain's Secret War against France in Syria and Lebanon, 1942–45 Part II', *Middle Eastern Studies*, 46/6, pp. 791–899.

Newspapers

BBC Summary of World Broadcasts
Ha'aretz (Israel)
Le Monde (France)
The Daily Mail
The Daily Telegraph
The Guardian
The London Review of Books
The Scotsman
The Sunday Telegraph
The Sunday Times
The Times
The Yorkshire Post
Yediot Aharonoth (Israel)

Broadcast Programmes

Television

'End of Empire: Aden', Channel 4 (UK), Broadcast 10 June 1985.

'SAS, The Real Story: Part IV – Who Cares Who Wins', Channel 4 (UK), Broadcast 1 December 2004.

'The Cost of Treachery', BBC1, Broadcast 30 October 1984.

'The Fallen', BBC2, Broadcast 15 November 2008.

'The Mayfair Set: David Stirling', BBC2, Broadcast 18 July 1999.

'Timewatch: The People's Coronation', BBC2, Broadcast 18 May 2007.

Radio

'Britain and the Yemen Civil War', *Document*, BBC Radio 4, Broadcast 8 March 2010.

'Britain's and the Oman Coup', *Document*, BBC Radio 4, Broadcast 23 November 2009.

'MI6: A Century in the Shadows – Part 1', BBC Radio 4, Broadcast 26 July 2010.

'The Albanian Operation', *Document*, BBC Radio 4, Broadcast 5 July 2016.

Index

Abel-Smith, Major Henry, 11
Abu Simbel, 33, 298
Abyssinia, 27–33, 48, 63, 68
Acre Convention, 50
Addis Ababa, 30
Aden, 22
  and British decision to withdraw from, 311, 314
Aden Group, 289, 297
Admoni, Nahum, 301
Afrika Korps, 34, 55, 60, 61, 65, 66
Alam Halfa (Battle of), 66
al-Amri, General Hassan, 314
al-Badr, Imam Muhammed, 288, 294–5, 305, 315, 331
Albania, 2, 4, 19, 44, 70, 72, 87, 88, 95, 326, 328
  and ethnic composition, 80
  and political history, 80–2
Aldrich, Richard J., 150
Aleppo, 46
Alexandria, 33, 34, 35
Al-Hussein, Prince Mohammed bin, 308–9, 315
al-Husseini, Haj Amin, 15
Ali, Imam Ghalib bi, 255, 256, 263, 268, 270, 273
Ali, Talib bin, 255, 276
Aliko, Turham, 235
al-Iriyani, Dr Abdul Karim, 328
Al-Kadhimain (Iraq), 42–3
Allen, Sergeant Derby, 229, 233
Allfree, Philip, 261
Al-Qaida, 329
Al-Qawuqjji, Fawzi al-Din, 46, 49

Al-Shamy, Ahmed, 297, 300, 306
Al-Wuhaybi, Said Salim, 278, 329
Amara, 302
American Joint Distribution Committee, 208
Amery, Julian, 73, 81, 83, 108, 117, 120, 122–4
  and communist influence in SOE, 130–1
  and Oman, 253, 257, 265, 268, 269, 270–1, 275
  and Operation Valuable, 222, 225, 230, 237, 240–1, 248
  and Smiley, 124, 136, 138, 336
  and Yemen, 289, 291, 297, 299, 314, 324, 328, 331, 334
Amery, Leo, 81
Amit, Meir, 301
Angleton, James, 236
Anglo-French Invasion of Suez, 246
Annamites, 186–9
Aqabat al-Dhafar, 273
ARAMCO (Arabian–American Oil Company), 256, 266
Aramitas, Ramiz, 92
Armja Krajowa (AK: Polish Home Army), 151, 203
Asllani, Xhemal, 234
Asquith, Herbert, 2
Astor, Gavin (Lord Hever), 198, 276
Aswan, 33
Atham, Kemal, 298, 214
Attaturk, Kemal, 51
Attlee, Clement, 209, 223
Avrahami, Colonel Eitan, 301

Index

Baghdad, 39, 45
Bahrain, 258, 268, 281
Bailey, Roderick, 118, 131
Bajraktar, Muharrew, 83
Balfour Declaratin, 15
Balli Kombetar (Balkom), 94, 95, 99, 106, 117, 118–22, 225, 228–30, 239
Baluchis, 259
Bangkok, 194
Banks, Major (OSS), 190, 191
Ban Non Han (Ascot), 158
Ban Tao Ngoi (Kempton), 161
Barclay, Sam, 232
Bardhok, 134
Bari, 90, 111, 120
Barisha, Sali, 328
Barmash, 95
Baron von Mitzlaff, 5
Bastor, 132–3
Batinah Coast, 268, 278
BBC, 199, 240
Beaton, Cecil, 5
Beaton, Nancy, 5
Begin, Menachem, 207
Beihan, 297, 298
Beirut, 20
Beit al-Falaj, 259, 279
Beniarbeig (Spain), 323
Beni Hinna (Omani tribe), 256, 267, 268, 270
Beni Riyam (Omani tribe), 255–6, 267, 270, 271, 272
Berat, 106
Berbera, 21
Bergan–Belsen, 167
Bethell, Nicholas, 236
Bevers, Don, 211
Bevin, Ernest, 207, 223, 226
Bey, Gani, 128
BGFIEND, 224; *see also* Operation Valuable
Bhanomyong, Nai Pridi *see* Pridi
Bir Hakeim, 58, 61
Bixha, 103, 104–5, 120, 132
Blackburn, Squadron Leader James 'Jimmy', 81, 211–12, 217, 240
Blathwayt, Major Chris, 174

BLOs (British Liaison Officers) *see* SOE
Boneng, 187
Boustead, Colonel Hugh, 264
Boutagy, Emil, 21, 73
Boyle, Flight Lieutenant Tony, 298, 301, 303, 307, 311
Branxholm Castle, Hawick, 286
Breene, Arnold, 112
Bridge on the River Kwai, 176
Brindisi, 107
British, Commonwealth and Dominion Military Units and Formations
  Balkan Air Force, 131, 137
  Blues *see* Royal Horse Guards
  British Army of the Rhine (BAOR), 221
  BRIXMIS, 202
  Coldstream Guards, 104
  Commandos, 23
  Durham Light Infantry, 25
  Eighth Army, 58–61, 66
  11th Hussars, 63
  Essex Regiment, 27
  5th Indian Division, 26, 32
  52 (Middle East) Commando, 24–37
  First Aid Nursing Yeomanry (FANY), 199
  1st Household Cavalry Regiment, 10, 17–18, 23, 36, 40, 41–4, 51–3, 54, 55
  Gocol, 44, 45
  Habforce, 40, 46, 47
  Highland Light Infantry, 26
  Intelligence Corps, 279
  Jedburghs, 116
  Kingcol, 40, 42, 44
  Layforce, 33, 36
  Life Guards, 7, 271, 273
  Long Range Desert Group, 67
  Middle East Command (Aden), 258, 264, 271
  Middle East Commandos, 50, 51, 52, 54
  Middlesex Yeomanry, 75
  MI(R) (Military Intelligence Research, 55

353

British, Commonwealth and Dominion Military Units and Formations (*cont.*)
1 Royal Tank Regiment (1RTR), 59–60
Parachute Regiment, 270
Relief of Allied Prisoners of War and Internees (RAPWI), 178
Royal Air Force (RAF)
No.2 Armoured Car Squadron, 41–2
148 Special Duties Squadron, 85
Royal Dragoon Guards, 60, 64
Royal Horse Artillery, 146
Royal Horse Guards (The Blues), 8, 10, 51, 58, 141, 146, 221–2, 241, 242, 337
Royal Marines, 259, 268
Royal Norfolk Regiment, 183
Royal Regiment of Artillery, 41
Royal Scots Greys, 229
Royal Warwickshire Regiment, 64
Scots Guards, 229
7th Armoured Division (Desert Rats), 65, 67
6th Australian Division, 45
Somaliland Camel Corps, 21, 26
Special Air Service (SAS), 74, 205, 206, 268, 286, 297, 303, 335
and assault on Jebel Akhdar, 271–6
10th Armoured Division, 51, 52
10th Indian Infantry Brigade, 26
13/18th Hussars, 259
21st Army Group, 146
British Mercenary Organisation (BMO), 298, 301, 306, 311, 313–14
Brittain-Catlin, Alexander, 329
Broadway (MI6 Headquarters, London), 225
Broz, Josip *see* Tito
Bruce-Lockhart, John, 291
Burgess, Guy, 130, 237
Burma, 148, 155, 157
Burrel, 132
Burrows, Sir Bernard, 262
Butka, Safet, 97

Cairncross, John, 130
Cairo, 50, 69, 71
and life in, 112–15
Çako, Ethem, 239
Calcutta, 149, 166
Camberley Staff College, 198, 200
Carpathian Mountains, 203
Casano, Squadron Leader Michael, 42
Casey, Sir Richard, 166
Cater, Mrs and Mrs, 4
Cavendish-Bentinck, Victor, 201
Cecil, Robert, 204
Četniks, 78, 80
Ceylon, 152
'Chat' *see* Sudhi Sudisakdi
Cherminika Massif, 103
Chida, Major, 176, 181
'Chin' *see* Subha Svasti
China, 151
Christie, John, 301
Churchill, Winston, 70, 150, 243, 268, 327
CIA (Central Intelligence Agency), 224, 240
Clark, Alan, 2
Clark, Kenneth, 2
Clark, Major General George, 48
Collins, Sergeant William 'Gunner', 123, 154, 157, 162–3, 166, 167, 174, 229, 232
Colombo, 152, 165
Colonial Office, 149, 288–9
Concensus missions *see* SOE
Constanza, 215
Cook, John, 86, 87
Cooling, Sergeant Terence, 229, 233
Cooper, Artemis, 113
Cooper, Major John, 273, 299, 301, 302
Cornwell, David (John le Carré), 333
Coughlin, John, 150
Crete, 1 22, 36, 62, 63
Cripps, Major Robert, 82
Crowe, Sir Colin, 293
Cruickshank, Charles, 173
Crusader tanks, 59
Curragh Mutiny, 2
Cyprus, 61, 63, 214

Index

Dahran, 256
Daimler Armoured Car, 67
Damascus, 45
Dammam (Saudi Arabia), 280
Darbyshire, Norman, 280
Das Englandspiel, 239
Da Silva, John, 280, 300–1
Davidson, Basil, 80, 326
Davies, Brigadier Edmund F
    'Trotsky', 104, 116–17, 226
D-Day, 116, 128
Deakin, William, 78
Deane-Drummond, Lieutenant
    Colonel Anthony, 272–6
de Chair, Somerset, 50
de Crespigny, Claude, 3
de Crespigny, Norman, 3
de Crespigny, Philip, 3, 9
de Crespigny, Sir Claude, 1–2, 243
de Crespigny, Vierville, 3
de Fay, Lieutenant, 185
de Gaulle, General Charles, 45, 50
de la Billière, Captain (later Major)
    Peter, 276, 298
Dennison, Major Malcolm, 260, 270,
    279, 280
Dentz, General Henri-Ferdinand, 39,
    45, 50
Derna Airfield, Cyrenaica, 84
Devji, 121
de Zulueta, Philip, 281
Dilo, Jani, 228
Dine, Fiqri, 129
Dine, Skender, 91–2
DIOs (Desert Intelligence Officers),
    280
Douglas-Home, Sir Alec, 289, 290,
    296
Drymades (Greece), 88–9
Dubai, 280
Duffy, Lieutenant Gavan 'Garry', 83,
    85, 87, 89, 97
Dukati, 106, 233, 234, 298
Dunkirk, 11
Durazzo, 81, 135–6
Dutch East Indies, 148, 180

East Anglia, 242
East Anglian Daily Times, 2

Eden, Sir Anthony, 115, 124, 327
Edinburgh University, 159
Egypt, 62
Egyptian army, 297
    and casualties in Yemen, 309
El Alamein, Battle of, 58, 61
ELAS/EDES, 87, 88, 90
Elbasan, 101
El-Ghalani, Rashid, 39, 41
Elizabeth, Princess, 232
Elliot, Air Vice-Marshal William,
    131
Elmaz, Faik, 84
Emwas Monastery, 55
Ephrat, Lieutenant Colonel Raphael,
    301
Epirus Mountains, 84, 120
Eritrea, 27, 75
Ermenji, Abas, 230
es Sa'id, Nuri, 39, 44
Essex, 1
Eton College, 323, 324, 332
Evans, Horace, 9
Eyre, Captain John, 130, 141

Faisal, Crown Prince (Later King),
    288, 290–1, 298, 305, 306
Faja, Baba, 83
Fallujah, 42
Falques, Colonel Roger, 306
Famagusta, 63
Farran, Rex, 206
Farran, Roy, 206
FAS (Federation of South Arabia),
    288, 290
Ferguson, Lieutenant Colonel
    Andrew, 43, 69
Fergusson, Brigadier Bernard, 206
Field, Major Jerry, 100, 106
Fielding, Xan, 22, 112–13, 146, 153
Fleming, Colonel Peter, 152, 332
Fleming, Ian, 152, 332
Flushing (Netherlands), 1
Foot, M. R. D., 114
Force 136 *see* SOE
Foreign Office
    and Albania, 82, 115, 131
    and Oman, 256–7, 262, 264, 269,
      275, 278

355

Foreign Office (*cont.*)
  and Thailand, 149–50, 194
  and Yemen, 288, 289, 297
Fort Benjimma, 226–7, 232
Fournier, Lieutenant Edith, 184
Fowler, Trooper, 47
Fox-Davies, Lieutenant Colonel Harry, 24
FRA (Federal Regular Army), 298
France, 11, 172, 184, 208
France, Major Rupert, 298
Franco-Laotian Forces, 189
Franks, Colonel Brian, 205
Frashëri, Mithat, 225
Free Albanian Committee, 225
Free French Forces, 45, 58
  and 'E' Group, 184
French Foreign Legion, 25, 45
French mercenaries, 298
FSM (Free Siam Movement), 149–51, 154, 155, 156, 159–60, 173, 184, 193
Fuller, Major Gerry, 48, 53

Gallabat, 26, 27, 28
Gausset, Lieutenant, 189
Gaza, 21, 55
Gazala, 58
Gedaref, 32
Geneifra, 24
Geneva, 300
Germanj, 91
Germany, 50, 241
Ghandi, Mahatma, 166–7
Gjinocaster, 89, 233, 234
Gjoles (Bridge at), 125, 131, 148
Glubb, Colonel John, 40, 44
Goddard, Major John, 261
'Golden Square', 39
Gooch, Lieutenant Colonel Eric, 44, 45, 69, 71
Gorgopotamos Viaduct, 87
Grant, Captain Alistair, 228
Greece, 35, 62, 80, 120, 208
Grobba, Dr Fritz, 44, 45
Gubbins, Major General Colin, 204
Guinness, Alec, 176
Gwadur, 259

Habbaniyah (RAF), 39, 40, 41, 54
Haifa, 11, 13, 16, 17, 36, 40, 71, 72
Haganah, 45, 73, 207, 208, 209
Hajja, 304, 305, 315
Hamid Ud-Din (Yemeni Imamate), 315
Hamilton, Lieutenant General, 271
Hands, Flight Lieutenant Andy, 95
Hare, Alan, 4, 104, 105, 116–17, 123, 132, 151, 154, 194, 234, 328, 331
Harib, 304
Harrison, Sergeant, 29
Hart, Major Tony, 272
Hasan, Veli, 125, 126
Hasluck, Frederick, 82, 84
Hasluck, Margaret 'Fanny', 81–2, 83
Hassan, Crown Prince, 299
Hataj, Ramiz, 234
Hawtrey's Preparatory School, 4
Heath, Air Vice-Marshal Maurice, 272
Hedley, Major John, 180
Heidelberg, University of, 265
Henrietta, 240
Hervey-Bathurst, Major Ben, 154
Herzog, Ya'acov, 300–1
Hibberdine, John, 125, 153
Hibbert, Reginald, 103, 326
Himeimat Ridge (Egypt), 67
Himyar, Sheikh Suleiman bin, 255, 267, 274
Hiram, Colonel Dan, 299
Hobbs, Tom, 150
Hod, Lieutenant General Mordechai, 301
Hodeidah (Yemen), 304
Holladay, Major John (OSS), 160
Holland, Lieutenant Colonel J. F. C., 55
Homs, 46
Hopkinson, Lieutenant Commander 'Hoppy', 154
Hoseda, Lieutenant, 181, 182
Hosumi, Colonel, 180–1, 186
Howarth, Patrick, 201
Hoxha, Enver, 89, 99, 103, 118, 129, 141, 206, 222–3, 227, 238, 241

Index

Hudson, Lieutenant Colonel Sidney 'Soapy', 156, 169, 176
Hussein, King of Jordan, 290
Hussein, Sharif of Beihan, 298

Imperial War Museum, 330
India, 151
India Office, 149
Indo-China, 173, 184, 191
Indonesia, 180
Inglis, Captain John, 227
Iran, 39
Iraq, 39, 56, 276
Irgun Zvai Leumi, 206–7
Ismalia (Egypt), 21
Israel, 299–304, 325
Israel Defence Forces, 30
Israeli air force, 301–2
Issacs, Major, 279
Italian army
  Alpini Division, 100
  Folgore Division, 68
  24th Colonial Brigade, 32
Izki (Oman), 270

Jacques, Brigadier Victor, 150, 155, 161, 168–9
Jalali prison, 277–8
Jannina, 84
Japan
  and occupation of Siam/Thailand, 148–50
Japanese Imperial Army, 161
  and *Kenpeitai* (military intelligence), 161–2
  and 22nd Imperial Japanese Division, 180–1, 192
Jávea (Spain), 313, 323
Jebel Ahmar (Yemen), 309
Jebel Akhdar (Oman), 255–6, 258, 264, 266, 267–75, 281, 334
Jeddah, 293, 309, 313
Jeffrey, Keith, 209, 216
Jenin, 17
Jenkins, Sergeant George, 95, 97, 123, 125–6, 140
Jericho, 55, 58
Jerusalem, 17, 50, 54, 55, 64
Jewish Agency, 208

Jinnah, Muhammed, 166–7
Johnson, Colonel James 'Jim', 297, 300, 301, 303, 306, 307, 311, 312, 314
Johnston, Sir Charles, 289, 297
Joint Intelligence Committee, 201, 208, 288, 290, 316
Jones, Sergeant, 95, 97, 123, 140
Jordan, 277, 290
Jordan Valley, 40
June 1967 war, 314

Kabrit, 74
Kafe-Thanes Road, 103, 133
Kameshle, 45
Karice, 132
Kassala, 32, 33
Keble, Brigadier C. M. 'Rolo', 82
Kelly, J. B., 226
Kelly, Jeffrey 'John', 229, 230
Kemp, Peter, 99, 100, 151, 153, 167, 168, 169, 173, 174, 184–93, 201, 325
Kenya, 198, 253, 281
Kermanshah, 51
Kerr, Elizabeth, 2
KGB (Soviet Foreign Intelligence Service), 331
Khanja, 296, 305
Kibbutz Degania, 19
King David Hotel (bombing of), 207
King Edward VIII, 8
King George VI (funeral of), 241
Kingstone, Brigadier John, 40–1
Kirkuk (Iraq), 40, 47, 51
Kitson, Major Frank, 270
Klotz, Lieutenant François, 184, 185, 186, 187, 190–1
Klugmann, Major James, 80, 130–1
Knox, Jimmy, 303
Kola, Halit, 135
'Kong' *see* Tosayanonda, Kris
Konitza, 89
Korcë, 89, 91, 93, 98, 100, 233, 234
Kosovo, 82, 128, 240
Kowma, suspected chemical weapons attack on, 293
Kozelli, Sulo, 90
Kra Isthmus, 150, 194

357

Kriepe, General Heinrich, 114
Kryeziu, Gani Bey, 128
Kryeziu, Hassan, 128
Kryeziu, Said, 128, 225, 303
Kuçove, 111
Kuka, Ahmet, 235
Kupi, Abas, 81, 83, 100, 121,123, 124, 127, 131, 132, 133, 136–9, 141, 225, 326–7
Kuqar, 94
Kurdistan, 45
Kuwait, 270, 276, 280

Labinot, 106
Lake Orchid, 100
Lancaster, Colonel Claude 'Jubie', 6
Lapanica, Sami, 234
Latham, John, 232
Latrun, 55
Lawson, Sergeant 'Spider', 168, 169
Laycock, Brigadier Bob, 33
Leake, Major Philip, 117
Lebanon, 39, 45
Leclerc, General Philippe, 194
Leeds, 83
Legaliteti, 239
Leigh-Fermor, Patrick, 112, 114
Leshnjë, 100
Leskovik, 90, 91, 98
Lincolnshire, 242
Liron, Major Ze'ev, 301
Lis, Michael, 201
Llengë, 100
LNC (*Levizje Nacional Çlirimtare*), 89, 94, 95, 100, 106, 117, 118–19
London Review of Books, 327
Low, Robert, 224, 225
Lublin, 202
Luftwaffe, 41, 59
Lyman, Robert, 39
Lyneham (RAF), 114
Lyon, Marcus, 104
Lytton family (Knebworth Estate), 199

McClean, Lieutenant Neil 'Billy', 73, 151, 334, 336
and Concensus I, 83–5, 86–90, 96, 99
and Concensus II, 117, 124, 136, 138
and Operation Valuable, 237, 240
and Yemen, 286, 290, 297, 298, 306–7, 311–12, 314, 316
background of, 22, 62
death of, 328
recommends Smiley for DSO, 127
recruits Smiley to SOE, 69
Macintyre, Ben, 332
Mackenzie, Colin, 149, 191
Maclean, Brigadier Fitzroy, 78, 103
Maclean, Donald, 130
Macmillan, Catherine, 222
Macmillan, Harold, 222, 248, 281, 290
McNeil, Sir Hector, 209
McTavish, Sergeant-Major Sandy, 175–6
Macukall, 132
Mafraq, 49
Maha Sarakham (Heston), 161, 163, 164
Major, Major, 227
Malaya, 148, 149, 157, 172, 271
Maldon, 10, 243
Malta, 212, 226–8, 231–2
Marib, 308–9
Marinowska, Countess Maria, 202, 204
Marmon Herrington Armoured Car, 20, 59, 60, 61, 67
Marseilles, 12
Maskelyne, Major Jasper, 72
Massey, Lewis, 201
Mati Valley, 132
Mau Mau, 270
Maxwell, Colonel Colin, 260
Mekong River, 156–7, 173
Menzies, Sir Stewart, 223
Mercenaries *see* British Mercenary Organisation (BMO)
Merrett, Captain Ian, 123, 140
Mesopotamia, 36
Metemma, 27, 28, 31
Micklethwaite, Guy, 87

Index

Middle East Cavalry School, 20
Middle East Centre, St Antony's College Oxford, 325, 330
MI5, 227, 326
Millot-Luz Road, 135
Mills, Major Bernard, 299, 305, 308, 311
MI9, 62
Minto Church, 330, 337
MI6, 70, 201, 203, 204
   Albania/Operation Valuable, 224, 232, 234, 235, 238, 280, 313, 331
   and Directorate of War Planning (D/WP), 205, 217
   and Palestine/Operation Embarrass, 209–17
   and Section 'D', 81
   and Yemen, 291, 300–1, 313, 325, 335
Monteith, William, 278
Montgomery, General Bernard, 63–4
Moshpina, 88
Moss, Captain William Stanley 'Billy', 112,113, 114, 146, 153, 194
Mossad, 206, 301
Mossad Le Aliyah Beth, 208, 212, 213, 214
Mountbatten, Admiral Lord Louis, 150, 155, 173, 232
Mount Carmel, 13, 71, 73
Mount Nemerçke, 106
Mount Ostravica, 93
Mount Vesuvius, 121
Muti, 266–7
Myers, Brigadier Eddie Myers, 86–7, 104

Nablus, 17
Najran, 290
Nakajima, Captain, 186
Nakhon Phanom, 186, 190
Nasser, President Gamal Abdel, 255, 263, 288, 289, 308, 309
NATO, 203, 245, 246
Nazareth, 49
Neel, Squadron Leader Tony, 95
Nehru, Jawaharlal, 166–7

Nequb, 298, 299
Netherlands, 1, 172
Nicholls, Lieutenant Colonel Arthur, 104, 116–17
Nivan, 88
Nizwa, 256, 265, 270, 273, 279
NKVD, 151
Nong Khai, 173, 192
Northrop, Tony, 201, 232, 331
North Sea Flood, 242
Norway, 70
Nosi, Fred, 97–8

O'Bryan Tear, Terry, 289, 325
O'Connor, Lieutenant General Ritchie, 34
Odey, Sergeant George, 230
Office of Policy Coordination (OPC), 224
Office of Special Operations, 230, 238
Office of Strategic Services (OSS), 150, 160, 176, 190, 224
Oman, 19, 44, 265–6, 277, 280–1, 329
   and air force, 264
   and Contract Officers, 260
   and Muscat and Oman Field force, 253–6, 259, 260
   and Muscat Regiment, 259, 271
   and Northern Frontier Regiment, 259–60, 271
   and oil, 278, 280, 224
   and Sultan's Armed Forces (SAF), 263–5, 266, 267, 268, 269–70, 271–3, 275–6, 279, 298, 329, 331, 334
   background to rebellion, 253–7
Oman Rebel Army (ORA), 256, 279–80
Operation Chariot (Raid on St Nazaire), 23
Operation Dermot, 270
Operation Embarrass, 206, 211, 217, 302
Operation Mango, 302, 304,
Operation Priest, 151
Operation Rotev, 312, 325
Operation Trespass, 209

359

Operation Valuable, 206, 222, 224–5,
 and Valuable BGFIEND, 224–8, 235, 237, 238, 332
Oz, Major Arieh, 301

Pahlevi, Mohammed Rez, 51
Pahlevi, Shah Reza, 50–1
Pai-Tak Pass, 51
Palestine, 11–12, 54–5, 206, 207–10
Palestine Police, 19, 206
Palmach, 73
Palmer, Major (later Lieutenant Colonel) Alan, 104, 120, 128, 131
Palmyra, 46, 47, 54, 199
Pangbourne Nautical College, 5
Paulson, Paul, 301
Peres, Shimon, 310
Perkins, Colonel Harold 'Perks', 151, 201, 203, 211, 214, 215, 222, 225, 335
Përmat, 106
Persia, 50, 54
Petroleum Development Oman (PD(O)), 255, 266, 279
Peza, Myslim, 83
Phannikhom, 169
Philby, Harold 'Kim', 218, 236–7
Philip, Prince, 232
Phillips, Major Tom, 183
'Pibul', 148–9
'Pixies', training of, 230–33, 240
'Pluto' (Nai Tieng Sirikhandra), 159–61, 166, 167, 168, 169
Poett, General Nigel, 233
Pogradec, 101, 102
Pointon, Lieutenant Colonel Peter, 154, 156
Poliçan, 88
Polish Home Army *see Armja Krajowa*
Polish Security Service (*Urzad Bezpiecznstwa*), 202
Porton Down, 293
Pot, Colonel Prom, 175
Power, Admiral Sir John, 227
Prajadhipok, King, 146

Pridi (codename Ruth), 149, 150, 154, 161
Primakov, Yevgeny, 331
Pun (Santa Sintari), 153, 163, 166
Przemysl, 203

Qabus bin Said, Sultan, 325, 329
Qatar, 280
Qattara Depression, 58, 66
Quayle, Major Anthony, 120
Queen's Coronation 1953, 243
Quebec conference, 150
Quereshnik, 106

Ramiz, Dani, 126, 134
Rangoom, 165
Raqqa, 70
Rashid Ali, 36, 44
Red Cross, 177
Reese, Lieutenant (OSS), 190
Romanon Monastery, 86, 87
Rommel, General Erwin, 55, 64
Roosevelt, President Franklin D, 150
Rowanduz Gorge, 45
Royal Air Force (RAF), 111, 126, 135, 158, 298
 and Special Duties Squadrons, 211, 259, 267–8, 273
 and in Oman, 267, 268–9
Royal Navy, 4, 34, 214
Rubowitz, Alexander, 206
Rumbold, Anthony, 234–5

'Sackcloth' *see* Kemp
Sada, 302
Sakon Nakon, 157, 158, 162, 167
Salalah, 267
Sallal, Brigadier Abdullah, 288, 290, 314
Sana'a, 296, 309
Sandhurst, 5, 7
Sandys, Duncan, 289
Santa Maria Monastery of, 100
Sarafand, 49
Saudi Arabia, 255–6, 266, 274, 278, 290, 293, 301
Schaathun, Major Birger, 293
Scott, Lieutenant David, 107
Scott, Lord Francis, 198

Index

SEAC, 149, 155, 159–60, 161, 166, 168, 172, 178, 187, 189
'Seaview', 107, 111, 233
Secret Intelligence Service, 55, 70 *see also* MI6
Sehu, Mehmet, 95, 99
Selbourne, Lord, 115
Sensui, Major, 182
Sète, 213
Seymour, George, 100
Shakespeare, Nicolas, 328
Shearer, Brigadier John, 23
Shëngjergi, 132
Shengjin, 140
Ships
  Exodus (*President Warfield*), 212–14
  HMS *Saumarez*, 223
  HMS *Volage*, 223
  Pan Crescent, 214–15, 216
  Pan York, 214–15
  SS *Patria*, 72, 213
Shkumbin River, 101–2
Shtyllë, 93–4, 95
Siam, 148–9, 152
Sigurimi (Albanian intelligence service), 238–9
Singapore, 172
Sino, Abdyl, 228
Smiley, Colonel David de Crespigny
  Albanian Assignment, 133, 325
  ambush on Leshovik-Korcë Road, 99
  and Arabs and Jews, 17–18
  and Commander SAF, 257–60
  and Deputy Military Attaché, Poland, 201–4
  and 1st Partisan Brigade, 90–1, 93–4, 97, 99, 131
  and French hostages, 185–7
  and 'meritocracy', 8–9
  and Sophie Tarnowska, 112–13, 114, 119, 120, 123, 146
  and trip to Israel, 300–2
  Arabian Assignment, 290, 312, 325
  attack on Shkumbin River bridge, 101
  awarded bar to MC, 148
  awarded Croix de Guerre, 194
  awarded MBE (military), 194
  awarded MC, 120
  birth of, 1–2
  burnt by 'briefcase', 162–5
  command of BMO, 311
  command of the 'Blues', 242–4
  commissioned into Royal Horse Guards, 8
  death of, 333
  denied DSO, 276, 334
  first experience of war, 28–9
  Gentleman at Arms, 313
  Gjoles Bridge, sabotage of, 125–7
  horse racing, 9
  intelligence gathering, 139
  Irregular Regular, 327, 336
  joins Force, 136, 152–3
  joins MO4 (SOE), 69, 71
  liberates Ubon Camp, 176–9
  leadership of Japanese troops, 187–8
  leadership of Tajiks and Turkestanis in Albania, 137–8
  leads 'Felt', 156, 157, 160, 161, 167, 168
  malaria, 126, 149
  marries Moy, 204
  Mentioned in Despatches, 48
  Military Attaché, Sweden, 245–8
  narrowly avoids being shot, 136
  offered command of SAS Regiments, 282
  Operation Embarrass, involvement in, 206, 211–17
  Operation Valuable, involvement in 225–41
  operations in Abyssinia, 26–34
  operations in Iraq, 41–5
  operations in Syria, 46–9
  operations in Western Desert, 58–60, 64–9
  parachute training, 74–5
  recommended for DSO, 194
  'Three Musketeers', 331
  training with SOE, 69–76
  upbringing, 3–6
  views of Abas Kupi, 121–2, 137, 139
  views of Australian troops, 34–5

361

Smiley, Colonel David de Crespigny (*cont.*)
  views of Concensus II, 133–4
  views of Hoxha, 95–6
  views of New Zealand troops, 34–5
  views of Royalists (Yemen), 304–5,
  views of 'Sapling' mission, 106
  views of SOE Bari, 130–1, 141, 146
  views of 'Spillway mission', 105
  views of Sultan Bin Taimur, 263–4, 265, 268, 272–6
  volunteers for Commandos, 20, 23, 24
  wartime London, 114–15
  weapons smuggling in Siam, 190–2
  Yemen, first trip to, 291–5
Smiley, John, 5, 75
Smiley, Lady Valerie (mother), 1–3, 167
Smiley, Moyra 'Moy', 198–200, 203, 229, 246, 258, 262, 266, 277, 296, 306, 312, 327, 329, 330, 333
Smiley, Patricia, 2, 48
Smiley, Philip David, 241, 266, 324
Smiley, Sir Hugh, 2
Smiley, Sir Hugh (elder brother of David Smiley), 5
Smiley, Sir John (father), 1–2
Smiley, Xan de Crespigny, 222, 248, 323–4, 332, 337
Smith, Captain Victor, 133
Smyth, Major E. A., 175
Soames, Christopher, 268, 269, 271
SOE, 4, 55, 62, 150, 195, 204, 205, 207, 211, 222, 232, 237, 302, 330, 331–2
  BLOs, 70, 72, 97, 100–1, 104, 115, 117, 122, 129, 335
  Concensus I, 83–4, 93, 107, 232
  Concensus II, 119, 122, 128, 132, 146, 334
  Force 136, 148, 149, 152, 154, 159, 162, 172, 184, 189
  Hoxha ultimatum to, 136, 141, 146, 326
  in Bari, 111, 128,
  in Cairo, 69, 100, 103
  ME25, 152
  MO4, 69
  Panicle Mission, 154–5
  Rustem Buildings, 70
  Siam Country Section, 154
  Spillway Mission, 103, 104–5, 226
  Starling Mission, 84, 86
  STS 102, 71, 83, 114, 212
Songgram, Field Marshal 'Pibul' *see* Pibul
Sons of the Eagle, 124
South East Asia Command *see* SEAC
Soviet Union, 50, 128, 315
Spahiu, Bedri, 89
Spain, 204, 313, 323
Special Operations Committee, 118
Special Operations Executive *see* SOE
Stafford, Davis, 137
Stephenson, Sir Hugh, 288
Stirling, Colonel David, 297, 298, 307
Stockholm, 244–5
Stone, Captain L. D., 175
Stormie Seas, 232
Subha Svasti, Prince (codename Chin), 146–8
Sudan, 26, 32
Suez Canal, 55, 74
Sultan bin Abdul Aziz, 294, 306
Sur, 279
Sweden, 244–8, 259
Swedish Legation (Tehran), 53
Sweet-Escott, Bickham, 69
Syria, 39, 45–9

Taiz, 309
Taimur, Sultan Said bin, 253–5, 278, 324–5, 329
Taji, 42, 44
Tanganyika, 3
Tara, 112–14, 146, 151
Tara (Spain), 323
Tariq, Sayyid, 265, 267
Tarnowska, Sophie, 112, 113, 123, 146, 201
Tegart, Sir Charles, 16
Tehran, 39, 53–4
Tel Aviv, 49, 55, 64, 300, 303

Index

Tel el Kabir, 33, 63, 69
Tershana, Rifaat, 135
Thai air force, 164
Thailand, 148, 157
Thakhek, 173, 184–8
The Daily Telegraph, 291, 328
The Household Brigade Magazine, 291
The Guardian, 217
The Observer, 217, 237
The Spectator, 211
The Times, 198, 276
Thorneycroft, Peter, 289
Tillman, Bill, 100
Tinker, Brigadier Edward, 262, 264, 268, 276, 281
Tinker, Tailor, Soldier, Spy (BBC drama), 332
Tirana, 103, 124, 125
Tito, 78, 103
Tobruk, 58, 59, 61
Toosey, Lieutenant Colonel Philip, 176, 178, 180–1
Toptani, Ihsan, 134, 140, 141, 228
Tosayanonda, Kris, 159, 163
Trami, Shaqir, 328
Trans-Jordanian Arab Legion, 40, 44, 47
Travaskis, Sir Kennedy, 289, 297
Trayhorn, Frank, 104
Tripoli (Lebanon), 46
Trucial Oman Scouts, 256, 273, 275, 281
Tulkarm, 17
Turkey, 44
Tweedie, Anna, 222, 323, 329
Tweedie, Lieutenant Alexander, 329–30
Tweedie, Major Gavin, 222, 323, 329
Tweedie, Major Hugo, 198–9
Tweedie, Philippa, 323

Ubon Camp, 162, 173–80, 181, 195
Ulster Reform Club, 2
United States
  dropping of Atomic bombs on Japan, 168
  involvement in Saudi Arabia, 255, 266

  policy toward Thailand, 149–50
United States Army Air Force (USAAF), 120–1, 124

Van Alting, Captain Gneisau, 182
Vanden Heuvel, Count Frederick, 211
Velijë, 140
Venereal Disease, threat of in Ubon camp, 179
Venice, 215
'Venona' Signals Traffic, 237
Verschoyle, Wing Commander Derek, 211–12
Vichy France, 45–9
Vientiane, 173, 190, 192
Viet Minh, 184, 189, 191
Vietnam, 184
Villa Bimbelli, Corfu, 233–4
Vinçani, Nexhip, 91–2, 94
Virginia Water, Surrey, 5, 116, 146, 167
Visani, 89
Višegrad, 80
Vithkuq, 93
Vlora, 239
Vodice, 91
Von Horn, General Carl, 245
Von Mitzlaff, Baron, 5
Voskopoj, 91

Wadi Humeidat, ambush at, 308–9
Walker, Captain Rory, 276
Warsaw, 201–2, 204
Waterfield, Brigadier Patrick, 257, 261–2, 264, 277, 281
Watts, Major John, 276
Waugh, Evelyn, 34
Wavell, Archibald (son of Lord), 7
Wavell, Lady Eugenie, 166–7
Wavell, Sir Archibald (later Lord), 7, 23, 64, 152, 166, 194, 198
Wehrmacht, 127, 137–8
Weizmann, Dr Chaim, 15
Weizmann, Major General Ezer, 300
Wennerström, Colonel Stig, 247–8
Whinney, Pat, 233
White, Sir Dick, 289, 335

363

Williamson, Corporal William 'Willie', 83, 85, 92, 97, 106
Wilson, Harold, 310, 316, 324
Wingate, Major General Orde, 206
Winn, Rowland, 112, 153, 168, 169, 173, 186, 326
Wisner, Frank, 224

Xhiber, 121-2, 124, 125, 132

Yemen, 44, 288, 314-15
   background to civil war, 288-9
   Jeddah agreement, 309
   Royalist Forces, 297, 308-9
   tribal confederations and tribes, 288
Yemen Arab Republic, 288
Yemen Peoples Democratic Republic, 325
Yishuv, 15, 208
Young, Lieutenant Colonel George, 36
Yugoslavia, 69, 70, 78-81, 103

Zaehner, Dr (Captain) Robert, 227-8
Zagros Mountains, 52,
Zamalek, Cairo, 112
Zeidi tribes, 294-5
Zog, King, 80, 81, 84, 115, 124, 225
Zogists, 100, 118-22
   and collaboration with Germans, 132-4, 137

EU representative:
Easy Access System Europe
Mustamäe tee 50, 10621 Tallinn, Estonia
Gpsr.requests@easproject.com